Dictionary of Musical Terms, Phrases & Abbreviations

DICTIONARY

of

musical terms, phrases and abbreviations

originating from

Italian, French, German, English

and other languages

by

JOHN HILES

New edition revised and enlarged by
W. B. Henshaw

PORTSMOUTH
BARDON ENTERPRISES

First published in 1871 by S. Brewer & Co.
Seventh Edition, 1882.

Copyright, this edition © 1997 by Bardon Enterprises

Newly typeset with additions.

This edition, published in 1997 by Bardon Enterprises

All rights reserved. No part of this publication may be reproduced, stored in a retrieval system, or transmitted, in any form or by any means, electronic, mechanical, photocopying, recording or otherwise, without the prior permission of the publishers.

ISBN: 0-9528184-1-8

Typeset and printed in England

by Bardon Enterprises.

Bound in England by Ronarturo.

Portsmouth, Hampshire, England.

Abbreviations

A.	*Altus,* or *Alto*
Accel.	*Accelerándo*
Accell°.	*Accelerándo*
Acc.	*Accompaniment*
Accomp.	*Accompaniment*
Accres	*Accresciménto*
Ad l.	*Ad libitum*
Ad lib.	*Ad libitum*
Ad°.	*Adagio*
Ad$^{g°}$.	*Adagio*
Affett°	*Affettuóso*
Ag°.	*Agitáto*
Agit°	*Agitáto*
All°.	*Allégro*
All^{tto}.	*Allegrétto*
All' ott.	*All' ottáva*
All' 8va	*All' ottáva*
Al Seg.	*Al Ségno*
Alt.	*Alto*
And^{no}	*Andantíno*
And^{te}.	*Andante*
Anim°.	*Animáto*
Arc.	*Arcáto*
Arp°.	*Arpéggio*
Ard.	*Ardíto*
à t.	*à tempo*
à tem.	*à tempo*
À temp.	*à tempo*
B.	*Básso*

B. C.	*Básso Continuo*
Brill.	*Brillánte*
₵	*Alla Bréve,* or *Alla Cappélla time*
₵	*Alla Bréve time*
Cad.	*Cadénza*
Cal°.	*Calándo*
Can.	*Cantóris*
Cant.	*Cánto*
Cantab.	*Cantábile*
C. B.	*Cóntra Básso*
C. B.	*col Básso*
C. D.	*cólla déstra*
Cello.	*Violoncéllo*
Cemb.	*Cémbalo*
Ch.	*Choir*
chalm	*chalumeau*
Cho. Org.	*Choir Organ*
Chor.	*Chorus*
c. l.	*col légno*
C. O.	*Choir Organ*
con 8va	*con ottáva*
con 8^{vi}	*con ottávi*
Clar.	*Clarinet*
Clar°.	*Claríno*
Clar^{tto}.	*Clarinétto*
co.	*cóme*

ABBREVIATIONS

col C.	col Cánto
Cotill.	Cotillon
con esp.	conespressióne
cres.	Crescéndo
cresc.	Crescéndo
c. s.	cólla sinístra
c. 8va	coll' ottáva
C° 1mo	Cánto Primo
C^{to}	Concérto
D.	Déstra, Droite
D. C.	Da Cápo
Dec.	Decáni
Decres.	
Decresc.	Decrescéndo
Delicatam.	Delicataménte
Dest.	Déstra
Diap.	Diapason
Dim.	Diminuéndo
Dimin.	Diminuéndo
Div.	Divísi
Dol.	Dólce
Dolciss.	Dolcíssimo
Dopp. Ped.	Dóppio pedále
D. S.	Dal Ségno
Energ°	Energicamète
Espr.	
Espress.	Espressívo
F.	Fórte
f	Fórte
Fag.	Fagótto
Falset.	Falsétto
FF.	Fortíssimo
ff	Fortíssimo
Fortiss.	Fortíssimo

FFF.	Fortissíssimo
fff	Fortissíssimo
Fl.	Fláuto, or Fláuti
For.	Fórte
F. O.	Full organ
F. Org.	Full Organ
Forz.	Forzándo
fz	Forzándo
fp	fórte, and then piáno; the note is to be strongly accented.
ffz	forzatíssimo: one note to be marked as strongly as possible.
G.	Gauche
G. O.	Great Organ
Grand°	Grandiósos
Graz°	Graziósо
Gr.	Great
Gt.	Great
Hauptw.	Hauptwerk
Haut.	Hautboy
H. C.	Haute Contre
H. p.	Hauptwerk
Hptw.	Hauptwerk
Introd.	Introduzióne
L.	Left
Leg.	Legáto
Leggieer.	Leggiéro
L.H.	Left Hand
Lo.	Lóco
Luo.	Luógo
Lusing.	Lusingándo

ABBRIVIATIONS

M.	Main, máno
M.	Mánual
Maest°	Maestóso
Magg.	Maggióre
Man.	Manual
Manc.	Mancándo
Man^{do}	Mancándo
Marc.	Marcáto
M. D.	Máno drítta
M. G.	Main gauche
M. S.	Máno sinístra
Mel.	Melody
Men.	Méno
Mez.	Mézzo
mf	mézzo fórte
Min.	Minóre
M. M.	Maelzel's Metronome
Mod°	Moderáto
Mod^{to}	Moderáto
Mov^{t}	Movement
mp	mézzo piáno
Mus. Bac.	Bachelor of Music
Mus. Doc.	Doctor of Music
m. v.	mézza vóce
Ob.	Oboè
Obb°	Obbligáto
Oberst.	Oberstimme
Oberw.	Oberwerk
Obw.	Oberwerk
Oh. Ped.	Ohne Pedal
Op.	Opus
Org°	Organo
8^a	ottáva
8va	ottáva
8va alta	ottáva álta
8va bassa	ottáva bássa
P.	Piáno
p	Piáno
Pia.	Piáno
Ped.	Pedal
Perd.	Perdendósi
Perden.	Perdendósi
P.F.	Pianoforte
pf	piáno, then fórte
piang.	Piangéndo
Pianiss.	Pianíssimo
pizz.	Pizzicáto
P^{mo}	Pianíssimo
PP	Pianíssimo
pp	Pianíssimo
ppp	Pianissíssimo: as soft as possible
1ma	príma
1mo	prímo
Prest^{mo}	Prestíssimo
Prim. Temp.	Prímo témpo
Raddol.	Raddolcéndo
Rallen.	
Rall°	Rallentándo
Recit.	Recitative
rf.	rinforzándo
rfz.	rinforzándo
R. H.	Right Hand
rinf.	rinforzándo
Risol.	Risolúto
Ritar.	Ritardándo
Ritard.	Ritardándo
Rit.	Ritenúto
Riten.	Ritenúto

ABBREVIATIONS

S.	*Sénza*
𝄋	*a Sign: see Ségno*
Scherz.	*Scherzándo*
Seg.	*Segue*
Sem.	*Sémpre*
Semp.	*Sémpre*
sf	*sforzándo*
sfz	*sforzándo*
Sim.	*Simile*
S.	*Sinístra*
Sin.	*Sinístra*
S. inter.	*Sénza interruzióne*
Slent.	*Slentándo*
Smorz.	*Smorzándo*
s. S.	*Sénza Sordíni*
s. sord.	*Sénza Sordíni*
Sost.	*Sostenúto*
Sosten.	*Sostenúto*
Spirit.	*Spiritóso*
s. T.	*sénza Témpo*
Stacc.	*Staccáto*
St Diap.	*Stopped Diapason*
String.	*Stringéndo*
2^{nda}	*secónda*
2^{ndo}	*secóndo*
Sw.	*Swell*
Sym.	*Symphony*
T.	*Tenóre*
T.	*Tútti*
T. C.	*Tre Córde*
T. S.	*Tásto Sólo*
Tem.	*Témpo*
Temp. Prim.	*Témpo Prímo*
Ten.	*Tenóre*
Ten.	*Tenúto*
Timb.	*Timballes*
Timp.	*Timpani*
Tr.	*Tríllo*
Trem.	*Tremolándo*
Tromb.	*Trombóne*
Tromp.	*Trompette*
u.	*und*
u. c.	*úna códa*
Unis.	*Unísoni*
V.	*Vóce*
V.	*Vólti*
V^a	*Vióla*
Var.	*Variation*
V^o	*Violíno*
V^{no}	*Violíno*
Viol.	*Violíno*
V^c	*Violoncéllo*
V^{llo}	*Violoncéllo*
V. S.	*Vólti Súbito*
V^{ni}	*Violíni*
V. V.	*Violíni*

In the following pages the words *Italian, French, German, English, Spanish, Greek,* &c., are abbreviated thus:- *It., Fr., Ger., Eng., Sp., Gr.,* &c.

DICTIONARY

OF

MUSICAL TERMS

A. The name given in England to the sixth note of the modern scale of Guido d'Arezzo; in France and Italy called *La*.

A, *or* **À** (*It.*) For, by, in to, &c.

AB (*Ger.*) *Off.*

ABACUS (*Lat.*) An ancient instrument for dividing the intervals of an octave.

À BALLÁTA (*It.*) In the style of a dance: see **BALLÁTA**.

ABANDON (*Fr.*) With ease; without restraint; with passionate expression.

À BATTÚTA (*It.*) *As beaten*: strictly in time.

ABBACCHIÁTO (*It.*) With a dejected, melancholy expression.

ABBADÁRE (*It.*) Take care.

ABBANDONAMÉNTE (*It.*) *see* **ABBANDÓNE**.

ABBANDONÁSI (*It.*) Without restraint; with ease: with passionate expression.

ABBANDONAMÉNTO (*It.*) Despondingly, in a dejected manner.

ABBANDONÁRE (It.) To quit, to leave.

ABBANDONATAMÉNTE (*It.*) Vehemently, violently; without any restraint as to time.

ABBANDÓNE (*It.*) Despondingly, with self-abandonment; making the time subservient to the expression.

ABBANDONEVOLMÉNTE | (*It.*) Vehemently, violently, desperately;
ABBANDÓNO | without any restraint as to time.

ABBASSAMÉNTO DI MANO (*It.*) The down-beat, or descent of the hand, in beating time.

ABBASSAMÉNTO DI VÓCE (*It.*) Sinking, diminution, or lowering of the voice.

ABBASSÁNDO (*It.*) See **DIMINUÉNDO**.

ABBATIMÉNTO (*It.*) The down beat.
ABBELLÁRE (*It.*) To embellish with ornaments.
ABBELLIMÉNTI (*It. pl.*) Ornaments, embellishments.
ABBELLIMÉNTO (*It.*) A grace note, or ornament.
ABBELLÍRE (*It.*) To embellish with ornaments.
ABBELLITÚRA (*It.*) An ornament, embellishment.
ABBELLITÚRE (*It. pl.*) Ornaments, embellishments.
ABBETONT (*Ger.*) With a *final* accent.
ABBLASEN (*Ger.*) To sound or flourish the trumpet; to sound the retreat; to sound for the last time.
ABBREVIAMÉNTI (*It.*) Abbreviations, in musical notation.
ABBREVIÁRE (*It.*) To abbreviate, or shorten the labour of notation.
ABBREVIATÚRE (*It. pl.*)
ABBREVIATUREN (*Ger. pl.*) } Abbreviations, in musical notation.
ABBREVIAZIÓNI (*It. pl.*)
ABBRUMMEN (*Ger.*) To hum over a tune.
ABDÄMPFEN (*Ger.*) To damp, to mute.
ABE-DIREN (*Ger.*) See **SOLMIZZÁRE**.
ABENDGLOCKE (*Ger.*) Evening bell, curfew.
ABENDLIED (*Ger.*) Evening song, or hymn.
ABENDMUSIK (*Ger.*) Evening or night music, serenade.
À BÊNE PLÁCITO (*It.*) *At pleasure*: the time may be retarded, or any ornaments may be introduced.
ABENTEUERLICH (*Ger.*) Adventurous.
ABER (*Ger.*) But; at the same time.
ABFASSEN (*Ger.*) To compose.
ABFASSER (*Ger.*) A composer, or author.
ABFLÖTEN (*Ger.*) To play on the flute.
ABGEHEN (*Ger.*) To go off, to make an exit, to retire.
ABGERUNDETES SPIEL (*Ger.*) A neat and finished style or execution.
ABGESANG (*Ger.*) *Aftersong*; the last section of a *Meisterlied*.
ABGESTOSSEN (*Ger.*) Struck off: *die letzte Note der Triolen nicht abgestossen*, the last note of the triplets not too short.
AB INITIO *Lat.*) An obsolete term, of the same meaning as **DA CAPO**.
ABKLANG (*Ger.*) Dissonance; echo.
ABKÜRZUNGEN (*Ger.*) Abbreviations.
ABNEHMENT
ABNEHMUNG } (*Ger.*) Decrescendo.
ABRÉGÉ (*Fr.*) Abridgement: also, the coupler in an organ.
ABRÉGER (*Fr.*) To curtail, to abridge.

Abreissung — Acathistus

ABREISSUNG (*Ger.*) A sudden stop, or pause.

A BRÍGLIA SCIÓLTA (*It.*) *With free bridle*: impetuously.

ABRUPT CADENCE. *See* **INTERRUPTED CADENCE**.

ABRUPT MODULATION. *See* **SUDDEN MODULATION**.

ABRUPTIO (*Lat.*) Breaking off; a sudden pause.

ABSATZ (*Ger.*) A musical sentence or passage; a phrase of melody, generally consisting of four bars. Also, a stop, or pause.

ABSCHLEIFER (*Ger.*) A staccato mark.

ABSCHNITT (*Ger.*) A Section.

ABSCHWELLEN (*Ger.*) *See* **DIMINUÉNDO**.

ABSETZEN
ABSTOSSEN (*Ger.*) Play the notes *Staccato*, or detached.

ABSINGEN (*Ger.*) To sing, or carol: also, to fatigue one's-self by singing.

ABSINGUNG (*Ger.*) Singing, carolling.

ABSPIELEN (*Ger.*) To play a tune; to finish playing; to tire one's-self by playing.

ABSTAND (*Ger.*) An interval.

ABSTEIGENDE TONARTEN (*Ger. pl.*) Descending scales or modes.

ABSTRAKEN (*Ger.*) *Trackers*: those pieces of wood, which connect the keys, to the sound board and pallets, of an organ.

ABSTUFEN (*Ger.*) Shading, in expression.

ABTEILUNG
ABTHEILUNG (*Ger.*) A part, movement, or division.

ABWÄRTSSCHREITEN (*Ger.*) To descend, in melody.

ABWECHSELND (*Ger.*) Alternating, changing; as *mit abwechselnden Manualen*, with alternate manuals, in organ-playing; in *abwechselnden Chören*, antiphonally. In dance music *abwechselnd* implies, returning from one movement, or strain, to another, &c.

ACADÉMIE DE MUSIQUE (*Fr.*) An academy of music, consisting of professors and scholars; a society for promoting the cultivation of music.

ACADÉMIE NATIONALE (*Fr.*) The principal opera house in Paris.

ACADÉMIE ROYALE DE MUSIQUE (*Fr.*) The name given to the Opera House in Paris.

ACADÉMIE SPIRITUELLE (*Fr.*) A performance, or concert, of sacred music.

À CAPPÉLLA (*It.*) *In the church style*; in the style of church music.

À CAPRÍCCIO (*It.*) In a capricious style: without adhering very strictly to the time.

ACATHISTUS (*Gr.*) A hymn of praise sung in the ancient Greek Church in honour of the Virgin.

Accablement — Accompagnaménto

ACCABLEMENT (*Fr.*) Depression, dejection.

ACCADÉMIA (*It.*) An academy: the word also means, a concert.

ACCAREZZÉVOLE
ACCAREZZEVOLMÉNTE | (*It.*) Blandishing: in a coaxing, caressing manner.

ACCELERAMÉNTO (*It.*) Celerity, swiftness.

ACCELERÁNDO
ACCELERÁTO | (*It.*) Accelerating the time; gradually increasing the rapidity.

ACCENT. A slight stress and distinctness given to certain sounds, to mark their particular position in the bar, and their relative importance with regard to the rhythm.

ACCENTÁRE (*It.*) *See* ACCENTUÁRE.

ACCENTÁTO (*It.*) Accented.

ACCÉNTI (*It.*)
ACCENTS (*Fr.*) | Accents.

ACCÉNTO (*It.*) Accent or emphasis laid upon certain notes; accentuation.

ACCENTOR. The leading singer, of a choir, &c.

ACCENTUÁRE (*It.*)
ACCENTUIREN (*Ger.*) | To accentuate: to mark with an accent.

ACCENTUS ECCLESIASTICI (*Lat.*) The precentor's chant, almost entirely upon one tone. These chants were formerly of seven kinds, viz., the *immutabilis*, *medius*, *gravis*, *acutus*, *moderatus*, *interrogatus*, and *finalis*.

ACCESSISTEN (*Ger.*) Unpaid choir-singers; supernumeraries.

ACCIACCÁTA
ACCIACCÁTO | (*It.*) Violently.

ACCIACCATÚRA (*It.*) A short beat, or grace note; an accessory note a semitone below the principal note, always played quickly but not kept down: it is marked ♪, or sometimes ♪.

ACCIDENT (*Fr.*) An accidental.

ACCIDENTALS (*Eng.*)
ACCIDÉNTI (*It.*)
ACCIDENTS (*Fr.*) | Occasional sharps, flats, or naturals, placed before notes in the course of a piece.

ACCIGLIAMÉNTO (*It.*) Sadness, melancholy.

ACCLAMAZIÓNE (*It.*) Acclamation.

ACCOLADE (*Fr.*) The *brace*, which connects two, three, or more staves together.

ACCOMMODÁRE (*It.*) To tune an instrument.

ACCOMPAGNAMÉNTO (*It.*) Accompaniment; the figured bass, or harmony.

Accompagnaménto — Accórdo

ACCOMPAGNAMÉNTO AD LÍBITUM (*It.*) An accompaniment that may be either played or dispensed with.

ACCOMPAGNAMÉNTO OBBLIGÁTO (*It.*) An accompaniment that must be played, being indispensable to the proper effect.

ACCOMPAGNÁRE (*It.*) To accompany; to play from the figured bass.

ACCOMPAGNATEUR (*Fr.*) \
ACCOMPAGNATÓRE (*It.*) } An accompanist; also, one who plays from the figured bass.

ACCOMPAGNÁTO (*It.*) Accompanied.

ACCOMPAGNATRÍCE (*It.*) A female accompanist.

ACCOMPAGNÉ (*Fr.*) Accompanied.

ACCOMPAGNEMENT (*Fr.*) Accompaniment.

ACCOMPAGNEMENTS (*Fr. pl.*) Accompaniments.

ACCOMPAGNER (*Fr.*) To accompany.

ACCOMPANIMENT. The figured bass; the chords or harmony: also, a part added to a solo, or other principal part in a composition, to enhance and enrich its effect.

ACCOMPANIMENT AD LIBITUM. *See* **ACCOMPAGNAMÉNTO AD LÍBITUM**.

ACCOMPANIMENT OBBLIGATO. *See* **ACCOMPAGNAMÉNTO OBBLIGÁTO**.

ACCOPPIÁTO (*It.*) Round, tied; joined together.

ACCORD (*Fr.*) A chord; a concord; consonance.

ACCORDABLE (Fr. & Eng.) Capable of being tuned.

ACCORDAMÉNTO (*It.*) Agreement; consonance.

ACCORDÁNDO (*It.*) Tuning; also, a burlesque imitation of tuning.

ACCORDANT (*Fr. & Eng.*) Consonant.

ACCORDÁNZA (*It.*) Agreement; consonance.

ACCORDÁRE (*It.*) To tune, to put an instrument in tune.

ACCORDÁTO (*It.*) Tuned: agreement in harmony, or tune.

ACCORDATÓIO (It.) A tuning-key; tuning-hammer.

ACCORDATÓRE (*It.*) One who tunes instruments.

ACCORDATÚRA (*It.*) Concord, harmony. Also, the scale or series of notes to which the open strings of an instrument are tuned. Thus, G, D, A, E, form the Accordatúra of the violin; C, G, D, A, that of the viola and violoncello; E, A, D, G, B, E, that of the guitar, &c.

ACCORD DE SIXTE AJOUTÉE (*Fr.*) A chord with an added sixth.

ACCORDER (*Fr.*) To tune an instrument; to sing or play in tune.

ACCORDION. A small wind-instrument, of modern invention, with keys and bellows; the tone is produced by the vibration of small springs, resembling those of the harmonium.

ACCÓRDO (*It.*) A chord; a concord; consonance.

ACCÓRDO CÔNSONO (*It.*) A concord.

ACCÓRDO DÍSSONO (*It.*) A discord.

ACCORDOIR (*Fr.*) A tuning-key; tuning-hammer; tuning-cone for organs.

ACCOUPLER (*Fr.*) To couple: *tirant à accoupler*, draw the coupler.

ACCRESCÉNDO (*It.*) Increasing, augmenting, in tone and force.

ACCRESCIMÉNTO (*It.*) Increase, augmentation.

ACCRESCIÚTO (*It.*) Increased, superfluous, augmented, speaking of intervals.

ACCURATÉZZA (*It.*) Care; accuracy.

À CÉMBALO (*It.*) For the harpsichord.

ACETABULUM (*Lat.*) An ancient Greek instrument, of percussion.

A CHAQUE ACCORD (*Fr.*) Press down the loud pedal, at each new chord, in pianoforte music.

ACHROMATIC MUSIC. Simple music, in which modulations seldom occur, and few accidental sharps or flats are used.

ACHT (*Ger.*) Eight.

ACHTEL (*Ger.*) Eighth; octave.

ACHTELNOTE (*Ger.*) A quaver, the eighth part of a semibreve.

ACHTELPASE (*Ger.*) A quaver-rest.

ACHTFÜSSIG (*Ger.*) For 8 feet pitch, in organ music.

ACHTKLANG (*Ger.*) Octave.

ACHTSTIMMIG (*Ger.*) For eight voices, or instruments.

A CHUFA, A FOFA
A CHULA | Portuguese dances, somewhat similar to the Fandango.

À CINQUE, *or*, **à 5** (*It.*) For five voices, or instruments; a quintet.

ACOCOTL. An ancient Mexican wind-instrument.

ACOLYTHIA (*Gr.*) The order of the service, in the Greek Church.

ACOUSTIC BASS. An organ register of 32 feet tone, but not of a true type. Produced from two pipes, one of 16 feet tone, and the other of the quint above, which produce a *beat*, giving the effect of the true note.

ACOUSTICS. The doctrine or theory of sounds; the mathematical rules and principals of sound.

ACTE (*Fr.*) An act; a part of an opera.

ACTE DE CADENCE (*Fr.*) A cadence, a final part.

ACTEUR (*Fr.*) An actor; an operatic performer.

ACTION (*Ger.*) The mechanical, or moving parts of an instrument.

ACTRICE (*Fr.*) An actress; female operatic performer.

ACT-TUNES. The pieces formally played between the acts of a drama.

ACÚSTICA (*It.*)
ACUSTIK (*Ger.*) | Acoustics; the doctrine of sounds.

ACÚTA (*It.*) Acute, shrill: also, a shrill-toned organ stop.

Acute — À deux

ACUTE. High, shrill, as to pitch.
ACUTÉZZA (*It.*) Sharpness of pitch.
ACÚTO (*It.*) Sharp, shrill, high, piercing.
ACUTUS (*Lat.*) Acute: the name of one of the ecclesiastical accents.
AD (Lat.) At, to, *ad libitum*, at pleasure.
ADAGIÉTTO (*It.*) A short *Adagio* movement.
ADÁGIO (*It.*) Slow, deliberate, but not so slow as *Lárgo*, or *Gráve*; requiring much taste and expression in performance.
ADÁGIO ADÁGIO (*It.*) Very slow.
ADÁGIO ASSÁSI (*It.*) Very slow, and with much expression.
ADÁGIO CANTÁBILE E SOSTENÚTO (*It.*) Slow, sustained, and in a singing style.
ADÁGIO CON GRAVITÀ (*It.*) Slow, with gravity and majesty.
ADÁGIO CON MOLT' ESPRESSIÓNE (*It.*) Slow, and with much expression.
ADÁGIO MÓLTO (*It.*) Very slow and expressive.
ADÁGIO NON MÓLTO
ADÁGIO NON TÁNTO   (*It.*) Not too slow.
ADÁGIO NON TRÓPPO
ADÁGIO PATÉTICO (*It.*) Slowly and pathetically.
ADÁGIO PESÁNTE (*It.*) Slowly and heavily.
ADÁGIO RELIGIÓSO (*It.*) Slowly, and in a devotional manner.
ADAGIOSÍSSIMO
ADAGÍSSIMO   (*It.*) Extremely slow.
ADÁSIO (*It.*) An old form of *Adágio*.
ADDITÁTO (*It.*) Fingered.
ADDITIONAL KEYS. Those keys of a pianoforte which extend above F in *alt*.
ADDOLCÉNDO (*It.*) Gradually softer.
ADDOLORÁTO (*It.*) Sorrowfully, with a melancholy expression.
A DÉFAUT DE (*Fr.*) *In the absence of.*
ADEL (*Ger.*) Majesty, nobility.
À DEMI-JEU
À DEMI-VOIX   (*Fr.*) With half the voice, or tone: synonymous with *Mézza voce.*
ADEPT. A thorough and accomplished composer, performer, or singer.
À DEUX (*Fr.*) For two voices or instruments.
À DEUX CORDES (*It.*) On two strings.
À DEUX HUIT (*It.*) In $\frac{2}{8}$ time.
À DEUX MAINS (*Fr.*) For two hands.

À DEUX TEMPS (*Fr.*) In two time: two equal notes in a bar, as $\frac{2}{2}, \frac{2}{4}$, &c.

ADIAPHONON (*Gr.*) A species of pianoforte with six octaves, invented in 1820 by Schuster, a watchmaker in Vienna.

ADIRATAMÉNTE
ADIRÁTO } (*It.*) Angrily, sternly.

À DIRITTÚRA (*It.*) Directly, straight.

ADJUNCT NOTES. Unaccented auxiliary notes.

ADJUVANT (*Ger.*) The deputy-master of the choristers; assistant to an organist.

ADLER (*Ger.*) An German organ stop, which starts in motion the winds of an eagle, in the case of the organ.

AD LIBITUM (*Lat.*) *At pleasure*, at will; changing the time of some particular passage at the discretion of the performer; or adding such ornaments as his fancy may suggest.

AD LONGAM (*Lat.*) In equal notes.

ADORNAMÉNTE (*It.*) Gaily, neatly, elegantly.

ADORNAMÉNTO (*It.*) An ornament, embellishment.

ADORNAMÉNTI (*It. pl.*) Embellishments.

ADOUCIR (*Fr.*) To lower: soften: flatten.

AD PLACITUM (*Lat.*) At pleasure.

À DÚE, *or*, **À 2** (*It.*) For two voices or instruments; a duet.

À DÚE CÓRDE (*It.*) Upon two strings.

À DÚE CÓRI (*It.*) For two choirs.

À DÚE STROMÉNTI (*It.*) For two instruments.

À DÚE VÓCI (*It.*) For two voices.

ADUFE. A Spanish tambourine.

A DUR (*Ger.*) The key of A major.

AD ÚNA CÓRDA (*Lat.*) For, or upon, one string.

AD VIVENDUM (*Lat.*) Written counterpoint, not improvised.

AENGSTLICH (*Ger.*) Anxiously.

ÆOLIAN. One of the ancient Greek modes.

ÆOLIAN HARP. An instrument invented by Kircher, about the middle of the seventeenth century. It is an oblong box of pine wood, with catgut strings distended upon the top, which, when acted upon by the wind, produce a variety of soft, murmuring tones. A kind of giant Æolian harp, or 'Meteorological Harmonica,' was invented at Milan by the Abbé Gattoni, who extended fifteen strings of iron wire from one tower of the Cathedral to another; they were tuned diatonically, and the tone was something like organ pipes, when the wind

Æolian — Affilar

caused them to vibrate strongly. The same effect is produced by the wind acting upon the telegraph wires.

ÆOLIAN PIANO. An *Æolodicon*, the springs of which are of wood, instead of metal.

ÆOLINE (*Gr.*) A reed stop, in an organ, in imitation of the Æolian harp: *see also* ÆOLODICON.

ÆOLODIAN
ÆOLODICON
ÆOLODION
(*Gr.*) A keyed instrument, the tone of which resembles that of the organ, and is produced by steel springs, which are put in vibration by means of bellows.

ÆOLOMELODICON. A kind of *Æolodicon*, improved by fixing brass tubes to the metal springs.

ÆOLOPANTALON. A pianoforte added to, or in connection with, the Æolodicon.

ÄOLSHARFE (*Ger.*) An Æolian harp.

ÆOLUS MODUS. The Æolian or fifth Authentic mode of the Greeks, nearly allied to the Phrygian mode; the scale is A, B, C, D, E, F, G, A, the same as the old scale of A minor, without any accidentals: *see* GREEK MODES.

ÆQUISONANS
ÆQUISONANT
ÆQUISONUS
(*Lat.*) A unison; of the same, or like, sound.

ÆQUIVAGANS (*Lat.*) Syncopation of all the parts.

ÆQUO ANIMO (*Lat.*) Quietly, with serenity.

ÆSTHETICS (*Gr.*) The rules of good taste, the laws of the beautiful in art, the principles of the Sublime and the Beautiful.

ÄUSSERSTE STIMMEN (*Ger. pl.*) The extreme parts.

AEVIA (*It.*) An abbreviation of the word *Allelúia*.

AFFÁBILE (*It.*) Pleasing, elegant.

AFFABILITÀ
AFFABILMÉNTE
(*It.*) With ease and freedom; with elegance; in a pleasing and agreeable manner.

AFFANNÁTO (*It.*) Sad, mournful, distressed.

AFFANNOSAMÉNTE (*It.*) Anxiously, restlessly.

AFFANNÓSO (*It.*) Languishing, mournful, sad.

AFFECTIRT (*Ger.*)
AFFECTTÁTO (*It.*)
With affectation.

AFFEKVOLL (*Ger.*) With fervour, passion.

AFFÉTTO (*It.*) Feeling, tenderness and pathos.

AFFETTUOSAMÉNTE (*It.*) With tenderness and pathos.

AFFETTUÓSO (*It.*) Tender, pathetic.

AFFICHE DE COMÉDIE (*Fr.*) A play-bill.

AFFILAR IL TUÓNO (*It.*) To sustain or *draw out* a tone steadily.

AFFINITÉ (*Fr.*) Relationship; affinity.

AFFIOCAMÉNTO (It.) Hoarseness.

AFFLÍTTO | (*It.*) Sorrowfully, with a sad and melancholy
AFFLIZIÓNE | expression.

AFFRETTÁNDO
AFFRETTÁTE | (*It.*) Hurrying, quickening, accelerating the time.

AFFRETTÓSO (*It.*) Quick, hurried, accelerated.

A FOFA. A Portuguese dance, resembling the Fandango.

AGENDE (*Ger.*) An agenda; things to be done.

AGÉVOLE
AGEVOLMÉNTE | (*It.*) Lightly, easily, with agility.

AGEVOLÉZZA (*It.*) Lightness, agility, facility.

AGGIUNTO (*It.*) Added.

AGGIUSTAMÉNTE (*It.*) Strictly in time.

AGGRADEVÓLE (*It.*) Pleasing; agreeable.

AGGRAVER LA FUGUE (*Fr.*) To augment the subject of a fugue.

AGIATAMÉNTE (*It.*) Indolently, lazily.

AGILITÀ (*It.*)
AGILITÉ (*Fr.*) | Agility, lightness, ease, fluency.

AGILMÉNTE (*It.*) Lightly, quickly.

AGITAMÉNTO (It.) Agitation, motion, restlessness.

AGITÁTO (*It.*) Agitated, hurried: *see* AGITAZIÓNE.

AGITAZIÓNE (*It.*) Agitation, restlessness, the time being somewhat quickened, and the tone generally increased.

AGITÁTO CON PASSIÓNE (It.) Passionately agitated.

AGITÉ (*Fr.*) Agitated.

AGLI (*It. pl.*) *See* ALLA.

AGNUS DEI (*Lat.*) *Lamb of God*. One of the principal movements in a Mass.

AGOGE (*Gr.*) Passages on the ascending and descending scale.

AGOGE RHYTHMICA (*Gr.*) Time; the measurement of time; rhythmical division.

AGRAFFÉ (*Fr.*) A device in pianofortes to reduce vibration.

A GRAND CHŒUR (*Fr.*) For the full choir or chorus.

A GRAND ORCHESTRE (*Fr.*) For the full or complete orchestra.

AGRÉMENTS (*Fr. pl.*) Graces, embellishments, ornaments: *see* GALANTÉRIEN: also, music and dancing in a play.

AGRESTE (*Fr.*) Rustic.

ÄHNLICH (*Ger.*) Like, similar.

AIGU (*Fr.*) Acute, high sharp, clear.

AIR (*Eng. & Fr.*) A melody, song, tune, with or without words. A series of sounds, so arranged as to have a certain relation to each other by their symmetry and regularity, and to produce that unity of effect which constitutes a tune. An *air* also implies any melodious succession of passages suited to vocal expression.

AIR À BOIRE (*Fr.*) A drinking song.

AIR CHANTANT (*Fr.*) *See* ARIA CANTÁBILE.

AIR DÉTACHÉ (*Fr.*) A single air, or melody, extracted from an opera, or larger work.

AIR ÉCOSSAIS (*Fr.*) A Scotch air.

AIR ITALIEN (*Fr.*) An Italian air.

AIRS DES BATELIERS VÉNÉTIENS (*Fr.*) Melodies sung by the Venetian *gondoliéri*, or boatmen.

AIRS TENDRES (*Fr. pl.*) Amatory airs, love songs.

AIR VARIÉ (*Fr.*) Air with variations: also, an air embellished and ornamented.

AIS (*Ger.*) The note A#.

AIS-DUR (*Ger.*) The key of A# major. This key is not in use, being represented by B♭ major.

AIS-MOLL (*Ger.*) The key of A-sharp minor. Not in use, being represented by B-flat minor.

AISÉ (*Fr.*) Glad, joyful; also, easy, facile, convenient.

AISÉMENT (*Fr.*) Easily, freely, readily.

AJAHLI KEMAN. A Turkish stringed instrument, of the violoncello species.

AJOUTEZ (*Fr.*) Add.

AKKORD (*Ger.*) *See* ACCORD.

AKROMAT (*Ger.*) A musician, a singer.

AKROMATISCH (*Ger.*) *See* ACHROMATIC.

AKT (*Ger.*) *See* ACTE.

AKUSTIK (*Ger.*) *See* ACOUSTICS.

À L'ABANDON (*Fr.*) Without restraint; with passionate expression.

À LA CHASE (*Fr.*) In the hunting style.

À LA FRANÇAISE (*Fr.*) In the French style.

À LA GRECQUE (*Fr.*) Choruses introduced by the French at the termination of the acts of their dramas, in imitation of the ancient Greek dramatists.

À LA MÊME
À LA MESURE (*Fr.*) In the original time.

À LA MILITAIRE (*Fr.*) In the military style. March style.

À LA POINTE D'ARCHET (*Fr.*) With the point of the bow.

À la polácca — Alla cámera

À LA POLÁCCA (*It.*) In the style or manner of a *Polácca*.
ALARGANDO (It.) *See* ALLARGÁNDO.
À LA SAVOYARDE (*Fr.*) In the style of the airs of Savoy.
ALBERTI BASS. An arpeggioed bass, of this particular kind,  &c. and thus named because it was first used by Domenico Alberti.
A L'ÉCOSSAISE (Fr.) In the Scotch style.
ALERTE (*Fr.*) Nimble, active, alert.
AL FÍNE, E PÓI LA CÓDA (*It.*) After playing to the place where *Fine* is marked, then go on to the *Códa*.
À L'IMPROVISTE (*Fr.*) Extempore.
ALIQUOTFLÜGEL (*Ger.*) A pianoforte invented by Blüther of Leipzig, with extra strings tuned an octave higher, to augment the tone.
ALIQUOT-TONES. Accessory, or secondary sounds; harmonics; sympathetic sounds.
À L'ITALIÉNNE (*Fr.*) In the Italian style.
À LIVRE OUVET (*Fr.*) *At the opening of the book*: at first sight.
AL
ALL'
ALLA
ALLE   (*It.*) *To the*; in the style or manner of.
AGLI
ALLO

ALLA BRÉVE (*It.*) A species of common time marked 𝄵, or sometimes 𝄵, and used in church music; each bar containing the value of a bréve - equal to two semibreves, or four minims; the minims being played quickly, as if they were crotchets, or twice as fast as usual.

Modern composers often subdivide these bars into two parts, each part containing two minims; and this is called *alla cappélla* time, to distinguish it from the *alla bréve* time, from which it is derived.

There are some differences of opinion, among musicians, as to the correct use and meaning of *alla bréve* and *alla cappélla*, but this is the generally received one.

ALLA BÚRLA, MA POMPÓSO (*It.*) In the burlesque style.
ALLA CÁCCIA (*It.*) In the style of hunting-music.
ALLA CÁMERA (*It.*) In the style of chamber-music.

Alla cappélla — Alle

ALLA CAPPÉLLA (*It.*) This term is generally applied to church music, containing two minims in a bar, and marked thus, 𝄵. It is derived from *alla bréve* time, the bar being subdivided. The minims are taken quickly, as if they were crotchets: *see* ALLA BRÉVE.

ALLA CÓDA (*It.*) Go back to the coda.

ALLA DIRÍTTA (*It.*) In direct ascending or descending intervals: proceeding diatonically.

ALLA FRANCÉSE \
ALLA FRANZÉSES (*It.*) In the French style.

ALLA HANÁCCA. A kind of dance, resembling the Polonaise.

ALLA MÁDRE (*It.*) *To the Virgin Mary.* Hymns and sacred songs addressed to the Virgin Mary.

ALLA MÁRCIA (*It.*) In the style of a march.

ALLA MILITÁIRE (*It.*) In the military style.

ALLA MODÉRNA (*It.*) In the modern style.

ALLA MORÉSCO (*It.*) In the Moorish style.

ALL' ANTÍCA (*It.*) In the ancient style.

ALLA PALESTRÍNA (*It.*) In the solemn ecclesiastical style, like that of Palestrina.

ALLA POLÁCCA (*It.*) In the time and style of a Polonaise, or Polish dance.

ALLA QUÍNTA (*It.*) In the fifth.

ALLARGÁNDO \
ALLARGÁTE (*It.*) Enlarged, spread out, amplified: to be performed in a broad, bold style.

ALLARMÁRE (*It.*) To sound the alarm, to beat to arms.

ALLA ROVÉSCIO (*It.*) *See* AL ROVÉSCIO.

ALLA RÚSSE (*It.*) In the style of Russian national airs.

ALLA SCOZZÉSE (*It.*) In the Scotch style.

ALLA SICILIÁNA (*It.*) In the style of the dance music of the Sicilian peasants: *see* SICILIÁNO.

ALLA STRÉTTA (*It.*) In a close, composed style, accelerating the time.

ALLA TEDÉSCA (*It.*) In the German style.

ALLA TÚRCA (*It.*) In the Turkish or Oriental style.

ALLA UNÍSSONO (*It.*) *See* ALL' UNÍSONO.

ALLA VENEZIÁNA (*It.*) In the Venetian style.

ALLA ZÍNGARA (*It.*) In a constrained, halting, limping style: *see* SYNCOPATION.

ALLA ZÓPPA (It.) In a lame, halting style.

ALLE (*Ger.*) All: *alle Instrumente*, all the instruments; the whole orchestra.

ALLEGRAMÉNTE (*It.*) \
ALLÉGREMENT (*Fr.*) } Gaily, joyfully, briskly, lively.

ALLÉGRESSE (*Fr.*) Joy, alacrity, gaiety.

ALLEGRETTÍNO (*It.*) A diminutive of *Allegrétto*, and rather slower.

ALLEGRÉTTO (*It.*) Rather light and cheerful, quicker than *Andánte*, but not so quick as *Allégro*.

ALLEGRÉTTO QUÁSI ANDANTÍNO (*It.*) A rather slow *allegrétto*.

ALLEGRÉTTO SCHERZÁNDO (*It.*) Lightly, cheerfully, in a playful and vivacious style.

ALLEGRÉTTO VILLERECIO (*It.*) Rather quick, and in the rural style.

ALLEGRÉZZA \
ALLEGRÍA } (*It.*) Joy, gladness, gaiety, cheerfulness, liveliness.

ALLEGRISSIMAMÉNTE (*It.*) Very joyfully, with great animation.

ALLEGRÍSSIMO (*It.*) Very joyfully, with great animation.

ALLÉGRO (*Fr. & It.*) Lively, briskly, merry, cheerful: the opposite to the pathetic, in music.

ALLÉGRO AGITÁTO (*It.*) Quick, with agitation.

ALLÉGRO ASSÁI (*It.*) Very quick, and animated.

ALLÉGRO CÓMODO (*It.*) A convenient degree of rapidity.

ALLÉGRO CON BRÍO (*It.*) Quick, with brilliancy.

ALLÉGRO CON FUÓCO (*It.*) Quick, with fire and animation.

ALLÉGRO CON MÓTO (*It.*) Quick, with more that the usual degree of motion.

ALLÉGRO CON SPÍRITO (*It.*) Quick, with much spirit.

ALLÉGRO DECÍSO (*It.*) Quick, with a well marked rhythm.

ALLÉGRO DI BRAVÚRA (*It.*) Quick, with brilliant and spirited execution.

ALLÉGRO DI MÓLTO (*It.*) Exceedingly quick and animated.

ALLÉGRO FURIÓSO (*It.*) Quick, with fury and impetuosity.

ALLÉGRO GIÚSTO (*It.*) Quick, with exactness; in a steady, precise time.

ALLÉGRO MA GRAZIÓSO (*It.*) Quick, but gracefully.

ALLÉGRO MA NON PRÉSTO (*It.*) Quick, but not so fast as *Présto*.

ALLÉGRO MA NON TÁNTO \
ALLÉGRO MA NON TRÓPPO } (*It.*) Quick, and lively, but not too rapid.

ALLÉGRO MODERÁTO (*It.*) Moderately quick.

ALLÉGRO MÓLTO (*It.*) Very quick and animated.

ALLÉGRO NON TÁNTO \
ALLÉGRO NON TRÓPPO } (*It.*) Quick, but not too fast.

ALLÉGRO RISOLÚTO (*It.*) Quick and vigorous, with decision.

ALLÉGRO VELÓCE (*It.*) Quick, with velocity.

Allégro — Almanes

ALLÉGRO VIVÁCE (*It.*) Quick, with vivacity; very lively and brisk.

ALLÉGRO VÍVO (*It.*) Quick, and lively.

ALLEIN (*Ger.*) Alone, single: *mit zarten Stimmen allein*, with delicate stops only.

ALLELÚIA (*It.*)
ALLELUJAH (*Eng.*) | *Praise the Lord!* A song of thanksgiving.

ALLEMANDE (*Fr.*) A German air: also a slow dance or air in $\frac{2}{4}$ or $\frac{4}{4}$ time, peculiar to Germany and Switzerland.

ALLE NEU EINTRETENDE STIMMEN HERVORTRETEND (*Ger.*) Each new entry, to be made prominent.

ALLENTAMÉNTO
ALLENTÁNDO | (*It.*) Relaxation, lingering, giving way, slackening the time.
ALLENTÁTO

ALLE SAITEN (Ger.) *All the strings*: see **TUTTE CORDE**.

ALL' ESPAGNUÓLA (*It.*) In the style of Spanish music.

ALLGEMEINER BASS (*Ger.*) See **THOUGH-BASS**.

ALLIÉVO (*It.*) A scholar, a pupil.

ALL' IMPROVVÍSO
ALL' IMPROVVÍSTA | (*It.*) Without previous study; extemporaneously.
ALL' IMPROVVÍSTO

ALL' INGLÉSE (*It.*) In the style of English music.

ALL' ITALIÁNA (*It.*) In the style of Italian music.

ALLMÄHLICH
ALLMÄHLIG | (Ger.) Gradually.
ALLMÄLIG

AL LÓCO (*It.*) In the right, or usual, place.

ALL' OTTÁVA (*It.*) *In the octave.* This is frequently met with in scores and orchestral parts, and means that one part must play an octave above, or below, another.

ALL' UNÍSONO (*It.*) *In unison*: a succession of unisons or octaves.

ALLONGER (*Fr.*) To lengthen; to prolong, to develop.

ALLONGEZ L'ARCHET (*Fr.*) Lengthen, or prolong, the stroke of the bow, in violin music.

ALLÓRA (*It.*) Then.

ALLZUGLEICH
ALLZUUMAL | (*Ger.*) Altogether.

ALMAIN
ALMAN | The name of an old slow dance, of a dignified character: see **ALLEMANDE**.
ALMAND

ALMANES (*pl.*) See **ALMAN**.

ALMA REDEMPTORIS (*Lat.*) A hymn to the Virgin.

ALMÉNO (*It.*) Becoming as soft as possible.

ALPENHORN
ALPHORN | (*Ger.*) The Alpine, or cow-horn.

AL PIACÉRE (*It.*) *At pleasure*: see À PIACÉRE.

AL PIÙ (*It.*) *The most.*

AL RIGÓRE DI TÉMPO
AL RIGÓRE DEL TÉMPO | (*It.*) In very strict and rigorous time.

AL RIVÉRSO
AL ROVÉSCIO | (*It.*) Reverse, backward motion: *see* RIVÉRSO and ROVÉSCIO.

ALS (*Ger.*) As, like; than; but; when.

AL SÉGNO (*It.*) To the sign: meaning that the performer must return to the sign 𝄋 in a previous part of the piece.

ALSO (*Ger.*) Thus, so; therefore: *Also nicht weniger geschwind*, Not less quick.

AL SÓLITO (*It.*) *As usual*: after the usual manner.

ALT (*It.*) *High*. This term is applied to the notes extending from G, above the fifth line of the treble stave, to the next F above, both inclusive.

ALT (*Ger.*) Counter-tenor, or alto.

ÁLTA (*It.*) *High*, or *higher*: *ottáva álta*, an octave higher; play he notes an octave above.

ALTCLARINETTE (*Ger.*) The alto clarinet; a fifth lower than the normal clarinet: *see* CLARINET.

AL TEDÉSCO (*It.*) In the German style.

ALTERÁRE (*It.*) To change, alter.

ALTERATIO (*Lat.*)
ALTERÁTO (*It.*)
ALTÉRÉ (*Fr.*) | *Changed, altered*: it generally means augmented, or doubling the value of a note, in counterpoint.

ALTÉRATION (*Fr.*)
ALTERÁZIO (*It.*) | Alteration; change of a note.

ALTERÉZZA (*It.*) Loftiness; pride.

ALTERNAMÉNTE
ALTERNÁNDO | *Alternating*; by turns, alternatively.

ALTERNATIONS. Changes, or melodies, composed for bells.

ALTERNATÍVO (*It.*) *See* ALTERNAMÉNTE.

ALTGEIGE (*Ger.*) The viola, or tenor violin.

ALTHOBOE (*Ger.*) *See* COR ANGLAIS.

ALTIERAMÉNTE (*It.*) With grandeur, nobly, haughtily.

ALTI NATURÁLI (*It.*) Natural male altos, or counter-tenors.

ALTÍSONO (*It.*) Sonorous.

Altíssimo — Amateur

ALTÍSSIMO (*It.*) *The highest*; extremely high or acute; applied to all the high treble notes, commencing from G on the fourth ledger line.

ALTIST (*Eng.*)
ALTÍSTA (*It.*)
ALTISTE (*Fr.*) | An alto singer; one who has an alto or counter-tenor voice.

ALTITONANS (*Lat.*) In the choral music of the sixteenth century this signified the *alto*, or highest part under the treble.

ÁLTO (*It.*) *High*. The highest male voice, sometimes called the counter-tenor. It also indicates the part for the viola, in instrumental music.

ÁLTO-BÁSSO (*It.*) An obsolete Venetian stringed instrument, played with some kind of bow.

ÁLTO-CLEF. The C clef, when played upon the third line.

ÁLT' OTTÁVA
ÁLTO OCTÁVO | (*It.*) The same notes, an octave higher.

ALTPOSAUNE (*Ger.*) Alto trombone.

ÁLTO-VIÓLA (*It.*) The viola, or tenor violin.

ÁLTRA (*It.*)
ÁLTRI (*It. pl.*)
ÁLTRO (*It.*) | Other, another; others.

ALTSÄNGER
ALTSTIMME | (*Ger.*) Counter-tenor singer, alto singer, alto voice or part.

ALTSCHLÜSSEL (*Ger.*) The alto-clef; the C clef on the third line.

ALTUS (*Lat.*) The alto, or counter-tenor.

ALTVIOLE (*Ger.*) The viola, or tenor violin.

ALTZEICHEN (*Ger.*) *See* ALTSCHLÜSSEL.

ALZAMÉNTO DI MÁNO (*It.*) Elevation of the hand, or up-beat, in conducting.

ALZÁNDO (*It.*) Raising, lifting up.

AM (*Ger.*) On the, at the, near the: *Am Stege*, near the bridge, in violin playing.

AMÁBILE (*It.*) Tender, graceful, gentle, amiable.

AMABILITÀ (*It.*) Gracefulness, gentleness, loveliness.

AMABILMÉNTE (*It.*) Gracefully, amiably.

AMARÉVOLE
AMARÉZZA | (*It.*) Bitterness, sadness, grief, affliction.

AMARISSIMAMÉNTE
AMARÍSSIMO | (*It.*) Very bitterly; in a very mournful and afflicted style.

AMÁRO (*It.*) Bitterness, grief, affliction.

AMATEUR (*Fr.*) A non-professional lover and performer of music: *see* DILETTÁNTE.

Ambitus — Amphimacer

AMBITUS (*Lat.*) Diapason: compass or range of sounds; also, the interval between deep and acute sounds.

AMBO | (*Gr.*) A desk, or pulpit.
AMBON |

AMBROSIAN CHANT. A series of sacred melodies or chants, collected and introduced into the Church by Ambrosius (St. Ambrose), Bishop of Milan, in the fourth century, and supposed to have been borrowed from the ancient Greek music: *see* **GREGORIAN MODES.**

AMBUBAJE (*Gr.*) The name of a society of strolling flute-players amongst the ancient Greeks.

AMBULANT (*Fr.*) Wandering; an itinerant musician.

ÂME (*Fr.*) The sound-post of a violin, viola, &c.

AMERICAN ORGAN. A variety of the harmonium, in which the arrangements for the production of the wind, and also of the *expression*, *tremolo* stops, &c., are different from the European harmoniums. The tone is sometimes produced by each reed being placed in a separate tube or very short pipe of soft wood.

A MESURE (*Fr.*) By the beat; in strict time.

À MÉZZA ÁRIA (*It.*) An air partaking of the style of recitative; between singing and speaking.

À MÉZZA FÓRZA | (*It.*) With half the power of the voice; in a
À MÉZZA VÓCE | subdued tone: the term is also applied to wind, and stringed, instruments.

A MI VOIX (*Fr.*) With half the voice.

A MOLL (*Ger.*) The key of A minor.

À MONOCORDE (*Fr.*) On one string only.

AMÓRE (*It.*) Affection, love, ardour, tenderness.

À MORÉSCO (*It.*) In the Moorish style; in the style of a Morésco, or Moorish dance.

AMORÉVOLE | (*It.*) Tenderly, lovingly, gently, affectionately.
AMOREVOLMÉNTE |

AMOROSAMÉNTE | (*It.*) In a tender, gentle, and affectionate style.
AMORÓSO |

AMORSCHALL | (*Ger.*) A French horn with valves, invented by
AMORSKLANG | Köbel, 1760.

AMPHIBRACH (*Gr.*) A musical foot, comprising one short, one long, and one short note or syllable, accented and marked thus, ⌣ — ⌣ .

AMPHIMACER (*Gr.*) A musical foot, comprising one long, one short, and one long note or syllable, accented and marked thus, — ⌣ — .

Amphion — Andanteménte

AMPHION (*Gr.*) The most ancient Greek musician. He played upon the lyre.

AMPOLLOSAMÉNTE
AMPOLLÓSO | (*It.*) Bombastically; in a pompous manner.

AMPOULÉ (*Fr.*) High-flown, bombastic: *un style ampoulé*, a high-flown, bombastic style.

AMT (*Ger.*) Office, ecclesiastical duty; mass.

AMUSEMENT (*Fr.*) A short and lively composition.

AMUSEMENTS (*Fr. pl.*) Short, entertaining compositions.

AMUSIA. Loss of musical faculty.

AN (*Ger.*) On; add; at, against, to; from: *An der Spitze*, at the point.

ANABASIS (*Gr.*) A succession of ascending sounds or tones.

ANACREONTIC. In the Bacchanalian, drinking style.

ANAKAMPTOS (*Gr.*) A succession of descending sounds, or tones.

ANAKARA. The kettledrum.

ANAKARISTA. A timpanist, or kettledrum-player.

ANAKRUSIS. The up-stoke, in conducting, or beating time.

ANÁLISI (*It.*)
ANALYSE (*Fr.*) | An analysis.

ANAPEST (*Gr.*) A musical foot, containing two short notes, or syllables, and a long one, accented and marked ⌣⌣—.

ANAPHORA (*Gr.*) The immediate repetition of a passage which has just been played.

ANARMONIA. Dissonance, false harmony.

ANBLASEN (*Ger.*) To blow, to sound.

ANCHE (*Fr.*) The reed, or mouth-piece, of the oboe, bassoon, clarinet, &c.: also, the various reed-stops in an organ.

ANCHE (*It.*) Also, too, likewise; even.

ANCHER (*Fr.*) To put a reed to a musical instrument.

ANCIA (*It.*) *See* ANCHE.

ANCILLA (*Gr.*) Those shields, by the clang of which the ancient Greeks marked the measure of their music on festive occasions.

ANCÓRA (*It.*) Again, once more: also, yet, still, &c.

ANCÓR PIÙ MÓSSO (*It.*) Still more motion; a little quicker yet.

ANDACHT (*Ger.*) Devotion.

ANDÄCHTIG (*Ger.*) Devoutly; devotional.

ANDÁNDO (It.) *See* ANDÁNTE.

ANDAMÉNTO (*It.*) A rather slow, stalking, movement: also, an episode, or accessory idea, in a fugue.

ANDÁNTE
ANDANTEMÉNTE | (*It.*) Going easily, fluently, steadily moving on, advancing, without interruption.

Andánte — Ánglico

ANDÁNTE AFFETTUÓSO (*It.*) Moving easily, with much pathos.

ANDÁNTE CANTÁBILE (*It.*) Moving easily, in a singing and melodious style.

ANDÁNTE CON MÓTO (*It.*) Moving easily, with motion, or agitation; rather lively.

ANDÁNTE GRAZIÓSO (*It.*) Moving easily, with a graceful expression.

ANDÁNTE MAESTÓSO (*It.*) Moving easily, with majesty.

ANDÁNTE MA NON TRÓPPO, E CON TRISTÉZZA (*It.*) Moving easily, but not too slow, and with pathos.

ANDÁNTE NON TRÓPPO (*It.*) Moving easily, not too slow.

ANDÁNTE PASTORÁLE (*It.*) Moving easily, in a pastoral style.

ANDANTÍNO (*It.*) A little slower than *Andánte*: see INO.

ANDANTÍNO SOSTENÚTO E SIMPLICEMÉNTE, IL CÁNTO UN PÓCO PIÙ FÓRTE (*It.*) Rather slowly, in a sustained and simple manner, with the melody a little louder than the other notes.

ANDÁR DIRÍTTO (*It.*) Go straight on.

ANDÁRE (*It.*) To go on; to move on.

ANDÁRE IN TÉMPO (*It.*) To go in time, to play or sing in time.

ANELANTEMÉNTE (*It.*) Ardently, anxiously.

ANELÁNZA \
ANÉLITO (*It.*) Shortness of breath.

ANEMOCHORD. See ANIMO CORDE.

ANEMOMETER. A *wind-gauge*, or machine for 'weighing the wind' in an organ.

ANFANG (*Ger.*) The beginning, commencement, entrance.

ANFÄNGER (*Ger.*) A beginner.

ANFANGSGRÜNDE (*Ger.*) Introductory symphony to an air, &c.

ANFITEÁTRO (*It.*) An amphitheatre.

ANFÜHRER (*Ger.*) Conductor; instructor.

ANGEBEN (*Ger.*) To give sound: *den Ton angeben*, to give out the time.

ANGELICA (*Ger.*) \
ANGÉLIQUE (*Fr.*) An organ stop: *see* VOIX CÉLESTES: also, an *Angelot*: see that word.

ANGELOPHONE. An early name for the harmonium, *which see*.

ANGELOT. An old instrument, somewhat resembling a lute.

ANGÉLUS (*Fr.*) Ave Maria; prayer time.

AGEMESSEN (*Ger.*) Appropriate, suitable.

ANGENEHM (*Ger.*) Agreeable, pleasing, sweet: *mit angenehm Registerm*, with pleasing stops, in organ playing.

ANGLAISE (*Fr.*) \
ÁNGLICO (*It.*) An English air, or country dance.

Angóre — Anschlag

ANGÓRE (*It.*) Passion, grief, anguish.

ANGOSCÉVOLE (*It.*) Dolorous, sorrowful.

ANGÓSCIA
ANGOSCIAMÉNTO | (*It.*) Anxiety, sorrow, anguish.

ANGOSCIOSAMÉNTE (*It.*) Anxiously, sorrowfully, in a dolorous manner.

ANGOSCIOSÍSSIMAMÉNTE (*It.*) With extreme sorrow, and dolorous expression.

ANGOSCIÓSO (*It.*) Sorrowful, afflicted.

ÄNGSTLICH (*Ger.*) Timidly, anxiously, restlessly.

ANHALTENDE CADENZ (*Ger.*) A protracted cadence; an organ point; a pedal point.

ANHANG (*Ger.*) Appendix, postscript; a coda.

ÁNIMA (*It.*) Soul, feeling.

ANIMATIO (*Lat.*) Animation, spirit.

ANIMÁTO (*It.*) Animated; with life and animation.

ANIMAZIÓNE (*It.*) Animation.

ANIMÉ (*Fr.*) Animated.

ANIMEZ PEU À PUE JUSQU'A LA FIN (*Fr.*) Quicker and quicker to the end.

ANIMO (*It.*) Spirit, courage, resolution, boldness.

ANIMO CORDE (*Lat.*) An instrument invented in 1789 by Joh. Jacob Schnell, of Paris, and which excited much admiration at the time. The tone is produced by wind passing over strings.

ANIMOSAMÉNTE (*It.*) Boldly, resolutely.

ANIMOSÍSSIMAMÉNTE
ANIMOSÍSSIMO | (*It.*) Exceedingly bold, and resolute.

ANIMÓSO (*It.*) Lively, energetic, bold, with spirit.

ANKLANG (*Ger.*) Accord, harmony, tune.

ANKLINGELN (*Ger.*) To ring a bell, to tingle.

ANKLINGEN (*Ger.*) To accord in sound.

ANLAGE (*Ger.*) Plan, or outline, of a composition.

ANLAUFEN (*Ger.*) To swell, to increase in sound.

ANLEITUNG (*Ger.*) An introduction, preface.

ANMUTH (*Ger.*) Sweetness, charm, grace, sauvity.

ÂNONNER (*Fr.*) Hesitating, stammering, want of confidence and decision; to blunder.

ANPFEIFEN (*Ger.*) To whistle at; to hiss at.

ANSATZ (*Ger.*) Mouth-piece of a wind instrument.

ANSCHLAG (*Ger.*) The percussion of a discord; the striking of a chord or key; the touch, in pianoforte-playing.

Amschlagen — Antiphone

AMSCHLAGEN (*Ger.*) To strike, touch, sound.
ANSCHMIEGEND (*Ger.*) Insinuating, yielding.
ANSCHWELLEN (*Ger.*) To swell: *see* CRESCÉNDO.
ANSINGEN (*Ger.*) To celebrate in song; to welcome with a song.
ANSIOSAMÉNTE (*It.*) Anxiously; hesitatingly.
ANSPIELEN (*Ger.*) To play first.
ANSPRACHE (*Ger.*) Intonation, sound, tone.
ANSPRECHEN (*Ger.*) To sound; to give, or emit, a sound.
ANSPRUCHSLOS (*Ger.*) Modest, unpretending.
ANSTATT (*Ger.*) Instead.
ANSTIMMEN (*Ger.*) To intone, to sing, to give a sound.
ANSTIMMUNG (*Ger.*) Intonation, singing, sounding.
ANTECEDENT (*Lat.*) The subject of a fugue, or of a point of imitation.
ANTELUDIUM (*Lat.*) Introduction, prelude.
ANTANZEN (*Ger.*) To begin to dance.
ANTHEM. A sacred vocal composition, the words of which are generally selected from the Bible, and the accompaniment is usually for the organ.
ANTHEMA. An ancient Greek dance.
ANTHOLOGIE (*Gr.*) A collection of choice pieces.
ANTHOLOGIUM (*Gr.*) *See* ANTIPHONARIUM.
ANTHROPOGLOSSA (*Gr.*) The *vox humana*, an organ stop, somewhat resembling the human voice.
ANTI-BACCHUS. A musical foot comprising two accented long notes or syllables, and a short or unaccented one, marked thus, ———◡.
ANTÍCA (*It.*) Anticipation.
ANTICIPATION. Sounding a note, or chord, before its natural and expected place.
ANTICIPAZIÓNE (*It.*) *See* ANTICIPATION.
ANTÍCO (*It.*) Ancient.
ANTIENNE (*Fr.*) An anthem.
ANTÍFONA (*It.*) An anthem; an antiphone.
ANTIFONÁRIO (*It.*) A book of anthems; an anthem-singer.
ANTIPHON. Alternate singing.
ANTIPHONAIRE (*Fr.*) A book of anthems, responses, &c.
ANTIPHONARIUM (*Gr.*) The collection of *Antiphons* used in the Roman Catholic service, sung alternately by the priest and congregation.
ANTIPHONARY. A book of anthems, responses, &c.
ANTIPHONE (*Gr.*) The response made by one part of the choir to another, or by the congregation to the priest. A part of the Roman Catholic musical service: also, singing alternately.

Antiphonie — À póco

ANTIPHONIE (*Gr.*) Antiphony; originally a species of sacred composition consisting of *octaves* and *fifteenths*; but the name was afterwards applied to hymns and anthems, which were sung responsively: *see* ANTIPHONE.

ANTIPHONIER (*Fr.*) A book of anthems.

ANTIPHONIZING. Singing in octaves, in the ancient Greek music.

ANTIPHONON (*Gr.*) In ancient Greek music it meant, accompaniment in the octave.

ANTIPHONS (*Gr. pl.*) See ANTIPHONE.

ANTIPHONY. See ANTIPHONE *and* ANTIPHONIE.

ANTISPAST (*Gr.*) A musical foot comprising two short, and two long syllables, marked thus ⏑ — — ⏑.

ANTISTROPHE. In an ode sung in parts, this is the second stanza of every three.

ANTITHESIS. In fugues this term is applied to the *answer*; and it generally signifies *contrast*.

ANTONEN (*Ger.*) To strike up; to intone.

ANTWORK (*Ger.*) The answer, in a fugue, &c.

ANWACHSEND (*Ger.*) Swelling: *see* CRESCÉNDO.

ÄOLSHARFE (*Ger.*) See ÆOLINE HARP.

ÄOLSKLAVIER (*Ger.*) See ÆOLINE PIANO.

A PÁRTE (*It.*) Aside.

À PÁSSO À PÁSSO (*It.*) Step by step.

APÉRTO (*It.*) *Open*: in pianoforte music this word means that the *damper pedal* is to be pressed down.

APERTUS (*Lat.*) *Open*: as, open canon, open diapason.

APFELREGAL (*Ger.*) *Apple-register*: a reed stop in old organs, now obsolete. It was of 8 or 4 feet tone: the body of the pipe (the longest of which did not exceed 4 inches) had at the top a round hollow knob, with little holes to let out the wind.

APHONIE (*Fr.*) Aphony, want of voice.

À PIACÉRE
À PIACIMÉNTO (*It.*) *At pleasure*: the time and expression are left to the pleasure of the performer, or a *cadenza* may be introduced.

À PIÉNA ORCHÉSTRA (*It.*) *For full orchestra.*

A PIENE ENTENDU (*Fr.*) Very soft; scarcely heard.

A PISTONS (*Fr.*) With pistons.

À PLOMB (*Fr.*) *Firm*: with exactness as to time.

APNŒA (*Gr.*)
APNÉA (*It.*) Want of breath, weakness of lungs.

À PÓCO (*It.*) By degrees, by little, gradually.

À PÓCO À PÓCO (*It.*) By little and little.

À PÓCO PIÙ LÉNTO (*It.*) A little more slowly.

À PÓCO PIÙ MÓSSO (*It.*) A little quicker.

APOGGIATÚRA
APOGIATÚRA } *See* APPOGGIATÚRA.

APOLLO. The Greek god of music, inventor of the lyre.

APOLLO-LYRA. An obsolete instrument, in shape like a lyre or small harp, 12 inches high, 6 inches broad, with 12 keys: it was played with a brass mouth-piece, like a horn.

APOLLONICON. A large organ, with six sets of keys, which may be played upon simultaneously by six performers. It also has immense self-acting cylinders or barrels, which bring the whole power of the instrument into operation, producing the most extraordinary effects, the tone resembling that of a full orchestra. Invented in 1828 by Flight and Robson.

APOTOME (*Gr.*) The larger half of a whole tone.

APPASSIONAMÉNTO
APPASSIONATAMÉNTE
APPASSIONÁTO } (*It.*) Passionately, with great emotion, and intensity of feeling.

APPEAU (*Fr.*) Bird-like tone.

APPELL (*Ger.*) A bugle call.

APPÉNA (*It.*) A little, somewhat.

APPENÁTO (*It.*) Grieved, afflicted: an expression of suffering and melancholy.

APPLAUDISSEMENT (*Fr.*)
APPLAÚSO (*It.*) } Applause.

APPLICÁTIO (*It.*)
APPLICATUR (*Ger.*) } The art of fingering.

APPOGGIÁNDO
APPOGGIÁTO } (*It.*) Leaning, held on, drawn out, dwelt upon.

APPOGGIATÚRA (*It.*) *Leaning note*, grace note, beat, note of embellishment.

APPÓGGIO (*It.*) Strength, support; breath-resistance.

APPRESTÁRE (*It.*) To prepare, or make playable.

APPUYER (*Fr.*) To sustain.

ÂPRE (*Fr.*) Harsh.

À PREMIÈRE VUE (*Fr.*)
À PRÍMA VÍSTA (*It.*) } At first sight.

À PRÍMO TÉMPO (*It.*) At the first speed.

À PÚNTA D'ÁRCO (*It.*) With the point of the bow.

À PÚNTO (*It.*) Punctually, correctly, exactly.

À quatre — Ardíto

À QUATRE MAINS (*Fr.*)
A QUÁTTRO MÁNI (*It.*)   For four hands: a pianoforte duet.

À QUÁTTRO, *or*, **A 4** (*It.*) For four voices or instruments; a quartet.

À QUÁTTRO PARTI (*It.*) In four parts.

À QUATRE VOIX (*Fr.*)
À QUÁTTRO VÓCI (*It.*)   For four voices.

À QUATRE SEULS (*Fr.*)
À QUÁTTRO SÓLI (*It.*)   For four solo voices, or instruments alone.

ARABESKEN (*Ger. pl.*) Ornamental variations.

ARABESQUE (*Fr.*) In the Arabian or Moorish style.

ARBÍTRIO (*It.*) Will, pleasure.

ARCÁTO (*It.*) *Bowed*: played with the bow.

ARCHE (*Ger.*) Sound-board.

ARCHEGGIÁRE (It.) To play with the bow.

ARCHEGGIAMÉNTO (*It.*) The management of the bow, in playing the violin, &c.

ARCHET (*Fr.*) The bow, of a violin, &c.

ARCHÉTTO
ARCHICÉLLO   (*It.*) A little bow.

ARCHICEMBALO (Fr.)
ARCHICYMBAL (Ger.)   *See* ARCICEMBÁLO.

ARCHILUTH (*Fr.*)
ARCILIÚTO (*It.*)   *See* ARCH-LUTE.

ARCHIVIOLE (*Fr.*) The celestina.

ARCH-LUTE. A theorbo, or lute, with two nuts, and sets of strings, one set for the bass. The strings of the theorbo were single; but in the arch-lute the bass strings were doubled with an octave, and the small strings with an unison.

ARCICEMBÁLO (It.) An instrument with six keyboards, and strings, to give all the tones of the ancient Greek modes.

ARCIVIÓLA DI LÍRA (*It.*) The largest type of lyre: *see* LIRÓNE.

ÁRCO (*It.*) The bow: *árco*, or *coll' árco*, in violin music, means that the notes are to be played with the bow, and not Pizzicáto.

ARDEMMENT (*Fr.*) Ardently, vehemently.

ARDÉNTE (*Fr. & It.*) Glowing, fiery, vehement, ardent.

ARDENTEMÉNTE (*It.*) Ardently, vehemently.

ARDENTÍSSIMO (*It.*) Very ardently and vehemently.

ARDITAMÉNTE (*It.*) Boldly, energetically, with ardour.

ARDITÉZZA (*It.*) Boldness.

ARDÍTO (*It.*) Bold, with energy.

ARETINIAN SYLLABLES. The syllables *ut, re, mi, fa, sol, la*, introduced by Guido d'Arezzo, to solfa his system of hexachords, or scales of six notes.

ARGHOOL. An Egyptian *reed* wind-instrument; a primitive type of clarinet.

ÁRIA (*It.*) An air, tune, song; a piece of music for a single voice, with or without instrumental accompaniment: *see* AIR.

ÁRIA AGGIÚNTE (*It. pl.*) Airs added to, or introduced into any opera, or other large work.

ÁRIA BÚFFA (*It.*) A comic, or humorous air.

ÁRIA CANTÁBILE (*It.*) An air in a graceful, melodious, and flowing, style.

ÁRIA CONCERTÁTA (*It.*) An air with elaborate orchestral accompaniments in a *Concertánte* style: see CONCERTÁNTE.

ÁRIA DA CHIÉSA (It.) *Church aria.*

ÁRIA D'ABILTÀ (*It.*) An air of difficult execution, requiring skill and ability in the performer.

ÁRIA DI BRAVÚRA (*It.*) A florid air, requiring great freedom of execution.

ÁRIA DI CANTÁBILE (*It.*) *See* ÁRIA CANTÁBILE.

ÁRIA FUGÁTA (*It.*) An air, the accompaniments of which are written in the fugal style.

ÁRIA PARLÁNTE (*It.*) An air in the declamatory style; much the same as recitative.

ÁRIA TEDÉSCA (*It.*) An air in the German style.

ARIÉTTA (*It.*) | A short air, or melody.
ARIETTE (*Fr.*)

ARIÉTTA ALLA VENEZIÁNA (*It.*) A short air, in the style of the Venetian Barcarolles.

ARIETTINA (*It.*) A short air, or melody.

ARIGOT (*Fr.*) A fife.

ARION. An ancient harp-player and poet of Greece, who lived 717 B.C.

ARIÓSE CANTÁTE (*It. pl.*) Airs in a style between melody and recitative, and with frequent changes in their time, manner, and humour.

ARIÓSO (*It.*) Melodious, vocal; a short piece in the style of an air, but less regular and symmetrical in its construction: *see* AIR.

ARMER LA CHEF (*Fr.*) The signature; or, the sharps or flats placed immediately after the clef.

ARMGEIGE (Ger.) *See* VIÓLA DA BRÁCCIO.

ARMONEGGIÁRE (*It.*) To sound in harmony.

Armonía — Ars

ARMONÍA (*It.*) Harmony, concord.

ARMONIÁLE (*It.*) Harmonious, musical.

ARMONÍA MILITÁRE (*It.*) Military band.

ARMONIÁTO (*It.*) Harmonised.

ARMÓNICA (*It.*) The earliest form of the accordion: also, a musical instrument the sounds of which are produced from glass.

ARMÓNICO (*It.*) Harmonious.

ARMONIE (*Fr.*) An old instrument of the 12th and 13th centuries.

ARMONIOSAMÉNTE (*It.*) Harmoniously.

ARMONIÓSO (*It.*) Harmonious.

ARMONÍSTA (*It.*) One who understands harmony.

ARMONIZZÁNTE (*It.*) That is harmonious, musical.

ARMONIZZÁRE (*It.*) To make harmony; to harmonise.

ARMURE (*Fr.*) The key-signature.

ÀRPA / ÀRPE (*It.*) The harp.

ÀRPA DÓPPIA (*It.*) The double-action harp: formerly it meant, a harp with two strings to each note.

ARPANÉTTA / ARPINÉLLA (*It.*) A small harp, or lute.

ARPÉGE (*Fr.*) See ARPEGGIO.

ARPÉGEMENT (*Fr.*) In the *arpéggio* style.

ARPÉGER (*Fr.*) To play *arpéggio*.

ARPEGGIÁNDO / ARPEGGIÁTO (*It.*) Harping; harp-music: chords, or harmonies, played *Arpéggio*, in imitation of the harp.

ARPEGGIÁRE (*It.*) To play on the harp.

ARPEGGIATÚRA (*It.*) A series of *arpéggio*.

ARPÉGGIO (*It.*) To play the notes of a chord, one after another, instead of striking them together.

ARPEGGIÓNE (*It.*) An instrument of the *Vióla da gamba* species, with six strings, invented by Stauffer of Vienna in 1823.

ARPICÓRDO (*It.*) A harpsichord.

ARPÓNE (*It.*) A species of harp, with horizontal, instead of vertical strings.

ARRACHÉ (*Fr.*) *Torn*: strongly *pizzicáto*.

ARRANGER (*Fr.*) / ARRANGIREN (*Ger.*) To arrange music for particular voices or instruments; also, to arrange orchestral music for the pianoforte, &c.

ARS CANENDI (*Lat.*) The art of singing with truth, judgement, and taste.

ARS COMPONENDI (*Lat.*) The art of composing.

Arsis — À súo

ARSIS (*Gr.*) The up-stroke, or elevation of the hand, in beating time.

ARS MUSICA (*Lat.*) Art and science of music.

ART (*Ger.*) Species, kind, mode.

ART DE L'ARCHET (*Fr.*) The art of bowing.

ÁRTE (*It.*) *Art*.

ARTICOLÁRE (*It.*) To pronounce the words distinctly, in vocal music; to articulate each note clearly.

ARTICOLÁTO (*It.*) Articulate, plain, distinct; clearly enunciated.

ARTICOLAZIÓNE (*It.*) Articulate and distinct pronunciation.

ARTICULER (*Fr.*) *See* **ARTICOLÁRE**.

ARTIGLICH (*Ger.*) Gracefully, neatly.

ARTÍSTA (*It.*) \
ARTISTE (*Fr.*) An artist: this term is only applied, musically, to singers, performers, or composers, of the highest class.

ARSÍLO (*It.*) Lively, sprightly.

AS (*Ger.*) The note A-flat.

A SCÉLTA DEL CANTÁNTE (*It.*) At the singers discretion.

ASCENDÉNTE (*It.*) Ascending.

AS DUR (*Ger.*) The key of A-flat major.

AS MOLL (*Ger.*) The key of A-flat minor.

A SÓLA VÓCE (*It.*) For one voice alone.

ASPERGES ME (*Lat.*) The opening of the Mass.

ASPIRÁRE (*It.*) To breathe loudly, a fault in singing.

ASPRÉZZA (*It.*) Roughness, coarseness, harshness.

ASSÁI (*It.*) Very, more, extremely; *Adágio assái*, very slow; *Allégro assái*, very quick.

ASSÁI PIÙ (*It.*) Much more.

ASSEMBLAGE (*Fr.*) Double-tonguing, on the flute; rapid passages executed on wind-instruments.

ASSEZ (*Fr.*) Enough, sufficiently.

ASSEZ LENT (*Fr.*) Rather slowly.

ASSIÉME (*It.*) *Ensemble*, concerted.

ASSOLÚTO (*It.*) Absolute, free, not slurred or bound.

ASSONÁNTE (*It.*) Consonant, harmonious.

ASSONANZ (*Ger.*) \
ASSONÁNZA (*It.*) Similarity, or consonance of tone.

A SÚO ARBÍTRIO \
À SÚO BÉNE PLÁCITO \
A SÚO CÓMODO (*It.*) At pleasure, at will, according to inclination or convenience; synonymous with *ad libitum*, the time, &c., being left to the will of the performer.

À SÚO LUÓGO (*It.*) Synonymous with *Loco*.

Asymphonie — Átto

ASYMPHONIE (*Gr.* & *Ger.*) Dissonance.

ATABAL. A kind of tabour used by the Moors.

À TABLE SEC / **À TABLE SÈCHE** (*Fr.*) The practice of vocal exercises, unaccompanied by an instrument.

À TÉMPO / **À TEM.** (*It.*) In time. After some short alteration in the time, this denotes that the first, or previous time, must be resumed.

À TÉMPO CÓMODO (*It.*) In a convenient time; an easy, moderate time.

À TÉMPO DI GAVÓTTA (*It.*) In the time of a Gavot; moderately quick.

À TÉMPO DI MINUÉTTO (It.) In the time of a minuet.

À TÉMPO GIÚSTO (*It.*) In just, exact, strict, equal time.

À TÉMPO ORDINÁRIO (*It.*) In a moderate, or ordinary time.

À TÉMPO PRÍMO (*It.*) The time, as at first.

À TÉMPO RUBÁTO (*It.*) See TÉMPO RUBÁTO.

ATHEM (*Ger.*) Breath, breathing, respiration.

ATHEMZUG (*Ger.*) Act of respiration, breathing.

À TRE, *or*, **À 3** (*Fr.*) For three voices, or instruments; a *Trio*, or *Terzétto*.

À TRE CÓRDE (*It.*) For three strings; with the three strings.

À TRE MÁNI (*It.*) For three hands.

À TRE PÁRTI (*It.*) In three parts.

À TRE VÓCI (*It.*) For three voices.

À TROIS, *or*, **À 3** (*Fr.*) For three voices, or instruments.

À TROIS MAINS (*Fr.*) For three hands.

À TROIS PARTIES (*Fr.*) For three parts.

À TROIS VOIX (*Fr.*) For three voices.

ATTÁCCA / **ATTÁCCA SÚBITO** (*It.*) Attack, or begin the next movement immediately.

ATTACCÁRE (*It.*) / **ATTAQUER** (*Fr.*) To attack, or commence, the performance.

ATTACCÁTO SÚBITO (*It.*) To be commenced immediately.

ATTASTÁRE (*It.*) To touch, to strike.

ATTENDANT KEYS. Those scales having most sounds in common with the scale of any given key; that is, having one sharp of flat more or less. In C major the attendant keys are, its relative minor A; the dominant G and its relative minor E; the sub-dominant F and its relative minor D.

In A minor the attendant keys are, the relative major C; the dominant E and its relative major G; the sub-dominant D and its relative major F.

ÁTTO (*It.*) An act of an opera.

ÁTTO PRÍMO (*It.*) The first act.
ATTÓRE (*It.*) An actor or singer in an opera.
ÁTTO SECÓNDO (*It.*) The second act.
ATTRÍCE (*It.*) An actress or singer in an opera.
AUBADE (*Fr.*) Morning music, morning concert in the open air.
AUCH (*Ger.*) But, also, so, likewise: *Auch in Zeitmass*, but in time.
AUDÁCE (*It.*) Bold, audacious.
AUF (*Ger.*) On, upon, in, at, &c.: *auf dem Claviere spielden*, to play upon the harpsichord.
AUFBLASEN (*Ger.*) To sound a wind-instrument.
AUF DEM OBERWERK (*Ger.*) Upon the *Upper-work*, or highest row of keys, in organ-playing.
AUF EINER SAITE (*Ger.*) On one string.
AUFFASSUNG (*Ger.*) The general conception, or *reading* of a piece.
AUFFÜHRUNG (*Ger.*) Performance.
AUFGEREGT (*Ger.*) In an agitated manner.
AUFGEWECKT (*Ger.*) Brisk, lively, sprightly, cheerful.
AUFGEWECKTHEIT (*Ger.*) Liveliness, sprightliness.
AUFHALTEN (*Ger.*) To stop, to keep back, to retard.
AUFHALTUNG (*Ger.*) *Keeping back*; a suspension, a retardation.
AUFLAGE (*Ger.*) Edition: met with in German titles.
AUFLÖSEN (*Ger.*) To resolve.
AUFLÖSUNG (*Ger.*) The resolution of a discord.
AUFLÖSUNGSZEICHEN (*Ger.*) The natural sign.
AUFPFEIFEN (*Ger.*) To play upon a pipe, fife, or flute.
AUFS (*Ger.*) To the, on the: *Vorspiel aufs Kyrie*, prelude to the Kyrie.
AUFSATZ (*Ger.*) The tube of the organ reed.
AUFSCHLAG (*Ger.*) *Up-beat*: the unaccented part of a bar.
AUFSCHLAGENDE ZUNGE (*Ger.*) The *beating* reed.
AUFSCHNITT (*Ger.*) The *mouth* of an organ pipe.
AUFSCHWUNG (*Ger.*) Soaring, exaltation, rapture.
AUFSINGEN (*Ger.*) To sing to, to awake by singing.
AUFSPIELEN (*Ger.*) To play upon, to strike up.
AUFSTEIGENDE TONARTE (*Ger. pl.*) Ascending scales, or modes.
AUFSTRICH (*Ger.*) An up-bow.
AUFTAKT (*Ger.*) *See* AUFSCHLAG.
AUFTRITT (*Ger.*) A scene in an opera, &c.
AUFWÄRTS (*Ger.*) Upwards.
AUFZUG (*Ger.*) The act of an opera, &c.
AUGMENTATIO (*Lat.*) *See* AUGMENTATION.

Augmentation — Auténtico

AUGMENTATION. In counterpoint this signifies that the subject or melody is imitated in notes of greater length, or double the original value.

AUGMENTÉ (*Fr.*) Augmented.

AUGMENTED INTERVALS. Those which include a semitone more than major, or perfect intervals; as, a perfect 5th, seven semitones; augmented 5th, eight semitones.

AUGUMENTAZIÓNE
AUGUMÉNTO (*It.*) Augmentation.

AULETES (*Gr.*) A flute-player.

AULOS (*Gr.*) The ancient flute.

AUMENTÁNDO
AUMENTÁTO (*It.*) Increased, crescendo; augmented.

AUMENTAZIÓNE (*It.*) Augmentation.

À ÚNA CÓRDA (*It.*) On one string.

AUS (*Ger.*) From, out of.

AUSARBEITUNG (*Ger.*) The last finish, or elaboration, of a composition.

AUSBLASEN (*Ger.*) To blow, or sound out, or about; to publish by sound of trumpet.

AUSDEHNUNG (*Ger.*) Expansion, extension, development.

AUSDRUCK (*Ger.*) Expression.

AUSFÜLLUNG (*Ger.*) The filling up, the middle parts.

AUSGABE (*Ger.*) Edition.

AUSGANG (*Ger.*) Going out, exit; conclusion, end.

AUSHALTEN (*Ger.*) To hold on, or sustain, a note.

AUSHALTUNGSZEICHEN (*Ger.*) A pause, ⌢.

AUSLAUTEN (*Ger.*) To emit a sound.

ÄUSSERST (*Ger.*) Extreme; extremely.

ÄUSSERST BEWEGT (*Ger.*) Extremely quick.

ÄUSSERST RASCH (*Ger.*) Extremely fast.

ÄUSSERST RUHIG (*Ger.*) Extremely tranquil.

ÄUSSERST STIMMEN (*Ger.*) The outer parts.

AUSSI (*Fr.*) Also.

AUSSINGEN (*Ger.*) To sing to the end, to cease singing.

AUSTROMMELN (*Ger.*) To drum about, or out, to punish by the drum.

AUSTROMPETEN (*Ger.*) A momentary, or transient change of key, or modulation.

AUTÉNTICO (*It.*) *Authentic*, in opposition to *Plagal*.

Authentic — Azióne

AUTHENTIC. Those *church modes* were thus called, where the melody was confined within the limits of the tonic, or final, and its octave: *see* **GREGORIAN MODES.**

AUTHENTIC CADENCE. The old name for a perfect cadence.

AUTHENTIQUE (*Fr.*) Authentic.

AUTOPHON. A species of barrel-organ, played from paper cards.

AUTÓRE (*It.*) Composer, author.

AUTRE (*Fr.*) Other, different.

AUXILIARY NOTES. Those standing on the next degree above, or below, an essential note; the harmony remaining stationary, and not moving from one essential note to another.

AUXILIARY SCALES. This name is sometimes given to the scales of the Relative, or Attendant, keys.

AVE (*Lat.*) Hail!

AVEC (*Fr.*) With.

AVEC DOULEUR (*Fr.*) With an expression of grief and tenderness.

AVEC GOÛT (*Fr.*) With taste, with expression and style.

AVEC GRANDE EXPRESSION (*Fr.*) With great expression.

AVEC LENTEUR (*Fr.*) With slowness; lingering.

AVEC LIAISON (*Fr.*) With smoothness.

AVEC LES PIEDS (*Fr.*) With the feet, in organ-playing.

AVE MARIA (*Lat.*) Hail Mary! The first words of a hymn, or prayer, to the Virgin Mary.

AVEMMARÍA (*It.*) A short prayer, or hymn, to the Virgin Mary. The term is also applied to the tolling of a bell, at break of day, at noon, and at the dusk of the evening, which, in Roman Catholic countries, calls to prayer.

AVÉNA (*It.*) Reed, pipe.

À VICÉNDA (*It.*) Alternately, by turns.

AVICINIUM (*Lat.*) An organ-stop which imitates the warbling of a bird.

À VÍSTA (*It.*) At sight.

À VÓCE SÓLA (*It.*) For one voice alone.

À VOLONTÉ (*Fr.*) At will, at pleasure.

À VUE (*Fr.*) At sight.

AZIÓNE SÁCRA (*It.*) A sacred musical drama; a species of oratorio.

B

B, called also in France and Italy *Si*, and by the Germans *H*, the seventh note of the modern scale of C. The Germans use the letter B to indicate *B-flat*.

BAARPYP (*Dutch*) *See* **BÄRPIPE**.

BAAZAS (*Fr.*) A sort of guitar.

BACCHIA. A Kamschatka dance, in $\frac{2}{4}$ time.

BACCHÉTTA (*It.*) A drum stick.

BACCHIUS (*Gr.*) A musical foot, consisting of one short, unaccented, and two long, accented notes or syllables, marked ⏑ — —.

BACCHUSLIED (*Ger.*) A Bacchanalian song.

BACCIOCÓLO (*It.*) A musical instrument common in some parts of Turkey.

BACHELOR OF MUSIC. The first musical degree taken at our universities.

BACKFALL. An ornament in harpsichord and lute music: also, one of the mechanical linkages in an organ, in the connexion of the keyboard, to the sound-board.

BADINAGE (*Fr.*) Playfulness, sportiveness: *avec badinage*, playfully, in a sportive style.

BAGATELLE (*Fr.*) Trifle, toy; a short, easy piece of music.

BAGPIPES. An ancient wind-instrument, consisting of a *bag* and two or three pipes, one of which is a *drone*, producing always the same sound, which serves as a perpetual bass for every tune. It appears to have been in general use not only in England, Wales, Scotland, and Ireland, but also, in different forms, in many European countries. The Irish had formerly two kinds: a large one for war purposes, and a smaller one for peace. In the excavations of Tarsus there was found a representation of a pair of bagpipes, which must have been delineated at least two centuries before the Christian era: *see also* **CORNAMÚSA**.

BAGUETTES (*Fr.*) Drumsticks.

BAISSER (*Fr.*) To lower, or flatten the pitch, or tone; to decrease or diminish the sound.

BAJETE (*Sp.*) A 4 foot pedal stop on Spanish organs.

BAJO (*Sp.*) Bass.

BAJÓN (*Sp.*) The bassoon: *see also* **BAXÓN**.

BALALAIKA. A Russian instrument, resembling a lute.

BALANCÉ (*Fr.*) A step of figure in dancing.

BALANCEMENT (*Fr.*) Quivering motion: *see* TRÉMOLO.

BALCKEN (*Ger.*) The bass-bar placed under the fourth string in a violin, &c.

BALDAMÉNTE (*It.*) Boldly.

BALDÁNZA } (*It.*) Audacity, boldness.
BALDÉZZA

BALG (*Ger.*) The wind chest, in an organ.

BALGENTRETEER } (*Ger.*) The bellows-treader, in old German organs.
BÄLGETRETER

BALKEN (*Ger.*) See BALCKEN.

BALLÁBILE (*It.*) In the style of a dance.

BALLAD. A popular song. In the fourteenth century this was a romantic or historical poem, such as 'Chevy Chase' set to music; or a short, familiar song, embodying some story or legend, and consisting of a few verses sung to the same tune. In the sixteenth century the term *Ballad*, *Ballet*, or *Ballette*, was applied to a light kind of music sung to a ditty, and also danced to. This latter term *Ballette*, or *Ballet*, also meant a light air for several voices, with a *fa la* burden. The word *Ballad* now means any unvaried, simple song, each verse being sung to the same tune.

BALLADE (*Ger.*) } A dance; dancing: also, a Ballad: see that word.
BALLÁTA (*It.*)

BALLÁRE (*It.*) To dance.

BALLATÉLLA
BALLATÉTTA } (*It.*) A short Balláyta: see that word.
BALLATÍNA

BALLATÓRE (*It.*) A dancer, a male dancer.

BALLATRÍCE (*It.*) A female dancer.

BALLEMATIA } Songs or melodies in the dance style.
BALLISTIA

BALLERÍNA (*It.*) A dancing-mistress, a female dancer.

BALLERÍNO (*It.*) A dancing-master, a male dancer.

BALLET } In old times this name was given to a song, or ditty, the tune of which was also used for dancing: *see also* BALLAD.
BALLETTE

BALLET (*Fr.*) } A dramatic representation of some fable, or story, by means of dances, with action; and in the seventeenth century this was intermixed with speaking in recitative. In the sixteenth century the name was also applied to a lively species of part-song, in the madrigal style, for several voices, with a *fa la* burden.
BALLÉTTO (*It.*)

Ballet — Bardóne

BALLET-MASTER. The artist who superintends the rehearsals and performance of the *Ballet*, and who is frequently the author of the fable and its details.

BÁLLI (*It. pl.*) Dances.

BÁLLI DELLA STÍRIA (*It. pl.*) Styrian dances resembling waltzes.

BÁLLI INGLÉSI (*It. pl.*) English country dances.

BÁLLI UNGARÉSI (*It. pl.*) Hungarian dances, in $\frac{2}{4}$ time, generally syncopated, or accented on the weak part of the bar.

BALLMÄSSIG (*Ger.*) In dance time, or style.

BÁLLO (*It.*) A dance, a dance tune: *da bállo*, in he style of a dance.

BALLÓNCHIO (*It.*) An Italian country dance; the dance of the Italian peasants.

BALLONZÁRE (*It.*) To dance artistically.

BAND. A number of instrumental performers assembled for the purpose of playing in concert.

BÁNDA (*It.*) | A band.
BANDE (*Fr.*) |

BANDOER. *See* BANDÓRE.

BANDOLA (*Sp.*) A species of lute.

BANDONION. A species of *concertina*, invented about 1830, by C. F. Uhlig.

BANDÓRA | (*It.*) A kind of lute, or cither, with twelve strings of
BANDÓRE | steel wire.

BANDURRÍA (*Sp.*) A species of the Spanish guitar.

BANJA | A species of guitar, used by the negroes.
BANJO |

BÄNKELSÄNGER (*Ger.*) A ballad singer.

BAR. Lines drawn down or across the stave, to divide the music into equal portions: the term *bar* is also applied to the music included between two of these lines: also, the *beard* of an organ pipe.

BARBITON. A name formerly applied to the viol and the violin.

BARCARÓLA (*It.*) | A song or air, with a kind of undulating effect,
BARCAROLLE (*Fr.*) | sung by the Venetian *gondoliéri*, or boatmen.

BARD. An old name for a poet-musician. Amongst the ancient Celtic tribes, the bard was a person of great importance and high consideration.

BÁRDÁHI. The Hindoo name for a bard.

BARDE (*Ger.*) Bard, minstrel.

BARDÓNE (*It.*) *See* BOURDON.

Barem — Basílica

BAREM
BAREN A stopped register, of soft 8 or 16 feet tone, in German organs.

BARI-BASSO. The deeper sort of barytone voice.

BARIOLAGE (*Fr.*) A passage for the violin, &c., in which the open strings are more especially used.

BARI-TENOR. The deeper sort of tenor voice.

BARITON-CLEF. The F clef, placed upon the third line: now obsolete.

BARITON (*Fr.*)
BARÍTONO (*It.*)
BARYTONE (*Eng.*) The barytone voice, or higher bass; intermediate, with respect to pitch, between the bass and the tenor voice. Also, a species of *Viola da gamba*, which had seven catgut strings, and also several strings of wire, and nine frets upon the fingerboard, to mark the semitones. It is now obsolete.

BARÓCCO (*It.*)
BAROCK (*Ger.*)
BAROQUE (*Fr.*) Strange, odd, eccentric music, in which the harmony is confused, and abounding in discords.

BÄRPFEIFE (*Ger.*) *Bear-pipe*: an obsolete reed stop of soft intonation, and 16 or 8 feet tone. The name is also given to an 8 feet stop of pleasant tone, belonging to the flue-work.

BARQUARDE (*Fr.*) An obsolete term for BARCAROLLE.

BARRA (*It.*) A bar-line.

BARRAGE (*Fr.*) In guitar-playing, a temporary nut or *fret*, formed by placing the fore-finger of the left hand across two, three or four strings.

BARRE DE LUTH (*Fr.*) The bridge of the lute.

BARRE DE MESURE (*Fr.*) The bar-line.

BARRE DE RÉPÉTITION (*Fr.*) A dotted double bar: also, a thick line used as an abbreviation, to mark the repetition of a group of notes.

BARREL-ORGAN. An organ, the tones of which are produced by the revolution of a cylinder; and the tunes, by the disposition of the pins and staples with which the cylinder is studded.

BARRURE (*Fr.*) The bar of a lute, &c.

BART (*Ger.*) The *beard* of an organ pipe.

BARYPHONUS. A man with a very deep, or very coarse voice.

BARYTON (*Fr.*) A kind of bass-viol, now obsolete; also, an organ reed stop.

BAS-DESSUS (*Fr.*) The mezzo-soprano, or second treble.

BASE
BASS The lowest, or deepest, male voice; the lowest part in a musical composition.

BASFLICÓRNO (*It.*) A baritone *Flügelhorn*.

BASÍLICA (*It.*) A cathedral.

Bássa — Básso-búffo

BÁSSA (*It.*) Low, down, deep: 8va bássa, play the notes an octave lower.

BASSANELLO (*Fr.*) An obsolete musical instrument, now unknown.

BÁSSA OTTÁVA or 8va **BÁSSA** (*It.*) The passage is to be played an octave lower than written.

BASSE (*Fr.*) The bass part.

BASSE CHANTANTE (*Fr.*) The vocal bass.

BASSE-CHIFFRE (*Fr.*) The figured bass.

BASSE-CLEF (*Fr.*) The bass, or F clef, placed upon the fourth line.

BASSE CONTINUE (*Fr.*) The continued bass, the figured bass, the thorough bass.

BASSE CONTRAINTE (*Fr.*) The constrained, or ground bass.

BASSE-CONTRE (*Fr.*) The double-bass: also, the deep bass voice, called by the Italians *básso profóndo*.

BASSE DE CRÉMONA | (*Fr.*) Old names for the fagótto, or bassoon.
BASSE DE HAUTBOIS |

BASSE D'HARMONIE (*Fr.*) The *túba*, or ophicleide, a large brass instrument used in military bands, and full orchestra, for playing the bass part.

BASSE DE VIOLE (*Fr.*) Bass-viol: the old name of the *viol da gámba*.

BASSE DE VIOLON (*Fr.*) The double-bass, or *cóntra básso*.

BASSE DOUBLE (*Fr.*) The largest kind of double-bass.

BASSE FIGURÉE (*Fr.*) The figured bass.

BASSE FONDAMENTALE (*Fr.*) The fundamental bass.

BASSE OSBSTINÉE (*Fr.*) Ground-bass.

BASSE RÉCITANTE (*Fr.*) A *reciting* bass.

BASSE TAILLE (*Fr.*) Barytone voice; low tenor voice.

BASSET-HORN. A long clarinet with a brass bell (like that of the French horn) at the end of it; the scale is extensive, and intermediate between those of the clarinet and the bassoon. The tone is of a melancholy character, somewhat resembling that of the *córno inglése*: see CÓRNO DI BASSÉTTO.

BASSETPOMMER (*Ger.*) A precursor of the bassoon.

BASSÉTTO (*It.*) An obsolete instrument with four strings: also, the little bass: also, a 4 feet reed organ stop of bright tone: see CLARION.

BASS-FLÖTE (*Ger.*) | Courtal, an old instrument of the bassoon
BASS-FLUTE (*Eng.*) | species: also, the name of an organ stop, of 8 feet tone, on the pedal.

BASS-GEIGE (*Ger.*) Bass-viol, violoncello.

BÁSSO (*It.*) The bass part: also, a bass singer: also, the double bass.

BÁSSO-BÚFFO (*It.*) The principal bass in a comic opera.

BÁSSO CANTÁNTE (*It.*) The vocal bass part: also, the principal bass singer in an opera.

BÁSSO CONCERTÁNTE (*It.*) The principal bass: those lighter and more delicate parts which are performed only by the principal violoncello, or bassoon.

BÁSSO CONTÍNUO (*It.*) The continued bass: a bass, in old music, with figures, to indicate the harmony.

BÁSSO FIGURÁTO (*It.*) The figured bass, a bass with figures to indicate the harmony.

BÁSSO FONDAMENTÁLE (*It.*) The fundamental bass.

BASSON (*Fr. & Ger.*) The bassoon.

BASSON-QUINTE (*Fr.*) A small bassoon, of the same compass as the ordinary bassoon, but the sounds produced are a *fifth* higher.

BÁSSO NUMERÁTO (*It.*) The figured bass.

BASSOON. A wind-instrument of wood, of the double reed species, forming the natural tenor and bass to the hautboy, indispensable in a full orchestra. The lower tones are strong and rough, the middle tones very rich and sonorous. Also, an organ reed stop, of a soft and slightly nasal tone, of 8 feet on the manual and 16 feet on the pedal.

BÁSSO RIPIÉNO (*It.*) A bass part, only intended to be played in the full, or *tútti* passages.

BÁSSO RIVOLTÁTO (*It.*) An inverted bass.

BASS-PFEIFE (*Ger.*) Bass-pipe; bassoon.

BASS-POSUNE (*Ger.*) Sackbut, bass trombone.

BASS-SAITE (*Ger.*) Bass-string.

BASS-SCHLÜSSEL (*Ger.*) Bass clef.

BASS-STIMME (*Ger.*) Bass voice; bass part.

BASS-TUBA (*Lat.*) *See* TUBA.

BASS-VIOL. An old name for the *viol da gamba*: now often given to the violoncello.

BASS-ZEICHEN (*Ger.*) Bass-clef.

BÁSTA (*Ger. & It.*) | Enough; sufficient: stop.
BASTÁNTE (*It.*)

BATÓCCHIO | (*It.*) The clapper of a bell.
BATTÁGLIO

BÂTON DE MESURE (*Fr.*) The stick, or rod, used by a conductor to beat the time.

BATTANTE (*Fr.*) Beating.

BATTEMENT (*Fr.*) An old term: *see* BATTIMÉNTO.

BÁTTERE (*It.*) The down-stroke, in beating time.

BATTERIE (*Fr.*) A roll of the military drum: also, a particular way of playing on the guitar, by striking the strings with the fingers of the right hand, instead of pulling them.

BATTIMÉNTO (*It.*) An old name for that kind of short shake called a *beat*.

BATTITÓRE DI MUSÍCA (*It.*) Time-beater; conductor.

BATTITÚRA (*It.*) The act of beating time.

BATTRE LA CAISSE | (*Fr.*) To beat the drum.
BATTRE LE TEMBOUR |

BATTRE LA MESURE (*Fr.*) To beat the time, to mark the time by beating with the hand, or with a stick.

BATTÚTA (*It.*) Time, or measure: the accented part of a bar: *portár la battúta*, to beat the time.

BAU (*Ger.*) The structure, the building, the fabric, of musical instruments.

BAUERNFLÖTE (*Ger.*) *Rustic flute*: a stopped register in an organ.

BAXÓN (*Sp.*) A bassoon: *see* BAJÓN.

BAXONCILLO (*Sp.*) A little bassoon: also, an organ stop, equivalent to the open diapason.

BAYLA | (*Sp.*) A dance; a comic dancing song.
BAYLE |

BAZUIB (*Dutch*) Trombone.

B CANCELLATUM (*Lat.*) The old name for a *sharp*, #.

B DUR (*Ger.*) The key of B-flat major.

B DURUM (*Lat.*) B *hard*, or major.

BEARBEITET (*Ger.*) Worked, elaborated: arranged, or adapted.

BEARBEITUNG (*Ger.*) A revision, adaptation.

BEARD. A small projection in front, or at the side of, the mouth of an organ pipe.

BEARINGS. The tuning scale, in tuning a pianoforte or organ.

BEAR-PIPE. See BÄRPFEIFE.

BEAT. An important musical ornament, or embellishment, consisting of the principal note, and the note *below* it: the short beat, or *acciaccatúra*, which is always a semitone below the principal note, is often used; but the longer beat, which somewhat resembles a short shake, is only met with in old music.

BEATING TIME. Marking the divisions, or parts of the bar, by means of the hand or foot.

BEAUCOUP (*Fr.*) Many; much: *en élargissant beaucoup*, broadening a great deal.

BEBEN (*Ger.*) To shake, to tremble; tremolo.

BEBENDE STIMME (*Ger.*) A trembling voice.

BEBUNG (*Ger.*) Shaking, oscillation, palpitation; also, a German organ stop: *see* SCHWEBUNG.

BÉCARRE (*Fr.*) The mark called a natural, ♮.

BEC (*Fr.*) \
BÉCCO (*It.*) The bill or beak: the mouth-piece of a clarinet, flageolet, &c.

BÉCCO POLÁCCO (*It.*) A large sort of bagpipe, used in some parts of Italy.

BECHER (*Ger.*) The *bell* of an instrument.

BECKEN (*Ger.*) A cymbal.

BECKENSCHLÄGER (*Ger.*) Cymbal-player.

BEDON (*Fr.*) An old name for a tabret, or drum.

BEDROHLICH (*Ger.*) Menacing, threatening.

BEFFROI (*Fr.*) Belfry: alarm-bell.

BEFILZEN (*Ger.*) To *felt* pianoforte hammers.

BEFINGERN (*Ger.*) To finger.

BEGEISTERUNG (*Ger.*) Inspiration, animation, enthusiasm, poetic excitement.

BEGLEITEN (*Ger.*) To accompany.

BEGLEITENDE STIMMEN (*Ger. pl.*) The accompanying parts.

BEGLEITEN (*Ger.*) An accompanist.

BEGLEITUNG (*Ger.*) An accompaniment.

BEHAGLICH (*Ger.*) Easy, agreeable.

BEHANDLUNG (*Ger.*) Management, treatment, manipulation.

BEHENDIG (*Ger.*) Dexterous, agile, nimble.

BEHERZT (*Ger.*) Resolute, determined; spirited.

BEI (*Ger.*) At, with, for, by.

BEIDE (*Ger.*) Both.

BEINAH (*Ger.*) Almost, nearly.

BEISPIEL (*Ger.*) An example.

BEISSER (*Ger.*) A mordent.

BEITÖNE (*Ger.*) Harmonics, partials, overtones.

BEIZEICHEN (*Ger.*) An accidental.

BEKLEMMT (*Ger.*) Oppressed, anxious.

BEL BÉLLO (*It.*) Gently, softly, sweetly.

BEL CÁNTO (*It.*) *Beautiful song*.

BELEBEND (*Ger.*) Animated; lively.

BELEBT (*Ger.*) Hoarse, veiled, covered.

BELIEBEN (*Ger.*) Pleasure.

BELLIEBT (*Ger.*) Beloved, popular.

BÉLIÈRE (*Fr.*) Bell-clappers.

Bell — Bergomask

BELL. In a trumpet, horn, &c., this is the wide circular opening at the end of the instrument.

BELL DIAPASON. *See* FLÛTE-À-PAVILLON.

BELLÉZZA (*It.*) Beauty of tone and expression.

BELLÉZZA DELLA VÓCE (*It.*) Beauty, sweetness of voice.

BELL GAMBA. A gamba stop in an organ, the top of each pipe spreading out like a bell.

BELLICOSAMÉNTE | (*It.*) In a martial and warlike style.
BELLICÓSO |

BELL METRONOME. A metronome with a small bell, which strikes at the beginning of each bar.

BÉLLO (*It.*) Beautiful.

BELLY. The sound-board of an instrument; that part over which the strings are distended.

BEL METÁLLO DI VÓCE (*It.*) A voice clear, full, and brilliant.

BELUSTIGEND (*Ger.*) Gay, joyful.

BEMERKBAR (*Ger.*) *Observable*, marked: to be played in a prominent manner.

BEMES. Old English horns, or trumpets.

BÉMOL (*Fr.*) | The mark called a *flat*, ♭.
BEMÓLLE (*It.*) |

BÉMOLISÉE (*Fr.*) A note preceded by a flat.

BÉMOLISER (*Fr.*) | To flatten notes, to lower the pitch by putting
BEMOLLIZZÁRE (*It.*) | a flat to them.

BÉN | (*It.*) Well; good.
BÉNE |

BENEDICTUS (*Lat.*) One of the principal movements in a Mass.

BÉNE MARCÁTO | (*It.*) Well marked, in a clear, distinct, and
BEN MARCÁTO | strongly accented manner.

BEN MISURÁTO (*It.*) In the exact time, as measured.

BEN MODERÁTO (*It.*) Very moderate time.

BÉNE PLÁCITO (*It.*) At will, at pleasure; the time may be retarded, and the passage ornamented.

BEN PRONUNZIÁTO (*It.*) Pronounced clearly and distinctly.

BE QUÁDRO (*It.*) | The mark called a natural, ♮.
BE QUARRE (*Fr.*) |

BEQUEM (*Ger.*) Convenient, easy.

BERCEUSE (*Fr.*) A lullaby, cradle song.

BERGAMÁSCA (*It.*) |
BERGAMASQUE (*Fr.*) | A kind of dance, in imitation of the clowns of Bergamo.
BERGOMASK (*Eng.*) |

BERGERET. A rustic dance or song.

BERGREIHEN (*Ger.*) Alpine melody, miners' song.

BERUHIGEND (*Ger.*) Becoming more tranquil.

BES (*Ger.*) The note B double-flat, B ♭♭.

BESAITEN (*Ger.*) To string an instrument.

BESCHLEUNIGEN (*Ger.*) Accelerate.

BESCHLÜSS (*Ger.*) Conclusion.

BESCHREIBUNG (*Ger.*) A description.

BESCHWINGT (*Ger.*) Hurried, hastened.

BESEELT (*Ger.*) Animated, spirited.

BESINGEN (*Ger.*) To sing, to celebrate in song.

BESONDERS GEBUNDEN (*Ger.*) Particularly *legáto*.

BESPANNEN (*Ger.*) To string an instrument.

BESPANNENE SAITEN (*Ger.*) *Wire-covered* strings.

BESTIMMT (*Ger.*) With decision; distinctly.

BESTIMMTHEIT (*Ger.*) Precision.

BETGLOCKE (*Ger.*) Prayer-bell.

BETONEND | (*Ger.*) Accented.
BETONT

BETONUNG (*Ger.*) Accent, stress, emphasis.

BETRÜBT (*Ger.*) Grieved, perturbed, sad.

BEWEGT (*Ger.*) Moved, stirred, animated.

BEWEGTER (*Ger.*) Quicker: *Bewegter werdend*, becoming more animated.

BEWEGUNG (*Ger.*) Motion, movement.

BEYSPIEL (*Ger.*) An example.

BEZEICHNETEN (*Ger.*) Sharply detached; very *staccáto*.

BEZIFFERTE BASS (*Ger.*) The figured bass.

BHÁT. The Hindoo name for a *bard*.

BIÁNCA (*It.*) A minim.

BIBELREGAL (*Ger.*) A regal shaped like a Bible.

BIBI (*Fr.*) A pianette.

BICHORD (*Lat.*) A term applied to instruments which have two strings to each note.

BICHORDON (*Lat.*) The *colachon*, with two strings only: *see* COLACHON.

BICINIUM (*Lat.*) A composition in two parts, a duet, or two-part song.

BIEN (*Fr.*) Well; good: *bien rhythmé*, the rhythm well marked.

BIFARA (*Lat.*) An organ stop, each pipe having two mouths, the speech of which is accompanied by a gentle undulation.

BIMMÓLLE (*It.*) The mark called a *flat*, ♭.

BINARY MEASURE. Common time of two in a bar.

BIND. A curved line, uniting two notes of the same name.

BINDE (*Ger.*) A tie, or bind.

BINDEBOGEN (*Ger.*) A tie, or slur.

BINDEN (*Ger.*) To tie, bind, connect; *legáto*.

BINDUNG (*Ger.*) Syncopation.

BINDUNGZEICHEN (*Ger.*) A tie, or bind.

BIRD ORGAN. A small organ, used for teaching birds to sing particular tunes.

BIRN (*Ger.*) That part of the clarinet, basset-horn, &c. into which the mouth-piece is inserted.

BIS (*Lat.*) Twice: indicating that the passage marked is to be played over again.

BISCANTÁRE
BISCANTERELLÁRE (*It.*) To sing often, to sing and sing again.

BISCÁNTO (*It.*) A kind of duet, where two are singing.

BÍSCHERO (*It.*) The pin of any instrument, the peg of a violin, violoncello, &c.

BISCRÓMA (*It.*)
BISCROME (*Fr.*) A semiquaver.

BIS-DIAPASON (*Gr. & Lat.*) A double octave, or fifteenth a compass of two octaves.

BISEAU (*Fr.*) The stopper of an organ-pipe, to make the tone sharper or flatter.

BISINIA (*Lat.*) A term meaning that the notes played by one hand, are regularly repeated by the other.

BISSÁRE (*It.*)
BISSER (*Fr.*) To encore.

BISSEX (*Lat.*) A kind of guitar with twelve strings.

BIS UNCA (*Lat.*) An old name for a semiquaver.

BITTEND (*Ger.*) Bitterness.

BIZZARRAMÉNTE (*It.*) Oddly, in a whimsical style.

BIZZARRÍA (*It.*) Written in an irregular and fantastic style: also, a sudden, unprepared, transition or modulation.

BIZZÁRRO (*It.*) Fantastical, whimsical, odd.

BLANCHE (*Fr.*) A minim.

BLANCHE POINTÉE (*Fr.*) A dotted minim.

BLASEBALG (*Ger.*) The bellows of an organ.

BLASEHORN (*Ger.*) Bugle horn, hunter's horn.

BLASE-INSTRUMENT (*Ger.*) A wind-instrument.

BLASE-MUSIK (*Ger.*) Music for wind-instruments.

BLASEN (*Ger.*) To blow, to sound.

BLASER (*Ger.*) A blower: an instrument for blowing.

BLATT (*Ger.*) A leaf, a sheet of music; reed of an instrument.

BLECH-INSTRUMENTE (*Ger.*) The brass instruments, as trumpets, trombones, &c.

BLOCKFLÖTE (*Ger.*) An organ stop, composed of large-scale pipes, the tone of which is very full and broad.

B-MOL (*Fr.*) *See* BÉMOL.

B MOLL (*Ger.*) The key of B-flat minor.

B MOLLE (*Lat.*) B *soft*, or minor.

BOB. A term used to express the changes, in bell ringing.

BOBIBATION | *Solféggi* adapted to the syllables of the Flemish, or
BOCEDISATION | Belgian language.

BOCAL (*Fr.*) | The mouth-piece of a horn, trumpet, trombone,
BÓCCA (*It.*) | serpent, &c.

BÓCCA RIDÉNTE (*It.*) *Smiling mouth*: a term, in singing, applied to an elongation of the mouth, approaching to a smile, produced by a particular conformation of the throat, mouth, and lips: this is believed to be most conducive to the production of a pure and equal tone, and a perfect intonation.

BOCCHÍNO | (*It.*) A small mouth-piece: *see* BÓCCA.
BOCCIUÓLA |

BOCKPFEIFE (*Ger.*) Bagpipe.

BOCK-SCHWEBUNG (*Ger.*) An organ tremulant stop, which a powerful beat.

BOCKSTRILLER (*Ger.*) A bad shake, with false intonation.

BODEN (*Ger.*) The *back* of a violin, viola, &c.

BOGEN (*Ger.*) The *bow* of a violin, &c.

BOGENCLAVIER | (*Ger.*) A piano-violin.
BOGENFLÜGEL |

BOGENFÜHRUNG (*Ger.*) The management of the bow, the art of bowing.

BOGEN-INSTRUMENT (*Ger.*) A bow-instrument: an instrument played on by means of a bow.

BOGENSTRICH (*Ger.*) A stroke of a bow.

BOIS (*Fr.*) Wood.

BOITE (*Fr.*) Box.

BOITE D'EXPRESSION | (*Fr.*) The swell box, in an organ.
BOITE EXPRESSIVE |

Boléro — Brace

BOLÉRO (*Sp.*) A graceful, lively, Spanish dance, in $\frac{3}{4}$ time, with castanets.

BOMBARD (*Ger.*)
BOMBARDE (*Fr.*) | A powerful reed stop in an organ, of 16 feet scale: also, an old wind-instrument of the hautboy species.
BOMBÁRDO (*It.*)

BOMBARDON (*Fr. & Ger.*) A large brass wind-instrument of brass, with valves: somewhat similar to the ophicleide.

BOMBIX (*Gr.*) An ancient Greek instrument, formed of a long reed, or tube.

BONS TEMPS DE LA MESURE (*Fr.*) The accented parts of a bar.

BORDÓNE (*It.*)
BOURDON (*Fr.*) | An organ stop, the pipes of which are stopped, or covered, and produce the 16 feet tone, or sometimes 32 feet tone: also, a drone bass.

BORDUN. See BOURDON.

BORDUN-FLÖTE (*Ger.*) An organ stop: *see* BORDÓNE.

BOUCHÉ (*Fr.*) Muted, closed; stopped pipe in organs.

BOUCHÉ FERMÉE (*Fr.*) With the mouth closed.

BOUFFE (*Fr.*) See BÚFFO.

BOURDON DE CORNEMUSE
BOURDON DE MUSETTE | (*Fr.*) The drone of a bagpipe.

BOURRÉE (*Fr.*) A lively old French dance, in $\frac{4}{4}$ time, always commencing with an odd crotchet, or quaver.

BOUTADE (*Fr.*) A kind of impromptu *ballet*, in a fanciful and capricious style, formerly very popular in France.

BOUT DE L'ARCHET (*Fr.*) The point of the bow, in violin playing, &c.

BOW. The instrument used in playing upon the violin, viola, &c. Its present length is from 27 to 30 inches, but formerly it was shorter.

BOW-HAND. The right hand: the hand which holds the bow.

BOWING. The art of using the bow, on the skilful management of which the tone of the violin, &c., materially depends, as well as the grace and freedom of the performance.

BOYAU (*Fr.*) Cat-gut strings, for violins, &c.

BOYAUDIER (*Fr.*) A maker of violin strings.

BOZZÉTTO (*It.*) A sketch.

B QUADRATUM
B QUADRUM | (*Lat.*) An old name for the *natural*, ♮ : formerly this was only applied to the note B.

B-QUARRE (*Fr.*) See BÉQUARRE.

BRÁCCIO (*It.*) The arm.

BRACE. The character {, used to connect together the treble and bass staves, &c.

BRANLE (*Fr.*) An old dance, in a ring.
BRANSLE (*Fr.*) An old dance, slow, and something like the *Alman*.
BRANSLE DE POICTOU | (*Fr.*) A dance in a quicker time than the
BRANSLE DOUBLE | preceding.
BRANSLE SIMPLE (*Fr.*) See **BRANSLE**.
BRATSCHE (*Ger.*) The viola, or tenor violin; formerly it was applied to the *viol da bráccia*.
BRAUL. See **BRAWL**.
BRAUT-LIED (*Ger.*) Bridal hymn, wedding song.
BRAUT-MESSE (*Ger.*) Music before the wedding ceremony: also, the ceremony itself.
BRÁVA (*It. fem.*)
BRÁVI (*It. pl.*) | Very well: very good: admirable: excellent.
BRÁVO (*It. masc.*)
BRAVÍSSIMA (*It. fem.*)
BRAVÍSSIMI (*It. pl.*) | Exceedingly good: exceedingly well.
BRAVÍSSIMO (*It. masc.*)
BRAVOUR-ARIE (*Ger.*) An *Ária di bravúra*.
BRAVÚRA (*It.*) Spirit, vigour; requiring great dexterity and skill: rapid and correct execution.
BRAWL
BRAWLE | A shaking, or swinging motion. An old round dance, in which the performers joined hands in a circle. The air was short, and *en rondeau*, and balls were usually opened with it.
BREIT (*Ger.*) Broad, slow, stately.
BRET-GEIGE (*Ger.*) A small pocket-fiddle.
BRÉVE (*It.*) *Short*: formerly the Breve was the shortest note; the notes then used were the *Large*, the *Long*, and the *Breve* or. The breve is equal to two semibreves, or four minims.
BRIDGE. That which supports the string in musical instruments.
BRIEF. See **BREVE**.
BRILLÁNTE (*It. & Fr.*) Bright, sparkling, brilliant.
BRILLÁNTE ASSÁI (*It.*) Very brilliant.
BRILLÁNTE ED ENÉRGICO (*It.*) Brilliant and energetic.
BRILLISÍMO (*It.*) As brilliant as possible.
BRILLÁRE (*It.*) To play, or sing, in a brilliant style.
BRÍLLO (*It.*) Joy, delight.
BRINDÍSI (*It.*) A drinking song.
BRÍO (*It.*) Fire, life, vigour, animation.

Brióso — Buffonescaménte

BRIÓSO (*It.*) Fiery, lively, vigorously.
BRISÉ (*Fr.*) Broke; sprinkled into an *arpéggio*.
BRODERIES (*Fr.*) Ornaments, embellishments.
BROKEN CADENCE. *See* **INTERRUPTED CADENCE.**
B ROTUNDUM (*Lat.*) The character called a *flat*, ♭ : formerly this was only applied to the note B.
BRUMMHORN. *See* **KRUMMHORN.**
BRUNETTES (*Fr. pl.*) Love songs.
BRUIT (*Fr.*) Noise, rattle, clatter.
BRUMMBASS (*Ger.*) Bourdon; drone; double-bass.
BRUMMEISEN (*Ger.*) A Jew's harp.
BRUMMER (*Ger.*) A drone.
BRUMMSTIMMEN (*Ger.*) Voice *humming* an accompaniment.
BRUMMTON (*Ger.*) A drone; a humming tone.
BRUNETTE (*Fr.*) A little tender, delicate, and simple air; a love song.
BRUSCAMÉNTE (*It.*)
BRUSQUEMENT (*Fr.*) } Abruptly, coarsely, bluntly.
BRÚSCO (*It.*) Coarse, rough, brusque.
BRUST (*Ger.*) Breast, chest.
BRUSTSTIMME (*Ger.*) The chest voice.
BRUSTTON (*Ger.*) Chest tone.
BRUSTWERK (*Ger.*) The pipes set up in the middle part of an organ; usually the *choir* or *swell*.
BÚCA (*It.*) The *sound-hold* of a lute, &c.
BÚCCINA (*It.*) An ancient wind-instrument, supposed to have resembled the trumpet.
BUCCINÁRE (*It.*) To sound a trumpet.
BUCCÓLICA (*It.*)
BUCOLIQUE (*Fr.*) } Pastoral songs, or verses.
BÜCHSE (*Ger.*) The boot or foot, of an organ reed.
BÚFFA | (*It.*) Comic, humorous, in the comic style: also, a
BÚFFO | vocalist who performed comic operatic parts.
BÚFFA CARICÁTA
BÚFFO CARICÁTO } (*It.*) A comic character in an Italian opera.
BUFFET D'ORGUES (*Fr.*) The buffet, or case, in which the keys of an organ are sometimes placed.
BUFFET ORGAN. A small organ: *see* **POSITIF.**
BUFFÓNE (*It.*) Comic singer in an opera.
BUFFONESCAMÉNTE (*It.*) Comically: in a burlesque manner.

BUGLE. A *curved* horn: the hunting horn: also, an instrument of copper or brass, not very unlike the French horn in tone, but higher, and more piercing. That species called the Kent bugle, is furnished with keys; and there is another kind with pistons, or cylinders.

BUGLE-HORN. A hunting horn.

BÜHNE (*Ger.*) Stage; scene, theatre.

BÚIOSO (*It.*) In a gloomy, obscure manner.

BUND (*Ger.*) The space between frets; a fret.

BUNGE (*Ger.*) A kettledrum.

BUON (*It.*) Good.

BUONACCÓRDO (*It.*) An instrument with a smaller keyboard than that of the pianoforte, for the use of young children.

BUÓNA MÁNO (*It.*) A good hand: a performer with a brilliant style of execution.

BUONAMÉNTE (*It.*) In a just and accurate style.

BUÓNA NÓTA (*It.*) Accented note.

BUÓN CANTÁNTE (*It.*) An accomplished singer.

BUÓN GÚSTO (*It.*) Good taste, refinement of style.

BURDEN. This was, originally, in very old English music, a kind of ground, or drone accompaniment to a song, which was sustained by another singer. It also means, a return of the same words and music, at the end of each verse of a song: *see also* **PES**.

BÚRLA
BURLÁNDO
BURLÉSCO
BURLESCAMÉNTE
(*It.*) Facetious, merry, comical: in a playful style.

BURLÉTTA (*It.*) A comic operetta: a light musical dramatic piece, with dialogue, songs, &c., somewhat in the nature of the English farce.

BURTHEN. See **BURDEN**.

BUSAUN (*Ger.*) A sackbut: a reed stop in an organ.

BÚSNA (*It.*) A species of trumpet.

BUSSÁNDO (*It.*) Thumping on the pianoforte.

BUSSÓNE (*It.*) A wind-instrument, now obsolete.

BUSSPSALMEN (*Ger.*) Penitential psalms.

BUXUS (*Lat.*) An ancient boxwood flute, with three finger holes.

BUZAIN (*Ger.*) See **BUSAUN**.

C

C, called by the French *Ut*, and by the Italians *Do*; the first note of the modern scale of Guido d'Arezzo. The major scale of C is called the *natural* scale, because it requires no sharps or flats.

CC This is generally the lowest note on the manuals of an organ, and is called an 8 feet note: that being the length of an open pipe required to produce it.

CCC. This note is an octave below CC, and is a 16 feet note.

CCCC. This is an octave below CCC, and is a 32 feet note.

c . C with *one stroke*: the German method of indicating middle C: the six notes above it are also marked in the same manner.

c . C with *two strokes*: C on the third space in the treble: the six notes above it are also marked in the same manner.

c . C with *three strokes*: the octave above the preceding.

c . C with *four strokes*: the octave above the preceding.

C Indicates common time or four crotchets, or the value of a semibreve, in each bar.

₵ This mark indicates either *álla bréve*, or *álla cappélla* time.

₵ A mark used by some of the old composers, to indicate *álla bréve* time, of four minims in a bar.

CABALÉTTA (*It.*) A pleasing melody of an attractive character: an operatic air, resembling the rondo in form, first a simple melody, then varied.

CABINET D'ORGUE (*Fr.*) The case, or cabinet, in which the keys of an organ are sometimes placed.

CABINET ORGAN. Reed organ; American organ.

CABINET PIANOFORTE. An upright pianoforte, about six feet in height: much larger than the cottage pianoforte, or the *pianino*.

CABISCOLA. The ancient name of the leader of the choristers in a church.
CÁCCIA (*It.*) Hunting: *see* ALLA CÁCCIA.
CACHÉE (*Fr.*) Hidden.
CACHÚCHA (*Sp.*) A popular Spanish dance, in triple time.
CACOFONÍA (*It.*) Cacophony.
CACOFÓNICO (*It.*) Cacophony; having a bad sound.
CACOPHONIE (*Fr.*) Cacophony.
CACOPHONY. Harsh and discordant combinations of sounds, bad tone, false intonation.
CADENCE (*Fr.*) A shake or trill: also, a cadence or close in harmony, as *Cadence parfaite*, a perfect cadence: *Cadence rompue*, or *interrompue*, an interrupted, or broken cadence.
CADENCE. A close in melody, or harmony: also, an ornamental passage: *see* CADÉNZA.
CADENCE ÉVITÉE (*Fr.*) An interrupted cadence.
CADENCE IMPARFAITE (*Fr.*) An imperfect cadence.
CADENCE INTERROMPUE (*Fr.*) An interrupted cadence.
CADENCE IRRÉGULIÈRE (*Fr.*) A half cadence.
CADENCE PARFAITE (*Fr.*) A perfect cadence.
CADENCE PERLÉE (*Fr.*) A brilliant cadence.
CADENCE ROMPUE (*Fr.*) A broken, or interrupted cadence.

CADENZ (*Ger.*)
CADÉNZA (*It.*) │ A cadence: an ornamental passage, sometimes extemporaneous, introduced near the close of a song, solo, or concerto. In modern music the *Cadénza* is usually written in small notes.

CADÉNZA D'INGÁNNO (*It.*) An interrupted, or deceptive cadence.
CADÉNZA FIORÍTA (*It.*) An ornate, florid cadence, with graces, and embellishments.
CADÉNZA SFUGGÍTA (*It.*) An interrupted, avoided, or broken cadence.
CADÉNZA SOSPÉSA (*It.*) A suspended cadence.

CÆSURA
CÆSURE │ (*Lat.*) A break, or section, in rhythm: the last accented note of a phrase, section, or period: the rhythmic termination of any passage containing two or more musical feet.

CAHIER (*Lat.*) A book; a part.
CAISSE (*Fr.*) A drum.
CAISSE CLAIRE (*Fr.*) The snare-drum.
CAISSE PLATE (*Fr.*) The shallow side-drum.
CAISSE ROULANTE (*Fr.*) The side-drum, the body of which is of wood, and rather long.
CAISSES CLAIRES (*Fr.*) The drums.

Calamus — Campanóne

CALAMUS PASTORALIS (*Lat.*) A reed, or pipe, used by shepherds.

CALÁNDO (*It.*) Gradually diminishing the tone, and a little slackening the time: becoming softer and slower, by degrees.

CALANDRONE (*Fr.*) A musical instrument used by the French peasants.

CALASCIONE (*It.*) A species of guitar.

CALÁTA (*It.*) An Italian dance in $\frac{2}{4}$ time.

CALCÁNDO (*It.*) Pressing forward, and hurrying the time.

CALCANT (*Ger.*) The bellows-treader, in old German organs.

CALCANTENGLOCKE (*Ger.*) Bells, sounded by means of pedals.

CALDAMÉNTE (*It.*) Warmly, ardently.

CALLIOPE. *Beautiful voice;* a harsh steam organ; an organ stop of 8, or 4 feet pitch.

CÁLMA
CALMÁTE (*It.*) Calmness, tranquillity.
CALMÁTO

CALMÁNDO (*It.*) Becoming calm; with tranquillity.
CALMÁTA

CALME ET PLACIDE (*Fr.*) Calm and serene.

CALÓRE (*It.*) Warmth, animation, fire.

CALORÓSO (*It.*) Very much fire, and animation.

CALUMEAU. A reed, or pipe.

CAMBIÁRE (*It.*) To change, to alter.

CAMENA
CAMOENA (*Lat.*) The Muse.

CÁMERA (*It.*) Chamber: *música da cámera*, chamber music.

CÁMERA MÚSICA (*It.*) *See* **CHAMBER MUSIC.**

CAMMINÁNDO (*It.*) Flowing: with easy and gentle progression.

CAMPAGNUOLO (*It.*) Rustic music.

CAMPÁNA (*It.*) A bell: also, a glass bell.

CAMPANÁJO (*It.*) A bell-ringer: a bell-founder: a performer upon the *campanétta*.

CAMPANE (*Fr.*) A bell.

CAMPANÉLLA
CAMPANÉLLO (*It.*) A little bell.

CAMPANELLÍNO (*It.*) A very little bell.

CAMPANÉTTA (*It.*) A set of bells, tunes diatonically, and played with keys, like the pianoforte.

CAMPANÍSTA (*It.*) A player upon the *campanétta*.

CAMPANOLOGY. The art of bell ringing.

CAMPANÓNE (*It.*) A great bell.

CAMPESTRE (*It.*) Rustic, pastoral.
CAN (*Welsh*). A song.
CAN Y PROPHWYD DAVYDD (*Welsh*). The song of David, the Prophet.
CANARIE (*Fr.*)
CANARIES (*Eng.*)
CANÁRIO (*It.*) An old dance, supposed to be of English invention, in lively $\frac{3}{8}$ or $\frac{6}{8}$ time, of two strains. It appears to have been popular in the time of Purcell.
CANCAN (*Fr.*) A boisterous dance.
CANCRIZANS (*Lat.*) Retrograde, or backward motion.
CANDORA. A species of the Spanish guitar.
CANGIÁRE (*It.*) To change, to alter.
CÁNNA (*It.*) A reed, or pipe.
CÁNNA D'ORGANO (*It.*) The pipe of an organ.
CANON. A species of fugue, with strict, and uninterrupted, imitation.
CÁNONE
CANÓNICO (*It.*) A canon: see that word.
CÁNONE AL SOSPÍRO (*It.*) A canon, the parts of which commence at the distance of a crotchet rest from each other.
CÁNONE APÉRTO (*It.*) An *open canon*: a canon of which the solution or development is given.
CÁNONE CHIÚSO (*It.*) A *close* or *hidden* canon, the solution or development of which must be discovered: also, an enigmatical canon.
CÁNONE ENIGMATÍCO (*It.*) An enigmatical canon.
CÁNONE SCIÓLTO (*It.*) A free canon, not in the strict style.
CANÓRO (*It.*) Canorous, harmonious.
CANOROUS. Musical, tuneful.
CANORIS (*Lat.*) Melody, song.
CANORUS (*Lat.*) Melodious, musical, sweet-sounding.
CANTÁBILE (*It.*) *That can be sung.* In a melodious, singing, and graceful style, smooth, elegant, and expressive.
CANTÁBILE, ORNAMÉNTI AD LIBITUM, MA PIÙ TÓSTO PÔCHI E BUÓNI (*It.*) In a melodious style, with embellishments at pleasure, but few, and well chosen.
CANTACCHIÁRE (*It.*) To sing often and badly: to hum.
CANTADOUR (*Fr.*) A singer of songs and ballads, in the tenth and following centuries.
CANTAFÉRA (*It.*) See **CANTILÉNA**.
CANTAJUÓLO
CANTAMBÁNCA (*It.*) A street singer: an itinerant musician: a contemptuous term for a singer.
CANTAMÉNTO (*It.*) The song: the melody.

CANTÁNDO (*It.*) The sounds must be blended gracefully and softly into each other, as in singing.

CANTÁNTE (*It.*) A singer: also, a part to be executed by the voice.

CANTÁRE (*It.*) To sing, to celebrate, to praise.

CANTÁRE À ÁRIA (*It.*) To sing without confining one's-self strictly to the music as written.

CANTÁRE À ORÉCCHIO (*It.*) To sing by ear, without a knowledge of musical notation.

CANTÁRE DI MANIÉRA (*It.*) To sing in a correct style, with grace and expression.

CANTÁRE MANIERÁTA (*It.*) To sing with a profusion of embellishments, but without taste or discernment.

CANTÁTA (*It.*)
CANTATE (*Fr. & Ger.*) | A poetical composition to be set to music. A vocal composition of several movements. Originally the *Cantáta* was for one voice, comprising airs, and recitative, but now it frequently takes the form of a short oratorio, or operetta, without action.

CANTATÍLLA (*It.*)
CANTATILLE (*Fr.*) | A short cantata: an air, preceded by a recitative.
CANTATÍNA (*It.*)

CANTATION (*Lat.*) The act of singing.

CANTÁTO (*It.*) Sung.

CANTATÓRE (*It.*) A male singer.

CANTATORIUM (*Lat.*) The book from which the priests in the Roman Catholic service chant, or recite, the responses.

CANTATRÍCE (*It.*) A female singer.

CANTELLERÁNDO (*It.*) Singing with a subdued voice, murmuring, trilling.

CANTERELLÁRE (*It.*) To chant, or sing.

CANTERÍNO (*It.*) A singer, a chanter.

CÁNTICA (*It.*)
CÁNTICI (*It. pl.*) | Canticles: the ancient *lcudi*, or sacred songs of the Roman Catholic Church.

CANTI CARNASCIALÉSCHI
CÁNTI CARNEVÁLI | (*It.*) Songs of the Carnival week.

CANTICCHIÁNDO (*It.*) See CANTELLERÁNDO.

CANTICCHIÁRE (*It.*) To sing, to hum.

CANTICLE (*Lat.*) A sacred hymn, or song; see CÁNTICA.

CÁNTICO (*It.*)
CANTICUM (*Lat.*) | A canticle: see CÁNTICA.

CANTILÉNA (*It.*) The air, the melody, the principal melodic theme, or part: generally the highest vocal part.

CANTILÉNA SCÓTICA (*It.*) A Scotch air, or tune.

Cantilenáccia — Cantríce

CANTILENÁCCIA (*It.*) Coarse, bad singing.

CANTILENÁRE (*It.*) To sing little songs: a contemptuous term, implying to sing, to make songs.

CANTILLATIO (*Lat.*) A singing style of declamation.

CANTÍNO (*It.*) The smallest string on the violin, guitar, &c.

CÁNTIO (*It.*) An air or song.

CANTIQUE (*Fr.*) A canticle, or hymn of praise.

CANTIQUE DES CANTIQUES (*Fr.*) Solomon's Song.

CÁNTO (*It.*) Song, singing; air, melody; the soprano, or highest vocal part.

CÁNTO À CAPPÉLLA (*It.*) Vocal church music.

CÁNTO ARMÓNICO (*It.*) A part-song for two, three, or more voices.

CÁNTO CROMÁTICO (*It.*) Singing in semitones, that is, in chromatic intervals, or passages.

CÁNTO FÉRMO (*It.*) Plain chant: an ancient chant or melody: choral singing in unison on a single, plain melody: a melody consisting of a few long, plain notes, given as a theme for counterpoint.

CÁNTO FIGURÁTO (*It.*) A florid, embellished chant, or melody: florid, artistic, vocal music.

CÁNTO FUNÉBRE (*It.*) A funeral song.

CÁNTO GREGORIÁNO (*It.*) The Gregorian chant.

CANTOLANO (*Sp.*)
CÁNTO LLÁNO (*Sp.*)   The plain chant, or song.
CÁNTO PLÁNO (*It.*)

CÁNTO PRÍMO (*It.*) The first treble, or soprano.

CANTÓR (*It.*) A singer, a chanter.

CANTOR
CANTOR CHORALIS   (*Lat.*) Precentor: leader of the choir.

CANTÓRE (*It.*) A singer, a chanter, a poet.

CÁNTO RECITATÍVO (*It.*) Recitative: declamatory singing.

CANTOREI (*Ger.*) A party, or class of choristers: the dwelling-house of the cantor.

CANTOREN (*Ger.*) Chanters: a choir of singers.

CANTOR FIGURALIS (*Lat.*) Oratorio singer; conductor of the choir.

CANTORIS (*Lat.*) A term used in cathedral music to mark the passages intended to be sung by those choristers which are placed on that side of the choir where the *cantor*, or *precentor*, sits; which is usually the left-hand side on entering the choir from the nave: *see* DECANI.

CÁNTO SECÓNDO (*It.*) The second treble, or soprano.

CANTRÍCE (*It.*) A female singer.

Cantus — Cápo orchéstra

CANTUS (*Lat.*) A song, chant, or melody: also, the treble, or soprano part.

CANTUS AMBROSIANUS (*Lat.*) Those four chants, or melodies, introduced into the church by Ambrosius (St. Ambrose), Bishop of Milan, in the fourth century, and which are supposed to be derived from ancient Greek melodies: *see* **GREGORIAN MODES**.

CANTUS FIGURATUS (*Lat.*) Embellished, or figurative chants, or melodies.

CANTUS FIRMUS (*Lat.*) The plain song, or chant: *see* **CÁNTO FÉRMO**.

CANTUS GREGORIANUS (*Lat.*) Those four chants, or melodies introduced into the church by St. Gregory (Pope Gregory I.), and which, with the Ambrosian chants, formed a series of eight *modes* or *tones*, as they were called: *see* **GREGORIAN MODES**.

CANTUS MENSURABILIS (*Lat.*) A regular, or measured melody.

CANZÓNA (*It.*) Song, ballad, canzonet: an air of graceful, and somewhat elaborate construction, in two or three strains or divisions: by Italian musicians the name is applied to airs in two or three parts, with passages of fugue and imitation, somewhat similar to the *madrigal*.

CANZONÁCCIA (*It.*) A vulgar, trivial song: a bad *canzóne*.

CANZONCÍNA (*It.*) A short *canzóne*, or song.

CANZÓNE (*It.*) See **CANZÓNA**.

CANZÓNE SÁCRA (*It.*) A sacred song.

CANZONET. A short *canzóne*, or song.

CANZONÉTTA (*It.*) A short *canzóne*.

CANZONIÉRE (*It.*) A book containing songs, or lyrical compositions.

CAOINAN (*Ir.*) A requiem, an Irish requiem: *see* **KEENERS**.

CAPELLE (*Ger.*) A chapel.

CAPELL-MEISTER (*Ger.*) The director, composer, or master of the music, in a choir.

CAPISCOLUS (*Lat.*) An old term, meaning the *chanter*, or *precentor* of a choir.

CAPISTRUM (*Gr.*) An implement used by the ancient trumpeters, to relieve the strain upon their cheeks, when blowing. It was almost universally used, the exertion required being so great.

CÁPO (*It.*) The head, the beginning, the first part, the top.

CAPODASTRE (*Fr.*) | See **CAPOTÁSTO**.
CAPODASTRO (*It.*) |

CÁPO D'ÓPERA. The finest or best work of any good composer.

CAPOLAVÓRO (*It.*) A master piece.

CÁPO MÚSICA (*It.*) The conductor.

CÁPO ORCHÉSTRA (*It.*) The conductor, or leader.

CAPOTÁSTO (*It.*) The nut, or upper part of the finger-board of a violin, &c.: also, a small instrument used by guitar players, to form a temporary nut upon the finger-board, to produce certain effects.

CAPPÉLLA (*It.*) A chapel, or church: also, a band of musicians that sing or play in a church.

CAPPÉLLA MÚSICA (*It.*) Chapel, or church music.

CAPRICCIÉTTO (*It.*) A short *capríccio*.

CAPRÍCCIO (*It.*) An irregular, fanciful composition: a caprice: a species of *Fantasia*, in a capricious, and free style.

CAPRICCIOSAMÉNTE (*It.*) Capriciously.

CAPRICCIÓSO (*It.*) In a fanciful capricious style.

CAPRICE (*Fr.*) *See* CAPRÍCCIO.

CAPRICIEUSEMENT (*Fr.*) Capriciously.

CAPRICIEUX (*Fr.*) In a fanciful, capricious style.

CAPRICIÖS (*Ger.*) Capricious.

CAPUT SCHOLÆ (*Lat.*) A precentor.

CARACTÈRES DE MUSIQUE (*Fr.*) All the marks, or symbols, belonging to musical notation.

CARÁTTERE (*It.*) Character, quality, degree, emphasis.

CARESSANT (*Fr.*) Caressing; tenderly.

CAREZZÁNDO
CAREZZÉVOLE } (*It.*) In a caressing, and tender style.

CARICÁTO (*It.*) Exaggerated, caricatured.

CARILLON (*Fr.*) *See* CARILLONS.

CARILLON À CLAVIER (*Fr.*) A set of keys, and pedals, acting upon the bells.

CARILLONNER (*Fr.*) To chime, or ring bells.

CARILLONNEUR (*Fr.*) A player, or ringer of chimes, or *carillons*.

CARILLONS (*Fr. pl.*) *Chimes*: a peal, or set of bells, or chimes: also, short simple airs, adapted for such bells: also, a set of bells in an organ, or a mixture-stop of three ranks, to imitate a peal of bells.

CARITÀ (*It.*) Tenderness, feeling.

CARMAGNOLE. A Savoyard dance, accompanied with singing.

CARMEN (*Lat. & Ger.*) A poem, song, ode.

CAROL. The old ditties sung at Christmas or Easter; a song of joy and exultation: a song of devotion. In olden times Christmas carols were sung in churches, instead of psalms or hymns.

CARÓLA (*It.*) A dance, with singing.

CAROLÁRE (*It.*) To dance.

CAROLÉTTA (*It.*) A little dance.

CARRÉE (*Fr.*) A breve.

CARTEL (*Fr.*) An obsolete word for the first sketch of a composition, or of a full score.

CARTELLE (*Fr.*) A sheet, a leaf.

CARTELLÓNE (*It.*) A large play-bill: the printed catalogue of operas to be performed during the season at Italian theatres.

CÁSSA
CÁSSA GRÁNDE (*It.*) The great drum.

CÁSSA ARMONÍCA (*It.*) The body of a violin, &c.

CASSATION (*Ger.*)
CASSAZÍONE (*It.*) A serenade, comprising of several movements.

CASTAGNÉTTA (*It.*)
CASTAGNETTES (*Fr.*)
CASTAGNOLE (*Sp.*) Snappers; castanets, used in dancing: *see* CASTANETS.
CASTAÑÉTAS (*Sp.*)

CASTANETS. Snappers, used to accompany dancing: pieces of hard wood, or shell-like instruments, which are struck together and make a rattling sound, used by dancers in Spain and other southern countries, to mark the rhythm of the *boléro, cachúcha,* &c.

CASTAÑUÉLAS (*Sp.*) *See* CASTANETS.

CASTRAT (*Ger.*)
CASTRÁTO (*It.*) A male singer, with a soprano voice, formerly very frequent, now seldom to be met with.

CÄSUR (*Ger.*) *See* CÆSURA.

CATCH. A humorous vocal piece, for several voices; supposed to be of English invention, and dating as far back as the first days of the Tudors. The melodies, or parts, are so contrived, that the singers catch up each other's words, and produce a whimsical kind of cross-reading.

CATÉNA DI TRÍLLI (*It.*) A chain, or succession of shakes.

CATHÉDRALE (*Fr.*)
CATTEDRÁLE (*It.*) A cathedral.

CATLINGS. The smallest size of lute strings.

CATTÍVO (*It.*) Bad.

CATTÍVO TÉMPO (*It.*) A weak beat of the bar.

CAVALLÉTTA (*It.*) *See* CABALÉTTA.

CAVALÉTTO (*It.*) *A little horse:* a little bridge; the break in the voice.

CAVALQUET (*Fr.*) Trumpet signal for the cavalry.

CAVÁTA (*It.*) The production of tone.

CAVATÍNA (*It.*) A graceful air of one strain only, of a dramatic kind, sometimes preceded by a recitative.

CAVÍGLIA (*It.*) The peg of a violin, &c.

C barré (*Fr.*) The character 𝄵 used to indicate *álla bréve*, or *álla cappélla* time.

C clef. The Tenor clef: thus called because, on whatever line it is placed, it gives to the notes on that line the name, and pitch, of *middle* C, indicated thus 𝄡.

C dur (*Ger.*) The key of C major.

Cebell. The name of an ancient air in common time; its distinguishing characteristic was, that it consisted of sudden alternations of high and low notes, or passages.

Cécilium (*Fr.*) A free-reed keyboard instrument, of the melodeon species.

Cédez (*Fr.*) See **Diminuéndo**.

Celeraménte (*It.*) With speed; quickly and easily.

Célere (*It.*) Quick, rapid: with velocity.

Celesta. A stop, in a French reed organ; a keyboard instrument in which steel plates, are struck with hammers.

Céleste (*Fr.*) *Celestial, heavenly.* In some pianofortes it indicates the employment of the pedal, which acts on a *Celestina* stop: *see also* **Voix céleste**.

Celestína (*It.*) An organ stop, of small 4 feet scale, producing a very delicate and subdued tone.

Célli. An abbreviation of *violoncélli*.

Céllo. An abbreviation of *violoncéllo*.

Cembalísta (*It.*) A player on the harpsichord: also, a player on the cymbals.

Cémbalo (*It.*) A harpsichord: also, the name for a cymbal.

Cembanélla (*It.*) A bag-pipe.

Cémbolo (*It.*) See **Cébalo**.

Cemmamélla (*It.*) Cymbal.

Cemmanélla (*It.*) A bag-pipe.

Cennamella (*It.*) A pipe, or flute.

Centone (*Lat.*) A cento, or medley, of different tunes or melodies.

Cercár délla nóta (*It.*) To seek, or feel for the note: gliding from one note to another, in singing, by anticipating the proper time of the second note.

Cervalet. An antique wind-instrument of the reed kind, the tone of which resembles that of the bassoon.

Ces (*Ger.*) The note C-flat.

Ces dur (*Ger.*) The key of C-flat major.

Cesúra (*It.*) See **Cæsura**.

Cétera — Chant

CÉTERA (*It.*) A cittern, or guitar.

CETERÁNTE (*It.*) A player upon the cittern, or guitar.

CETERÁRE (*It.*) To play upon the cittern, or guitar.

CETERATOJO (*It.*) A song accompanied upon the cittern.

CETERATÓRE \
CETERÍSTA } (*It.*) A player upon the cittern, or guitar.

CETERIZZÁRE (*It.*) To sing with, or play upon the cittern.

CETRARCIÉRO (*It.*) Carrying the bow and lyre.

CETRÁRE (*It.*) *See* CETERÁRE.

CHACÓNA (*Sp.*) \
CHACONNE (*Fr.*) } A chacone, a graceful slow Spanish air or dance movement, in $\frac{3}{4}$ time, and composed upon a ground-bass. It is supposed to be of Arabian, or Moorish origin, and is always in a major key. The first and third beats of each bar are strongly emphasised.

CHAIR ORGAN. This occurs in old organ music: *see* CHOIR ORGAN.

CHALEMIE (*Fr.*) A kind of pipe.

CHALMEY. *See* CHALUMEAU.

CHALMEAU \
CHALUMEAU } (*Fr.*) An ancient rustic flute, resembling the hautboy, and blown through a *calamus*, or reed. The term is also applied to some of the low notes of the clarinet, which are distinguished by a great peculiarity of tone: also a reed stop on an organ, *see* SCHALMEIE.

CHAMBER MUSIC. Music composed for private performance, or for small concerts; such as instrumental duets, trios, quartets, &c.

CHAMPÊTRE (*Fr.*) Rustic, pastoral.

CHANG. A Persian harp.

CHANGEABLE. A term applied to chants which may be sung either in the major or minor mode of the key or tonic in which they are written.

CHANGER DE JEU (*Fr.*) To change the stops, or registers, in an organ.

CHANGES. The varied or altered passages, produced by a peal of bells.

CHANGING NOTES. A term applied by some theorists to passing notes, or discords, which occur on the *accented* parts of a bar.

CHANSON (*Fr.*) A song.

CHANSONNETTE (*Fr.*) A little, or short song, or canzonet.

CHANSONNIER (*Fr.*) A maker of ballads.

CHANSONS DE GESTE (*Fr.*) The romances formerly sung by the wandering *jongleurs*.

CHANT. A simple melody, generally harmonised in four parts, to which the daily psalms are sung in cathedrals, &c., part of the words being recited, *ad libitum*, and part sung in strict time. There are two kinds, the single chant, and the double chant. The name is also applied to some Ambrosian, and Gregorian melodies, supposed to be derived from the ancient Greek music.

CHANT (*Fr.*) The voice part: a song, or melody: singing.

CHANTANT (*Fr.*) Tuneable: in a melodious, and singing style.

CHANT DES OISEAUX (*Fr.*) Singing of the birds.

CHANT DE TRIOMPHE (*Fr.*) A triumphal song; a song of victory.

CHANTÉE (*Fr.*) Sung.

CHANT EN ISON (*Fr.*) An obsolete style of psalmody, confined to the singing of only two different sounds.

CHANTER. The superintendent, or leader of a cathedral choir.

CHANTER (*Fr.*) To sing, to celebrate.

CHANTER À LIVRE OUVERT (*Fr.*) To sing at sight.

CHANTERELLE (*Fr.*) Treble string: the smallest or most acute string of the violin.

CHANTER JUSTE (*Fr.*) To sing true, or perfect, as to intonation, &c.

CHANTERRES (*Fr.*) The singers of songs, and ballads, in the tenth and following centuries.

CHANTEUR (*Fr.*) A male singer.

CHANTEUSE (*Fr.*) A female singer.

CHANT FUNÈBRE (*Fr.*) A funeral song.

CHANTOR. An old name for the precentor, or chanter, in a choir.

CHANT PASTORAL (*Fr.*) A pastoral melody.

CHANTRE (*Fr.*) Chanter, chorister.

CHANTRERIE (*Fr.*) \
CHANTRY (*Eng.*) Institutions established and endowed for the purpose of singing the souls of the founders out of purgatory.

CHANTRY PRIESTS. Priests selected to sing in the chantry.

CHANT SUR LE LIVRE (*Fr.*) A barbarous kind of counterpoint, or *descant*, as it was termed, on the plain chant or *cánto férmo*, in use as early as the eighth century, and performed by several voices, each singing extempore.

CHAPEAU CHINOIS (*Fr.*) A crescent, or set of small bells, used in military music.

CHAPELLE (*Fr.*) *See* **CAPPÉLLA**.

CHARFREITAG (*Ger.*) Good Friday.

CHARIVARI (*Fr.*) Paltry music: clatter: mock music.

CHARLATAN (*Fr.*) A noisy, rattling, scrambling, unfinished performer: a superficial artist who makes great pretensions, which are not justified in performance.

CHASSE (*Fr.*) Hunting: in the hunting style.

Che — Chirogymnast

CHE (*It.*) Than, which: *póco più lénto che Andánte*, rather slower than Andante.

CHEF-D'ATTAQUE (*Fr.*) The leader, or principal first violin performer: also, the leader of the chorus.

CHEF-D'ŒUVRE (*Fr.*) A master-piece: the principal or most important composition: *see* CAPO D'ÒPERA.

CHEF-D'ORCHESTRE (*Fr.*) The conductor of an orchestra.

CHEF DU CHANT (*Fr.*) Trainer, or conductor of an opera house.

CHELYS (*Gr.*) A species of lute, or viol.

CHENG. A Chinese mouth organ.

CHEST OR VIOLS. A set of six viols, two of which were basses, two tenors, and two trebles, each with six strings: these were the instruments to which those compositions called *Fantasias* were adapted.

CHEVALET (*Fr.*) The bridge of a violin, viola, &c.

CHEVILLE (*Fr.*) The peg of a violin, viola, &c.

CHEVROTEMENT (*Fr.*) Singing with a trembling voice.

CHEVROTER (*Fr.*) To sing with a trembling voice: to make a bad, or false shake.

CHIÁRA (*It.*) Clear, pure, as to tone: pure, perfect, as to intervals.

CHIARAMÉTE (*It.*) Clearly, neatly, purely.

CHIÁRA VÓCE (*It.*) A clear pure voice.

CHIÁRA QUÁRTA (It.) A perfect fourth.

CHIARÉZZA (*It.*) Clearness, neatness, purity, brightness.

CHIARÍNA (*It.*) A clarion.

CHIÁRO (*It.*) Clear, brilliant: *see* CHIÁRA.

CHIAROSCÚRO (*It.*) Light and shade: the various modifications of *piáno*, and *fórte*.

CHIÁVE (*It.*) A key, or clef.

CHIÁVE DI BÁSSO (*It.*) The bass clef.

CHIÁVE DI VIOLÍNO (*It.*) The *violin* or treble clef.

CHIÉSA (*It.*) A church: *música di chiésa*, music for the church.

CHIFFRES (*Fr.*) *Figures*, used in Harmony, and Thorough-Bass.

CHIFLA (*Sp.*) A whistle.

CHIFONIE (*Fr.*) The old name for the *hurdy-gurdy*.

CHIKARA. A Hindoo fiddle, with fourth or five strings.

CHIME. A clarion.

CHINNOR \
CHINOR (*Heb.*) An instrument of the harp or psaltery species, supposed to have been used by the ancient Hebrews.

CHIRÍMIA (*Sp.*) The hautboy.

CHIROGYMNAST (*Gr.*) A square board, on which are placed various mechanical contrivances for exercising the fingers of a pianist.

CHIROPLAST (*Gr.*) A small machine invented by John Bernard Logier, about 1815, to keep the hands and fingers of young pianoforte players in the right position.

CHITÁRRA (*It.*) A guitar; a cithara.

CHITARRÁTA (*It.*) To imitate the guitar, on the pianoforte.

CHITTÁRRA COLL' ARCO (*It.*) A species of guitar played with a bow, like that of a violin.

CHITTARRÍNA | (*It.*) The small Neapolitan guitar.
CHITTARRÍNO |

CHIUCCHIURLÁJA (*It.*) A buzzing, or humming sound.

CHIUDÉNDO (*It.*) Closing, ending with.

CHIUDÉNDO COL MOTÍVO (*It.*) Concluding with the subject.

CHIURLÁRE (*It.*) The singing of a cuckoo.

CHIÚSO (*It.*) Close, hidden, speaking of canons.

CHŒUR (*Fr.*) The choir; the chorus.

CHOIR. That part in a cathedral, or church, set apart for the singers, and where service is performed: also, the singers themselves taken collectively.

CHOIR ORGAN. In a large organ, the lowest row of keys is called the choir organ, and contains some of the softer and more delicate stops, used to accompany the principal singers in solos, duets, &c. It also contains several of the *sólo* stops. The choir organ is often placed in a case by itself, in front of the other part of the instrument.

CHOR (*Ger.*) Choir, chorus: quire of a church: *Arie und Chor*, air and chorus.

CHORAGUS (*Lat.*) The leader of the ancient dramatic chorus; a musical official at Oxford University.

CHORAL. Belonging to the choir: full, or for many voices.

CHORAL (*Ger.*) Psalm or hymn tune: choral song or tune plain-song.

CHORAL-BUCH (*Ger.*) Choral book: antiphonal: book of hymn tunes.

CHORÄLE (*Ger. pl.*) Hymn tunes.

CHORALEON. See ÆOLODICON.

CHORALIST (*Ger.*) Chorister, choral-singer.

CHORALITER | (*Ger.*) In the style, time, or measure, of a psalm
CHORALMÄSSIG | tune, or choral.

CHORAL PRELUDE. An organ piece, based on a *choral* melody.

CHOR-ALTAR (*Ger.*) The high, or great altar.

CHOR-AMT (*Ger.*) Cathedral service; choral service.

CHORAULA (*Gr.*) The flute-player who accompanied the Greek chorus.

CHORD. A combination of several sounds, heard at the same time.

CHORDA (*Lat.*) A string.

CHORDA CHARACTERISTICA (*Lat.*) The leading, or characteristic, note or tone: *see* NOTA SENSIBILIS.

CHORDÆ ESSENTIALES (*Lat.*) These are, the tonic or key-note, the third, and the fifth, of each mode or diatonic scale.

CHORD A VIDO (*Lat.*) The open string of a violin, &c.

CHORDAULODION | The name given to an instrument like a large barrel-organ, self-acting: invented by Kaufmann, of Dresden.
CHORDOMELODION |

CHOR-DIENST (*Ger.*) Choir, or choral service.

CHORDOMETER. An instrument for measuring strings.

CHORDS ÉTOUFFÉS (*Fr.*) Stifled chords, on the harp, the sounds of which are damped by placing the palm of the left hand upon the strings.

CHÖRE (*Ger. pl.*) Choir, chorus: *see* CHOR.

CHORIAMBUS. A musical foot, accented thus, — ◡ ◡ —.

CHORION (*Gr.*) A hymn in praise of Cybele.

CHORIST (*Gr.*) | A chorister, a choral singer.
CHORISTE (*Fr.*) |

CHORISTER. A member of the choir, or chorus.

CHOR-REGENT (*Ger.*) Leader, or director, of the choristers.

CHOR-SÄNGER | (*Ger.*) A chorister, a choral singer, a member of the choir.
CHOR-SCHÜLER |

CHOR-STIMMEN (*Ger.*) Chorus parts.

CHOR-TON (*Ger.*) *Choral-tone*: the usual pitch, or intonation, of the organ, and therefore of the choir, in a church.

CHORUS. A company of singers: also, a composition written for performance by a number of singers. With the ancient Greeks, the chorus was a band of singers and dancers, who assisted at their dramatic representations. The name is also applied to the mixture-stops in an organ.

CHORUS-TONE. *See* CHORTON.

CHRISTE ELEISON (*Gr.*) A part of the Kyrie, or first movement in a Mass.

CHRISTMESSE | (*Ger.*) Christmas matins.
CHRISTMETTE |

CHROMA (*Gr.*) The chromatic signs: a *sharp* ♯, or a *flat* ♭.

CHROMA DIESIS (*Gr.*) A semitone, or half-tone.

CHROMA DUPLEX. The *double-sharp*, marked by the sign ×, 𝕏 or ♯♯; a semiquaver.

CHROMAMETER. A tuning-folk.

CHROMA SIMPLEX (*Lat.*) A sharp; a quaver.

CHROMATIC. Proceeding by semitone.

CHROMATIQUE (*Fr.*) \
CHROMATISCH (*Ger.*) Chromatic: moving by semitones.

CHROMATISHES KLANGGESCHLECHT (*Ger.*) The chromatic genus, or mode.

CHROTTA. See **CROWD**.

CHURCH CADENCE. Another name for the *Plagal* cadence.

CIACCÓNA \
CIACCÓNNE (*It.*) A slow Spanish dance, generally constructed on a ground-bass: see **CHACONNE**.

CIARAMÉLLA (*It.*) A bagpipe.

CICUTE (*Fr.*) An *appoggiatúra*, or a slide.

CICUTRÉNNA (*It.*) A musical pipe.

CIFRÁTO (*It.*) Figured: see **FIGURED BASS**.

CIGÓGNA (*It.*) The mouth pipes of a wind-instrument.

CIMBALE. See **CIMBEL**.

CÍMBALI (*It. pl.*) \
CIMBALLES (*Fr. pl.*) Cymbals: military instruments used to mark the time: see **CYMBALS**.

CIMBÁLO (*It.*) A cymbal: a harpsichord: a tambourine: a dulcimer.

CIMBÁLON (*It.*) An Hungarian dulcimer.

CIMBEL (*Ger.*) A mixture-stop, of acute tone.

CIMBÉLI (*It.*) Cymbals.

CIMBEL-STERN (*Ger.*) *Cymbal-star.* An organ stop, consisting of five bells, and composed of circular pieces of metal, cut in the form of a star, and placed at the top of the instrument, in front. It is acted upon by a foot-pedal, which sets it in rotation, and plays the five bells Arpeggio, so as to produce a chord: as, for instance, E, G#, B, E, and G#.

CINELLEN. See **CIMBALLES**.

CINK (*Ger.*) A small reed stop in an organ: see **KINKHORN**.

CINQ (*Fr.*) \
CINQUE (*It.*) Five: the fifth voice, or part, in a quintet.

CINYRA. An old name for the harp.

CIPHER. The continuous sounding of an organ pipe, due to some defect.

CIRCA (*Lat.*) About.

CIRCÓLO (*It.*) The old symbol for triple time, marked thus O.

CIRCÓLO MÉZZO (*It.*) A turn.

CIRCULAR CANON. A canon which goes through the twelve major keys.

CIS (*Ger.*) The note C#.

Cis — Clan marches

CIS-CIS (*Ger.*) The note C-double-sharp.
CIS DUR (*Ger.*) The key of C# major.
CIS MOLL (*Ger.*) The key of C# minor.
CISTELLA (*Lat.*) See DULCIMER.
CISTRE (*Fr.*) A cittern: see that word.
CISTRUM. See CITTERN.
CÍTARA (*It.*) A cittern, a guitar: see CITTERN.
CITARÍSTA (*It.*) A minstrel, a player on the cittern.
CITARIZZÁRE (*It.*) To play upon the cittern.
CITHÁRA (*Lat. & Sp.*) The lute, an old instrument of the guitar kind: see CITTERN.
CITHÁRA BIJUGA (*Lat.*) See CITHERA BIJUGA.
CITHÁRA HISPÁNICA (*Sp.*) The Spanish guitar.
CITHARODIA (*Gr.*) The art of singing to the lyre.
CITHER
CITHERA
CITHERN
CITTERN
CYTHORN
An old instrument of the lute or guitar species. The oldest on record had only three strings, but these were afterwards increased to eight, nine, and up to twenty-four; they were of wire, and twanged with a *plectrum*, usually made of quill, or a piece of whalebone. The *cither* was very popular in the sixteenth century, and commonly found in barbers' shops, and other places of resort. The names of the *cittern* or *gittern*, and *guitar*, appear to be derived from the same Greek word, and it may be inferred from the similarity of appellation, and from the remains of antique art, that the modern instruments resemble the ancient ones
CITHERA BIJUGA (*Lat.*) A Theorbo, a lute with two necks, or rather two nuts, which severally determined the lengths of two sets of strings: the longest of which gave the deepest, and gravest sounds, serving as a bass in accompanying the voice.
CITOLE (*Lat.*) An old instrument of the dulcimer species, and supposed to be synonymous with it.
CIVETTERÍA (*It.*) Coquetry; in a coquettish manner.
CLAIR (*Fr.*) Clearly, plainly.
CLAIRON (*Fr.*) Trumpet: also, the name of a reed stop, in an organ.
CLANGOR (*Lat.*) The tone of the trumpet, when blown with vehemence.
CLANGOR TUBARUM (*Lat.*) A military trumpet used by the ancient Romans, consisting of large tube of bronze, surrounded by seven smaller pipes, terminating in one point.
CLAN MARCHES. These are composed for the Scotch bagpipe, and formed upon peculiar scale of the instrument, with a strong accent, and marked rhythm.

CLAPPER. The tongue of a bell.

CLAQUEBOIS (*Fr.*) A musical instrument.

CLARA VOCE (*Lat.*) A clear, loud voice.

CLARABELLA (*Lat.*) An organ stop, invented by J. C. Bishop, of 8 feet scale, and a thick, powerful, fluty tone; the pipes being made of wood, and not stopped.

CLARIANA. An organ stop of the dulciana or string species.

CLARIBEL-FLUTE. An organ stop of the flute species.

CLARICHORD. *See* CLAVICHORD.

CLARICORDE (*Fr.*) The clarichord, or clavichord.

CLARIN (*Ger.*) Clarion: also, the name of a 4 feet reed stop in German organs.

CLARINBLASEN (*Ger.*) Soft tones, or notes upon the trumpet.

CLARINET. A rich and full-toned wind-instrument, of wood, of the single reed species; said to have been invented by Johann Christopher Denner, of Nuremburg, about 1659.

CLARINETTE (*Fr.*) The clarinet: also, the name of an organ stop: *see* CLARIONET.

CLARINETTÍSTA (*It.*) | A performer upon the clarinet.
CLARINETTISTE (*Fr.*) |

CLARINÉTTO (*It.*) A clarinet.

CLARÍNO (*It.*) | A small, or octave trumpet: also, the name of a 4
CLÁRION (*Eng.*) | feet organ reed stop, tuned an octave above the trumpet stop, and of a sharp, clear tone. The term is also used to indicate the trumpet parts, in a full score.

CLARION HARMONIQUE (*Fr.*) An organ reed stop: *see* HARMONIQUE.

CLARIONET. A wind-instrument, of the single reed species, of full, rich tone. Also, an organ reed stop of 8 feet scale, and soft quality of tone: *see also* CLARINET.

CLARIONET-FLUTE. An organ stop of a similar kind to the stopped diapason; the tone is of a very agreeable, reedy quality.

CLARSEACH. The ancient Irish harp.

CLARTÉ DE VOIX (*Fr.*) Clearness of voice.

CLAUSEL (*Ger.*) | A close, a cadence; a concluding musical phrase.
CLAUSULA (*Lat.*) |

CLAUSULA AFFINALIS (*Lat.*) A cadence in a key nearly related to the original key of the piece.

CLAUSULA DISSECTA (*Lat.*) A half-cadence.

CLAUSULA DOMINANS (*Lat.*) A cadence on the dominant.

CLAUSULA FALSA (*Lat.*) A false, or deceptive, cadence.

Clausula — Clavicytherium

CLAUSULA FINALIS
CLAUSULA PRIMARIA (*Lat.*) A final cadence, or close, in the original key.
CLAUSULA PRINCIPALIS

CLAUSULA IMPROPRIO (*Lat.*) An uncommon, or deviation, cadence.

CLAUSULA MEDIANS (*Lat.*) A cadence on the third, in a piece in the minor mode.

CLAUSULA PEREGRINA (*Lat.*) A close in a distinct, or extraneous key.

CLAUSULA PROPRIA
CLAUSULA PURA (*Lat.*) A proper, or natural close.

CLAUSULA SECUNDARIA (*Lat.*) A cadence on the dominant.

CLAUSULA TERTIARIA (*Lat.*) *See* CLAUSULA MEDIANS.

CLAVÆOLINE. An organ free-reed stop, of 8, or 16 foot pitch.

CLAVE (*Lat.*) A key: a clef.

CLAVECIN (*Fr.*) The harpsichord.

CLAVECIN D'AMOUR (*Fr.*) A species of harpsichord.

CLAVECÝMBALA (*It.*) The harpsichord.

CLAVES SIGNATA (*Lat.*) The coloured lines used by Guido to express the pitch of the notes, and which were in use until clefs were invented.

CLAVIARIUM (*Lat.*)
CLAVIATUR (*Ger.*) The keys of a pianoforte, harpsichord, organ, &c.

CLAVICÉMBALO (*It.*)
CLAVICEMBALUM (*Lat.*) The harpsichord.

CLAVICHORD. A small, keyed instrument, of the spinet, or virginal species, and the precursor of the pianoforte. It was used by the nuns in convents, and that the sound might not disturb the sisters in the dormitory, the strings were muffled with small pieces of fine woollen cloth, the tone being produced by little iron pins, or wedges, called *tangents*, which pressed under the brass strings when the keys were struck; and not with 'jacks and crow-quills' like the harpsichord, spinet, and virginal. The tone of the Clavichord was pleasant, soothing, and impressive, though weak.

CLAVICHORDIUM (*Lat.*) *See* CLAVICHORD.

CLAVICOR (*Fr.*) A species of horn with pistons or keys.

CLAVICYLINDER. A keyboard instrument, containing a revolving glass cylinder and steel bars, instead of strings.

CLAVICYMBALUM (*Lat.*) The harpsichord: spinet.

CLAVICYMBEL (*Ger.*) A clavichord.

CLAVICYTHERIUM (*Lat.*) A species of upright harpsichord, said to have been originally in the form of a harp or lyre, with catgut strings, and to have been invented in Italy about 1300.

Clavier — Colascióne

CLAVIER (*Fr. & Ger.*) The keys, or key-board, of a pianoforte, organ, &c.: also, an old name for the *Clavichord*.

CLAVIER-AUSZUG (*Ger.*) An arrangement, or reduction of a full score, for the use of pianoforte players.

CLAVIER-DRATH (*Ger.*) Wire, for the pianoforte, &c.

CLAVIS (*Lat. & Ger.*) A key: a clef.

CLEAR-FLUTE. An organ stop, of 4 feet scale, the tone of which is exceedingly firm, clear, and full. It was invented by Messrs. Kirkland and Jardine, of Manchester.

CLÉ | (*Fr.*) A key: a character used to determine the name and
CLEF | pitch of the notes: there are three kinds, the G or Treble clef, the C or Tenor clef, and the F or Bass clef.

CLEF D'ACCODEUR (*Fr.*) A tuning-key.

CLEF DE FA (*Fr.*) The F, or Bass clef.

CLEF DE SOL (*Fr.*) The G, or Treble clef.

CLEF D'UT (*Fr.*) The C clef.

CLIQUETTE (*Fr.*) The bones.

CLOCCA (*Lat.*) | A bell.
CLOCHE (*Fr.*) |

CLOCHETTE (*Fr.*) A little bell; a hand-bell.

CLOSE HARMONY. Harmony in which the notes, or parts, are kept as close together as possible.

CLYNKE-BELL. A chime.

C MOLL (*Ger.*) The key of C minor.

COALOTTINO. *See* **CONCERTINO.**

COCCHIÁTA (*It.*) A serenade in a coach.

CÓDA (*It.*) *The end: the tail*: a few bars added at the end of a piece of music, to produce a more complete and effective termination.

CODÉTTA (*It.*) A short coda, or passage added to a piece or serving to connect one movement with another.

CODON. A bell.

COFFRE (*Fr.*) The belly, of a lute, guitar, &c.

COGLI (*It. pl.*) With the.

COGLI STROMENTI (*It. pl.*) With the instruments.

COI (*It. pl.*) With one: *coi bássi*, with the basses: *coi violíni*, with the violins.

COL (*It.*) With the: *coll' árco*, with the bow: *col básso*, with the bass.

COLACHON (*Fr.*) An Italian instrument, much like a lute, but with a longer neck.

COL ÁRCO (*It.*) *With the bow*: see **COLL' ÁRCO.**

COLASCIÓNE (*It.*) An instrument like a guitar, with two strings only.

Col cánto — Cóme il

COL CÁNTO (*It.*) With the melody, or voice: *see also* COLLA VÓCE.
COLL' \
COLLA / (*It.*) With the.
COLLA DÉSTRA (*It.*) With the right hand.
COLLA PÁRTE (*It.*) With the part, or principal performer: indicating that the time is to be accommodated to the sólo singer, or player.
COLLA PIÙ GRAN FÓRZA E PRESTÉZZA (*It.*) As loud, and as quick as possible.
COLLA PÚNTA D'ÁRCO (*It.*) With the point, or tip of the bow.
COLL' ÁRCO (*It.*) *With the bow*: the notes are to be played with the bow, and not *pizzicáto*.
COLLA SINÍSTRA (*It.*) With the left hand.
COLLA VÓCE (*It.*) *With the voice*: implying that the accompanist must accommodate, and take the time from the singer.
COLLEGE YOUTHS. A name given to a society of bell-ringers, formerly in high repute, and including gentlemen of great learning and respectability amongst its members.
COLLEGIÁTA (*It.*) \
COLLEGIAT-KIRCHE (*Ger.*) / A collegiate church.
COL LÉGNO DELL' ÁRCO (*It.*) *With the bow-stick*: strike the strings with the wooden part, or wrong side of the bow, to produce particular effects.
COLLINET (*Fr.*) A flageolet.
COLLO (*It.*) See COLLA.
COLL' OTTÁVA (*It.*) With octaves: to be played in octaves.
COLOFANE (*Fr.*) \
COLOFÓNIA (*It.*) \
COLOPHANE (*Fr.*) } Resin: used for the hair, in the bow of the violin, &c., to enable the performer to obtain a better, and firmer hold, or *bite*, upon the strings.
COLOPHON (*Fr.*) \
COLOPHONIUM (*Ger.*) \
COLOPHONY (*Eng.*) /
COLORÁTO (*It.*) *Coloured*, florid, embellished.
COLORATÚRA (*It.*) Ornamental passages, roulades, divisions, &c., in vocal music.
CÓLPO (*It.*) Suddenly, immediately.
COMBINATION PEDALS. *See* COMPOSITION PEDALS.
CÓME (*It.*) As, like, the same as.
COMÉDIE (*Fr.*) Comedy, play.
COMÉDIEN (*Fr.*) Comedian, actor.
COMÉDIENNE (*Fr.*) An actress.
CÓME IL PRÍMO TÉMPO (*It.*) In the same time as the first.

CÓME PRÍMA (*It.*) As before; as at first.

COMES (*Lat.*) A *companion*: this term was used by Fux, and other old theorist, to indicate the *answer*, in a fugue.

CÓME SÓPRA (*It.*) *As above; as before*: indicating the repetition of a previous, or similar passage.

CÓME STA (*It.*) *As it stands*: exactly as it is written, without any alteration, or embellishment.

CÓME TÉMPO DEL TÉMA (*It.*) In the same time as the theme.

CÓMICO (*It.*)
COMIQUE (*Fr.*) } Comic: also, a comic actor: a writer of comedies.

COMINCIÁNTE (*It.*) A beginner, in music, &c.

COMINCIÁRE (*It.*) To begin: *al cominciáre*, at the beginning.

COMINCIÁTA (*It.*) The beginning: the commencement.

CÓMMA (*It.*) The ninth part of a tone. A comma is a small interval, used in treating of the analysis of musical sounds, and which may be described as something like the difference between D-sharp, and E-flat, as played upon the violin by the best performers.

The interval of a *tone* is divided into nine almost imperceptible intervals, which are called *commas*, five of which constitute the major semitone and four the minor semitone.

COMMÉDIA (*It.*) A play, a comedy: also, a theatre.

COMMEDIÁNTE (*It.*) A comedian.

COMMENÇANT (*Fr.*) A beginner, in music, &c.

COMMENCER (*Fr.*) To begin, to commence.

COMME UN MURMURE (*Fr.*) Like a murmur; very soft.

CÓMMODO (*It.*) See CÓMODO.

COMMON CHORD. A chord consisting of a bass note or root, together with its third and fifth, to which the octave is generally added. It is called a *triad*.

COMMON TIMES. Those which have an *even* number of parts in a bar, as *two*, *four*, *six*, &c.

COMODAMÉNTE
CÓMODO } (*It.*) Conveniently, easily, with ease; quietly, with composure.

COMPANY OF MUSICIANS. One of the old chartered societies of London, originally instituted by Charles I.

COMPENSATION MIXTURE. An organ mixture-stop, in the pedals, of a peculiar composition, and intended to assist the intonation of the pedal bass.

COMPIACÉVOLE
COMPIACIMENTO } (*It.*) Agreeable, pleasing, attractive.

COMPIÉTA (*It.*) Complin: evening prayers.

Complement — Con alcúna

COMPLEMENT. The interval, which, when added to another, completes the octave.

COMPLÉSSO (*It.*) A term applied to a chord which is complete.

COMPLIN (*Lat.*) Evening service, during Lent, in the Roman Catholic Church.

COMPONASTER (*Ger.*) A bad composer.

COMPÓNERE (*It.*)
COMPONIREN (*Ger.*) | To compose music.
COMPÓRRE (*It.*)

COMPONITÓRE (*It.*) A composer, author.

COMPONITRÍCE (*It.*) A female composer, an authoress.

COMPOSER (*Fr.*) To compose music.

COMPONIST (*Ger.*)
COMPOSITEUR (*Fr.*) | A composer of music.
COMPOSITÓRE (*It.*)

COMPOSITION. Any musical production, or invention. The art of inventing, or composing music.

COMPOSITION PEDALS. Pedals connected with a system of mechanism for arranging the stops in an organ. The invention is due to J. C. Bishop.

COMPOSITÚRA
COMPOSIZIÓNE | (*It.*) A composition, or musical work.

COMPOSIZIÓNE DI TAVOLÍNO (*It.*) Table-music; music sung at table; such as, part-songs, glees, catches, rounds, &c.

COMPÓSTO (*It.*) Composed; set to music.

COMPOUND INTERVALS. Those which exceed the extend of an octave: as, a ninth, tenth, &c.

COMPOUND TIMES. Those which include, or exceed *six* parts in a bar, and contain *two*, or more, principal accents; as $\frac{6}{4}, \frac{6}{8}, \frac{9}{4}, \frac{9}{8}, \frac{12}{8}$, &c.

COMPRESSED HARMONY. *See* **CLOSE HARMONY.**

CON (*It.*) With.

CON ABBANDÓNO (*It.*) With passion and sentiment; with ardent feeling.

CON ABBANDÓNO ED ESPRESSIÓNE (*It.*) With passionate feeling, and expression.

CON AFFÉTTO
CON AFFEZIÓNE | (*It.*) With warmth, and intensity of expression.

CON AFFLIZIÓNE (*It.*) With affliction; mournfully.

CON AGILITÀ (*It.*) With agility, neatly; with clean and light expression.

CON AGITAZIÓNE (*It.*) With agitation; hurriedly.

CON ALCÚNA LICÉNZA (*It.*) With a certain degree of licence, as regards time, expression.

CON ALLEGRÉZZA (*It.*) With lightness: joyfully, cheerfully, gaily.

CON ALTERÉZZA (*It.*) With an elevated, and sublime, expression.

CON AMABILITÀ (*It.*) With grace, and gentleness.

CON AMARÉZZA (*It.*) With affliction, mournfully.

CON AMÓRE (*It.*) With an affectionate, ardent, expression.

CON ÁNIMA (*It.*) With soul, resolution, boldness.

CON ANIMAZIÓNE (*It.*) With animation, decision, boldness.

CON AUDÁCE (*It.*) With boldness, audacity, firmness.

CON BELLÉZZA (*It.*) With beauty of tone, and expression.

CON BRÍO (*It.*) With life, fire, spirit, brilliancy.

CON BRÍO ED ANIMÁTO (*It.*) With spirit, and resolution.

CON CÁLMA (*It.*) With calmness, and tranquillity.

CON CALÓRE (It.) With warmth: with fire.

CONCATENAZIÓNE ARMÓNICA (*It.*) Harmony in which some of the parts are changed, or moving, while others are held on, or sustained.

CON CELERITÀ (*It.*) With celerity, with rapidity.

CONCÉNTO (*It.*) | Concord, agreement, harmony. This name is
CONCENTUS (*Lat.*) | sometimes given to a collection of pieces.

CONCERTRÁRE (*It.*) To concentrate the sounds: it also sometimes means, to veil the sounds with mystery.

CONCERTÁNTE (*It.*) A piece in which each part is alternately principal, and subordinate, as in a *dúo concertánte*. It also implies, an orchestral piece, in which several of the instruments have occasional solos, or passages for the display of execution, and taste.

CONCERTÁTO (*It.*) In an irregular, extemporaneous manner: *see also* **CONCERTÁNTE**.

CONCERTED MUSIC. Music in which several voices, or instruments, are heard at the same time; in opposition to *sólo* music.

CONCERT-GERBER (*Ger.*) Concert-giver.

CONCÉRTI (*It. pl.*) The pural of the word *concerto*.

CONCERTÍNA (*It.*) A small instrument, of sexangular shape, held in the hands. The sounds are produced from metal tongues, or vibrators, by pressing the fingers upon the keys, which are placed on each side of the instrument, and moving the bellows at the same time, to obtain the requisite supply of wind. The tones are soft, and delicate.

CONCERTÍNO (*It.*) A short concerto: the word also denotes a principal part in a concerto, or other full orchestral piece; *violíno prímo concertíno*, principal first violin: *violíno secóndo concertíno*, principal second violin.

CONCERTIREN (*Ger.*) To accord, to agree in sound: also, to contend, or emulate with the voices, or instruments, in the parts of refined music, as in the *sóli* of concerts.

CONCERTIREND (*Ger.*) See **CONCERTÁNTE**.

CONCERT-MEISTER (*Ger.*) Master, or conductor of the concert: manager, or conductor of the musical academy.

CONCÉRTO (*It.*) A concert: harmony: also, a composition for a solo instrument, with orchestral accompaniment.

CONCÉRTO GRANDE (*Fr.*) | A grand orchestral composition, for many instruments, some Principal, some Auxiliary.
CONCÉRTO GRÓSSO (*It.*) |

CONCÉRTO SPIRITUÁLE (*It.*) A miscellaneous concert, chiefly consisting of sacred, or classical music.

CONCERT OVERTURE. See **OVERTURE**.

CONCERT-SAAL (*Ger.*) Concert room: music room.

CONCERT-SPIELER (*Ger.*) A solo player, concerto player.

CONCERT SPIRITUEL (*Fr.*) See **CONCÉRTO SPIRITUÁLE**.

CONCERT-STÜCK (*Ger.*) A concert piece: a concerto.

CONCITÁTO (*It.*) Perturbed, agitated.

CON CIVETTERÍA (*It.*) With coquetry, in a coquettish manner.

CONCLUSIÓNE (*It.*) The conclusion, or winding up.

CON CÓMODO (*It.*) With ease; without constraint, or effort: in a convenient time.

CONCORD. An agreeable combination of sounds: the opposite to a discord: *see* **CONSONANCE**.

CONCORDANT. Harmonious, consonant.

CONCORDANTEN (*Ger.*) Those sounds which, in combination, produce a concord: as C, E, G.

CONCORDÁNZA | (*It.*) Concord, harmony.
CONCÓRDIA |

CON DELICATÉZZA (*It.*) With delicacy, and softness.

CON DESIDÉRIO (*It.*) With an ardent, longing expression.

CON DEVOSIÓNE (*It.*) With devotion and fervour.

CON DILIGENZA (*It.*) With care and accuracy.

CON DISCREZIÓNE (*It.*) With discretion: at the discretion, or pleasure of the performer, not allowing the accompaniment to overpower the voice.

CON DISPERAZIÓNE (*It.*) With despair, desperation, violence of expression.

CON DIVOZIÓNE (*It.*) With religious feeling: in a devotional and solemn manner.

Con dólce maniéra / **Con dolcézza** (*It.*) With sweetness, delicacy, softness.

Con colóre (*It.*) Mournfully, with grief and pathos.

Conduciménto (*It.*) A melody consisting of a regular succession of conjunct degrees.

Conductor. The master, or chief of an orchestra, who directs the time and performance of every piece with has baton, and occasionally with his hand.

Conductus (*Lat.*) A very old species of descant, of which all that is known is, that instead of being founded upon some chosen, or popular melody, it was entirely original, supplied its own theme, and, unlike other modes of descant, was independent of everything but the composer's imagination.

Con duólo (*It.*) Mournfully, with grief and pathos.

Conduttóre (*It.*) A conductor.

Cone gamba. An organ stop of the gamba species, with conical pipes.

Con elegánza (*It.*) With elegance.

Con elevazióne (*It.*) With elevation, in a lofty, elevated, grand style.

Con energía (*It.*) With energy and emphasis.

Con entusiásmo (*It.*) With enthusiasm.

Con espressióne (*It.*) With expression.

Con espressióne dolorósa (*It.*) With a mournful expression.

Con éstro poético (*It.*) With poetic fervour and fury: with poetic rage.

Con facilità (*It.*) With facility.

Con fermézza (*It.*) With firmness.

Con festività (*It.*) With festive gaiety.

Con fidúcia (*It.*) With hope, with confidence.

Con fierézza (*It.*) With fire: fiercely.

Con fiochézza (*It.*) With hoarseness: hoarsely: as occasionally in *búffo* parts.

Con flessibilità (*It.*) With flexibility, with freedom.

Con fórza (*It.*) With force, with vehemence.

Confrérie de St. Julien (*Fr.*) An ancient French association, or club, of ballad singers, and itinerant fiddlers.

Con frétta (*It.*) Hurriedly: with haste.

Con fuóco (*It.*) With fire, with passion.

Con fúria / **Con furóre** (*It.*) With fury, impetuosity, rage, vehemence.

Confusióne (*It.*) Confusion: want of clearness, and order.

Con gárbo (*It.*) With elegance and taste.

Con gentilézza — Con mólto

CON GENTILÉZZA (*It.*) With grace, and elegance.
CON GIUSTÉZZA (*It.*) With justness, and precision.
CON GIUSTÉZZA DELL' INTONAZIÓNE (*It.*) With just, and correct, intonation.
CON GLI (*It. pl.*) With the.
CON GRANDÉZZA (*It.*) With dignity, and grandeur.
CON GRAVITÀ (*It.*) With gravity, and majesty.
CON GRÁZIA (*It.*) With grace, and elegance; usually in a moderate time.
CON GÚSTO (*It.*) With taste.
CON ÍMPETO
CON IMPETUOSITÀ | (*It.*) With impetuosity, and vehemence.
CON ÍMPETO DOLORÓSO (*It.*) With pathetic force, and energy.
CON INDIFFERÉNZA (*It.*) With indifference: a dramatic expression, intimating that the performer is to assume an air of indifference, and ease.
CON INNOCÉNZA (*It.*) In a simple, artless, and innocent style.
CON INTIMÍSSIMO SENTIMÉNTO (*It.*) With very much feeling: with great expression.
CON INTREPIDÉZZA (*It.*) With intrepidity, with boldness.
CON ÍRA (*It.*) With anger: angrily.
CONJUNCT (*Lat.*) A term applied by the ancient Greeks to tetrachords, when the highest note of one tetrachord formed the lowest note of the succeeding one.
CON JÚSTO (*It.*) With exactness.
CON LEGGERÉZZA
CON LEGGIERÉZZA | (*It.*) With lightness, and delicacy.
CON LENÉZZA (*It.*) With mildness, sweetness.
CON LENTÉZZA (*It.*) With slowness: lingering.
CON MAESÀ (*It.*) With majesty, and grandeur.
CON MALANCONÍA
CON MALENCONÍA
CON MALINCONÍA | (*It.*) With an expression of melancholy and sadness.
CON MÁNO DÉSTRA
CON MÁNO DRÍTTA | (*It.*) With the right hand.
CON MÁNO SINÍSTRA (*It.*) With the left hand.
CON MISTÉRIO (*It.*) With mystery; in a mysterious manner.
CON MODERAZIÓNE (*It.*) With a moderate degree of quickness.
CON MÓLTA EXPRESSIÓNE (*It.*) With more expression.
CON MÓLTO CARÁTTERE (*It.*) With much character and emphasis.
CON MÓLTO PASSIÓNE (*It.*) With much passion, and feeling.

Con mólto SeNtiménto (*It.*) With much feeling, and expression.
Con morbidézza (*It.*) With softness, smoothness, delicacy, and tenderness.
Con móto (*It.*) With motion: keeping up a lively movement: not dragging.
Con negligénza (*It.*) With negligence; in a careless manner, without restraint.
Connoisseur (*Fr.*) One skilled in music, and who is a competent judge of it.
Con osservánza (*It.*) With scrupulous care and accuracy in regard to time and expression.
Con ottáva
Con 8va (*It.*) With octaves: to be played in octaves.
Con passióne (*It.*) With passion, with feeling.
Con piacevolézza (*It.*) With a pleasing, and graceful, expression.
Con precipitazióne (*It.*) With precipitation, in a hurried manner.
Con precisióne (*It.*) With exactness, and precision.
Con prestézza (*It.*) With rapidity.
Con rábbia (*It.*) With rage, fury, impetuosity.
Con rapidità (*It.*) With rapidity.
Con réplica (*It.*) With repetition; to be repeated.
Con risoluzióne (*It.*) With firmness, and resolution.
Con sdégno (*It.*) With wrath; in an angry and scornful style.
Consecutive. A series of similar intervals, or chords, immediately following one another.
Consecutives. Consecutives of the like character, in succession, between two parts: such as are forbidden by the laws of harmony.
Con semplicità (*It.*) With simplicity.
Con sensibilità (*It.*) With sensibility, and feeling.
Con sentiménto (*It.*) With feeling, and sentiment.
Consequent (*Lat.*) An old term, meaning the *answer*, in a fugue, or of a point of imitation.
Conservatoire (*Fr.*)
Conservatório (*It.*) A public school or academy of music, in which every branch of the art is taught.
Conservatorium (*Ger.*)
Consolánte (*It.*) In a consoling, comforting manner.
Consolataménte (*It.*) Quietly, comfortably, cheerfully.
Console. That part of an organ, which the performer uses to control the pipes, and contains the keyboards.
Con solennità (*It.*) With solemnity.
Con sómma espressióne (*It.*) With very great expression.

Consonance — Cóntra-gámba

CONSONANCE. The opposite to a discord, or dissonance: an interval, or chord, pleasing, satisfactory, and agreeable to the ear, and which does not necessarily require another to follow it.

CONSONANT. A chord composed entirely of consonances.

CONSONANZ (*Ger.*) \
CONSONÁNZA (*It.*) A consonance: a concord: harmony.

CONSONÁRE (*It.*) To tune in unison, or concord, with another.

CONSONIREN (*Ger.*) To concord: to agree in sound.

CON SONORITÀ (*It.*) With full, sonorous, vibrating kind of tone.

CON SORDÍNI (*It. pl.*) *With mutes*, in violin playing: in pianoforte music it means *with dampers*, indicating that the dampers are not to be raised by the pedal.

CON SORDÍNO (*It.*) *With the mute*: meaning that a mute, or damper, is to be affixed to the bridge of the violin, viola, &c.

CONSORT. A company of musicians.

CON SPÍRITO (*It.*) With spirit, life, energy.

CON STRÉPITO (*It.*) With noise: in a boisterous manner.

CON STROMÉNTI \
CON STRUMÉNTI (*It.*) *With the instruments*: meaning that the orchestra and voices are together.

CON SUAVÉZZA \
CON SUAVITÀ (*It.*) With sweetness, and delicacy.

CONTADÍNA (*It.*) A country dance.

CONTADINÉSCO (*It.*) Rustic: in a rural style.

CONTÁNO (*It.*) The parts so marked, are to rest.

CON TENERÉZZA (*It.*) With tenderness, softness.

CON TEPIDITÀ (*It.*) With coldness, and indifference.

CON TIMIDÉZZA (*It.*) With timidity.

CON TÍNTO (*It.*) With various shades of expression.

CONINUÁTO (*It.*) Continued, held on, sustained.

CONTEUARS (*Fr.*) Troubadours.

CONTINUED BASS. *See* **BÁSSO CONTÍNUO.**

CONTÍNUO (*It.*) *Continued:* see **BÁSSO CONTÍNUO.**

CONTRABÁSSIST. A double-bass player.

CÓNTRA-BÁSSO (*It.*) The double bass, the deepest toned stringed instrument of the bow species.

CONTR' ÁCO (*It.*) Bowing (the violin, &c.) in a manner contrary to rule.

CONTRADDÁNZA (*It.*) A country dance.

CÓNTRA-FAGÓTTO (*It.*) The double bassoon: also, the name of an organ stop of 16, or 32 feet scale: *see* **DOUBLE BASSOON.**

CÓNTRA-GÁMBA (*It.*) An organ stop of 16 feet scale.

CONTRÁLTO (*It.*) The deepest species of the female voice, the scale of which somewhat resembles that of the alto, or counter-tenor voice.

CON TRANQUILLÉZZA | (*It.*) With tranquillity, with calmness:
CON TRANQUILLITÀ | quietly.

CONTRA-POSAUNE (*Ger.*) Double trombone: a 16, or 32 feet reed stop, in an organ.

CONTRAPPUNTÍSTA (*It.*) One skilled in counterpoint.

CONTRAPPÚNTO (*It.*) Counterpoint: see that word.

CONTRAPPÚNTO ALLA MÉNTE (*It.*) *See* CHANT SUR LE LIVRE.

CONTRAPPÚNTO ALLA ZÓPPA (*It.*) *Lame, halting*: syncopated counterpoint.

CONTRAPPÚNTO DÓPPIO (*It.*) Double counterpoint.

CONTRAPPÚNTO DÓPPIO ALLA DUODÉCIMA (*It.*) Double counterpoint in the twelfth.

CONTRAPPÚNTO SÓPRA IL SOGGÉTTO (*It.*) Counterpoint above the subject.

CONTRAPPÚNTO SÓPRO IL SOGGÉTTO (*It.*) Counterpoint below the subject.

CONTRAPUNKT (*Ger.*) Counterpoint.

CONTRAPUNTAL. Belonging, or relating to counterpoint.

CONTRAPUNTIST. One skilled in counterpoint.

CONTRÁRIO (*It.*) Contrary: *see* CONTRARY MOTION.

CONTRARY MOTION. Motion in an opposite direction to some other part, one rising as another falls.

CON TRASPÓRTO (*It.*) With passion, excitement, anger.

CONTRASSOGGÉTTO (*It.*) The counter-subject, secondary subject, or counter-theme, in a fugue.

CONTRATÉMPO (*It.*) *Against the time*: that is, one part moving in a slower progression than the other parts: syncopation.

CONTRA-TENOR. See COUNTER-TENOR.

CONTRATÖNE (*Ger.*) A term applied to the deeper tones of the bass voice.

CÓNTRA VIOLÓNE (*It.*) | The double bass: *see* CÓNTRA-BÓSSO.
CONTRE-BASSE (*Fr.*) |

CONTREDANSE (*Fr.*) A country dance: a quadrille: a dance in which the parties engaged stand against each other, in two opposite ranks.

CON TREMÓRE (*It.*) With tremor, in a trembling manner.

CONTRE-PARTIE (*Fr.*) A counterpart, the second part: a second voice, singing different notes from those of the first.

CONTRE-POINT (*Fr.*) Counterpoint.

CONTREPOINTISTE (*Fr.*) A contrapuntist.

Contre-sujet — Corde à boyau

Contre-sujet (*Fr.*) The counter-subject, or second subject in a fugue.

Contre-temps (*Fr.*) Syncopation: driving notes.

Con tristézza (*It.*) With sadness, heaviness.

Con tútta fórza
Con tútta la fórza | (*It.*) With the whole power, with all possible force; as loud as possible.

Con un díta (*It.*) With one finger.

Con veeménza (*It.*) With vehemence, earnestness, force.

Con velocità (*It.*) With velocity, rapidity.

Conversio (*Lat.*) Inversion, in counterpoint.

Con vigóre (*It.*) With vigour, force, sprightliness, strength.

Con violénza (*It.*) With violence, force; boisterously.

Con vivacità
Con vivézza | (*It.*) With liveliness, vivacity, fire, sprightliness.

Con vóce ráuca (*It.*) With a hoarse, or rough voice.

Con volubilità (*It.*) With volubility; with freedom and fluency of performance.

Con zélo (*It.*) With zeal, eagerness, ardour.

Copérto (*It.*) Covered, muffled; *timpani copérti*, muffled drums.

Copist (*Ger.*)
Copiste (*Fr.*) | A music copyist.

Coppel-flöte (*Ger.*) Coupling-flute: an organ stop of the clarabella, or stopped diapason species, intended to be used chiefly in combination with some other stop.

Cópula (*It.*)
Copule (*Fr.*) | An appliance in an organ, by which two rows of keys can be connected together; or the keys coupled with the pedals.

Cor (*Fr.*) A horn: commonly called French horn.

Coràle (*It.*) Choral: the plain-chant: relating to the choir.

Coranach. A Scottish funeral dirge.

Cor anglais (*Fr.*) *English horn*: the tenor hautboy, and sounding a fifth lower: *see* **Córno Inglése**. The name is also applied to a reed stop in an organ.

Coránte
Coránto | (*It.*) A slow dance in $\frac{3}{2}$ or $\frac{3}{4}$ time, moving in quavers, with two strains or reprises, each commencing with an odd quaver.

Córda (*It.*) A string: *úna córda*, one string.

Cordatúra (*It.*) The scale, or series of notes, to which the open strings of an instrument are tuned: *see* **Accordatúra**.

Corde (*Fr.*) A string: *une corde*, one string.

Corde à boyau (*Fr.*) Catgut; strings for the violin, harp, &c.

CORDE À JOUR / **CORDE À VIDE** (*Fr.*) An open string, on the violin, viola, &c.

COR DE BASSET (*Fr.*) A basset horn.

COR DE CHASSE (*Fr.*) The hunting horn; the French horn.

CORDE FAUSSE (*Fr.*) A false, or dissonant string.

CORDE FILÉE (*Fr.*) A covered string.

COR DE POSTILLON (*Fr.*) A post-boy's horn; post-horn.

CORDES DE NAPLES (*Fr.*) The strings imported from Naples, for the violin, harp, &c.

COR DE SIGNAL (*Fr.*) A bugle.

CODE SOURDE (*Fr.*) A muted string.

COR DE VACHES (*Fr.*) The cowherd's horn.

CORDE VUIDE (*Fr.*) An open string, on the violin, &c.

CORDIÁLY (*It.*) Cordially; with heartiness.

CORDIER (*Fr.*) / **CORDIÉRA** (*It.*) The tail-piece, of a violin, viola, &c.

CORDOMÉTRO (*It.*) A string-gauge.

COREGRAFÍA (*It.*) The art of describing the figures of a dance.

CÓRICA / **CÓRICO** (*It.*) Choral.

CORIFÉO (*It.*) The leader of the dances, in a ballet.

CORIMAGÍSTRO (*It.*) The head of a choir.

CORIPHÆUS (*Gr.*) See **CORIFÉO**.

CORÍSTA (*It.*) A chorister.

CORMORNE. *A soft-toned horn.* This name is sometimes given to a reed stop in English organs, of 8 feet scale, and soft intonation: *see also* **CREMÓNA**.

CORNAMÚSA (*It.*) The bagpipes, consisting of a bourdon or drone, a small pipe in which is inserted a wheaten straw, and another pipe called the calumeau, with seven holes. These two pipes are inserted into the neck of a calf-skin bag, resembling in shape a chemist's retort, on the back of which the whole instrument is inflated by the mouth of the performer. The shape differs very little from that of the common or Scotch bagpipe, which was not peculiar to Scotland, but also used in Italy, and other southern countries, and formerly in Ireland.

CORNAMUSÁRE (*It.*) To play on the bagpipes.

CORNÁRE (*It.*) To sound, or wind a horn, or cornet.

CORNATÓRE (*It.*) One who blows, or plays on a horn.

CORNEMUSE (*Fr.*) See **CORNAMÚSA**.

CORNER (*Fr.*) To sound a horn, or cornet.

Cornet — Córno secóndo

CORNET. An organ stop, consisting of several ranks of pipes: in German organs the name is sometimes applied to a large reed stop on the manuals, or to a small reed on the pedal. Also, a small horn, of which there were three kinds, treble, tenor, bass, and they were formerly used in churches, and cathedrals, to assist the choir. The tones of the cornet were powerful, but capable of being much softened and modulated by a skilful performer.

CORNETA
CORNETTO — A name sometimes applied to a reed stop in an organ, of 16 feet scale.

CORNET À BOUQUIN (*Fr.*) Cornet; bugle horn; small shawm.

CORNET À PISTONS (*Fr.*) A small brass instrument resembling a trumpet, but shorter, and softer in tone, with valves, or pistons, to produce the semitones.

CORNET DREIFACH (*Ger.*) Cornet, with three ranks, in German organs.

CORNETT (*Ger.*)
CORNÉTTA (*It.*) — A cornet.

CORNETTÍNO (*It.*) A small cornet: an octave trumpet.

CORNÉTTO (*It.*) A cornet.

CÓRNI (*It. pl.*) The horns.

CÓRNO (*It.*) A horn, a French horn.

CÓRNO ÁLTO (*It.*) A horn of a high pitch.

CÓRNO BÁSSO (*It.*) A horn of a low pitch.

CÓRNO CROMÁTICO (*It.*) The chromatic horn: *see* **CÓRNO VENTÍLE**.

CÓRNO DI BASSÉTTO (*It.*) The basset-horn: a large clarinet with a brass bell mouth; the notes sound a fifth lower than written, and the tone is very fine. The name is also given to a delicate toned reed stop, in an organ, of 8 feet scale, and of the cremorna, or clarinet species.

CÓRNO DI CÁCCIA (*It.*) The hunting, or French horn.

CÓRNO DÓLCE (*It.*) *Soft horn*: an organ stop, occurring both in the manuals and pedals.

CORNO-FLUTE. An organ reed stop of 8 feet scale, producing a soft, agreeable quality of tone.

CÓRNO INGLÉSE (*It.*) The English horn: a long hautboy, of deeper pitch, the tones of which are very beautiful, melancholy, and expressive.

CORNOPEAN. An organ reed stop of 8 feet, on the manuals; the tone is more sonorous than that of the trumpet, and smoother than that of the horn, though not quite so powerful. The name is also given to a wind-instrument of the trumpet species: *see* **CORNET À PISTONS**.

CORNOPHONE (*Fr.*) A tenor *sax-horn*, played with a horn mouthpiece.

CÓRNO PRÍMO (*It.*) The first horn.

CÓRNO SECÓNDO (*It.*) The second horn.

CÓRNO VENTÍLE (*It.*)
COR OMNITONIQUE (*Fr.*) Chromatic horn, with valves or keys, for producing the semitones as perfectly as the open notes.

CÓRO (*It.*) A chorus, or piece for many voices.

CÓRO DÉLLA CHIÉSA (*It.*) A church choir; a sacred chorus.

CORÓNA (*It.*) A pause, ⌒.

CORONACH (*Ir.*) Funeral hymn, burying song.

CORPS DE VOIX (*Fr.*) Body, or fullness of voice.

CORRECTORIUM (*Lat.*) A tuning-cone, for tuning organs.

CORRÉNTE (*It.*) An old dance tune, in slow triple time: *see* CORÁNTO.

CORRÉPÉTITEUR (*Fr.*)
CORRIPETITORE (*It.*) The musician who instructs the chorus-singers, and teaches them the choruses of new operas.

CORYPHÆUS (*Gr.*) The conductor of the chorus: *see also* CORIFÉO.

CORYPHÉE (*Fr.*) The leader, or chief of the groups of dancers in a ballet.

COSTRÉTTO (*It.*) Constrained, forced.

COTILLON (*Fr.*) A lively, animated old dance, in $\frac{6}{8}$ time.

COUAC (*Fr.*) The quacking sound produced by bad playing of the hautbois, or clarinet.

COUCHED HARP. A name formerly applied to the *spinet*.

COULÉ (*Fr.*) A group of two notes, connected by a slur.

COULISSE (*Fr.*) The slide of a trumpet or trombone.

COUNTERPOINT. *Point against point.* The art of adding one, or more parts, either plain and simple, or elaborate, to a given melody, theme, or subject. Before the invention of notes, the various sounds were expressed by *points*.

COUNTER-SUBJECT. The second subject, in a fugue composed on two subjects.

COUNTER-TENOR. *High-tenor*: the highest male voice, sometimes called the *alto*. It is generally a *falsétto*.

COUNTER-TENOR CLEF. The C clef, when placed on the third line of the stave.

COUNTRY-DANCE. An old species of dance, said to be of English invention, the earliest known specimen dating from about the fifteenth century: *see also* CONTRE-DANSE.

COUP (*Fr.*) A stroke.

COUP D'ARCHET (*Fr.*) The stroke of the bow, in violin playing, &c.

COUP DE FOUET (*Fr.*) The sudden application of brilliance, to the conclusion, of a passage or movement.

COUP DE LA GLOTTE (*Fr.*) A distinct, sudden attack.

Coup — Croches

COUP DE LANGUE (*Fr.*) *Tonguing* in wind-instrument playing.
COUPER LE SUJET (*Fr.*) To curtail, or contract, the subject or theme.
COUPLER. See CÓPULA.
COUPLET (Fr.) A stanza, or verse; a song in a vaudeville, or comic opera.
COUPLING FLUTE. A name given to a stop which may be coupled to, or used with any other register.
COUPS D'ARCHET (*Fr.*) Strokes of the bow, in violin playing: ways, or methods of bowing.
COUPURE (*Fr.*) A cut.
COURANTE (*Fr.*) *Running*: an old dance in triple time, somewhat resembling a country-dance.
COURONNE (*Fr.*) See CORONA.
COURT (*Fr.*) Short.
COURTAL
COURTAUD (*Fr.*) An old instrument: a species of short bassoon.
COURTAUT
COVERED CONSECUTIVES. See HIDDEN CONSECUTIVES.
CRACOVIENNE. A Polish dance, in $\frac{2}{4}$ time.
CRÉCELLE (*Fr.*) A rattle.
CREDO (*Lat.*) *I believe*. One of the principal movements of the Mass.
CREMÓNA (*It.*) A small town in Italy, celebrated as having been the residence of the renowned violin makers, *Amati*, *Stradivari* or *Stradivarius*, *Guarnerius*, &c.; and whose instruments are often called *Cremonas*.
CREMÓNA. An organ reed stop, of delicate quality of tone, tuned in unison with the diapasons: *see* CROMORNE, and KRUMM-HORN.
CRESCÉNDO (*It.*) With a gradually increasing power of tone.
CRESCÉNDO E INCALCÁNDO PÓCO À PÓCO (*It.*) Increasing the tone, and hurrying the time by degrees.
CRESCÉNDO PÓCO À PÓCO (*It.*) Increasing the tone by little and little.
CRESCÉNDO PÓI DIMINUÉNDO (*It.*) Increasing, and then diminishing, the tone.
CRETICUS (*Lat.*) A musical foot, comprising of one short syllable, followed by two long ones, marked thus, —— ‿ ——.
CREYGHTONIAN SEVENTH. A dominant seventh, followed by one on the sub-dominant, said to have been first used by Creyghton.
CRIARDE (*Fr.*) Bawling, shouting: relating to the quality of the tone, of the voice.
CROCHE (*Fr.*) A quaver.
CROCHES LIÉES (*Fr.*) Quavers with joined stems.

CROCHET (*Fr.*) The *hook* of a quaver, semiquaver, &c.
CROCHETA (*Lat.*) A crotchet.
CROISEMENT (*Fr.*) The crossing of parts.
CRÓMA (*It.*) A quaver.
CROMÁTICA | (*It.*) Chromatic, with respect to intervals, and scales.
CROMÁTICO |
CRÓME (*It. pl.*) Quavers.
CROM-HORN (*Ger.*) A reed stop in an organ: *see* KRUM-HORN.
CRÓMMO (*It.*) A choral lamentation.
CROMORNE. An English reed stop, in an organ: *see* CORMORNE.
CROOKS. Small curved tubes applied to horns, trumpets, &c., to change their pitch, and adapt them to the key of the piece in which they are to be used.
CROQUE-NOTE (*Fr.*) An unskilful musician.
CROTALE (*Fr.*) | An ancient musical instrument, used by the
CRÓTALO (*It.*) | priests of Cybele. It differs from the Sistrum,
CROTALUM (*Gr.*) | though the names are often confounded. From the allusions made to it by Virgil, Lucretius, and others, it appears to have been a small *Cymbal*, or species of castanet.
CROTCHET. A note equal in duration and value to one-half of a minim: made thus ♩ or thus ♩ .
CROTCHET REST. A mark of silence, equal in duration to a crotchet: made thus 𝄽 , or sometimes thus 𝄽 or thus 𝄽 , to distinguish it the more readily.
CROWD. An old name for the fiddle: *see* CRWTH.
CROWDER. An old term for a performer on the *Crwth*, or *Cruth*: the name was afterwards applied to a common fiddler; hence, undoubtedly, the common surname *Crowther*, or *Crowder*.
CROWLE. An old English wind-instrument, of former times, a kind of bass-flute, or bassoon.
CROWTH. The English name of the *Crwth*: see that word.
CROWTHER. *See* CROWDER.
CRUCIFIXUS (*Lat.*) Part of the *Credo*, in a Mass.
CRUPEZIA (*Gr.*) Wooden clogs, worn by the Greek musicians.
CRUTH (*Sax.*) See CRWTH.
CRWTH (*Welsh*) An ancient Welsh instrument, resembling the violin; with six strings, and played on with a bow: the bridge differed from that of a violin, in that it was flat, and not convex on the top, from

which it is supposed that the strings were struck at the same time, so as to give a succession of cords. It was sometimes corruptly called a *Crowd*.

C SCHLÜSSEL (*Ger.*) The C clef.

CUIVRE (*It.*) *Brass*.

CUM CANTU
CUM DISCANTU (*Lat.*) With song; with singing: applied to the celebration of certain festivals in the Roman Catholic Church.

CUM SANCTO SPIRITU (*Lat.*) Part of the *Gloria*, in a Mass.

CUPO (*It.*) Dark, mysterious, close; sombre.

CURRENDANER (*Ger.*) A school or choir boy, of the singing processions.

CURRENDE (*Ger.*) Schoolboys, or young choristers, chanting in procession through the streets: procession of young choristers, singing plain-chant through the streets in Germany, at Christmas, and other festivals.

CURRENDSCHÜLER (*Ger.*) See **CURRENDANER**.

CURRENS SALTATIO (*Lat.*) See **CORÁNTO**.

CUSTOS (*Lat.*) A *Direct*, W.

CUVETTE (*Fr.*) The pedestal of a harp.

CYMBALES (*Fr.*) See **CYMBALS**.

CYMBALISTA (*Lat.*) A cymbal player.

CYMBALS. Circular metal plates used in military bands, usually in combination with the great drum: they are clashed together, producing a brilliant, ringing effect. Cymbals are traceable to remote antiquity, and were formerly of a more cup-like shape, and much smaller, than at present, being now nearly flat. In the Museum at Naples there are some no larger than a dollar. They were consecrated to Cybele, and used by her priests. The name is also applied to a compound, or mixture stop, in German organs, of very shrill quality of tone.

CYMBALE (*Fr.*)
CYMBEL (*Ger.*) A mixture stop of very acute quality of tone.

CYTHORN. See **CITHER**.

CZAKAN. A Bohemian cane or bamboo flute.

CZARDAS. An Hungarian national dance, with constantly changing tempo.

CZIMBAL (*Hung.*) A dulcimer.

CZIMKEN. A Polish country dance.

D

D, called in France and Italy *Re*; the second note, or tone of the modern scale of Guido d'Arezzo.

DA (*It.*) By, from, for, through, &c.

DA BÁLLO (*It.*) In the style of a dance, like a dance.

DABBUDÀ (*It.*) A psaltery.

DA CÁMERA (*It.*) For the chamber: *see* **CHAMBER MUSIC**.

DA CAPPÉLLA (*It.*) For the church: in the church style.

DA CÁPO (*It.*) *From the beginning*; from the commencement; often placed at the end of a movement, to indicate that the performer must return to the first strain.

DA CÁPO AL FÍNE | (*It.*) Return to the beginning, and conclude
DA CÁPO SIN' AL FÍNE | where the word *Fíne* is placed.

DA CÁPO AL SÉGNO (*It.*) Return to where the *Sign* 𝄋 is placed at the beginning.

DA CÁPO, E PÓI LA CÓDA (*It.*) Begin again, and then play the *Códa*.

DA CÁPO SÉNZA REPETIZIÓNE, E PÓI LA CÓDA (*It.*) Begin again, but without repeating the strain, and then proceed to the *Códa*.

DA CÁPO SIN' AL SÉGNO (*It.*) Return to the beginning, and conclude at the *Sign*, 𝄋.

D'ACCORD (*Fr.*) In tune.

DA CHIÉSA (*It.*) For the church.

DACHSCHWELLER (*Ger.*) A swell-box, in an organ.

DACTYL (*Lat.*) A metrical foot, consisting of one long note or syllable, followed by two short ones, marked thus, —◡◡.

DACTYLION (*Gr.*) A machine invented by Henri Herz. For strengthening, and giving independence to the fingers, in pianoforte playing.

DACTYLUS (*Lat.*) See **DACTYL**.

DÁGLI | (*It.*) From the, of the, to the, &c.
DAI |

DAINA | A term, in Lithuania, for the amatory songs.
DAINOS |

DAIRE. The tambourine, or hand-drum.

Daktylus — Darm

DAKTYLUS (*Ger.*) A *dactyl*: see that word.

DAL
DALL'
DALLA   (*It.*) From the, by the, &c.
DALLE
DALLO

DA LONTÁNO (*It.*) *At a distance*: the music is to sound as if distant.

DAL SÉGNO (*It.*) *From the sign*: a mark directing a repetition from the place where the *sign* is placed.

DAMENISATION. *Solféggi* to which are adapted the syllables used by Graun for vocal exercises, *da, me, ni, po, tu, la, be*.

DAMPER PEDAL. That pedal in a pianoforte, which raises the dampers from the strings, and allows them to vibrate fully. In pianoforte music its use is indicated by the abbreviation *ped*.

DAMPERS. That mechanism in a pianoforte, intended to check, or stifle, the vibration of the strings, and prevent a confusion of sounds.

DÄMPFER (*Ger.*) A mute, or damper, used to deaden the tone of the violin, &c.

DÄMPFUNG (*Ger.*) Damping, smothering the tone.

DANKLIED (*Ger.*) Thanksgiving song.

DANN (*Ger.*) Then, immediately.

DANSE (*Fr.*) Dance tune.

DANSER (*Fr.*) To dance.

DANSERIES (*Fr.*) A name formerly given to all collections of dance tunes.

DANSEUR (*Fr.*) A male dancer.

DANSEUSE (*Fr.*) A female dancer.

DANS UNE EXALTATION CROISSANTE (*Fr.*) With increasing enthusiasm.

DÁNZA (*It.*) A dance.

DANZÁNTE (*It.*) A dancer.

DANZÁRE (*It.*) To dance.

DANZATÓRE (*It.*) A male dancer.

DANZATRÍCE (*It.*) A female dancer.

DANZÉTTA (*It.*) A short dance, a little dance.

DA PRÍMA (*It.*) At first: from the beginning.

DA QUESTA PÁRTE FÍNO AL MAGGIÓRE PÓCO À PÓCO PIÙ ANIMÁTO E PIÙ FÓRTE (*It.*) From this place, as far as the major, gradually more animated, and louder.

DARM-SAITE (*Ger.*) A gut-string.

DARM-SAITEN (*Ger. pl.*) The strings of gut, used for the harp, violin, guitar, &c. Those called 'Roman strings' are made in the kingdom of Naples.

DARSTELLER (*Ger.*) Performer.

DA SCHÉRZO (*It.*) In jest; in a playful manner.

DAS DOPPELT LANFSAMER (*Ger.*) Twice as slow.

DAS LEBEWOHL (*Ger.*) The farewell.

DAS SELBE TEMPO (*Ger.*) *See* L'ISTÉSSO TÉMPO.

DAS WIEDERSEHN (*Ger.*) The return.

DAS ZWEITE MAL (*Ger.*) The second time.

DA TEÁTRO (*It.*) For the theatre: music composed in a dramatic style.

DÁTTILO (*It.*) A *dactyl*: see that word.

DAUER (*Ger.*) The length, or duration, of notes.

DAUM / **DAUMEN** (*Ger.*) The thumb.

DAUMENAUFSATZ (*Ger.*) A thumb position, in violoncello playing.

DAVID'S-HARFE (*Ger.*) David's harp.

D DUR (*Ger.*) The key of D major.

DÉBILE / **DÉBOLE** (*It.*) Feeble, weak, faint.

DÉBUT (*Fr.*) First appearance; the first time of singing or playing in public.

DÉBUTANT / **DÉBUTANTE** (*Fr.*) A singer, or performer, who appears for the first time before the public.

DÉBUTER (*Fr.*) To begin, to play first.

DECACHORDON (*Lat.*) / **DECACÓRDO** (*It.*) An obsolete instrument of the harp or psaltery species, with a sound-board, and ten strings. The ancient Hebrew name was *Hasur*.

DECAMERÓNE (*It.*) A period of ten days: a collection of ten musical pieces.

DECANI (*Lat. Pl.*) In cathedral music this term implies that the passages thus marked must be taken by those singers who are placed on that side of the choir where the *Dean* sits, which is usually the right hand side on entering the choir from the nave: but in some cathedrals the Dean sits on the left side.

DECEM (*Ger.*) An organ stop, *see* DECIMA.

DECEPTIVE CADENCE. A close on the triad of the subdominant: also, when after a succession of regularly connected chords, the cadence concludes in a foreign key. These cadences are called Ingánni: *see also* INTERRUPTED CADENCE.

Deceptive — Deductio

DECEPTIVE MODULATION. A modulation by which the ear is deceived; that is, led to an unexpected harmony.

DÉCHANT (*Fr.*) Discant.

DÉCIDÉ
DÉCIDÉMENT } (*Fr.*) With decision, resolution.

DECIMA (*Lat.*) *A tenth*: an interval of ten degrees in the scale: also, the name of an organ stop, sounding the tenth.

DECIMA QUARTA (*Lat.*) The interval of a fourteenth.

DECIMA QUINTA (*Lat.*) The interval of a fifteenth.

DECIMA TERTIA (*Lat.*) The interval of a thirteenth.

DÉCIME (*Fr.*) A tenth: *see* DECIMA.

DECIMOLE. A musical figure, formed out of the division of any note or chord, into ten parts, or notes, of equal value.

DÉCISIF (*Fr.*) Decisive, clear, firm.

DECISÍSSIMO (*It.*) Very decided, with extreme decision and firmness.

DÉCISIVEMENT (*Fr.*) Decisively.

DECISÍVO
DECISO } (*It.*) Decisive: with decision: firmly, boldly.

DECKE (*Ger.*) The belly, or sound-board, of a violin, viola, &c. Also, the cover, or top, in those organ stops which are *stopped*, or *covered*.

DECLAMÁNDO (*It.*) With declamatory expression.

DECLAMATION. Dramatic singing: the art of speaking words to music in such a manner, that their meaning is well expressed and understood, and the correct verbal accent carefully preserved.

DECLAMÁTO (*It.*) *See* DECLAMÁNDO.

DECLAMAZIÓNE (*It.*) Declamation.

DÉCLAVER (*Fr.*) To go out of the key.

DÉCOMPOSÉ (*Fr.*) Incoherent, unconnected.

DÉCOMPTER (*Fr.*) To sing *portaménto*.

DÉCORATION (*Fr.*) Some French theorists use this word to indicate the *signature*.

DÉCOUPLEZ (*Fr.*) To uncouple, in organ playing.

DÉCOUSU (*Fr.*) Disconnected; lacking in form, or unity.

DECRESCÉNDO (*It.*) Gradually decreasing in power of tone: diminishing in force or loudness.

DECUPLET. A group of ten notes, to be performed in the time of eight.

DEDICÁTO (*It.*)
DÉDIÉ (*Fr.*) } Dedicated.

DEDUCTIO (*Lat.*) The ascending scale or syllables in the Aretinian form solmisation.

DEFECTIVE. *See* DIMINISHED.

DEFICIÉNDO (*It.*) Dying away.

DEGRÉ (*Fr.*) A degree of the stave.

DEGREE. A step of the stave: moving from a line to a space, or from a space to a line. The term *Degree* is also applied to certain distinction granted by the Universities to eminent composers, &c.

DEHNEN (*Ger.*) To prolong, extend, expand.

DEHNUNG (*Ger.*) Extension, prolongation.

DEHNUNGSTRICH (*Ger.*) A long stroke with the bow, in playing the violin, &c.

DEI (*It. pl.*) Of the; from the.

DEKLAMATION (*Ger.*) *See* DECLAMATION.

DEL (*It.*) Of the.

DÉLASSEMENT (*Fr.*) A light, entertaining composition.

DELIBERATAMÉNTE | (*It.*) Deliberately.
DELIBERÁTO

DELICATAMENTE (*It.*) Delicately, softly, smoothly.

DÉLICATESSE (*Fr.*) | Delicacy, refined execution, softness and
DELICATÉZZA (*It.*) | smoothness.

DELICATISSIMAMÉNTE | (*It.*) With extreme delicacy.
DELICATÍSSIMO

DELICÁTO (*It.*) Delicately, smoothly, softly.

DÉLIÉ (*Fr.*) Light, easy.

DELIRÁNTE (*It.*) Excited; frenzied.

DELÍRIO (*It.*) Frenzy, excitement.

DELIZIOSAMÉNTE | (*It.*) Sweetly, deliciously.
DELIZÍOSO

DELL'
DELLA | (*It.*) of the.
DELLE
DELLO

DELYN (*Welsh*) The Welsh harp.

DEM (*Ger.*) To the.

DÉMANCHÉ | (*Fr.*) To shift, or change position.
DÉMANCHEMENT

DÉMANCHER (*Fr.*) To change, or alter, the position of the hand: to shift, on the violin, &c.: to cross hands on the pianoforte, making the left hand play the part of the right, and *vice versa*.

DEMANDE (*Fr.*) The question, or proposition of a fugue: called also *dux*, or leading subject.

DEMI (*Fr.*) Half.

DEMI-BÂTON (*Fr.*) A breve rest.
DEMI-CADENCE (*Fr.*) A half-cadence, or cadence on the dominant.
DEMI-CROCHE (*Fr.*) A semiquaver.
DEMI-DITONE. See SEMI-DITONE.
DEMI-JEU (*Fr.*) Half the power of the organ, harmonium, &c.: the same as *mézzo fórte*.
DEMI-MESURE
DEMI-PAUSE (*Fr.*) A minim rest.
DEMI-QUART DE SOUPIR (*Fr.*) A demi-semiquaver rest.
DEMI-SEMIQUAVER. A short note, equal in duration to one half the semiquaver, made thus, ♪, or thus, ♫.
DEMI-SEMIQUAVER REST. A mark of silence, equal in duration to a demi-semiquaver, made thus, 𝄿.
DEMI-SOUPIR (*Fr.*) A quaver rest.
DEMI-TEMPS (*Fr.*) A half-beat.
DEMI-TON (*Fr.*) A semitone.
DEMOISELLE (*Fr.*) An organ tracker.
DEM SÄNGER FOLGEND (*Ger.*) See COLLA VÓCE.
DÉNOUEMENT (*Fr.*) Conclusion, the catastrophe of an opera, &c.
DE PLUS EN PLUS VITE (*Fr.*) More and more quickly, quicker by degrees, gradually.
DE PROFUNDIS (*Lat.*) One of the seven penitential psalms.
DERB (*Ger.*) Firm, vigorous, heavy, hearty: *Mit derbem Humor*, with hearty humour.
DERIVATIVES. Chords derived from others, by inversion.
DÉRIVÉ (*Fr.*) Derived; derivative.
DER MELODIE FOLGEND (*Ger.*) See COLLA PÁRTE.
DERNIÈRE FOIS (*Fr.*) The last time.
DES (*Ger.*) The note D-flat.
DÉSACCORDÉ (*Fr.*) Untuned, put out of tune.
DÉSACCORDER (*Fr.*) To untune, to put out of tune.
DESCANT. An extemporaneous, or other counterpoint, on a given subject, melody, or theme.
DESCENDANT (*Fr.*) Descending.
DESCENDERE (*It.*)
DESCENDRE (*Fr.*) To descend.
DESCENDRE D'UN TON (*Fr.*) To sing a note lower.
DES DUR (*Ger.*) The key of D-flat major.

DESIDÉRIO (*It.*) Desire.
DESINVOLTURÁTO (*It.*) See DISINVOLTURÁTO.
DES MOLL (*Ger.*) The key of D-flat minor.
DESPERAZIÓNE (*It.*) See DISPERAZIÓNE.
DESSAUER MARSCH (*Ger.*) A famous instrumental march, one of the national airs of Germany, particularly of Prussia. It is supposed to be of Italian origin, and was brought over by Prince Leopold of Dressau, after the siege of Turin, 1706.
DESSIN (*Fr.*) The design, or sketch, of a composition.
DESSINER (*Fr.*) To make the sketch, or design, of a composition.
DESSUS (*Fr.*) The treble, or upper part.
DESTERITÀ (*It.*) Dexterity.
DÉSTO (*It.*) Brisk, sprightly.
DÉSTRA (*It.*) Right: *déstra máno*, the right hand.
DÉTACHÉ (*Fr.*) Detached, staccato.
DETERMINATÍSSIMO (*It.*) Very determined, very resolutely.
DETERMINÁTO (*It.*) Determined, resolute.
DETERMINAZIÓNE (*It.*) Determination, resolution.
DÉTONATION (*Fr.*) See DÉTONNATION.
DETONIREN (*Ger.*) See DISTONIREN.
DÉTONNATION (*Fr.*) False intonation, out of tune.
DÉTONNER (*Fr.*) To sing, or play, out of tune.
DÉTTO (*It.*) The same: *il détto stroménto*, the same instrument.
DEUTLICH (*Ger.*) Distinctly: *Deutlicher und stets gut hervor tretend*, more distinctly and always well-defined.
DEUTSCHE FLÖTE (*Ger.*) A German flute.
DEUTSCHE TÄNZE (*Ger.*) German dances.
DEUX (*Fr.*) Twice.
DEUXIÈME POSITION (*Fr.*) The second position of the hand, or finger, in playing the violin, &c.
DEVÓTO (*It.*) Devout, religious.
DEVOZIÓNE (*It.*) Devotion, religious feeling.
DEXTRA (*Lat.*) } The right hand.
DEXTRE (*Fr.*)
DEXTRÆ (*Lat. pl.*) Applied by the ancient Romans, to those flutes which were to be played on with the right hand. The Roman flute player blew two instruments at the same time, and those which were played with the left hand were called sinistræ.
DEZEM (*Ger.*) See DECIMA.
DEZIME (*Ger.*) The interval of a tenth.
DI (*It.*) Of, with, for, in.

Dia — Diatonic

DIA (*Gr.*) Through: throughout: as *diapente*, though the fifth: *diapason*, through the octave.

DIACHISMA. An interval produced by the division of another interval.

DIACONICON (*Gr.*) The set of collects chanted by the *diaconus*, in the service of the Greek Church.

DIADROM. The tremulance, or vibration, of sounds.

DIAGRAMMA (*Gr.*) The ancient Greek scale, or system of sounds, which consisted of a *bisdiapason*, or double octave, and was dignified by the name of *Sistema-Perfectum*.

DIÁLOGO (*It.*)
DIALOGUE (*Fr.*) A composition in which two parts, or voices, respond alternately to each other.

DIÁNA (*It.*)
DIANE (*Fr.*) The reveille: the beat of the drum at daybreak.

DIAPÁSON (*Gr.*) An *octave*: also, the *compass*, or *scale*, of a voice, or instrument: also, certain important *stops*, or *registers*, in an organ, which usually extend through the entire compass, and are called 8 feet stops, the lowest note CC having a pipe of that length or tone, as *open diapason*, *stopped diapason*, &c. In Germany the *diapason* is called *principal*, 8 *feet*.

DIAPASON CUM DIAPENTE (*Gr.*) An *octave and fifth*: the interval of a *twelfth*.

DIAPASON CUM DIATESSARON (*Gr.*) An *octave and fourth*: the interval of an *eleventh*.

DIAPENTE (*Gr.*) A perfect *fifth*: also, an organ stop: *see* QUINT.

DIAPENTE COL DITONO (*Gr.*) A major seventh.

DIAPENTE COL SEMIDITONO (*Gr.*) A minor seventh.

DIAPENTER (*Fr.*)
DIAPENTISARE (*Gr.*) To *descant*, or modulate in fifths.

DIAPHONE. An organ stop, of powerful tone, invented by Hope Jones, which can be made to have various sounds.

DIAPHONIE
DIAPHONY Clear, transparent: two sounds heard together.

DIASCHISMA (*Gr.*) *See* INTERVAL.

DIASTEMA (*Gr.*) An interval, a space.

DIASTOLIK (*Gr.*) The system of musical division, and periods.

DIATESSARON (*Gr.*) A perfect fourth.

DIATONIC (*Gr.*) *Naturally*: that is, according to the degrees of the scale, proceeding by tones and semitones; moving from *line* to *space*, or from *space* to *line*, the name (or letter) of the note being changed each time.

DIATÓNICO (*It.*)
DIATONIQUE (*Fr.*) Diatonic.
DIATONISCH (*Ger.*)

DIATONIQUEMENT (*Fr.*) Diatonically.

DIAZEUXIS (*Gr.*) In ancient Greek music, two tetrachords separated by the interval of a tone.

DI BEL NUÓVO (*It.*) Again.

DIBRACH
DIBRACHIS (*Gr.*) A metrical foot of two short syllables shown thus, ⌣⌣.

DI BRAVÚRA (*It.*) In a floris, and brilliant style.

DICÉLIE (*It.*) Farces.

DI CHIÁRO (*It.*) Clearly.

DICHORD (*Gr.*) The two-stringed lyre: *see also* BICHORD.

DICHTER (*Ger.*) Poet, minstrel, bard.

DI CÓLTO (*It.*) Suddenly, instantly, at once.

DICTÉE MUSICALE (*Fr.*) Musical dictation.

DIE ABWESENHEIT (*Ger.*) Absence.

DIE AKKORDE MÖGLICHST GEBUNDEN (*Ger.*) The chords are to be played, as smooth as possible.

DIE BÄSSE DURCHAUS LEICHT UND FREI (Ger.) The bass is to be *light* throughout.

DIECÉTTO (*It.*) A piece for ten instruments, or voices.

DIE FERMATEN SEHR LANG UND BEDEUTUNGSVOLL (*Ger.*) The pauses are to be very long and impressive.

DIE LETZTE NOTE DER TRIOLEN NICHT ABGESTOSSEN (*Ger.*) The last notes of the triplets, not too staccato.

DIE NOTEN DER LINKEN HAND DURCH GÄNGIG GEBUNDEN (*Ger.*) The notes for the left hand *legáto* throughout.

DIESÁRE (*It.*) To sharpen notes, either at the signature, or in the
DIÉSER (*Fr.*) course of a composition, by means of a sharp.

DIÈSE (*Fr.*) A *sharp*.

DIEAS ARÆ (*Lat.*) A principal movement in a Requiem.

DIÈSIS (*Fr.*) A quarter of a tone: half a semitone; a small
DIÉSIS (*Gr. & It.*) interval used in the mathematical computation of intervals. The ancient Greeks applied this word to the smallest intervals used in their music. In modern music it means a *sharp*.

DIESIS CHROMATICA (*Gr.*) The third part, or fraction, of a whole tone.

DIESIS ENHARMONICA (*Gr.*) A quarter tone: this interval may be described as the difference between G-sharp and A-flat, or between D-sharp and E-flat, on the violin.

Diesis — Diminúto

DIESIS MAGNA (*Gr.*) A semitone.

DIÈZE (*Fr.*) A *sharp*, #.

DIEZMONOVENA (*Sp.*) A *larigot*.

DIFFÍCILE (*It.*) Difficult.

DI GÁLA (*It.*) Merrily, cheerfully.

DIGNITÀ
DIGNITÁDE (*It.*) Dignity, greatness.
DIGNITÁTE

DI GRÁDO (*It.*) *By degrees*: step by step: in opposition to **DI SÁLTO**, which see.

DI LEGGIÉRE
DI LEGGIÉRO (*It.*) Easily, lightly.

DILETANT (*Ger.*) A lover of music or painting, an amateur, who
DILETTÁNTE (*It.*) composes or performs, without making the art his express vocation.

DILETTÁRSI DI MÚSICA (It.) To love music.

DILICATAMÉNTE (*It.*) Delicately, deliciously.

DILICATÉZZA (*It.*) Delicateness, niceness, softness, neatness.

DILICATISSIMAMÉNTE (*It.*) Very delicately: with excessive
DILICATÍSSIMO softness and delicacy.

DILICÁTO (*It.*) Soft, delicate.

DILIGÉNZA (*It.*) Diligence, care.

DILUDIUM (*Lat.*) An interlude.

DILUÉNDO (*It.*) A gradual dying away of the tone, until it is extinct: fading away: diminishing.

DILUNGÁNDO (*It.*) Prolonging; *rallentándo*.

DIMETER. Consisting of two measures.

DIMINISHED. This word is applied to intervals, or chords, which are less than minor, or perfect.

DIMINISHED INTERVALS. Those which are *one semitone less* than minor, or perfect intervals.

DIMINISHED TRIAD. A chord composed of the minor third, and the diminished or imperfect fifth.

DIMINUÉ (*Fr.*) Diminished: *see* **DIMINUÍTO**.

DIMINUÉNDO (*It.*) Diminishing gradually the intensity, or loudness, of the tone: decreasing in power.

DIMINEUR (*Fr.*) To diminish in loudness.

DIMINUÍTO
DIMINÚTO Diminished, lessened, in speaking of intervals or chords.

Diminution — Discant

DIMINUTION. In counterpoint this means, the imitation of a given subject, or theme, in notes of *shorter* length, or duration: in opposition to *augmentation*.

DIMINUZIÓNE (*It.*) Diminution.

DI MÓLTO (*It.*) *Very much*: a great deal. This term augments the meaning of the word to which it is added: as *allégro di mólto*, very quick: *ardíto di mólto*, with much passion.

DI NÉTTO (*It.*) Neatly, cleverly.

DINGÁNDO (*It.*) Unexpected.

DI NUÓVO (*It.*) Newly, again, once more.

DIOXIA. A perfect fifth: the fifth tone, or sound.

DI PESO (*It.*) At once.

DIPHONIUM. A vocal duet.

DI PÓSTA (*It.*) At once.

DI QUIETO (*It.*) Quietly.

DIRECT. A mark W placed sometimes at the end of a staff, to indicate the note next following.

DIRECTEUR (*Fr.*) A director, or manager, of an orchestra, or of a musical performance.

DIRECT MOTION. Similar motion: the parts rising or falling simultaneously.

DIRECTRICE (*Fr.*) A female manager, or director.

DIRÉTTA (*It.*) Direct, straight.

DIRÉTTO (*It.*) Directed: conducted.

DIRETTÓRE (*It.*) *See* DIRECTEUR.

DIRETTRÍCE (*It.*) *See* DIRECTRICE.

DIRGE. A funeral song: a song of lamentation.

DIRIGENT (*Ger.*) Director, conductor.

DIRÍTTA (*It.*) Straight on: direct: in ascending, or descending intervals.

DIRIZZATÓRE (*It.*) *See* DIRECTEUR.

DIS (*Ger.*) The note D#.

DISACCENTÁTO (*It.*) Unaccented.

DISACCORDÁRE (*It.*) To be out of tune.

DI SÁLTO (*It.*) *By leaps, by skips*: in opposition to DI GRÁDO, which see.

DISARMONÍA (*It.*) Discord, want of harmony.

DISARMONICHÍSSIMO (*It.*) Extremely discordant.

DISARMÓNICO (*It.*) Disharmonious, discordant.

DISCANT. The upper part: *see also* DESCANT.

Discant-clef — Disperáto

DISCANT-CLEF (*Ger.*) The soprano clef: the C clef placed upon the first line, the note upon which line is called C (the middle C). This is seldom used now.

DISCANT-GEIGE (*Ger.*) An obsolete term for the violin.

DISCANTIST (*Ger.*) Treble, or soprano singer.

DISCANT-SAITE (*Ger.*) Treble string.

DISCANT-SÄNGER (*Ger.*) Treble, or soprano singer.

DISCANT-SCHLÜSSEL (*Ger.*) The treble clef.

DISCENDÉNTE (*It.*) Descending.

DISCENDERE (*It.*) To descend.

DISCÉPOLA (*It.*) A female pupil.

DISCÉPOLO (*It.*) Pupil, scholar, disciple.

DISCIÓLTO (*It.*) Skilful, dexterous.

DISCONCÓRDIA (*It.*) Discord.

DISCORD. A dissonant combination of sounds: a peculiar species of harmony requiring to be resolved into, or to proceed to, a concord, in order to satisfy the ear.

DISCORDÁNTE (It.) Discordant.

DISCORDANTEMÉNTE (*It.*) Discordantly.

DISCORDÁNZA (*It.*) Discord.

DISCORDER (*Fr.*) To be out of tune.

DISCRÉTO (*It.*) Discreetly.

DISCREZIÓNE (*It.*) Discretion, discreetly: not too loud: as *con discreziòne*, moderately; agreeably to the composer's intentions.

DIS-DIAPASON (*Gr.*) A double octave: an interval of two octaves; a fifteenth.

DIS DUR (*Ger.*) The key of D# major.

DISEURS (*Fr. pl.*) The itinerant vocalist who formerly recited romances, and metrical histories, in the French metropolis and the provinces.

DISHARMONISCH (*Ger.*) Discordant, dissonant.

DISINVÓLTO
DISINVOLTURÁTO (*It.*) Free, dexterous, in an easy manner: not forced: naturally.

DISJUNCT. A term applied by the Greeks to those tetrachords where the lowest sound of the upper one was one degree higher than the acutest sound of the lower: *see* CONJUNCT.

DISKANT (*Ger.*) *See* DISCANT.

DIS MOLL (*Ger.*) The key of D# minor.

DISPÁRI (*It.*) Unequal.

DISPERABILE (*Fr.*)
DISPERÁTO (*It.*) Despaired of: with extreme emotion: with desperation.

DISPERAZIÓNE (*It.*) Despair, desperation: as, *con disperazióne*, with great emotion.

DISPERSED HARMONY. Harmony in which the notes, or sounds, forming the carious chords, are separated from each other by wide intervals.

DISPOSITION. The arrangement of the stops in an organ, disposing them according to their relative power, and quality of tone, &c.

DISSONANCE. A discord: an interval, or chord, displeasing to the ear, and requiring to be followed by another in which the dissonant note is resolved.

DISSONANT. An inharmonious combination of sounds.

DISSONÁNTE (*It.*) Dissonant, out of tune, discordant.

DISSONANZ
DISSONÁNZA | (*It.*) Discord: dissonance.

DISSONÁRE (*It.*)
DISSONIREN (*Ger.*) | To sound out of tune.

DISTANCE. The interval between any two sounds differing in pitch.

DISTÁNZA (*It.*) Distance, interval, space between.

DISTINTAMÉNTE (*It.*) Clearly, distinctly.

DISTÍNTO (*It.*) Clear, distinct.

DISTONÁRE (*It.*) To be out of tune.

DISTONIREN (*Ger.*) To go out of tune: to jar: to produce discord either in singing, or playing.

DITEGGIATÚRA (*It.*) Fingering.

DITHYRAMBE (*Fr. & Ger.*) A song, or ode, sung in ancient times, in honour of Bacchus: a wild, rhapsodical composition.

DITHYRAMBIC (*Gr.*) A song in honour of Bacchus: any poem written with wildness.

DITHYRAMBIQUE (*Fr.*)
DITHYRAMBISCH (*Ger.*) | Dithyrambic.

DITHYRAMBUS (*Lat.*) *See* **DITHYRAMBE**.

DITIRÁMBICA
DITIRÁMBICO | (*It.*) Dithyrambic.

DITIRÁMBO (*It.*) *See* **DITHYRAMBE**.

DÍTO (*It.*) The finger.

DÍTO GRÓSO (*It.*) The thumb.

DITON (*Fr.*)
DITONE (*Gr.*)
DÍTONO (*It.*)
DITONUS (*Lat.*) | Of two parts, or tones: a major third, or interval of two whole tones.

DITTIED. Sung: adapted to music.

Ditty — Doigt

DITTY. A poem to be sung: a pathetic song in a simple, unaffected style: a short, simple tale, sung in verse, to an appropriate melody.

DIVA (*It.*) A specially gifted female singer.

DIVAGAZIONE (*It.*) A wandering; a digression.

DIVÉRBIO (*It.*) A musical dialogue, often used by the ancients to enrich their drama.

DIVERTIMÉNTO (*It.*) A short, light composition, in a pleasing and familiar style.

DIVERTISSEMENT (*Fr.*) A series of airs and dances, resembling a short ballet, introduced between the acts, or at the conclusion, of an opera: also, a composition in a light and pleasing style.

DIVINARE. A stopped organ register, of a beautiful tone.

DIVÍSI (*It.*) Divided: separated. In orchestral parts this word implies that one half of the performers must play the upper notes, and the others the lower notes: the term has a similar meaning when it occurs in vocal music.

DIVISION. A series of notes sung to one syllable. Formerly, this word implied, a sort of variation upon a given subject.

DIVOTAMÉNTE \
DIVÓTO } (*It.*) Devoutly: in a solemn style.

DIVOZIÓNE (*It.*) Devotion.

DIX-HUITIÈME (*Fr.*) The *eighteenth*, or double octave to the fourth.

DIXIÈME (*Fr.*) The *tenth*, or octave to the third.

DIX-NEUVIÈME (*Fr.*) The *nineteenth*, or double octave to the fifth.

DIX-SEPTIÈME (*Fr.*) The *seventeenth*, or double octave to the third.

DIZAIN (*Fr.*) Stanza of ten verses.

D MOLL (*Ger.*) The key of D minor.

DO (*It.*) A syllable applied to the note C, in solfaing.

DOCH (*Ger.*) Still, nevertheless, but.

DOCKE (*Ger.*) The *jack* of a harpsichord.

DOCTOR OF MUSIC. The highest musical degree conferred by the universities. It is obtained by composing certain exercises, and passing an examination, with the payment of certain fees. The title is sometimes presented, as a distinction, to eminent composers.

DODEDACHORDON (*Gr.*) The twelve ancient modes.

DODECÚPLA DI CRÓME (*It.*) $\frac{12}{8}$ time.

DODECUPLET. A group of twelve notes, to be played in the time of eight.

DODINETTE (*Fr.*) A lullaby.

DÓGLIA (*It.*) Grief, affliction, sadness.

DOIGT (*Fr.*) Finger.

DOIGTÉ (*Fr.*) Fingered.

DOIGTER (*Fr.*) To finger: the art of fingering any instrument.

DOLCAN. An organ stop, of 8 feet scale, the pipes of which are larger diameter at the top than the bottom: the tone is very agreeable. The name *dulcan*, or *block-flute*, are sometimes erroneously applied to this stop.

DÓLCE (*It.*) Sweetly, softly, gently, expressively: applied also to organ stops of pleasing tone.

DÓLCE CON GÚSTO (*It.*) Softly and sweetly, with taste and delicacy.

DÓLCE E LUSINGÁNDO (*It.*) In a soft, and insinuating style.

DÓLCE E PIACEVOLMÉNTE ESPRESSÍVO (*It.*) Soft, and with pleasing expression.

DÓLCE MA MARCÁTO (*It.*) Soft and delicate, but marked and accented.

DÓLCE MANIÉRA (*It.*) A delicate and expressive style of delivery.

DOLCEMÉNTE (*It.*) Agreeably, gently, sweetly, softly.

DOLCÉZZA (*It.*) Sweetness: softness or tone and expression.

DOLCIÁNO / **DOLCÍNO** (*It.*) A small bassoon, formerly much used, as a tenor to the hautboy.

DOLCICANÓRO (*It.*) Harmonious.

DOLCÍSSIMO (*It.*) Very sweet and soft: with extreme sweetness and delicacy.

DOLÉNTE (*It.*) Sorrowful, mournful, pathetic.

DOLENTEMÉNTE (*It.*) Dolefully, plaintively, mournfully.

DOLENTÍSSIMO (*It.*) Very plaintively: with much doleful and pathetic expression.

DOLÓRE (*It.*) Grief, sorrow.

DOLOROSAMÉNTE / **DOLORÓSO** (*It.*) Dolorously, sorrowfully, sadly, tenderly, pathetically.

DOLZAÍNA / **DOLZAÍNO** (*It.*) The hautboy.

DOLZFLÖTE (*Ger.*) The old German flute; an organ pedal stop of 8 feet pitch, with a sweet-tone.

DOM (*Ger.*) A cathedral.

DOM-CHOR (*Ger.*) The cathedral choir.

DOMINANT. The name applied by theorists to the *fifth* note of the scale. In the ancient Greek, and the Ecclesiastical, or Church modes, the term Dominant was applied to that sound which was the prevailing one, and which was most frequently heard of any in the mode: in some, but not in all the modes, the dominant was a fifth above the *final*, or key-note: see GREEK MODES, *and* GREGORIAN MODES.

DOMINANTE (*Fr. & Ger.*) The dominant.

Domine — Dorien

Domine salvum fac (*Lat.*) A prayer for the reigning Sovereign, sung after the Mass.

Dom-kirche (*Ger.*) A cathedral.

Dona nobis pacem (*Lat.*) The concluding movement of the Mass.

Dónna (*It.*) Lady: applied to the principal female singers in an opera: as, *prima dónna assolúta*, first, or principal female singer.

Dónne (*It. pl.*) Ladies: see **Dónna**.

Donner du cor (*Fr.*) To blow a French horn.

Dópo (*It.*) After.

Doppel (*Ger.*) Double.

Doppel-be (*Ger.*) A double-flat, ♭♭, lowering a note a whole tone, or two semitones.

Doppel-fagot (*Ger.*) A double bassoon.

Doppel-flöte (*Ger.*) *Double flute*, a stop in an organ, the pipes of which have two mouths, which make the tone particularly bright and agreeable.

Doppel-fuge (*Ger.*) Double fugue.

Doppel-gedact (*Ger.*) Double stopped diapason: see **Gedact**.

Doppel-geige (*Ger.*) See **Viola d'amour**.

Doppel-gesang (*Ger.*) A duet.

Doppel-griffe (*Ger.*) Double stop, on the violin, &c.

Doppel-kreuz (*Ger.*) A double sharp, ×, or ✖, or ♯♯, raising a note two semitones

Doppel-schlag (*Ger.*) A turn, ∞.

Doppelt (*Ger.*) Double.

Doppel-triller (*Ger.*) A double shake.

Doppel-zunge (*Ger.*) Double tonguing.

Dóppio (*It.*) Double, twofold: sometimes indicating that octaves are to be played.

Dóppio moviménto (*It.*) Double movement, or time: that is, *as fast again*.

Dóppio pedále (*It.*) Playing a bass passage on the organ, with the pedals moving in octaves, &c.; that is, using both feet at the same time.

Dóppio più lénto (*It.*) Twice as slow.

Dóppio témpo (*It.*) Double time: that is, *as fast again*.

Dóppo (*It.*) See **Dópo**.

Dorian (*Gr.*) The name of one of the ancient modes, or scales: see **Greek modes**.

Dorien (*Fr.*) See **Dorian**.

DOSSOLÓGIA (*It.*) Doxology.

DOT. A mark, which, when placed *after* a note, or rest, increases its duration one half, making it one half as long again. If there are *two* dots, the second dot is equal to half the preceding one. When the dot is placed *over* a note, it means that the note is to be played detached, or *staccáto*.

DOTS. When placed at the side of a bar, or a double bar, they shew that the music on that side is to be repeated.

DOUBLE. The old name for a *Variation*: used by Scarlatti, Handel, and others.

DOUBLE A, *or* **AA.** *See* DOUBLE G.

DOUBLE ACTION HARP. A harp with pedals, by which each string can be raised two semitones.

DOUBLE B, *or* **BB.** *See* DOUBLE G.

DOUBLE BACKFALL. An obsolete ornament.

DOUBLE BAR. Two thick strokes drawn down through the staff, to divide one strain, or movement, from another.

DOUBLE BARRE (*Fr.*) *See* DOUBLE BAR.

DOUBLE BASS. The largest and deepest toned of all bow-instruments. There are two kinds, one with three strings, the other with four. The real sounds of the double bass are an octave below the notes written. It had originally five rather thick gut strings, the two lowest of which were covered; and also frets for each semitone on the fingerboard: but the frets have disappeared.

DOUBLE BASSOON. A large bassoon, the sounds of which are an octave deeper than those of the bassoon: also, a 16 feet or 32 feet organ reed stop, of similar scale, and softer tone than the double trumpet.

DOUBLE BEMOL (*Fr.*) Double-flat.

DOUBLE C, *or* **CC.** *See* DOUBLE G.

DOUBLE CHANT. A simple, harmonised melody, in four strains, or phrases; to be sung to *two* verses of a psalm, or canticle.

DOUBLE COUNTERPOINT. A counterpoint which admits of the parts being inverted in such a manner, that the upper part becomes the lower, and *vice versa*.

DOUBLE CROCHE (*Fr.*) Double-hooked: a semiquaver.

DOUBLE D, *or* **DD.** *See* DOUBLE G.

DOUBLE-DEMISEMIQUAVER. A note the value of which is one half the *Demisemiquaver*. It is sometimes called the *half-demisemiquaver*, or *semi-demisemiquaver*. It is marked thus ♪, or thus ♫.

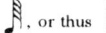

Double-demi — Double stopped

DOUBLE-DEMISEMIQUAVER REST. A mark of silence, equal in duration to a *double-demisemiquaver*: made thus .

DOUBLE DIAPASON. An organ stop, tuned an octave below the diapasons. It is called a 16 feet stop, on the manuals, the lowest key, CC, having a pipe of that length, or tone: on the pedals it is a 32 feet stop.

DOUBLE DIÈSE (*Fr.*) A double sharp, ×, or ✖, or ♯ .

DOUBLE DRUM. A large drum, used in military bands, and beaten at both ends. It is carried horizontally in front of the performer, and the tone serves to mark the rhythm.

DOUBLE DULCIANA. An organ stop of small 16 feet scale, and delicate tone.

DOUBLE E, *or* **EE** | *See* **DOUBLE G.**
DOUBLE F, *or* **FF** |

DOUBLE FLAGEOLET. A flageolet consisting of two tubes, sounds into through one mouth-piece, and producing two sounds at the same time; the holes in one tube being for the fingers of the right hand, and those of the other tube for the fingers of the left hand.

DOUBLE FLUTE. *See* **DOPPEL-FLÖTE.**

DOUBLE FUGUE. A fugue on two subjects.

DOUBLE G, *or* **GG.** In England the term *double* is applied to all those bass notes from inclusive: in Germany the rule is slightly different.

DOUBLE GRAND PIANOFORTE. A remarkable instrument invented by James Pirsson, a pianoforte manufacturer at New York: it has two sets of keys, one at each end.

DOUBLE HAUTBOY. A 16 feet reed stop, of small scale, in an organ.

DOUBLE OPEN DIAPASON. *See* **DOUBLE DIAPASON.**

DOUBLE QUARTET. A composition written for eight instruments, (or two sets): as, four violins, two violas, and two violoncellos.

DOUBLE REED. *See* **REED.**

DOUBLES. An old term for *variations*: *see* **DOUBLE.**

DOUBLE SHAKE. Two notes shaken simultaneously.

DOUBLE SONATA. A sonata composed for two instruments, concertánte: as, the pianoforte, and violoncello.

DOUBLE STOPPED DIAPASON. An organ stop, of 16 feet tone, on the manuals: the pipes are stopped, or covered, at the top. On the pedals it is called the *Sub-bourdon*, and is of 32 feet tone.

DOUBLE STOPPING. Stopping two, or more, strings on a violin, &c., at the same time, to play multiple notes.

DOUBLE TIERCE. An organ stop, tuned a tenth above the diapasons, or a major third above the principal.

DOUBLE TONGUEING. A method of articulating quick notes, used by flute and brass players.

DOUBLE TOUCH. A mechanism on organs, to play another manual, or stop, on the keyboard being played, when extra pressure is applied, to a particular note, or chord.

DOUBLE TRUMPET. An organ reed stop, of 16 feet scale: sometimes the lowest octave of pipes are omitted, and it is called the *Tenoroon Trumpet*. The tone is a little weaker than the Unison Trumpet, to which it, of course, sounds the octave below: *see* **TENOROON**.

DOUBLE TWELFTH. An organ stop, sounding the fifth above the foundation stops: it is generally composed of stopped pipes, though sometimes of open ones. On the manual it us usually of $5^1/_3$ feet, and on the pedal $10^2/_3$ feet tone: *see* QUINT.

DOUBLETTE (*Fr.*) An organ stop, tuned an octave above the principal: in England it is called the *Fifteenth*. The term *Doublette* is sometimes applied by English organ builders to a stop containing two pipes to each note, sounding a fifteenth and a twenty-second above the diapasons.

DOUCE (*Fr.*) Soft, sweet, gentle.

DOUCEMENT (*Fr.*) Softly, gently, sweetly.

DOULEUR (*Fr.*) Grief, sorrow, pathos, tenderness.

DOULOUREUSEMENT (*Fr.*) Plaintively, pathetically.

DOULOUREUX (*Fr.*) Sorrowful, tender, plaintive.

DOUX (*Fr.*) Soft, sweet, smooth, gentle.

DOUZIÈME (*Fr.*) A twelfth.

DOXOLOGIA (*Gr.*) A doxology.

DOXOLOGY. A hymn, or praise, to God.

DRAHT-SAITE (*Ger.*) Music wire: wire string.

DRAMA. A poem, accompanied with action: a play, a comedy, a tragedy.

DRAMATIQUE (*Fr.*) | Dramatic.
DRAMATISCH (*Ger.*) |

DRAMATISCHER DICHTER (*Ger.*) A dramatist: a writer for the stage.

DRAMATIS PERSONÆ (*Lat.*) The characters of a play or opera.

DRAME (*Fr.*) | A drama.
DRÁMMA (*It.*) |

DRÁMMA BURLÉSCA (*It.*) A comic, or humorous drama: *see* **BURLÉTTA**.

DRÁMMA LÍRICO
DRÁMMA PÉR MÚSICA } (*It.*) An opera, or musical drama.

DRAMMATICAMÉNTE (*It.*) Dramatically, in a theatrical or declamatory style.

DRAMMÁTICO (*It.*) Dramatic.

DRÄNGEND (*Ger.*) Hurrying; pressing on.

DREH-ROGEL (*Ger.*) Barrel organ.

DREH-STUHL (*Ger.*) Music stool.

DREHER (*Ger.*) A slow waltz, or German dance.

DREHLEIR (*Ger.*) A hurdy-gurdy.

DREHORGEL (*Ger.*) A barrel-organ.

DREI (*Ger.*) Three.

DREIACHTELTACT (*Ger.*) Time, or measure, of three quavers.

DREIANGEL (*Ger.*) Triangle.

DREICHÖRIG (*Ger.*) A grand pianoforte, with three strings to each note.

DREIDOPPELT
DREIFACH } (*Ger.*) Three-fold: triple: of three ranks.

DREIGESANG (*Ger.*) Trio; for three voices.

DREIKLANG (*Ger.*) A triad, a chord of three sounds, a common chord.

DREILING (*Ger.*) Tierce.

DREIREM (*Ger.*) Triplet: stanza of three verses.

DREISANG
DREISPIEL } (*Ger.*) A trio.

DREIST (*Ger.*) Bold, confident.

DREISTIGKEIT (*Ger.*) Boldness, confidence, resolution.

DREISTIMMIG (*Ger.*) See DREYSTIMMIG.

DREIVIERTELTACT (*Ger.*) Time, or measure, of three crotchets.

DREIZWEITELTACT (*Ger.*) Time, or measure, of three minims.

DREYKLAND (*Ger.*) See DREIKLANG.

DREYSTIMMIG (*Ger.*) In three parts: for three voices.

DRINGENDER (*Ger.*) Hurrying; pressing on.

DRÍTTA
DRÍTTO } (*It.*) Right: *máno drítta*, the right hand.

DRIVING NOTES. An old term applied to a passage consisting of long notes placed between shorter ones, and accented contrary to the usual and natural flow of the rhythm: *see* SYNCOPATION.

DROHEND (*Ger.*) Threatening.

DROITE (*Fr.*) Right: *main droite*, the right hand.

DRONE. The largest of the three tubes of the bagpipe. It only sounds one deep note, which serves as a perpetual bass to every tune.

DRÜCKBALG (*Ger.*) A wind-reservoir, in an organ.

DRUCKER (*Ger.*) A very brilliant climax, or special effect.

DRUCKWERK (*Ger.*) The complete *sticker* action, of an organ.

DRUM. A well-known instrument of percussion, consisting of a cylinder, covered at each end by a skin, which may be tightened by means of cords.

DRUM MAJOR. The principal drummer, in a military band.

DRUMSLADE. An old name for a drummer.

DUDELKASTEN (*Ger.*) Barrel organ.

DUDELKASTENSACK (*Ger.*) A bagpipe, a cornamuse, a hornpipe.

DUDELSACK (*Ger.*) A bagpipe.

DUDELN (*Ger.*) To play on the bagpipe: also, a contemptuous term for playing badly on the flute, &c.

DUDLER (*Ger.*) A bagpiper, a player on the bagpipe.

DÚE (*It.*) Two: in two parts: *see* À DÚE.

DÚE CÓRDE (*It.*) Two strings: *À dúe córde*.

DÚE CÓRI (*It.*) Two choirs, or choruses.

DÚE PEDÁLI (*It.*) The two pedals are to be used.

DUET. A composition for two voices, or instruments: also, a pianoforte composition for four hands, or two performers.

DUETT (*Ger.*) A duet.

DUETTE (*Ger. pl.*) Duets.

DUETTÍNO (*It.*) A short duet.

DUÉTTO (*It.*) A duet.

DÚE VÔLTE (*It.*) Twice.

DULCAN. A name sometimes erroneously applied to the *Dolcan*.

DULÇANA
DULÇAYNAS } (*Sp.*) See Dolciáno.

DULCET. An organ stop: *see* DULCIANA PRINCIPAL.

DULCIAN (*Fr.*) A small bassoon: *see* DOLCIÁNO. The name is also applied to a stop in an organ.

DULCIANA (*Lat.*) An 8 feet organ stop, of a soft and sweet quality of tone.

DULCIANA PRINCIPAL. A delicate and sweet-toned organ stop, of 4 feet scale.

DULCICANÓRO (*It.*) Harmonious.

DULCIMER. A triangular chest, or box, strung with wires, which are struck with little rods. This is also the name of an ancient Hebrew instrument, of the form, tone, and compass of which we are ignorant.

DULCÍNO (*It.*) See DOLCIÁNO.

Dulzaginas — Durchführung

Dulzaginas (*Sp.*) A dulciana.

Dulzain. *See* Dolciáno.

Dulzaína (*Sp.*) The dulcimer: also a flute or pipe.

Dulz-flöte (*Ger.*) An open organ stop of 8 or 4 feet scale, and pleasant tone.

Dumb Spinet. Another name for the *Clavichord*.

Dumpf / **Dumpfig** (*Ger.*) Of a dull, hollow, dead sound.

Dumpfigkeit (*Ger.*) Hollowness, dullness of sound.

Dúo (*It.*) Two: in two parts: a composition for two voices, or instruments: a duet.

Duodécima / **Duodécimo** (*It.*) The twelfth: the twelfth note from the tonic: the name is also applied to an organ stop, tuned a twelfth above the diapasons.

Duodecimóle (*It.*) A musical phrase, formed by a group of twelve notes.

Duodrámma (*It.*) A kind of melodrama, in which only two persons act and sing.

Duólo (*It.*) Sorrow, grief, sadness.

Duómo (*It.*) A cathedral.

Duple Time. Time with two beats in a bar, as, *álla cappélla* time, &c.

Duplicasióne (*It.*) Duplication; doubling a note, part, &c.

Dúplo (*It.*) Double.

Dur (*Ger.*) Major, in speaking of keys and modes: as, *C dur*, C major.

Dur (*Fr.*) Hard, coarse, harsh: *see also* Duráte.

Dúra (*It.*) Delay, stop, stay.

Duraménte (*It.*) Roughly, coarsely, harshly: also meaning that the passage is to be played in a firm, bold style, and strongly accented.

Duráte (*It.*) Hard, coarse, harsh: also implying false relations in harmony.

Durchaus (*Ger.*) Throughout.

Durchaus fantastich und leidenschaftlich vorzutragen (*Ger.*) To be performed throughout with a fantastic style, and with passionate emotion.

Durchblasen (*Ger.*) To play a piece through.

Durchcomponiren (*Ger.*) To set a song, through all its stanzas, to music.

Durchdringend (*Ger.*) Penetrating, piercing.

Durchdringende Stimme (*Ger.*) A shrill voice, or tone.

Durchführung (*Ger.*) Development.

DURCHGÄNGIG
DURCHGÄNGLICH (*Ger.*) Throughout: *die Noten der linken Hand durchgängig gebunden*, the notes of the left hand *legáto* throughout.

DURCHGEHEND (*Ger.*) Passing, transient: passing through.

DURCHSCHALLEN (*Ger.*) To sound through, to penetrate with sound.

DURCHSCHLAGEND (*Ger.*) A term applied to some organ-stops, indicating that they extend through the whole compass of the manual: it also signifies a *free reed* stop: which see.

DURCHSPIELEN (*Ger.*) To play, to act over: to try a musical instrument by playing upon it: to hurt one's fingers by playing too long: to perform a musical piece thoroughly.

DURCHWEG LEISE ZU HALTEN (*Ger.*) To be generally soft.

DURÉE (*Fr.*) Length, duration of notes.

DUREMENT (*Fr.*) Hard, harsh.

DURETÉ (*Fr.*) See DURÁTE.

DURÉZZA (*It.*) Hardness, harshness, roughness of tone or expression.

DÚRO (*It.*) See DURAMÉNTE.

DURUS (*Lat.*) Hard.

DÜSTER (*Ger.*) Gloomy, mournful, sombre.

DU TALON (*Fr.*) With the *nut* of the bow, in violin playing.

DUTCH CONCERT. A term of ridicule, when each performer plays his own tune, and in his own time.

DÜTCHEN
DÜTE (*Ger.*) A cornet.

DUTEN
DÜTEN (*Ger.*) A contemptuous term, meaning to *toot*, or blow on a horn.

DUX (*Lat.*) *Leader, guide*: the subject, or leading melody of a fugue.

DYSTONIE (*Gr. & Ger.*) Discord, or false intonation.

E

E, called in France and Italy *Mi*: the third note of the modern scale of Guido d'Arezzo.

E | (*It.*) *And:* as *fláuto e violíno,* flute and violin: *nobilménte ed animáto,* with grandeur and animation.
ED |

E. The smallest, and most acute string, on the violin and guitar.

EBENFALLS (*Ger.*) Likewise; similarly.

EBOLLIMÉNTO | (*It.*) *Ebullition*; a sudden and energetic expression
EBOLLIZIÓNE | of emotion.

ECART (*Fr.*) A wide *stretch* on the pianoforte.

ECCEDÉNTE (*It.*) *Augmented*, in speaking of intervals: *see* AUGMENTED.

ECCHEGGIÁNTE (*It.*) Resounding, echoing.

ECCHEGGIÁRE (*It.*) To resound, echo.

ECCHEIA (*Lat.*) *See* ECHEIA.

ECCLÉSIA (*It.*) Church.

ECCLESIASTICAL MODES. *See* CHURCH MODES.

ÉCCO (*It.*) An echo, the rebounding of a sound: *see also* ECHO.

ECHAPPÉE (*Fr.*) A *hanging*, or *anticipatory* note.

ECHAPPEMENT (*Fr.*) An escapement; the *hopper* of a pianoforte.

ECHEGGIÁRE (*It.*) To echo; to resound.

ECHEIA (*Gr.*) Vases used by the ancients, at their dramatic performances, &c., to increase the effect of their voice.

ECHELETTE (*Fr.*) A xylophone.

ÉCHELLE (*Fr.*) The scale, or gamut.

ÉCHELLE CHROMATIQUE (*Fr.*) The chromatic scale.

ÉCHELLE DIATONIQUE (*Fr.*) The diatonic scale.

ÉCHELON (*Fr.*) Step, or degree, of the scale.

ÉCHO (*Fr.*) In organ music this term means, a repetition, or imitation, of a previous passage, with some remarkable modification in regard to tone. In old organs the stops forming the 'echo' were enclosed in a solid wooden box, to give the effect of distance; this was afterwards altered and improved by Abraham Jordan, in 1712, who invented the 'swell,' by opening one of the sides of the box, and furnishing it with a moveable 'shutter'; and this afterwards gave place to a series of Venetian 'shades,' or 'shutters,' forming the *Venetian swell* of the present day. Some of the large modern organs contain an 'echo,' which is enclosed within the swell-box, the pipes of the 'echo' organ being of very small scale, with their own soundboards, &c., and voiced upon an extremely light pressure of wind.

ECHO CORNET. An organ stop, the pipes of which are of small scale, with a light delicate tone. It is usually placed in the swell.

ECHOMETRE (*Gr.*) An instrument for measuring the powers of echoes and other sounds.

ECHT (*Ger.*) Genuine.

ECLAT (*Fr.*) Brilliancy; dash.

ECLATANT (*Fr.*) Piercing; loud.

ÉCLISSES (*Fr.*) The *sides*, or hoops, of a violin, guitar, &c.

ECLOGUE (*Fr.*) A pastoral song, or poem.

ÉCO (*It.*) An echo, the rebounding of a sound: the repetition of a previous passage, in a softer tone: *see also* ECHO.

ÉCOLE (*Fr.*) A school, a method, or course of instruction: a style of playing, singing, or composing, formed by some eminent artist.

ÉCOLIER (*Fr.*) A pupil.

ÉCOSSAIS / **ÉCOSSAISE** (*Fr.*) Scotch: a dance tune, or air, in the Scotch style.

ED (*It.*) And.

EDEL (*Ger.*) Noble; refined, lofty.

E DUR (*Ger.*) The key of E major.

EFFEKT (*Ger.*) / **EFFET** (*Fr.*) / **EFFÉTTO** (*It.*) The effect, or operation of music, upon an audience.

ÉGALEMENT (*Fr.*) Equally, evenly, smoothly.

ÉGALITÉ (*Fr.*) Equality, evenness.

ÉGLISE (*Fr.*) Church: *musique d'église*, church music, music for the church.

EGLOGUE (*Fr.*) An eclogue.

EGUAGIÁNZA (*It.*) Equality, evenness.

EGUÁLE (*It.*) Equal, even, alike: this word is also applied to a composition for several voices, or instruments, of one kind, as, male voices only, or female voices only.

EGUALÉZZA (*It.*) Equality, evenness.

EGUALMÉNTE (*It.*) Equally, evenly, alike.

EIFERIG / **EIFRIG** (*Ger.*) Passionate, ardent, full of zeal, eager.

EIGENTLICH (*Ger.*) Real, actual, proper.

EIGENTON (*Ger.*) The real, or natural tone, of an instrument.

EIGHTH. An octave.

Eighth — Einsang

EIGHTH-NOTE. A quaver.

EIN (*Ger.*) A, an: one: *für ein oder zwei Claviere und Pedal*, for
EINE one or two manuals and pedals.

EINBLASEN (*Ger.*) To blow into.

EINCHÖRIG (*Ger.*) An undivided choir.

EINEM (*Ger.*) A, one: *mit einem Finger*, with one Finger.

EINE SAITE (*Ger.*) Upon one string only.

EINFACH (*Ger.*) Simple, plain, unornamented.

EINFACHER CHORAL (*Ger.*) Plain choral: without any variation, or ornament.

EINFALT (*Ger.*) Simplicity.

EINGANG (*Ger.*) Introduction, preface, prologue, prelude.

EINGANG DER MESSE (*Ger.*) Introit.

EINGANG EINER MUSIK (*Ger.*) Prelude.

EINGANG-SCHLÜSSEL (*Ger.*) Introductory key.

EINGESTRICHEN (*Ger.*) Note of the treble, marked with *one stroke*: this refers to the octave from middle C to the B above.

EINGESTRICHENE OCTAVE (*Ger.*) The notes from middle C to the B above, both inclusive: in Germany these are marked with *one stroke*; thus, $\overline{c}$, or c^1.

EINGLIED (*Ger.*) *One-linked*, or, *one chord*, in speaking of sequences.

EINHÄLLIG (*Ger.*) Unison: harmonious.

EINHALTEN (*Ger.*) To pause, to stop.

EINHAUCHEN (*Ger.*) To breathe into.

EINHEIT (*Ger.*) Unity.

EINHELFEN (*Ger.*) To prompt.

EINHELFER (*Ger.*) Prompter.

EINIGEM (*Ger.*) Some, any: *mit einigem Ausdruck*, with some expression.

EINIGKEIT (*Ger.*) Concord, harmony, unity.

EINKLANG (*Ger.*) Unison, accord, harmony.

EINKLINGEN (*Ger.*) To accord.

EINLANG (*Ger.*) A short piece, between two longer ones.

EINLAUT (*Ger.*) Monotonous.

EINLEITUNG (*Ger.*) Introduction.

EINLEITUNGS-SATZ (*Ger.*) An introductory movement.

EINLEITUNGS-SPIEL (*Ger.*) Overture, prelude.

EINMAL (*Ger.*) Once.

EINMÜTHIGKEIT (*Ger.*) Concord, unanimity.

EINSANG (*Ger.*) A solo.

Einsatz — Elegiac

EINSATZ (*Ger.*) The entry, or attack of an instrument.
EINSATZSTÜCK (*Ger.*) *See* CROOKS.
EINSCHLAFEN (*Ger.*) To die away, to slacken the time, and diminish the tone.
EINSCHMEICHELND (*Ger.*) Insinuating.
EINSCHNITT (*Ger.*) A phrase, or incomplete musical sentence.
EINSETZEN (*Ger.*) To enter after a pause or rest.
EINSTIMMEN (*Ger.*) To agree in tune, to be concordant.
EINSTIMMIG (*Ger.*) Unanimity of tone, of one voice.
EINSTIMMIGKEIT (*Ger.*) Concord, agreement, unanimity.
EINTONIG (*Ger.*) Monotonous.
EINTRACHT (*Ger.*) Concord, unity.
EINTRÄCHTIG (*Ger.*) Concordant, harmonious.
EINTRÄCHTIGKEIT (*Ger.*) Concordance, harmony.
EINTRETEND (*Ger.*) Entering, beginning: *ale neu eintretende Stimmen hervortretend*, each newly entering part to be played very prominently.
EINTRITT (*Ger.*) Entrance, entry, beginning.
EINVERSTÄNDNISS (*Ger.*) Harmony, agreement, concord.
EINZELN
EINZELNE } (*Ger.*) Solo, single, alone.
EINZUG (*Ger.*) Entry, entrance.
EIS (*Ger.*) The note E-sharp.
EISENVIOLINE (*Ger.*) An iron fiddle; nail-fiddle.
EISTEDDFOD (*Welsh*). A bardic congress, an assemblage of bards, first held in 1078, when Prince Gryffydd invited a number of bards from Ireland to Wales, to confer with his own, for the improvement and fostering of music.
EKLOGE
EKLOGUE } (*Ger.*) *See* ECLOGUE.
ELARGI (*Fr.*) Broadened, slackened.
ÉLÉGAMMENT (*Fr.*)
ELEGANTEMÉNTE (*It.*) } Elegantly, gracefully.
ELEGANT (*Fr.*)
ELEGÁNTE (*It.*) } Elegant, graceful.
ELEGÁNZA (*It.*) Elegance, grace.
ELEGÍA (*It.*) An elegy, or monody: music of a mournful, or funereal character.
ELEGIAC. Plaintive, mournful, sorrowful.

Elegiáco — Émpito

ELEGIÁCO (*It.*)
ÉLÉGIAQUE (*Fr.*) } Mournful, plaintive, elegiac.

ÉLÉGIE (*Fr.*) See **ELEGÍA**.

ELEGY. Funeral song, mournful song.

ÉLÉMENS (*Fr.*)
ELEMÉNTI (*It.*) } The rudiments, or elements, of musical science.

ELEVÁTO (*It.*) Elevated, sublime, lofty.

ELEVAMÉNTE
ELEVAZIÓNE } (*It.*) Grandeur, sublimity, loftiness of expression.

ÉLÈVE (*Fr.*) Pupil.

ELEVENTH. An interval comprising an octave and a fourth.

ÉLEVER (*Fr.*) To raise, or lift up the hand, in beating time.

ELFTE (*Ger.*) See **ELEVENTH**.

ELINE (*Gr.*) The ancient *song of the weavers*.

ELLENLÄNDE
ELLIG } (*Ger.*) *Ell-length*, or *two foot* size, speaking of the scale of pipes.

ELOGE (*Fr.*) Praise, eulogy.

EMBELLIMÉNTE (*It.*) Embellishments.

EMBELLIR (*Fr.*) To embellish, to adorn, to ornament.

EMBELLISSEMENT (*Fr.*) Embellishment.

EMBOUCHURE (*Fr.*) The mouth-piece of a flute, hautboy, or other wind-instrument: that part to which the lips are applied, to produce the sound. The term also refers to the position which the mouth muse assume, in playing the instrument.

ÉMÉRILLONNÉ (*Fr.*) Sprightly, merry, brisk.

ÉMÉRITE (*Fr.*) Said of a professor who has retired from the duties of his profession.

E MOLL (*Ger.*) The key of E minor.

EMOZIÓNE (*It.*) Emotion, agitation.

EMPÂTER LES SONS (*Fr.*) To sing, or play, in a masterly, flowing style, without defects, or imperfections.

EMPFINDSAM (*Ger.*) Sensitive, emotional.

EMPFINDUNG (*Ger.*) Emotion, passion, feeling.

EMPHASE (*Ger.*) Emphasis.

EMPHATIQUE (*Fr.*) Emphatical.

EMPHATIQUEMENT (*Fr.*) Emphatically.

EMPHATISCH (*Ger.*) Emphatical.

EMPHASIS. Marked expression: a particular stress, or accent, on any note, generally indicated by $>$ $\wedge$ $\vee$ fz sf , &c.

ÉMPITO (*It.*) Impetuosity.

EMPITUOSAMÉNTE (*It.*) Impetuously.
EMPLUMER (*Fr.*) To *pen*, or put quills into the *jacks* of a spinet, &c.
EMPORTÉ (*Fr.*) Passionate, hurried.
EMPORTEMENT (*Fr.*) Passion, transport.
EMPRESSÉ (*Fr.*) In haste, eager, hurried.
EMPRESSEMENT (*Fr.*) Haste, eagerness, in a hurried manner.
EN ANIMANT PEU À PEU (*Fr.*) Quicker by degrees.
ENARMÓNICO (*It.*) Enharmonic.
EN AUGMENTANT (*Fr.*) Increasing the tone.
EN BADINANT (*Fr.*) Playfully, jestingly; *scherzándo*.
EN BOUSULADE (*Fr.*) Precipitately.
EN CÉDANT (*Fr.*) Slackening the speed.
EN CHANTANT (*Fr.*) In a singing style.
EN CHŒUR (*Fr.*) In chorus.
ENCORE (*Fr.*) Again, one more, over again: demand for the repetition of a piece.
ENDE (*Ger.*) End.
ENDECASÍLLABO (*It.*) Consisting of eleven syllable: a short lyric poem, composed of verses consisting of eleven syllables each.
EN DEHORS (*Fr.*) In the distance.
EN DESCENDANT (*Fr.*) In descending.
EN DIMINUANT LA FORCE (*Fr.*) Diminuéndo.
ENDSCHLUSS (*Ger.*) End, conclusion, concluding piece.
EN ÉLARGISSANT BEAUCOUP (*Fr.*) With much more breadth.
ENERGETICAMÉNTE (*It.*) Energetically, forcibly.
ENERGÉTICO (*It.*) Energetic: with emphasis.
ENERGÍA (*It.*) Energy, force, emphasis, vigour.
ENERGICAMÉNE (*It.*) Energetically, forcibly.
ENÉRGICO (*It.*) Energetic, forcible, vigorous.
ÉNERGIE (*Fr.*) Energy, force, emphasis.
ÉNERGIQUE (*Fr.*) Energetic: with emphasis.
ÉNERGIQUEMENT (*Fr.*) Energetically, forcibly.
ENERGISCH (*Ger.*) Energetical.
ENFANT DE CHŒUR (*Fr.*) Singing boy.
ÉNFASI (*It.*) Emphasis, earnestness.
ENFATICAMÉNTE (*It.*) Emphatically.
ENFÁTICO (*It.*) Emphatical: with earnestness.
ENFIATAMÉNTE (*It.*) Proudly, pompously.
ENFLER (*Fr.*) To swell, to increase the tone.

Enge — En passant

ENGE (*Ger.*) Close, condensed, compressed: this term is applied to the *strétto* in a fugue. Also, narrow, straight, in speaking of organ pipes.

ENGE HARMONIE (*Ger.*) Contracted, or close harmony, the intervals, or sounds, being near together.

ENGELSTIMME (*Ger.*) *See* VOX ANGELICA.

ENGFÜHRUNG (*Ger.*) The *strétto* of a fugue.

ENGUICHURE (*Fr.*) The mouth-piece of a trumpet.

ENHARMONIC (*Gr.*) One of the ancient scales, or modes, proceeding by quarter tones. On the pianoforte these cannot be expressed, but on the violin, oboe, &c., they may be described as something like the difference between G-sharp and A-flat: or between D-sharp and E-flat: &c.

In modern music it also means, such a change in the nature of an interval or chord, as can be effected by merely altering the notation of one or more notes; thus,

ENHARMONIC INTERVALS. Such as have only a nominal difference (on the pianoforte): for instance: the minor third C, E-flat, and the extreme second, C, D-sharp: or, the extreme fifth, C, G-sharp, and the minor sixth, C, A-flat: &c.

ENHARMONIC KEYS. Such as include (on the pianoforte) the same notes, and have the same scales, but under different names: for instance, the scales of F-sharp and G-flat: B-natural, and C-flat: D-sharp and E-flat: A-sharp and B-flat: E-sharp and F: G-sharp and A-flat: C-sharp and D-flat.

ENHARMONIC CHANGE. This may take place upon a note, chord, or entire passage, the signature being changed, (to avoid complexity,) either for convenience in writing, or to obtain a passing modulation into another key, which can only be properly written by substituting flats for sharps, or sharps for flats.

ENHARMONIQUE (*Fr.*) \
ENHARMONISCH (*Ger.*) } Enharmonic.

ENJOUÉ (*Fr.*) Cheerful, gay.

ENJOUEMENT (*Fr.*) Cheerfulness, sprightliness, gaiety.

ENLEVER (*Fr.*) To lift up the hand, in beating time.

ENLEVEZ LA SOURDINE (*Fr.*) *Take of the mute.*

EN MESURE (*Fr.*) A témpo; in time.

ÉNONCER (*Fr.*) To enunciate, to declare, to proclaim.

ÉNONCIATION (*Fr.*) Enunciation, declaration.

ENOPLIA (*Gr.*) War songs of the ancient Spartans.

EN PASSANT (*Fr.*) In passing; by the way.

EN RENFORÇANT (*Fr.*) With force.

EN RONDEAU (*Fr.*) Resembling a *Rondeau*.

EN SCÈNE (*Fr.*) On the stage.

EN S'ÉLOIGNANT (*Fr.*) Growing fainter.

EN SE PERDANT (*Fr.*) Dying away.

ENSEIGNEMENT (*Fr.*) Instruction.

ENSEIGNER (*Fr.*) To instruct, to teach.

ENSEMBLE (*Fr.*) *Together, the whole*: a concerted vocal piece. Applied to concerted music when the whole is given with that perfect smoothness, and oneness of style and feeling, as to leave nothing further to be desired.

EN SERRANT (*Fr.*) *Stringéndo*, hurrying the pace.

ENTFERNT (*Ger.*) Distant, remote, far off; *echo-like*.

ENTGEGEN / **ENTGEGENGESETZT** (*Ger.*) Contrary, opposite, speaking of motion.

ENTHALLEN (*Ger.*) To sound fourth.

ENTHOUSIASME (*Fr.*) / **ENTHUSIASMUS** (*Ger.*) Enthusiasm, warmth of expression

ENTHUSIASTISCH (*Ger.*) Enthusiastically: with warmth of expression.

ENTONER (*Fr.*) To give out the tune, to begin singing.

ENTR'ACTE (*Fr.*) Music played by the orchestra between the acts of a drama: a dramatic interlude, or prelude.

ENTRÁDA / **ENTRÁNTE** / **ENTRÁTA** (*It.*) An entrance, introduction, prelude, beginning.

ENTRÁRE (*It.*) To enter, to begin.

ENTRÁRE IN BÁLLO (*It.*) To begin to dance.

ENTRÉE (*Fr.*) Entry, entrance, beginning.

ENTREMESE (*Sp.*) A short burlesque musical comedy.

ENTREMET (*Fr.*) A short entertainment between two longer ones.

ENTRETAILLE (*Fr.*) The interchange of the foot, in dancing.

ENTSCHEIDUNG (*Ger.*) Decision, determination.

ENTSCHIEDEN (*Ger.*) Decided: in a determined manner.

ENTSCHLAFEN (*Ger.*) To die away, to diminish gradually the tone, &c.

ENTSCHLIESSUNG (*Ger.*) Resolution, determination.

ENTSCHLOSSEN (*Ger.*) Determined, resolute.

ENTSCHLOSSENHEIT (*Ger.*) Resoluteness, firmness.

ENTSCHLUSS (*Ger.*) Resolution.

Entusiásmo — Epitalámio

ENTUSIÁSMO
ENTUSIASTÍCO (*It.*) Enthusiasm, warmth.
ENTWURF (*Ger.*) Sketch, outline, or design, of a composition.
ENTZÜCKEND (*Ger.*) Charming, delightful.
ENUNCIÁRE (*It.*) To enunciate, to declare, to proclaim.
ENUCIATÍVA (*It.*) Enunciation, declaration.
ENUNCIÁTO (*It.*) Enunciated, declared, proclaimed.
ENUNCIAZIÓNE (*It.*) Enunciation, declaration.
EÓLIA (*It.*)
EOLIAN (*Gr.*)
ÉOLIEN (*Fr.*) One of the ancient modes: *see* GREEK MODES.
EÓLIO (*It.*)
ÉOLIQUE (*Fr.*) Eolic: *see* EOLIAN.
EPIAULA (*Gr.*) The ancient Greek *song of the millers.*
EPIC (*It.*) In a heroic, narrative style.
EPICAMÉNTE (*It.*) In an epic style.
EPICÉDIO (*It.*)
EPICEDION (*Gr.*) An elegy, dirge, funeral song or ode.
EPICEDIUM (*Gr.*)
ÉPICI (*It.*) Epic, heroic.
EPIDOTONOS (*Gr.*) The third above.
EPIGONION
EPIGONIUM (*Gr.*) An ancient Greek instrument, with forty strings, played with the fingers without a plectrum: the shape of the instrument is, however, unknown.
EPILENIA (*Gr.*) The ancient *song of the grape-gatherers.*
EPILOGUE. A conclusion; an after-word.
ÉPINETTE (*Fr.*) A spinet: see that word.
EPINICIA
EPINICIUM (*Gr.*) Triumphal songs, songs of victory: festival to commemorate a victory.
EPINÍCIO (*It.*)
EPINICION (*Gr.*) A triumphal song: *see* EPINICIA.
EPIODION (*Gr.*) A funeral lament.
EPISODE. An intermediate passage: a digression: a portion of a composition not founded upon the principal subject or theme.
EPISODICAMÉNTE (*It.*) In the manner of an episode.
EPISÓDICO (*It.*) Episode, digression.
EPISODISCH (*Ger.*) In the manner of an episode.
EPISTROPHE (*Gr.*) A repetition of the concluding melody.
EPITALÁMIO (*It.*) A marriage song: a nuptial song or ode.

EPITASIS (*Gr.*) The progress of the plot in a play or poem; the raising of the voice.

EPITHALAMION (*Gr.*)
EPITHALAMIUM (*Gr.*) A marriage song: a nuptial song or ode.
ÉPITHALMAE (*Fr.*)

EPODE (*Gr.*) An *after-song*; a refrain; the third part or stanza of a Greek ode.

E PÓI (*It.*) *And then*: as, *e pói la códa*, and then the coda.

ÉPOUMONER (*Fr.*) To tire the lungs.

EPTACORDE (*Fr.*)
EPTACÓRDO (*It.*) A heptachord, a lyre with seven strings.

EQUÁBILE (*It.*) Equal, alike, even, uniform.

EQUABILMÉNTE (*It.*) Smoothly, equally, evenly.

EQUALE. *See* EGUÁLE.

EQUAL TEMPERAMENT. That equalisation, or tempering, of the twelve sounds included in an octave, which renders all the scales equally in (or out of) tune; the imperfection being divided equally amongst the whole: *see* WOLF, *and* UNEQUAL TEMPERAMENT.

EQUAL VOICES. This term is applied to those compositions in which either all adult male, or all female voices are employed: all the voices being *one* species, either male, or female.

EQUISONANT. Of the same, or like sound: a unison. In guitar music the term is often used, to express the different ways of stopping the same note.

EQUISONNANCE (*Fr.*) In unison.

EQUÍSONO (*It.*) Having the same sound: *see* EQUISONANT.

EQUIVOCAL. Such chords as may, by slight change in the notation, belong to more than one key.

EQUIVOCÁLE (*It.*) *See* EQUIVOCAL.

ERFREULICH (*Ger.*) Joyful, rejoicing.

ERGRIFFEN (*Ger.*) Stirred, agitated, moved.

ERHABEN (*Ger.*) Elevated, sublime: a lofty and exalted expression.

ERHEBEN (*Ger.*) To raise, to elevate, to lift up the hand, in beating time.

ERHEBUNG (*Ger.*) Raising: elevation of the hand in beating time.

ERHÖHEN (*Ger.*) *See* ERHEBEN.

ERHÖHUNG (*Ger.*) *See* ERHEBUNG.

ERHÖHUNGS-ZEICHEN (*Ger.*) A sharp, or other mark for raising a note a semitone.

ERINNERUNG (*Ger.*) Reminisce.

ERKLINGEN (*Ger.*) To sound: to resound.

ERLEHREN (*Ger.*) To acquire by teaching.

Erleichterung — Esecutóre

ERLEICHTERUNG (*Ger.*) Simplified arrangement.
ERLÖSCHEND (*Ger.*) Extinguished; dying away; *calándo*.
ERMATTET (*Ger.*) Wearied, exhausted, jaded.
ERMUNTERUNG (*Ger.*) Animation, rousing, excitation.
ERNIEDRIGUNG (*Ger.*) Lowering: depression of a note by means of a flat, or natural.
ERNIEDRIGUNGS-ZEICHEN (*Ger.*) A flat, or other sign for lowering a note a semitone.
ERNST / **ERNSTHAFT** (*Ger.*) Earnest, serious: in a grave, severe, and earnest style.
ERNSTHAFTIGKEIT (*Ger.*) Earnestness, seriousness.
ERNSTLICH (*Ger.*) Earnest, fervent, ardent, grave.
ERNSLICHKEIT (*Ger.*) Earnestness.
ERNST, UND MIT STEIGENDER LEBHAFTIGKEIT (*Ger.*) Earnestly, and with increasing vivacity.
ERNTELIED (*Ger.*) Harvest song.
ERÖFFNUNG (*Ger.*) Opening, beginning.
ERÖFFNUNGS-STÜCK (*Ger.*) Overture.
EROTIC. Amatory.
ERÓTICA (*It.*) Erotical: love songs, amatory ditties.
ERREGT (*Ger.*) Excited, agitated.
ERSATZ (*Ger.*) Artificial, substitute, equivalent.
ERST (*Ger.*) First, at first: *erstes Heft*, first book, or part.
ERSTERBEN (*Ger.*) To die away, to fade or become extinct.
ERTONEN (*Ger.*) To sound, to resound.
ERWECKUNG (*Ger.*) Animation, awaking, excitation.
ERWEITERN (*Ger.*) To expand, augment.
ERWEITERT (*Ger.*) Expanded, extended, developed.
ERZÄHLER (*Ger.*) The *narrator* in a Passion play; also, an organ stop of 8 feet tone, invented Ernest Skinner.
ERZLAUTE (*Ger.*) *See* ARCHLUTE.
ES (*Ger.*) The note E-flat.
ESÁCORDO (*It.*) Hexachord.
ESALTAZIÓNE (*It.*) Exaltation, sublimity.
ESÁMETRO (*It.*) Hexameter.
ESÁTTA (*It.*) Exact, strict.
ESÁTTA INTONAZIÓNE (*It.*) Exact intonation.
ESCHALOT. *See* SHALLOT.
ESCLAMÁTO (*It.*) Well defined; *marcáto*.
ES DUR (*Ger.*) The key of E-flat major.
ESECUTÓRE (*It.*) A performer.

ESECUZIÓNE (*It.*) Execution, facility of performance, whether vocal, or instrumental.

ESECUTRÍCE (*It.*) A female performer.

ESEGUÍRE (*It.*) To execute, or perform, either vocally, or on an instrument.

ESÉMPIO (*It.*) Example, model, pattern, copy.

ESERCÍZIO (*It.*) An exercise, study for the acquirement of execution, whether instrumental or vocal.

ESERCÍZJ (*It. pl.*) Exercises: *see* ESERCÍZIO.

ES ES (*Ger.*) The note E-double-flat.

ESITAMÉNTO
ESITAZIÓNE } (*It.*) Hesitation.

ES MOLL (*Ger.*) The key of E-flat minor.

ESORNÁRE (*It.*) To adorn, to embellish.

ESPACE (*Fr.*) A space of the stave.

ESPAGNOL (*Fr.*)
ESPAGNUÓLO (*It.*) } Spanish: *all' espagnuólo*, in the Spanish style.

ESPANSIÓNE (*It.*) Expansion, breadth.

ESPÉRTO (*It.*) Skilful, expert.

ESPIRÁNDO (*It.*) Breathing deeply: with anxious endeavour.

ESPRESSÍVO (*It.*) Expressive: the movement must be performed with expression.

ESPRESSIÓNE (*It.*) Expression, feeling.

ESPRIT (*Fr.*) Spirit.

ESSAI (*Fr.*) An essay.

ESSÉMPIO. *See* ESÉMPIO.

ESSENTIAL NOTES. The notes forming any chord: in contradistinction to all merely accidental, passing, or ornamental notes.

ESSENTIAL SEVENTH. The dominant seventh.

ESTEMPORÁLE
ESTEMPORÁNEO } (*It.*) Extemporaneous.

EXTENSIÓNE (*It.*) The compass of a voice.

ESTINGUÉNDO
ESTÍNTE
ESTÍNTO } (*It.*) Becoming extinct, expiring, dying gradually away, in regard to tone and time.

ESTRAVAGÁNTE
ESTRAVAGÁNZA } (*It.*) Extravagant and wild, both as to composition, and performance.

ESTREMAMÉNTE (*It.*) Extremely, very much.

ESTRIBILHO. A popular Portuguese song, in $\frac{6}{8}$ time.

ESTRIBÍLLO (*Sp.*) A verse often repeated, the burden of the song.

Estrinienda — Eufónico

ESTRINIENDA (*It.*) A close, binding way of execution the notes of any passage: extremely *legáto*.

ESTRINCIÉNDO (*It.*) Playing a passage with force and precision.

ESTRINIÉNDA (*It.*) Very *legáto*; *legatissímo*.

ÉSTRO POÉTICO (*It.*) Poetic inspiration, poetic rage, inspired fury, imaginative power in a composer.

ESULTAZIÓNE (*It.*) Exultation: in a joyful, rejoicing style.

ET (*Lat.*) And: *pedale et manuale*, pedal and manual: that is, the hand and the feet play the same notes.

ÉTEIGNEZ LE SON (*Fr.*) Let the sound die away.

ÉTEINTE (*Fr.*) See ESTÍNTE.

ÉTENDUE (*Fr.*) The extent, range, compass, of a voice or instrument.

ET INCARNATUS (*Lat.*) A portion of the *Credo*.

ÉTOUFFÉ (*Fr.*) Stifled, smothered, damped, in harp playing: in pianoforte music it means, an exceedingly soft style of playing.

ÉTOUFFOIRS (*Fr. pl.*) The dampers: on *lève les étouffoirs*, the dampers are to be raised.

ET RESURREXIT (*Lat.*) Part of the *Credo*.

ETTA | (*It.*) An Italian final diminutive: as, *trómba*, a trumpet,
ETTO | *trombétta*, a little trumpet: see INO.

ÉTUDE (*Fr.*) A study, an exercise.

ET VITAM (*Lat.*) A part of the *Credo*.

ETWAS (*Ger.*) Some, somewhat, a little.

ETWAS BELEBEND (*Ger.*) A little accelerated.

ETWAS BETONT, DOCH SEHR INNIG (*Ger.*) Somewhat accented, bet very feelingly.

ETWAS BEWEGT (*Ger.*) Rather animated.

ETWAS DRÄNGEND (*Ger.*) Hurrying a little.

ETWAS FLÜSSIGEER ALS ZU ANFANG (*Ger.*) Rather more flowing, than at the beginning.

ETWAS GESCHWIND (*Ger.*) Rather quicker.

ETWAS LANGSAMER (*Ger.*) A little slower.

ETWAS RALLENT (*Ger.*) Becoming gradually a little slower.

ETWAS RASCHER (*Ger.*) Rather quicker.

ETWAS SANFTER (*Ger.*) Rather softer.

ETWAS SCHNELL (*Ger.*) Rather quick.

ETWAS ZÖGERND UND SEHR RUHIG (*Ger.*) Somewhat retarding and very tranquil.

EUFONÍA (*It.*) Euphony.

EUFÓNICO (*It.*) Harmonious, well-sounding.

Euphone — Expressivo

EUPHONE (*Fr.*) A reed stop in an organ, of 16 feet scale this stop is generally a *free* reed.

EUPHONIE (*Fr.*) Euphony.

EUPHONY (*Gr.*) Sweetness of tone, agreeable sounds.

EUPHONIOUS. Sweetly sounding.

EUPHONIUM. A brass wind-instrument of modern invention, used in military bands.

EURYTHMY. Harmony: regular and symmetrical measure.

EUTHIA (*Gr.*) With the Greeks, a regularly ascending succession of sounds.

EUTIMÍA (*It.*) Alacrity, vivacity.

ÉVEILLÉ (*Fr.*) Lively, gay, sprightly.

EVERSÍO (*It.*) Reversing the parts.

EVIRÁTI (*It.*) Men with soprano voices, who formerly took the treble parts both in the church and the theatre, but are not nearly, if not quite, extinct.

EVOÈ (*It.*) An acclamation to Bacchus.

EVOLUTIO (*Lat.*) Inversion: referring to the fugal parts, or imitations, in double counterpoint.

EXABRUPTO (*Lat.*) Suddenly, abruptly, without preparation.

EXACTEMENT (*Fr.*) Exactly; with precision.

EXALTATION (*Fr.*) In an exalted, and dignified manner.

EXALTÉ (*Fr.*) Exalted; inspired; raised up.

EXÉCUTANT (*Fr.*) A performer, either vocal or instrumental.

EXÉCUTER (*Fr.*) To perform, to execute, either vocally or instrumentally.

EXECUTION. Dexterity, and skill, either vocal or manual: agility in performance.

EXEQULÆ (*Lat.*) Dirge.

EXEQUIEN (*Ger.*) Masses for the dead.

EXERCITIUM (*Ger.*) An exercise.

EXERCITIEN (*Ger. pl.*) Exercises.

EXERCIZI. See ESERCIZJ.

EXIT (*Lat.*) A word set in the margin of operas, &c., to mark the time when the actor is to leave the stage.

EXPIRANT PEU À PEU (*Fr.*) Gradually dying away.

EXPRESSIF (*Fr.*) Expressive.

EXPRESSION. Observing the various modifications of *piáno*, and *fórte*, *legáto* and *staccáto*, &c., and imparting to the performance of any composition a peculiar charm arising from the impulse and feeling of the performer.

EXPRESSIVO. See ESPRESSÍVO.

Extempore — Extrêmenent

EXTEMPORE (*Lat.*) Unpremeditated, improvised, on the spur of the moment.

EXTEMPORIREN (*Ger.*) To extemporise.

EXTEMPORISE. To perform extemporaneously, without premeditation.

EXTENDED HARMONY. *See* **DISPERSED HARMONY**.

EXTRANEOUS. Foreign, far-fetched, belonging to a remote key.

EXTRANEOUS MODULATION. A modulation into some remote key, far distant from the original key and its relatives.

EXTRAVAGÁNZA (*It.*) A cadence, or ornament, which is redundant, or in bad taste: an extravagant, eccentric, and irregular composition: *see also* **EXTRAVAGÁNZA**.

EXTREME. A term referring to the most distant parts, as the treble and bass. Relating also to intervals in an augmented state: as, *extreme sharp sixth*, *extreme fifth*, &c. *See* **AUGMENTED INTERVALS**.

EXTREME KEYS. An old term implying those keys which have many sharps, or flats, as B, F-sharp, F-flat, G-flat.

EXTRÊMENENT LENT (*Fr.*) Extremely slow.

F

F, called in France and Italy *Fa*, the fourth note of the modern scale of Guido d'Arezzo.

FABLIAU (*Fr.*) An ancient tale of verse.

FA BÉMOL (*Fr.*) The note F-flat.

FA-BURDEN. An old term applied to several ancient species of counterpoint. It also sometimes means a succession of chords of the sixth, where the interval of the sixth is formed by the extreme parts, and that of the third by the inner part.

FAÇADE D'ORGUE (*Fr.*) The front of an organ case.

FACE (*Fr.*) Appearance; presentation.

FACES D'UN ACCORD (*Fr.*) The various positions of a chord.

FACH (*Ger.*) Ranks: as, *Cornet, fünf-fach*, cornet, five ranks.

FÄCHERFÖRMIGES PEDAL (*Ger.*) A radiation pedal-board, on an organ.

FÁCILE (*Fr. & It.*) Easy.

FACILEMENT (*Fr.*) Easily, with ease, with facility.

FACILITÀ (*It.*) / **FACILITÉ** (*Fr.*) Facility: facilitated: an easier arrangement or adaptation.

FACKEL-TANZ (*Ger.*) Dance with flambeaux.

FACILMÉNTE (*It.*) With ease, easily.

FACTEUR D'ORGUE (*Fr.*) An organ-builder.

FACTURE (*Fr.*) The composition, or workmanship, of a piece of music.

FACTURE D'ORGUES (*Fr.*) Dimensions, or scale, of the pipes of an organ.

FA DIÈSE MAJEUR (*Fr.*) The key of F-sharp major.

FA DIÈSE MINEUR (*Fr.*) The key of F-sharp minor.

FADING. An old Irish dance; the refrain, or burden of a song.

FAGGIÓLO (*It.*) The *fláuto píccolo*, or *petite flûte à bec*: the flageolet.

FAGOTT (*Ger.*) A bassoon.

FAGOTTÍNO (*It.*) A small bassoon.

FAGOTTIST (*Ger.*) / **FAGOTTÍSTA** (*It.*) A performer on the bassoon.

FAGÓTTO (*It.*) A bassoon: also, an organ stop: *see* BASSOON.

FAGOTTÓNE (*It.*) A double bassoon.

Faggotzug — Fanfare

FAGGOTZUG (*It.*) An organ reed stop.

FAHNEN-MARSCH (*Ger.*) The march, or tune, which is played when the colours are lodged.

FAIBLE (*Fr.*) Feeble, weak.

FAIRE DES FREDONS (*Fr.*) To run a division, to trill, or quaver.

FAIRE RESSORTIR LE CHANT (*Fr.*) Bring out the melody.

FAITES BIEN SENTIR LA MÉLODIE (*Fr.*) Play the melody very distinctly.

FA LA. The burden, chorus, or refrain, of many old songs, &c.

FALÓTICO (*It.*) Fantastical, whimsical.

FALSA (*Lat. & It.*) False.

FALSCH (*Ger.*) False, wrong: *falsch singen*, to sing out of tune.

FALSE CADENCE. An imperfect, or interrupted cadence: a cadence in which the chord of the dominant is not followed by that of the tonic, but by some other chord, such as the sub-mediant, or sixth degree of the scale, &c.: *see also* **INTERRUPTED CADENCE**.

FALSE FIFTH. An old term for an imperfect, or diminished fifth: a fifth containing only *six* semitones, as C, G-flat.

FALSE RELATION. When a note which has occurred in one chord, is found chromatically altered in the following chord, but in a *different part*.

FALSE STRING. A bad violin string, giving faulty notes.

FALSETT (*Ger.*)
FALSÉTTO (*It.*) Head-voice: *feigned voice*: certain notes in a man's voice which are above its natural compass, and which con only be produced in an artificial, or feigned tone: called also *vóce di tésta*.

FALSETTSTIMME (*Ger.*) A *falsétto* voice.

FÁSO BORDÓNE (*It.*) *See* **FA-BURDEN**.

FA MAJEURE
FA MAJOR (*Fr.*) The key of F major.

FANÁTICO (*It.*) A fanatic, or passionate admirer: *un fanático per la música*, an ardent lover of music.

FANCIES. A term applied by old composers to their lighter compositions.

FANDÁNGO (*Sp.*) An expressive lively Spanish national dance in $\frac{3}{4}$ time, generally accompanied with castanets, and having a strong emphasis on the second beat in each bar.

FANDANGUÉRO (*Sp.*) One who is skilled in dancing the *fandángo*: also, one who is fond of festive entertainments.

FANFÁRA (*It.*)
FANFARE (*Fr.*) A trumpet tune, a flourish of trumpets.

FANTAISIE (*Fr.*)
FANTASÍA (*It.*)
FANTASIE (*Ger.*) — Fancy, imagination, caprice: a species of music in which the composer gives free scope to his ideas, without regard to those regular, systematic, and symmetrical forms, which govern other compositions.

FANTASIOSAMÉNTE (*It.*) Fantastically, capriciously.

FANTASIÓSO (*It.*) Fantastic, capricious.

FANTASIREN (*Ger.*) To improvise, to play extemporaneously.

FANTASTICAMÉNTE (*It.*) In a fantastic style.

FANTÁSTICO (*It.*)
FANTASTIQUE (*Fr.*)
FANTASTISCH (*Ger.*) — Fantastical, whimsical, capricious, in relation to style, form, modulation, &c.

FARANDÓLA (*It.*)
FARANDOLE (*Fr.*)
FARANDOULE (*Fr.*) — A lively dance, in $\frac{6}{8}$ time, peculiar to Provence.

FAR FIÁSCO (*It.*) To fail, to make no impression, to displease the public.

FAR FURÓRE (*It.*) To produce enthusiastic admiration.

FARNETICAMÉNTO (*It.*) Frenzy, madness.

FÁRSA IN MÚSICA (*It.*) Musical farce, a species of little comic opera in one act.

FÁSCIA (*It.*) A tie or a bind.

FÁSCIE (*It. pl.*) The sides, or hoops, of a violin, viola, &c.

FAST DASSELBE TEMPO (*Ger.*) Almost the same speed.

FASTOSAMÉNTE (*It.*) Pompously, proudly.

FASTÓSO (*It.*) Proud, stately, in a lofty and pompous style.

FATTÚRA (*It.*) See FACTURE.

FAUSSE (*Fr.*) False.

FAUSSE CORDE (*Fr.*) A false string, out of tune.

FAUSSE QUINTE (*Fr.*) A diminished fifth.

FAUSSET (*Fr.*) A falsetto, feigned voice: *see* FALSÉTTO.

FAUX (*Fr.*) False, untrue: *chanter faux*, to sing out of tune.

FAUX ACCORD (*Fr.*) A dissonance.

FAUX BOURDON (*Fr.*) See FA-BURDEN.

F CLEF. The bass clef, 𝄢.

F DUR (*Ger.*) The key if F major.

FEATHERING. A term sometimes applied to a particularly delicate, and lightly detached manner of bowing certain rapid passages on the violin.

FEDER-BRET (*Ger.*) The spring-board of an organ.

Federclavier — Férvido

FEDERCLAVIER \
FEDERKLAVIER } (*Ger.*) A *spinet*.

FÉERIE (*Fr.*) A fair opera or play.

FEIER (*Ger.*) Festival, celebration, solemnity.

FEIER-GESANG (*Ger.*) Solemn hymn, anthem.

FEIERLICH (*Ger.*) Solemn, festive: solemnly.

FEIERLICHKEIT (*Ger.*) Solemnity, pomp.

FEIGNED-VOICE. See FALSÉTTO.

FEILEN (*Ger.*) To tough-up, polish, refine.

FEIN (*Ger.*) *Fine*: refined, delicate.

FELD-FLÖTE (*Ger.*) A fife; or rustic flute.

FELD-MUSIK (*Ger.*) Military music.

FELD-PFEIFE (*Ger.*) A *rustic pipe*; *fláuto travérso*.

FELD-STÜCK (*Ger.*) A military signal or call.

FELD-TONE (*Ger.*) The tone, or key-note, of the trumpet, and other military wind-instruments.

FELD-TROMPETE (*Ger.*) Military trumpet.

FÉMA (*It.*) Firm, resolute, steady.

FERMAMÉNTE (*It.*) Firmly, steadily.

FERMÁTA (*It.*) \
FERMATE (*Ger.*) } A pause, ⌢.

FERMÁTE \
FERMÁTO } (*It.*) Firmly, steadily, resolutely.

FERMEMENT (*Fr.*) Firmly, resolutely.

FERMETÉ (*Fr.*) \
FERMÉZZA (*It.*) } Firmness, resolution, steadiness.

FÉRMO (*It.*) Firm, resolute, steady: *cánto férmo*, the plain-chant.

FERNE (*Ger.*) Distance.

FERN-WERK (*Ger.*) Distant, or remote-work: a term applied to a particular row of keys in German organs.

FERÓCHE \
FEROCEMÉNTE } (*It.*) Fierce, resolute, bold: with a rough, ferocious expression.

FEROCITÀ (*It.*) Fierceness, boldness.

FERTIG (*Ger.*) Quick, nimble, dexterous: quickly.

FERTIGKEIT (*Ger.*) Quickness, dexterity, facility.

FERVEMMENT (*Fr.*) Fervently, vehemently.

FERVÉNTE (*It.*) Fervent, vehement.

FERVENTEMÉNTE \
FERVIDAMÉNTE } (*It.*) Fervently, vehemently.

FÉRVIDO (*It.*) Fervent, vehement.

FERÓRE (*It.*) Fervour.

FES (*Ger.*) The note F-flat.

FEST (*Ger.*) Feast, festival: also, firm, steadily.

FESTE
FESTIGKEIT | (*Ger.*) Firmness, steadiness.

FESTIGLICH (*Ger.*) Firmly, steadily.

FESTIVAMÉNTE (*It.*) Gaily, brilliantly.

FESTIVITÀ (*It.*) Festivity, gaiety.

FESTÍVO (*It.*) Merry, cheerful, gay.

FESTLICH (*Ger.*) Festive, festival, solemn.

FESTLICHKEIT (*Ger.*) Festivity, solemnity.

FESTLIED (*Ger.*) A festal song.

FESTÓSO (*It.*) Merry, cheerful, gay.

FEST-OVERTURE (*Ger.*) Festival overture: an overture in a vigorous, brilliant, style.

FESTZEIT (*Ger.*) Festival day.

FEUER (*Ger.*) Fire, ardour, spirit, passion.

FEURIG (*Ger.*) Fiery, ardent, passionate, brisk.

FEYER (*Ger.*) Festival, celebration.

F F, principalménte il básso (*It.*) Very loud, particularly the bass.

FIÁCCA
FIÁCCO | (*It.*) Feeble, weak, languishing, faint, speaking of the tone.

FIÁSCO (*It.*) A failure: as to intonation, &c.

FIÁTO (*It.*) The breath: the voice.

FICTA
FICTUM | (*Lat.*) False; feigned.

FIDDLE. A common name for the violin.

FIDDLER. A violin player, a violinist.

FIDICINAL (*Lat.*) Of the fiddle, or violin species.

FIDÚCIA (*It.*) Confidence.

FIEDEL (*Ger.*) Fiddle, violin.

FIEDEL-BOGEN (*Ger.*) Fiddle-stick, violin bow.

FIEDELN (*Ger.*) To play upon the fiddle, to fiddle, to scrape.

FIEDLER (*Ger.*) Contemptuous term for a fiddler, gut scraper.

FIEL. An old name for the fiddle, or violin.

FIER (*Fr.*) Proud, lofty, fierce.

FIERAMÉNTE (*It.*) Fiercely, boldly, vehemently.

FIÈRE (*Fr.*) Proud, lofty, fierce.

FIÈREMENT (*Fr.*) In a lofty, fierce manner.

FIÉRO (*It.*) Bold, energetic, lively, spirited.

Fierté — Finger

FIERTÉ (*Fr.*) Fierceness, stateliness.

FIFE. A small, shrill-toned instrument, of the flute species: only used in military music.

FIFER. One who plays the fife.

FÍFFARO (*It.*) A fife: *see* PÍFFERO.

FIFRE (*Fr.*) A fife: also, a fifer: the name is also applied to one of the stops in a harmonium.

FIFTEENTH. A double octave, an interval of two octaves: also, the name of an organ stop, tuned two octaves above the diapasons.

FIFTH. An interval containing seven semitones: this is called a *perfect* fifth: the imperfect fifth contains only six semitones: the augmented fifth contains eight semitones: also, an organ stop, tuned a fifth above the diapasons.

FIGUR (*Ger.*) A musical figure, phrase, or idea.

FIGURA (*Lat.*) A *figure*; a note in old music.

FIGURAL-GESANG (*Ger.*) | Varied, and ornamented chant, as
FIGURAL-GESÄNGE (*Ger. pl.*) | opposed to plain-chant.

FIGURANTE (*Fr.*) An opera dancer, a figure dancer.

FIGURÁTO (*It.*) | Figured, florid, embellished: *see* BÁSSO FIGURÁTO,
FIGURÉ (*Fr.*) | and CÁNTO FIGURÁTO.

FIGURED BASS. A bass with figures placed over or under the notes, to indicate the harmony.

FILÁR LA VÓCE (*It.*) To spin out, to prolong the tone, gradually augmenting and diminishing the sound of the voice.

FILARMÓNICO (*It.*) Philharmonic, music-loving.

FILER LE SON (*Fr.*) See FILÁR LA VÓCE.

FILET DE VOIX (*Fr.*) A very thin voice.

FILPEN (*Ger.*) See FISTULIREN.

FILUM (*Lat.*) The *stem* of a note.

FIN (*Fr.*) The end, the conclusion.

FINAL. The name given to the *first* sound, or note, in each of the ancient Greek, or ecclesiastical modes, that being the note with which all the Gregorian antiphones, responses, &c., terminated: *see* GREGORIAN MODES.

FINÁLE (*It.*) Final, concluding: the last piece of any act of an opera, or a concert: or the last movement of a sonata, or symphony, &c.

FÍN À QUI (*It.*) To this place.

FÍNE (*It.*) The end, the termination.

FINGER-BRETT (*Ger.*)) Fingerboard; the place on a violin, guitar, &c. where the fingers are placed, to shorten the strings.

FINGER-LEITER (*Ger.*) Finger-guides.

FINGER-SATZ (*Ger.*) Fingering.

FINGER-WECHSEL (*Ger.*) *Finger change*: the change of finger on the same note or key.

FINIMÉNTO (*It.*) Conclusion, end.

FINÍRE IL TUÓNO (*It.*) *See* MÉSSA DI VÓCE.

FINÍTA (*It.*) Finished, ended, concluded.

FINITE CANON. A canon which is not repeated.

FINÍTO (*It.*) Finished, ended, concluded.

FÍNO (*It.*) Up to, as far as, till, until.

FÍN QUÌ (*It.*) To this point.

FÍNTO (*It.*) Feigned, false, interrupted, in respect to cadences: a feint, or deceptive close.

FIÓCA (*It.*) Hoarse, faint, feeble: *vóce fióca*, a faint voice.

FIOCHÉZZA (*It.*) Hoarseness.

FIÓCO (*It.*) *See* FIÓCA.

FIÓRE (*It.*) A flower, or blossom: ornate.

FIOREGGIANTE (*It.*) Too ornate: tricked out with roulades, cadences, &c.

FIORÉTTI (*It.*) Little graces or ornaments, in vocal music.

FIORISCÉNTE | (*It.*) Flourishing, florid, abounding with ornaments.
FIORÍTO

FIORITÚRE | (*It.*) Embellishments and graces in singing: divisions
FIORITÚRI | of rapid notes.

FIÓTOLA (*It.*) Flute.

FIS (*Ger.*) The note F-sharp.

FIS DUR (*Ger.*) The key of F-sharp major.

FIS FIS (*Ger.*) The note F-double-sharp.

FIS MOLL (*Ger.*) The key of F-sharp minor.

FISTEL | (*Ger.*) Feigned voice, falsetto.
FISTELSTIMME

FISTOLA | (*Lat.*) A pipe, Pan's pipe, pitch-pipe, flute.
FISTULA

FISTULA GERMANICA (*Lat.*) The German flute.

FISTULA PANIS | (*Lat.*) The Pandean-pipes, the shepherd's
FISTULA PASTORALIS | pipe.

FISTULIREN (*Ger.*) To sing in a feigned voice; to over blow an organ pipe.

FITHELE. The ancient name of the violin or fiddle.

FLACH-FLÖTE (*Ger.*) *Shallow-flute*: flageolet: also, an organ stop or rather thin tone.

FLAGEOLET (*Fr. & Ger.*) An instrument resembling a small hautboy, but blown through a small ivory tube: the tone is agreeable, but very

Flageolet — Flessibilità

weak and fluty. Also, an organ stop of two feet scale, and wood pipes: the tone is smaller and sharper than that of the piccolo stop.

FLAGEOLET TONES. Those produced on instruments of the violin species, by drawing the bow very lightly over the strings, the fingers only just touching them: *see* HARMONICS.

FLAGIOLÉTTA. *See* FLAGEOLET.

FLASCHINETT (*Ger.*) The flageolet.

FLAT. A character which lowers a note one semitone, ♭.

FLATTER LA CORDE (*Fr.*) To play the violin, &c., in a soft, expressive manner.

FLAUTA AMABILIS (*Lat.*) *See* FLÁUTO AMÁBILE.

FLAUT À BECQ. *See* FLÛTE À BEC.

FLAUTÁNDO | (*It.*) Flute-like tone: the flageolet-tones, or harmon-
FLAUTÁTO | ics, on the violin, which are obtained by lightly touching the strings at certain points, with the fingers of the left hand.

FLAUTÍNA | (*It.*) A small flute, an octave flute: a *píccolo*, or small
FLAUTÍNO | flute: *see also* FLAUTÁNDO, *and* PÍCCOLO.

FLAUTÍSTA (*It.*) A performer on the flute.

FLÁUTO (*It.*) A flute.

FLÁUTO AMÁBILE (*It.*) The name of an organ stop, of soft and delicate tone.

FLÁUTO AMORÓSO (*It.*) A 4 feet organ stop of delicate tone.

FLÁUTO DI PAN (*It.*) *Pan's flute:* an organ stop of small size.

FLÁUTO DÓLCE (*It.*) An organ stop of a tranquil and agreeable flute-like tone.

FLAUTO DORIS. | *See* FLÁUTO DÓLCE, *and* FLÛTE DOUCE.
FLAUTO DOUCE. |

FLÁUTO GRÁVE (*It.*) An organ stop of 8 feet tone.

FLAUTÓNE (*It.*) The bass flute, not in use: the name is also applied to a 16 feet pedal stop in an organ, of soft tone.

FLÁUTO PÍCCOLO (*It.*) An octave flute, a small flute of very shrill tone: also, a flageolet.

FLÁUTO TRAVÉRSO (*It.*) The *transverse flute*, thus named because it is held *across*, and blown at the side, contrary to the *flûte à bec*: it is also often called the German flute. The name is also applied to an organ stop, the pipes of which are cylindrical, of pear-tree wood, and sounding their octave, or harmonic, in the treble: *see* FLUTE.

FLÉBILE (*It.*) Mourning, doleful, sad.

FLEBILMÉNTE (*It.*) Dolefully, sadly, mournfully.

FLESSÍBILE (*It.*) Flexible, pliant.

FLESSIBILITÀ (*It.*) Flexibility of voice, or finger.

Flickoper — Flûte à bec

FLICKOPER (*Ger.*) See PASTICCIO.
FLICORNO (*It.*) See FLÜGEL-HORN.
F-LÖCHER (*Ger.*) The *f* holes, or sounds holes, of a violin, &c.
FLON-FLON (*Fr.*) *Bad music, trash*: also, the burden of certain old vaudevilles. It is now a contemptuous term for any air resembling them in style.
FLORID. Ornamental, figured, embellished.
FLÖTE (*Ger.*) Flute.
FLÖTEN (*Ger.*) To play upon flute.
FLÖTEN-BEGLEITUNG (*Ger.*) Flute accompaniment.
FLÖTEN-BLÄSSER (*Ger.*) Flute-player.
FLÖTE TRAVERSO (*Ger.*) The German flute: also, an organ stop: *see* FLÁUTO TRAVÉRSO.
FLÖTIST (*Ger.*) A flute-player.
FLÜCHTIG (*Ger.*) Lightly, fleetly.
FLÜCHTIGKEIT (*Ger.*) Lightness, fleetness.
FLUGBLATT (*Ger.*) A fugitive piece.
FLÜGEL (*Ger.*) A harpsichord.
FLÜGEL-PIANOFORTE (*Ger.*) Grand pianoforte, in the form of a harpsichord.
FLÜSIG (*Fr.*) Fluid; flowing evenly.
FLUTE. A wind-instrument, generally made of wood, though sometimes of metal. The compass extends from middle C to the third C above, three octaves, with semitones. Formerly the flute was very imperfect in many respects, but since the improvements introduced by Boëhm and others, the instrument is as complete, and the intonation as true and equal, and as sonorous as can be desired. It is often called the German flute, though the well-known antique statute of the piping faun seems to be proof that it is not of German invention: and in the tessellated pavement of a temple of Fortuna Virilis, erected by Sylla, at Rome, a young man was represented playing on a traverse pipe, with an aperture to receive his breath, exactly corresponding with the German flute.

There was also another flute, of a pastoral kind, which was blown at the end, or beak, (like a clarinet,) and called the English flute. This is now obsolete. *See* FLÁUTO TRAVÉRSO, *and* FLÛTE À BEC.

FLUTE. An organ stop of the diapason species, the tone of which resembles that of the flute.
FLÛTE (*Fr.*) A flute: see that word.
FLÛTE À BEC (*Fr.*) *Flute with a beak:* the old English flute, with a lip or *beak:* it was held long-ways from the lips, and blown at the end,

Flûte à cheminée — Folâtre

like a clarinet: also, the name of an organ stop: *see also* FLÛTE DOUCE.

FLÛTE À CHEMINÉE (*Fr.*) *See* ROHR-FLÖTE.

FLÛTE ALLEMANDE (*Fr.*) The German flute.

FLÛTE À PAVILLON (*Fr.*) An organ stop, of French invention, with a powerful tone: in England it is sometimes called the 'Bell Diapason.'

FLUTE-BASS. *See* Bass-flute.

FLÛTE CONIQUE (*Fr.*) Conical flute: an organ stop.

FLÛTE COUVERTE (*Fr.*) An organ flute stop of 8 feet pitch, of a liquid and brilliant tone.

FLUTED. A term applied to the upper notes of a soprano voice, when they are of a thin and flute-like tone.

FLÛTE D'AMOUR (*Fr.*) A flute, the compass of which is a minor third below that of the German flute: the name is also applied to an organ stop of 8 or 4 feet scale.

FLÛTE D'ANGLETERRE (*Fr.*) English flute; the *flageolet* or *flûte à bec*.

FLÛTE DESSUS (*Fr.*) Treble flute.

FLÛTE DOUCE (*Fr.*) *Soft flute:* the *flûte à bec:* there were four kinds, the treble, alto, tenor, and bass.

FLÛTE DU POITOU (*Fr.*) The *bagpipe*, or *cornamúsa*.

FLÛTÉE (*Fr.*) Soft, sweet: *voix flûtée*, a soft, sweet voice.

FLÛTE HARMONIQUE (*Fr.*) *See* HARMONIC FLUTE.

FLÛTE OCTAVIANTE (*Fr.*) Octave flute, an organ stop.

FLÛTE OUVERTE (*Fr.*) An organ stop, of the diapason species.

FLÛTER (*Fr.*) To play the flute.

FLÛTE TRAVERSIÈRE (*Fr.*) The traverse, or German flute.

FLÛTEUR (*Fr.*) A flute player.

FLUTTUAN. An organ stop, of a horn-like tone.

FLYING CADENCE. *See* FALSE CADENCE.

F MOLL (*Ger.*) The key of F minor.

FÓCO (*It.*) Fire, ardour, vehemence.

FOCOSAMÉNTE (*It.*) Ardently, vehemently.

FOCOSÍSSIMO (*It.*) Very ardently, much passion.

FOCÓSO (*It.*) Fiery, animated, vehement.

FOGLIÉTTO (*It.*) Copy of the first violin part, in which the *sólo* passages of the other instruments, and the voice parts, are indicated, for the use of the leader; or for the conductor, in the absence of a full score.

FOIS (*Fr.*) Time: *première fois*, the first time; *deuxieme fois*, the second time.

FOLÂTRE (*Fr.*) Playful, wild, frolicsome.

Folge — Franchise

FOLGE (*Ger.*) Sequence, consecution.

FOLÍA (*Sp.*) A species of Spanish dance.

FONDAMENTÁLE (*Fr. & It.*) Fundamental: fundamental bass.

FONDAMÉNTO (*It.*) The fundamental bass: the roots of the harmony.

FOND D'ORGUE (*Fr.*) The most important stop in an organ, called in England the open diapason, 8 feet scale. In Germany this is called principal 8 feet.

FOOT. A certain number of syllables, constituting a distinct part of a verse: also, in very old English music it was a kind of ground, or drone accompaniment, to a song, which was sustained by another singer: *see also* PES.

FORLÁNA (*It.*) \
FORLANE (*Fr.*) A lively Venetian dance in $\frac{6}{8}$ time.

FORMÁRE IL TUÓNO (*It.*) See MÉSSA DI VÓCE.

FORT (*Fr.*) \
FÓRTE (*It.*) Loud, strong.

FORTEMÉNTE (*It.*) Loudly, stoutly, vigorously, with force.

FORTÉZZA (*It.*) Force, power, rigour.

FÓRTE-PIÁNO (*It. Fr. & Ger.*) The piano-forte: thus called on account of its capability of modifying the intensity of the sounds.

FÓRTE POSSÍBILE (*It.*) As loud as possible.

FORTFAHREND (*Ger.*) Resuming, continuing.

FORTÍSSIMO (*It.*) Very loud, vary vigorous.

FORTSCHREITEN (*Ger.*) To progress.

FORTSETZUNG (*Ger.*) A continuation: further development.

FORTSINGEN (*Ger.*) To proceed with a song, to continue singing.

FÓRZA (*It.*) Force, strength, power.

FORZÁNDO \
FORZÁTO (*It.*) *Forced:* laying a stress upon *one* note, or chord: sometimes marked $\wedge$, $\vee$, $>$.

FOUGEUX (*Fr.*) Ardent, impetuous.

FOURCHETTE TONIQUE (*Fr.*) A tuning fork.

FOURLANE (*Fr.*) See FORLÁNA.

FOURNITURE (*Fr.*) A mixture stop, on organs, consisting of several ranks of pipes.

FOURTH. An interval comprising five semitones.

FOURTH FLUTE. A flute sounding a fourth higher than the concert flute.

FRANÇAISE (*Fr.*) A graceful dance, in $\frac{3}{4}$ time.

FRANCAMÉNTE (*It.*) With freedom; boldly.

FRANCHÉZZA (*It.*) \
FRANCHISE (*Fr.*) Freedom, confidence, boldness.

FRANÇOISE (*Fr.*)
FRANZÉSE (*It.*) French: in the French style.
FRANZÖSISCH (*Ger.*)

FRANZTON (*Ger.*) An intonation below that of the received concert pitch.

FRAPPÉ (*Fr.*) *Stamping, striking:* a particular manner of beating time: or striking notes with force.

FRAPPER (*Fr.*) To beat the time: to strike.

FRASÈ (*It.*) To one's self; aside.

FRÁSE (*It.*) A phrase.

FRÁSI (*It.*) Phrases, short musical sentences.

FRAUENCHOR (*Ger.*) A female chorus.

FREDDAMÉNTE (*It.*) Coldly, frigidly.

FREDDÉZZA (*It.*) Coldness, frigidity, heaviness.

FRÉDDO (*It.*) Cold, frigid, devoid of sentiment.

FREDON (*Fr.*) Trilling, quavering: a flourish, or other extemporaneous ornament: a roulade with a shake upon each note.

FREDONNER (*Fr.*) To trill, to quaver, to shake: also, to hum, or sing low.

FREE-MEN'S SONGS. Little compositions for three or four voices, a sort of *roundelay,* or country ballad, in use about 1600.

FREE-REED. A reed stop in an organ, in which the tongue, instead of striking on the edges of the reed, is impelled into the opening, and its rapid vibratory motion to and fro produces the sound. The tone of a *free* reed is particularly smooth and free from rattling, but is not usually so strong as that of a *striking* reed. The vibrators in a harmonium are of the free reed species.

FREGIÁRE (*It.*) To adorn, to embellish.

FREGIÁTO (*It.*) Embellished, ornamented.

FREGIATÚRA (*It.*) An ornament, an embellishment.

FREI (*Ger.*) *See* FREY.

FREMÉNTE (*It.*) Furiously.

FRÉMISSEMENT (*Fr.*) Humming, singing in a low voice.

FRENCH HORN. *See* HORN.

FRENCH SIXTH. One form of the augmented sixth: a chord composed of a major third, extreme fourth, and extreme sixth: as

FRENÉTICO (*It.*) Frantically.

FRESCAMÉNTE
FRÉSCO (*It.*) Freshly, vigorously, lively.

Frétta — Fuga contraria

FRÉTTA (*It.*) Increasing the time: haste, speed: accelerating the movement.

FRETS. Small projecting divisions placed across the finger-boards of guitars, &c., to mark where the notes are to be stopped.

FREUDE (*Ger.*) Joy, joyfulness, joyousness.

FREUDEN-GESANG (*Ger.*) Hymn of rejoicing.

FREUDIG (*Ger.*) Joyously, joyfully.

FREUDIGKEIT (*Ger.*) Joyousness, joyfulness.

FREY (*Ger.*) Free, unrestrained, as to style.

FREYE SCHREIBART (*Ger.*) The free style of composition.

FRICASSÉE (*Fr.*) An 18th century Parisian dance, with pantomimic action.

FRISCH (*Ger.*) Freshly, briskly, lively.

FRÍVOLO (*It.*) Frivolous, trifling, trashy.

FROHBEWEGT (*Ger.*) Gaily animated.

FROHGESANG (*Ger.*) Frolicsome; gay, joyous.

FRÖHLICH (*Ger.*) Joyous, gladsome, cheerful, gay.

FRÖHLICHKEIT (*Ger.*) Joyfulness, gaiety, joyousness.

FROIDEMENT (*Fr.*) Coldly.

FRONTPFEIFEN (*Ger.*) *Front pipes*: the pipes displayed in the case of an organ.

FROSCH (*Ger.*) The lower part, or nut, of a violin bow.

FRÓTTOLA (*It.*) A ballad, a song.

FROTTOLÁRE (*It.*) To compose ballads.

FRÜHER (*Ger.*) Before, earlier.

FRÜHLINGSLIED (*Ger.*) A spring song.

F SCHLÜSSEL (*Ger.*) The F, or bass clef.

FUCHS-SCHWANZ (*Ger.*) *Fox-tail*: in old organs this is a *Nebenzuq* to which is attached a real fox's tail, as a sort at joke: if any over-curious, or ignorant person draws out the register, the *fox-tail* is drawn out with it, into the hand, and there is much trouble to put it in again.

FÚGA (*It.*) *A flight, a chace*: see FUGUE.

FUGA AD QUINTUM (*Lat.*) A fugue on the 5th.

FUGA ÆQUALIS MOTUS (*Lat.*) A fugue in which the answer has a similar tonal progression to that of the subject.

FUGA AUTHENTICA (*Lat.*) A fugue with an *authentic* theme, or subject.

FUGA CANONICA (*Lat.*) A canon.

FUGA COMOSITA (*Lat.*) A fugue which moves by conjunct degrees.

FUGA CONTRARIA (*Lat.*) A fugue in which the answer is always, or for the most part, inverted.

FÚGA DÓPPIA (*It.*) A double fugue: a fugue on two themes, or subjects.

FUGA HOMOPHONA (*Lat.*) A fugue with an answer at the octave.

FUGA IMPROPRIA (*Lat.*) An irregular fugue.

FUGA INÆQUALIS (*Lat.*) A fugue by inversion.

FUGA INCOMPOSITA (*Lat.*) A fugue in which the subject move by skips.

FUGA IN CONTRARIO TEMPORE (*Lat.*) A fugue in broken rhythmical division.

FUGA IN NOMINE (*Lat.*) A free fugue; a fugue by *name* only.

FUGA IRREGULARIS (*Lat.*) An irregular fugue.

FUGA LIBERA (*Lat.*) A free fugue.

FUGA LIGATA (*Lat. & It.*) A fugue developed entirely from the subject and counter subject.

FUGA MIXTA (*Lat.*) A mixed fugue.

FUGA OBLIGATA (*Lat.*) A strict fugue.

FUGA OBSTINATA \
FUGA PERFIDA (*Lat.*) A fugue in which one finger is steadily adhered to.

FUGA PARTIALIS \
FUGA PERIODICA (*Lat.*) The common, or usual form of the fugue, with episodical passages intermixed.

FUGA PERPETUA (*Lat.*) A *canonic* fugue.

FUGA PROPRIA (*Lat.*) A regular fugue, strictly according to rule.

FUGARA (*Lat.*) An organ stop, of the gamba species, of bright and cutting tone, but slow speech.

FUGA RECTA (*Lat.*) *See* FUGA ÆQUALIS MOTUS.

FUGA REGULARIS (*Lat.*) *See* FUGA PROPRIA.

FUGA RETROGRADA (*Lat.*) A fugue in contrary motion.

FÚGA RICERCÁTA (*It.*) An artificial fugue.

FÚGA SCIÓLTA (*It.*) A free fugue, not fettered by the rules, with episodes of light and graceful ideas.

FUGA SOLUTA (*Lat.*) A free fugue.

FUGÁTO (*It.*) In the style of a fugue.

FUGA TOTALIS (*Lat.*) A canon.

FUGE (*Ger.*) A fugue: the term is also applied to the ranks of a mixture stop, in an organ.

FUGE GALANTE (*Ger.*) A free fugue, in the style of chamber music.

FUGGÍRE LA CADÉNZA (*It.*) An interrupted cadence.

FUGHÉTTA (*It.*)
FUGHETTE (*Ger.*) } A short fugue.
FUGHÉTTO (*It.*)

FUGIERTES } (*Ger.*) In the style of a fugue: *fugirt* is also applied to
FUGIRT the ranks of a mixture stop, in an organ.

FUGUE. A composition in the strict style, in which a melody, or subject, is proposed or given in one part, and afterwards imitated and repeated, or answered, by each of the other parts in succession, according to certain rules.

FUGUE RENVERSÉE (*Fr.*) A fugue, the answer in which is made in contrary motion to that of the subject.

FÜHRER (*Ger.*) Conductor, director, leader: also, the subject, or leading theme in a fugue.

FULGÉNTE (*It.*) Effulgent, bright; brilliant.

FULL. For all the voices, or instruments. In cathedral music it means, that the passage is to be sung by both sides of the choir.

FULL ANTHEM. An anthem in four, or more, parts, without verses, or solo passages; to be sung by the whole choir, in chorus: *see* **VERSE ANTHEM**.

FULL CADENCE. *See* **PERFECT CADENCE**.

FÜLL-FLÖTE (*Ger.*) *Filling-flute*: a stopped organ register, of 4 feet tone.

FÜLL-PFEIFE (*Ger.*) A *dummy* organ pipe.

FULL SCORE. A score containing the whole of the vocal and instrumental parts of any composition, written on separate staves, placed under each other.

FULL SERVICE. A service for the whole choir in chorus, without any verse, or solo, parts: *see* **VERSE SERVICE**.

FÜLL-STIMME (*Ger.*) An accessory part.

FUNDAMENTAL BASS. A bass containing the roots of the chords only. This bass is not intended to be played, but merely to serve as a test of the correctness of the harmony.

FUNDAMENTAL TONES. The tonic, dominant, and sub-dominant, of any key or scale.

FUNÈBRE (*Fr.*)
FUNERÁLE (*It.*) } Funereal: mournful.
FUNÉREO (*It.*)

FUNEBREO. *See* **FUNÉREO**.

FÜNF (*Ger.*) Five.

FÜNF-FACH (*Ger.*) *Five-fold*: five ranks: speaking of organ pipes.

FÜNF-STIMMIG (*Ger.*) For five voices, or parts.

FÜNFTE (*Ger.*) A fifth.

Funzióne — Fütterung

Funzióne (*It.*) Function, or ceremony in a church: a festival.
Funióni (*It. pl.*) Oratorios, masses, and other sacred musical performances.
Fuóco (*It.*) Fire, energy, passion, ardour.
Fuocóso (*It.*) Fiery, ardent, impetuous.
Fuoridisè (*It.*) In a dreaming manner; absently.
Für das ganze Werk
Für das volle Werk │ (*Ger.*) For the full organ.
Fureur (*Fr.*) Fury, rage, madness.
Für Harmoniemusik (*Ger.*) For wind instruments.
Fúria (*It.*) Fury, passion, rage, impetuosity.
Furibóndo (*It.*) Mad and furious, extreme vehemence.
Furie (*Fr.*) Fury, passion, impetuosity.
Furieusement (*Fr.*)
Furiosaménte (*It.*) │ Furiously, madly.
Furiosíssimo (*It.*) Very furiously.
Furióso (*It.*) Furious, fierce, vehement.
Furlándo
Furláno │ (*It.*) An antiquated dance.
Furniture. An organ stop, consisting of several ranks of pipes, of very acute pitch.
Furóre (*It.*) Fury, rage, passion, madness.
Fürsich (*Ger.*) Aside.
Für zwei Manuale (*Ger.*) For two manuals: in organ playing.
Fusa (*Lat.*) A quaver.
Fusée (*Fr.*) A very rapid roulade, or passage: a skip, &c.
Fusella (*Lat.*) A demi-semiquaver.
Fuss (*Ger.*) Foot: the lower part of an organ pipe.
Füsse (*Ger. pl.*) Feet: *see* **Fuss**.
Füssig (*Ger.*) Footed: as *8-füssig*, of 8 feet size, or scale.
Fusston (*Ger.*) The *tone, or pitch*: as 8 *Fusston*, a pipe of 8 feet tone: *see* **Diapáson**.
Fütterung (*Ger.*) The *linings* of a violin, &c.

G

G, called in France and Italy *sol*, the fifth note or sound of the modern scale of Guido d'Arezzo.

GABEL (*Ger.*) A folk.

GABELKLAVIER (*Ger.*) A keyboard instrument, with the sound being produced by striking *tuning-folks*.

GABELTON (*Ger.*) *Tuning-folk tone*: generally the A of the tuning-folk.

GAGLIÁRDA (*It.*) A *galliard*: which see.

GAGLIARDAMÉNTE (*It.*) Briskly, vigorously, gaily.

GAGLIÁRDO (*It.*) Spirited, merry, vigorous.

GAI (*Fr.*) Gay, merry, lively.

GAIEMENT | (*Fr.*) Merrily, lively, gaily.
GAÎMENT

GAILLARDE (*Fr.*) Merry, brisk, lively: also, a *galliard*: which see.

GAILLARDEMENT (*Fr.*) Merrily, gaily, briskly.

GAÍTA (*Sp.*) A bagpipe: also, a sort of flute: the name is also given to a street organ.

GAITÉRO (*Sp.*) A player upon the bagpipes.

GÁJA | (*It.*) Gay, merry, lively.
GÁJO

GAJAMÉNTE (*It.*) Merrily, lively, gaily.

GALANT (*Ger.*) Free.

GALÁNTE | (*It.*) Gallantly, boldly, gracefully.
GALANTEMÉNTE

GALANTERIE-FUGUE (*Ger.*) A fugue in the free style.

GALANTEERIEN (*Ger. pl.*) *Fashionable ornaments*: the turns, trills, shakes, slidings, &c., with which the old harpsichord music was embellished.

GALANTERIE-STÜCKE (*Ger. pl.*) Pieces in the free, ornamental style.

GALANT-STYL (*Ger.*) Free style, ideal style.

GALLIARD. A lively old dance, formerly very popular; in $\frac{3}{4}$ time.

GALOP (*Eng.*)
GALOPADE (*Fr.*)
GALOPP (*Ger.*)
GALÓPPO (*It.*) } A quick dance, generally in $\frac{2}{4}$ time.

GALOUBÉ / **GALOUBET** (*Fr.*) A small, ancient kind of flute, with three holes, sometimes to be met with in France.

GÁMBA (*It.*) The *viol di gámba*, or *bass viol*, an old instrument the predecessor of the violoncello, and thus termed because it was held between the knees of the player. It is also the name of an organ stop, of an agreeable, and rather reedy tone.

GAMBA-BASS. A 16 feet organ stop, on the pedals.

GÁMBA MAJOR (*It.*) A name given to the 16 feet organ stop, or double gamba.

GAMBE (*Ger.*) Viol di gamba: bass viol: *see* **GÁMBA**.

GAMBETTE (*Ger.*) A small, or octave gamba stop, in an organ.

GAMBIST. A performer upon the *viol di gamba*.

GÁMMA (*It.*) / **GAMME** (*Fr.*) The gamut, or scale.

GAMME CHROMATIQUE (*Fr.*) The chromatic scale.

GAMME DIATONIQUE (*Fr.*) A diatonic scale.

GAMME MAJEURE MONTANTE (*Fr.*) An ascending major scale.

GAMMES. Exercises on the scales.

GAMUT. The scale, of any key.

GAMUT G. That G which is on the first line of the bass stave.

GANASCIÓNE (*It.*) An Italian lute.

GANG (*Ger.*) Pace, rate of movement or motion.

GANZ (*Ger.*) Whole, perfect, entire, full: also, all, very.

GANZE NOTE / **GANZE TACTNOTE** (*Ger.*) A *whole note*, or semibreve.

GANZE STÄRKE (*Ger.*) Very loud.

GANZE-TON (*Ger.*) A whole tone.

GANZE-WERK (*Ger.*) The full organ.

GANZ LANGSAM (*Ger.*) Very slowly.

GANZ LEISE (*Ger.*) Quite soft.

GANZSCHLUSS (*Ger.*) A final cadence.

GANZ VERHALLEND (*Ger.*) Entirely dying away, very faintly.

GARBATAMÉNTE (*It.*) Gracefully.

GARBÁTO (*It.*) Graceful.

GÁRBO (*It.*) Simplicity, grace, elegance.

GARDER (*Fr.*) To keep, hold.

GARNIR UN VIOLON DE CORDES (*Fr.*) To string a violin.

GARRÍRE (*It.*) To chirp, to sing, to warble like a bird.

GASSENHAUER (*Ger.*) Formerly a popular street song; now applied to a vulgar melody.

GAUCHE (*Fr.*) Left: *main gauche*, the left hand.

GAUDÉNTE (*It.*) Blithe, merry, sprightly.
GAUDENTEMÉNTE (*It.*) Merrily, joyfully.
GAUDIOSO (*It.*) Merry, joyful, blithe.
GAUMENTON (*Ger.*) A throaty, guttural tone.

GAVOT (*Eng.*)
GAVÓTTA (*It.*)
GAVOTTE (*Fr.*) | A lively, but stately, species of dance, in common time, popular in the seventeenth and eighteenth centuries. It consisted of two strains, each commencing, and ending, with a half bar.

GAZOUILLANT (*Fr.*) Chattering, warbling.
G DUR (*Ger.*) The key of G major.
GEBERDENSPEIL (*Ger.*) Pantomime, dumb show.
GEBIETERISCH (*Ger.*) Commanding, peremptory, domineering.
GEBLASE (*Ger.*) Trumpeting, blowing.
GEBLÄSE (*Ger.*) Bellows: apparatus for blowing.
GEBLÜMT (*Ger.*) Ornamented; embellished.
GEBROCHEN (*Ger.*) Broken: see ARPÉGGIO.

GEBROCHENE AKKORDE
GEBROCHENER ACCORD | (*Ger.*) Broken chords, chords played in *arpéggio*.

GEBUNDEN (*Ger.*) Bound, connected, slurred, syncopated: *besonders gebunden*, particularly *legáto*.
GEBUNDENE NOTE (*Ger.*) A tied note, which is to be sustained, and not repeated.
GEBUNDENER STIL (*Ger.*) Style of strictly connected harmony; style of counterpoint.
GEBURTS-LIED (*Ger.*) Birth-day song.

GEDACKT
GEDECKT | (*Ger.*) Stopped, covered with a lid: certain registers of pipes in an organ; as, the stopped diapason, &c.

GEDACT. See GEDACKT.
GEDÄMPFT (*Ger.*) Damped, muffled, muted.
GEDECKTE STIMMEN (*Ger. pl.*) Stops with covered pipes, as the stopped diapason, &c., in an organ.
GEDEHNT (*Ger.*) Prolonged, sustained; slow.
GEDICHT (*Ger.*) Poem, fable, tale, verses.
GEFÄHRTE (*Ger.*) The answer, in a fugue.
GEFALLEN (*Ger.*) To please, agree.
GEFÄLLIG (*Ger.*) Pleasingly, agreeably.
GEFEILTER STRICH (*Ger.*) *Detached stroke*, in violin playing.
GEFIEDEL (*Ger.*) Fiddling, playing on the fiddle.
GEFÜHL (*Ger.*) Feeling, sentiment, expression.
GEGEIGE (*Ger.*) Fiddling.
GEGEN (*Ger.*) Against.

Gegenbewegung — Gelassenheit

GEGENBEWEGUNG (*Ger.*) Contrary motion.

GEGENGESANG (*Ger.*) Antiphonal singing.

GEGENHALL
GEGENSCHALL } (*Ger.*) Resonance, echo, repercussion of sound.

GEGENPUNKT (*Ger.*) Counterpoint.

GEGENSTIMME (*Ger.*) Counter-tenor, or alto, part.

GEGENSTIMMIG (*Ger.*) Discordant, dissonant.

GEGENSUBJECT (*Ger.*) Counter-subject, in a fugue.

GEHALTEN (*Ger.*) Sustained, held on; steady.

GEHAUCHT (*Ger.*) Very soft and light; whispered.

GEHEIMNISVOLL (*Ger.*) Mysterious.

GEHEND (*Ger.*) Going, moving easily; of the same meaning as *andánte*.

GEHÖRIG (*Ger.*) Suitable, convenient.

GEIGE (*Ger.*) The violin: the fiddle.

GEIGEN (*Ger.*) To play upon the violin; to fiddle.

GEIGEN-BLATT (*Ger.*) *Fingerboard* on which the fingers are placed to shorten the strings, on a violin.

GEIGEN-BOGEN (*Ger.*) Violin bow: fiddle-stick.

GEIGEN-DIAPASON. Violin diapason: *See* **GEIGEN PRINCIPAL.**

GEIGEN-FUTTER (*Ger.*) Case for a violin.

GEIGEN-HALS (*Ger.*) The neck of a violin.

GEIGEN-HARZ (*Ger.*) Colophony, Spanish resin, hard resin.

GEIGEN-HOLZ (*Ger.*) Fiddle wood: the wood used in making violins.

GEIGEN-MACHER (*Ger.*) Violin maker.

GEIGEN-PRINCIPAL (*Ger.*) Violin, or crisp-toned, diapason, a German organ stop with a pungent tone, very like that of the gamba, but a fuller quality.

GEIGEN-SAITE (*Ger.*) Violin string.

GEIGEN-SATTEL
GEIGEN-STEG } (*Ger.*) The bridge of a violin.

GEIGEN-WIRBEL (*Ger.*) A peg, in a violin.

GEIGER (*Ger.*) Violin player, fiddler.

GEIST (*Ger.*) Soul, spirit; genius, intellect.

GEISTREICH
GEISTVOLL } (*Ger.*) Spirited, full of life and spirit.

GEKLINGEL (*Ger.*) Tinkling.

GEKNEIPT (*Ger.*) *See* **PIZZICÁTO.**

GELASSEN (*Ger.*) Calmly, quietly, tranquilly.

GELASSENHEIT (*Ger.*) Calmness, tranquillity.

GELAUFE   (*Ger.*) Running passages, scale passages, rapid
GELAUFEN   movements.

GELÄUFIG (*Ger.*) Easy, fluent, rapid.

GELÄUFIGKEIT (*Ger.*) Fluency, easiness, volubility.

GELÄUT (*Ger.*) Ringing of bells, peal of bells.

GELINDE (*Ger.*) Softly, gently, smoothly.

GELINDIGKEIT (*Ger.*) Softness, smoothness, sweetness, gentleness.

GELLEN (*Ger.*) To sound loudly.

GELLFLÖTE (*Ger.*) Clarionet.

GELTUNG (*Ger.*) Value, or duration, of a note or rest.

GEMÄCHLICH   (*Ger.*) Softly, slowly, easily.
GEMACHSAM

GEMÄHLIG (*Ger.*) Gradually, by degrees.

GEMÄSSIGT (*Ger.*) See MODERÁTO.

GEMEBÓNDO   (*It.*) Moaning; plaintive, doleful
GEMÉNDO

GEMISCH (*Ger.*) Mixed: mixture, or compound stops, in an organ.

GEMS-HORN (*Ger.*) *Goat's horn, chamois-horn*: an organ stop with conical pipes, more pointed than those of the spitz-flute. The tone is light, but very clear.

GEMS-HORN-QUINT (*Ger.*) An organ stop with conical pipes, sounding a fifth above the foundation stops.

GEMÜTH (*Ger.*) Mind, soul: *mit Gemüth*, with much feeling and expression.

GEMÜTHLICH (*Ger.*) Agreeable, expressive.

GENERA   (*Lat.*) The different methods of dividing the octave; as,
GENUS   by tones and semitones conjointly, called the *diatonic* or natural genus: by semitones only, called the *chromatic* genus: and, theoretically, by quarter-tones alone, which is called the *enharmonic* genus.

GENERAL-BASS (*Ger.*) Thorough-bass, figured bass.

GÉNERE (*It.*) See GENERA.

GENERÓSO (*It.*) Nobly: in a grand and dignified manner.

GENIAL (*Ger.*) Showing genius; talented.

GÉNIE (*Fr.*)   Genius, talent, spirit.
GÉNIO (*It.*)

GENRE (*Fr.*) Style, manner: *see also* GENERA.

GENRE CHROMATIQUE (*Fr.*) The chromatic genus.

GENRE DIATONIQUE (*Fr.*) The diatonic, or natural genus.

GENRE ENHARMONIQUE (*Fr.*) The enharmonic genus.

GENRE EXPRESSIF (*Fr.*) The expressive style.

GENTÍLE (*It.*) Noble, pleasing, graceful, elegant.
GENTILÉZZA (*It.*) Grace, elegance, refinement of style.
GENTILMÉNTE (*It.*) Gently, nobly, gracefully.
GENUS (*Lat.*) See **GENERA**.
GENUS CHROMATICUM (*Lat.*) The chromatic genus or mode.
GENUS DIATONICUM (*Lat.*) The diatonic genus or mode.
GENUS ENHARMONICUM (*Lat.*) The enharmonic genus or mode.
GENUS INFLATILE (*Lat.*) Wind-instruments.
GENUS PERCUSSIBILE (*Lat.*) Instruments of percussion.
GENUS SYNTONUM (*Lat.*) An old term of musical theorists for the *diatonic scale*.
GENUS TENSILE (*Lat.*) Stringed instruments.
GERADE BEWEGUNG (*Ger.*) Similar motion, direct motion.
GERADE TAKTART (*Ger.*) Common time.
GERMON FLUTE. See **FLÁUTO TRAVÉRSO**.
GERMAN SIXTH. A name given to a chord composed of a major third, perfect fifth, and extreme sixth: as
GES (*Ger.*) The note G-flat.
GESANG (*Ger.*) Singing: the art of singing a song, melody, hymn, air.
GESANGARTIG (*Ger.*) In a singing style.
GESANGBUCH (*Ger.*) Song book, hymn book.
GESANG DUR VÖGEL (*Ger.*) Singing of birds.
GESÄNGE (*Ger. pl.*) Songs, hymns.
GESANGREICH (*Ger.*) Very smooth and *cantábile*.
GESANGSWEISE (*Ger.*) In the style or manner of song.
GESANGWEISE (*Ger.*) Melody, tune.
GESÄUSEL (*Ger.*) Murmuring, rustling.
GESCHICK (*Ger.*) Skill, dexterity.
GESCHLECHT (*Ger.*) Genus; mode, species.
GESCHLEIFT (*Ger.*) Slurred; *legáto*.
GESCHLOSSENE LÖCHER (*Ger.*) Closed holes, in flute playing.
GESCHMACK (*Ger.*) Taste.
GESCHWIND (*Ger.*) Quick, rapid.
GESCHWINDIGKEIT (*Ger.*) Swiftness, rapidity, speed.
GESCHWINDMARSCH (*Ger.*) A quick march.
GES DUR (*Ger.*) The key of G-flat major.
GESICHT (*Ger.*) Front, face.
GESINGE (*Ger.*) Constant singing, bad singing.
GESPONNEN (*Ger.*) Spun.

Gesprochen — Giocóndo

Gesprochen (*Ger.*) Spoken.
Gesteigert (*Ger.*) Crescéndo; sforzándo.
Gestopft (*Ger.*) Stopped, in horn playing.
Gestossen (*Ger.*) Struck, hit, touched: *kurz gestossen*, struck detached, staccáto.
Gestrichen (*Ger.*) Stroked; cut.
Getern
Getron } Old names for the *cittern*.
Getragen (*Ger.*) Sustained; sostenúto.
Getrost (*Ger.*) Confidently, resolutely.
Geübtere (*Ger.*) Expert performers.
Gewandt (*Ger.*) Active, nimble, dexterous.
Gewichtig (*Ger.*) Heavily; pesánte.
Gewidmet (*Ger.*) Dedicated to.
Gewirbel (*Ger.*) A roll on the drums.
Gewiss (*Ger.*) Firm, steady, resolute.
Gewissheit (*Ger.*) Firmness, steadiness, resolution.
Gewitter (*Ger.*) Thunderstorm, tempest.
Geworfener Strich (*Ger.*) A light dancing stroke, in violin playing.
Gezogen (*Ger.*) Drawn out, sustained.
G Gamut. That G which is on the first line of the bass stave.
Ghazal. An Arabic melody, with an often returning theme.
Ghijghe. An old name for the fiddle: *see* GEIGE.
Ghiribízzi (*It.*) Unexpected skips, or fantastical passages.
Ghiribizzóso (*It.*) Fantastical, whimsical.
Ghirónda (*It.*) The hurdy-gurdy.
Ghittern. An old name for the *cittern*.
Gicheróso (*It.*) Merry, playful.
Gíga (*It.*)
Gigue (*Fr. & Ger.*) } A jig, a lively species of dance, in $\frac{6}{8}$ or $\frac{12}{8}$ time: the name is supposed to be derived from the German word *Geig*, or *Geige*: the air being peculiarly adapted to instruments of the class: *see* GEIGE.
Gighardo (*It.*) A sort of jig.
Ginglarus. A small Egyptian flute.
Giochévole (*It.*) Merry, sportive, gay.
Giochevolménte
Giocolarménte } (*It.*) Merrily, sportively.
Gióco (*It.*) A joke.
Giocondaménte (*It.*) Merrily, joyfully, cheerfully.
Giocóndo (*It.*) Cheerful, merry, gay.

GIOCOSAMÉNTE
GIOCÓSO | (*It.*) Humorously, sportively, merrily, gaily.

GIÓJA (*It.*) Joy, mirth, gladness.

GIOJÁNTE (*It.*) Blithe, merry, joyful.

GIOJOSAMÉNTE (*It.*) Joyfully, merrily.

GIOJÓSO (*It.*) Joyous, merry.

GIOVIÁLE (*It.*) Jovial, pleasant, gay, merry.

GIOVIALITÀ (*It.*) Gaiety, joviality.

GIRAFFE. A species of ancient *spinet*.

GIRO (*It.*) A *turn*.

GIS (*Ger.*) The note G-sharp.

GIS MOLL (*Ger.*) The key of G-sharp minor.

GITÁNA
GITTÁNA | (*It.*) A Spanish gypsy dance.

GITTERN. A species of *cittern*, but strung with gut strings.

GIUBBILÓSO (*It.*) Jubilant, exulting.

GIUBILAZIÓNE
GIUBILÍO | (*It.*) Jubilation, rejoicing.
GIÚBILO

GIUCANTE
GIUCHEVOLE | *See* GIOJÁNTE.

GIULIVAMÉNTE (*It.*) Joyfully, lively.

GIULIVÍSSIMO (*It.*) Very joyful, very lively.

GIULÍVO (*It.*) Cheerful, merry, gay.

GIUOCÓSO. *See* GIOCÓSO.

GIUSTAMÉNTE (*It.*) Justly, with precision.

GIÚSTO (*It.*) Just, exact: *see* TÉMPO GIÚSTO.

GLAIS (*Fr.*) The passing bell.

GLÄNZEND (*Ger.*) Brilliant, resplendent.

GLAPISSANT (*Fr.*) Shrill, squeaking: *voix glapissante*, a shrill, squeaking voice.

GLATT (*Ger.*) Smooth, even.

GLÄTTE (*Ger.*) Smoothness, evenness.

GLEE. A term originally applied to vocal music of various kinds, The glee, in its present form, first appeared about the middle of the eighteenth century, and is a composition peculiar to England, noting similar being found by any foreign composer of the last century [18th]. It is written for three or more solo voices, without accompaniment, generally in a cheerful style; abounding in melody, and requiring a though knowledge of part-writing of the most refined kind, the melodies moving pretty much together, and not with points of imitation, as in a madrigal, from which it differs in every particular of style and form.

GLEEK. An old word signifying *music*, or *musician*.

GLEICH (*Ger.*) Equal, alike, consonant.

GLEICHKLANG (*Ger.*) Consonance, conformity of sound.

GLEICHMÄSSIG (*Ger.*) Equal, uniform, similar.

GLEICHSAM (*Ger.*) Almost; as it were.

GLEICHSTIMMIG (*Ger.*) Harmonious, accordant.

GLEITEN (*Ger.*) To slide, to glide the finger.

GLI (*It. pl.*) The.

GLIED (*Ger.*) Link: the term is used to express a *chord*: see EINGLIED, ZWEIGLIED.

GLISSADE (*Fr.*) A slip, slipping, sliding the fingers.

GLISSÁNDO (*It.*)
GLISSÁTO (*It.*)
GLISSEMENT (*Fr.*) } Slurred, smooth; in a gliding manner: *see also* GLISSER.

GLISSER (*Fr.*) To glide lightly along the key-board, by turning the nails and drawing them rapidly over the keys.

GLISSICÁNDO
GLISSICÁTO } (*It.*) Slurred, smooth: in a gliding manner: *see also* GLISSER.

GLI STROMÉNTI (*It.*) The instruments.

GLITSCHEN (*Ger.*) To glide the finger: see GLISSER.

GLÖCKCHEN (*Ger.*) A little bell, small bell.

GLOCKE (*Ger.*) A bell.

GLOCKENIST (*Ger.*) Player on the chimes.

GLOCKENKLANG (*Ger.*) Sound of bells.

GLOCKENKLÖPPEL (*Ger.*) Bell clapper.

GLOCKENLÄUTER (*Ger.*) Bell ringer.

GLOCKENSPIEL (*Ger.*) Chimes: a set of bells put in vibration by the mechanism of keys: also, a stop in imitation of bells, in German organs.

GLÖCKLEIN-TON (*Ger.*) An organ stop of very small scale, and wide measure: *see also* GLOCKENSPIEL.

GLORIA (*Lat.*) A principal movement in a Mass.

GLOTTIS (*Gr.*) A kind of reed used by the ancient flute players, which they held between their lips, and blew through in performance.

GLÜHEND (*Ger.*) Glowing, ardent.

G MOLL (*Ger.*) The key of G minor.

GNACCARE. *See* CASTANETS.

GOL. One of the funeral lamentations of the Irish.

GÓLA (*It.*) The throat: also, a guttural voice: *see* VÓCE DI GÓLA.

Gondellied — Graduale

GONDELLIED (*Ger.*)
GONDOLIERA (*It.*) } Gondolier's song: see BARCAROLLE.

GONDOLIN. A species of *zither*.

GONG. An Indian pulsatile instrument, consisting of a large circular plate of bell-metal, which, when struck, produces an exceedingly loud noise.

GORGHÉGGI (*It. pl.*) Rapid divisions, or passages, as exercises for the voice, to acquire facility.

GORGHEGGIAMÉNTO (*It.*) Trilling, quavering.

GORGHEGGIÁRE (*It.*) To trill, to quaver, to shake.

GOSIER (*Fr.*) The throat.

GOTO. A Japanese *dulcimer*.

GOTTESDIENST (*Ger.*) Divine service.

GOÛT (*Fr.*) Taste, style, judgement, skill.

GRAB-GESANG
GRAB-LIED } (*Ger.*) Dirge, funeral song.

GRACES. Ornamental notes and embellishments, either written by the composer, or else spontaneously introduced by the performer. The principal embellishments are the *appoggiatúra*, the *turn*, and the *shake*.

GRACIEUX (*Fr.*) Graceful.

GRÁCILE (*It.*) Thin, weak, small: referring to the tone.

GRAD (*Ger.*) Step, degree: see GRADO.

GRADÁRE (*It.*) To descend, step by step.

GRADATAMÉNTE (*It.*)
GRADATION (*Fr.*) } By degrees, gradually: a gradual increase, or diminution, of speed, or intensity of tone.

GRADAZIÓNE. See GRADUAZIÓNE.

GRADÉVOLE
GRADEVOLMÉNTE } (*It.*) Gracefully, pleasingly.

GRADÍRE (*It.*) To ascend, step by step.

GRADITAMÉNTE (*It.*) In a pleasing manner.

GRADITÍSSIMO (*It.*) Very sweet, most gracefully.

GRADLEITER (*Ger.*) Scale.

GRÁDO (*It.*) A step, a degree: *di grádo* means, that a melody moves by degrees ascending and descending, and not *di sálto*, by skips of greater intervals.

GRÁDO ASCENDÉNTE (*It.*) An ascending degree.

GRÁDO DESCENDÉNTE (*It.*) A descending degree.

GRADUALE (*Lat.*) A gradual: that part of the Roman Catholic service which is sung between the Epistle and the Gospel, and which was anciently sung on the steps of the alter.

GRADUALMÉNTE \
GRADUATAMÉNTE (*It.*) Gradually, by degrees or steps.

GRADUAL MODULATION. Modulation in which some chord is taken before the modulating chord, which may be considered as belonging either to the original key, or to the new key.

GRADUAZIÓNE (*It.*) See GRADATAMÉNTE.

GRADUELLEMENT (*Fr.*) Gradually, by degrees.

GRADWEISE (*Ger.*) By degrees, gradually.

GRAILLEMENT (*Fr.*) A hoarse sound.

GRÁN \
GRÁNDE (*It.*) Great, grand.

GRÁN CÁSSA (*It.*) The great drum.

GRAND-BARRÉ (*Fr.*) In guitar playing this means, laying the first finger of the left hand upon all six strings of the guitar, at once.

GRAND BOURDON. Great, or double bourdon: an organ stop of 32 feet tone, in the pedal.

GRAND CORNET. This name is sometimes given to a reed stop of 16 feet scale on the manuals of an organ.

GRANDE MASSE (*Fr.*) High Mass.

GRANDE MESURE À DEUX TEMPS (*Fr.*) Common time of *two beats* in a bar, marked $\frac{2}{2}$, or sometimes $\frac{4}{4}$ or **C**: see also ÁLLA CAPPÉLLA.

GRANDÉZZA (*It.*) Grandeur, dignity.

GRANDIÓSO (*It.*) Grand, noble, lofty, elevated.

GRANDISONÁNTE (*It.*) Very sonorous, full sounding.

GRAND JEUX (*Fr.*) Full: full organ: all the stops: in organ and harmonium playing.

GRAND ORGUE (*Fr.*) Great organ.

GRÁN GÚSTO (*It.*) Great taste: in a grand style.

GRÁN TAMBÚRO (*It.*) The great drum.

GRANULÁTO (*It.*) *Granular*, disconnected; slightly *staccáto*.

GRÁPPA (*It.*) The brace, or character used to connect two or more staves together.

GRATIAS AGIMUS (*Lat.*) Part of the *Gloria*, in a Mass.

GRATIOSO. See GRAZIÓSO.

GRÁVE (*It.*) Majestical, slow, weighty, grave: a very slow and solemn movement: also, a deep, low pitch, in the scale of sounds.

GRAVECEMBALUM (*Lat.*) An old name for the harpsichord.

GRAVEMENT (*Fr.*)
GRAVEMÉNTE (*It.*) | With gravity, in a dignified and solemn manner.

GRAVE MIXTURE. An organ stop of two ranks, comprising a twelfth and a fifteenth, above the fundamental.

GRAVÉZZA (*It.*) Gravity, solemnity.

GRAVICÉMBALO (*It.*)
GRAVICÉMBOLO (*It.*) | An old name for the harpsichord.

GRAVITÀ (*It.*)
GRAVITÄT (*Ger.*) | Gravity, majesty.
GRAVITÉ (*Fr.*)

GRÁZIA (*It.*)
GRAZIE (*Ger.*) | Grace, elegance.

GRAZIÖS (*Ger.*) Graceful, gracefully.

GRAZIOSAMÉNTE (*It.*) Gracefully, smoothly, agreeably.

GRAZIÓSO (*It.*) Graceful, smooth, elegant.

GREATER SIXTH. A name sometimes given to the major sixth.

GREATER THIRD. A name sometimes given to the major third.

GREAT OCTAVE. The name given in Germany to the notes between [music notation] and C inclusive: these notes are expressed by capital letters, as C.

GREAT ORGAN. In an organ with three rows of keys, this is, usually, the middle row; and where there are four rows, the great organ is the second row from the bottom. It is thus named because, formerly, it contained the greatest number of stops, and also, because the pipes are of a larger scale, and are voiced louder than those in the swell, or choir organ.

GRECO (*It.*) Grecian, Greek.

GREEK MODES. The ancient Greek modes, or scales, were twelve in number: of these, six were *Authentic*, and six *Plagal*. The sounds are supposed to have been somewhat similar to those in the scale of C.

Authentic.

The Dorian	d	e	f	g	A	b	c	d
The Phrygian	e	f	g	a	b	C	d	e
The Lydian	f	g	a	b	C	d	e	f
The Mixolydian	g	a	b	c	D	e	f	g
The Æolian	a	b	c	d	E	f	g	a
The Ionian or Iastian	c	d	e	f	G	a	b	c

The six Plagal modes were formed by taking these a fifth higher, with the exception of the second Plagal mode, which commenced on C (the fifth of B being imperfect). So the Plagal Doric was similar to the Æolian, but the *dominant* of each was different. In the above example the dominant is shown by the capital letter: *see* DOMINANT, *and* GREGORIAN MODES.

GREGORIANISCH (*Ger.*) Gregorian.

GREGORIANISCHER GESANG (*Ger.*) The Gregorian chant.

GREGORIAN MODES \
GREGORIAN TONES Those chant, or melodies, used for the Psalms in the Roman Catholic service, and also in many English churches. They are taken from the ancient Greek modes, and the sounds are supposed to have been somewhat similar to those in the modern natural scale of C.

The 1st, 3rd, 5th, and 7th of these modes were adopted by St. Ambrose, in the fourth century, and in the sixth St. Gregory added the 2nd, 4th, 6th, and 8th. The former are called *Authentic*, the latter *Plagal*.

1st tone	d	e	f	g	A	b	c	d	Authentic
2nd tone	d	e	F	g	a	b	c	d	Plagal
3rd tone	e	f	g	a	b	C	d	e	Authentic
4th tone	e	f	g	A	b	c	d	e	Plagal
5th tone	f	g	a	b	C	d	e	f	Authentic
6th tone	f	g	A	b	c	d	e	f	Plagal
7th tone	g	a	b	c	D	e	f	g	Authentic
8th tone	g	a	b	C	d	e	f	g	Plagal

These eight tones, or modes, are regulated by two sounds, one of which is termed the *Dominant*, or most prevailing sound in the melody; and the other the *Final*, or terminating sound.

In the above example the Dominant is shown by the capital letter: the Final is the same as the first note of each mode: *see also* DOMINANT, *and* FINAL.

There is also another tone called by some *Il tuóno Pellegríno*, or, the Wandering tone; and by others *Tuóno Místo*, or the Mixed tone.

GREGORIÁNO (*It.*) \
GRÉGORIEN (*Fr.*) Gregorian.

GRELL (*Ger.*) Shrill, acute.

GRELLHEIT (*Ger.*) Sharpness, hardness, shrillness.

GRELOTS (*Fr.*) Sleigh bells.

GRIFF (*Ger.*) Fingering; touch, grip, stretch.

GRIFFBRET (*Ger.*) Finger-board of a violin, guitar, &c.

GRILLIG (*Ger.*) Capricious, fanciful.

GRINGOTTER (*Fr.*) To hum.

Grisoller — G-schlüssel

GRISOLLER (*Fr.*) To sing like a lark.
GROB (*Ger.*) Deep, low voice, bass.
GROB-GEDACKT (*Ger.*) Large stopped diapason, of full tone.
GROPPÉTTO. *See* GRUPPÉTTO.
GRÓPPO (*It.*) A group of notes, a rapid vocal passage.
GROS-FA. A name formerly given to old church music in square notes, semibreves, and minims.
GROSSE (*Ger.*) Major, speaking of intervals: also, grand, in respect to style.
GROSSE CAISSE (*Fr.*) The great drum.
GROSSE NASARD
GROSSE NASAT
GROSSE NASSAT
GROSSE NAZARD (*Ger.*) An organ stop, sounding a fifth above the diapasons.
GROSSE PRINCIPAL (*Ger.*) An organ stop of 32 feet scale, of the open diapason species.
GROSSE QUINT
GROSSE-QUINTEN-BASS (*Ger.*) An organ stop, in the pedals, sounding a fifth, or twelfth, to the great bass of 32 feet, or 16 feet.
GROSSE SONATE (*Ger. pl.*) Grand sonatas.
GROSSE TIERCE (*Ger.*) Great third sounding stop in an organ, producing the third, or tenth, above the foundations stops.
GROSSE TROMMEL (*Ger.*) The great drum.
GROSS-GEDACT (*Ger.*) Double-stopped diapason, of 16 feet tone, in an organ.
GRÓSSO (*It.*) Large, great, full: *see* CONCÉRTO GRÓSSO.
GRÖSSTER (*Ger.*) Greatest.
GROS TAMBOUR (*Fr.*) The great drum.
GROTTÉSCO (*It.*) Grotesque.
GROUND. A bass consisting of a few notes, or bass, unceasingly repeated, and each time accompanied by a new or varied melody.
GROUP. Several short notes tied together.
GRUND-BASS (*Ger.*) A ground bass.
GRUND-STIMME (*Ger.*) The bass part.
GRUND-TON (*Ger.*) The bass note: fundamental, or principal tone: the tonic of any scale.
GRUPPÉTTO (*It.*) A turn: also, a small group of grace, or ornamental notes.
GRUPPE (*Ger.*)
GRÚPPO (*It.*) A group of notes: formerly it meant a trill, shake, or turn.
G-SCHLÜSSEL (*Ger.*) The G, or treble clef.

GUARÁCCA
GUARÁCHA A lively Spanish dance: it is also used by the Neapolitans.
GUARÁCHE

GUDDOK. A rustic violin with three strings, used by the Russian peasants.

GUERRIÉRO (*It.*) Martial, warlike.

GUET (*Fr.*) A military trumpet piece.

GUÍDA (*It.*) Guide: also, the mark called a *direct*.

GUÍDA ARMÓNICA (*It.*) A guide to harmony.

GUÍDA BÁNDA (*It.*) A conductor's condensed score.

GUIDE-MAIN. The hand-guide, an instrument invented by Kalkbrenner, for assisting young players to acquire a good position of the hands, on the pianoforte.

GUIDON (*Fr.*) The mark called a *direct*.

GUIDONIAN HAND. The figure of a left hand, used by Guido, and upon which was marked the names of the sounds forming his three hexachords.

GUIDONIAN SYLLABLES. The syllables *ut, re, mi, fa, sol, la*, used by Guido d'Arezzo, and called the Aretinian scale: the syllable *si* was introduced afterwards.

GUIGUE. See GÍGA.

GUILTERN. See GITTERN.

GUIMBARDE (*Fr.*) A Jew's harp.

GUITAR (*Eng.*)
GUITARE (*Fr.*) An instrument with six strings, which are twitched by the fingers of the right hand: the
GUITÁRRA (*Sp.*) neck of the guitar is furnished with frets.
GUITARRE (*Ger.*) There are three kinds: the German, Italian, and Spanish guitar. It is supposed to be of Spanish invention, and is very popular, and much used in that country.

GUITARRERO (*Sp.*) A guitar maker.

GUITARÍLLA (*Sp.*) A little guitar.

GUITARRÍSTA (*Sp.*) A guitar player.

GUITARRÓN (*Sp.*) A large guitar.

GUITERNE. A species of lute, formerly used.

GUNST (*Ger.*) Grace, tenderness.

GURÁCHO (*Sp.*) See GUARÁCHE.

GÚSTO (*It.*) Taste, expression.

GUSTOSAMÉNTE (*It.*) Tastefully, expressively.

GUSTÓSO (*It.*) Expressive, tasteful.

GUT (*Ger.*) Good, well.

GUT BETONT (*Ger.*) Well accented.

GUT GESTOSSEN (*Ger.*) Very *staccáto*.

GUTTURAL. Formed too much in the throat, instead of coming freely from the chest.

H

H. This letter is used by the Germans for B-natural, which note is called by the French and Italians *si*.

HABANERA. A Cuban dance in $\frac{3}{4}$, $\frac{6}{8}$ or time.

HABER-ROHR (*Ger.*) Shepherd's flute.

HACKBRETT (*Ger.*) The dulcimer.

HACKE (*Ger.*) The heal.

HAGEBÜCHEN / **HAHNBÜCHEN** (*Ger.*) Coarse, clumsy.

HALB (*Ger.*) Half.

HALB-BASS (*Ger.*) A small double bass.

HALB-CADENZ (*Ger.*) Half-cadence: see that word.

HALB-CELLO (*Ger.*) A small violoncello.

HALBE TAKTNOTE / **HALB-NOTE** (*Ger.*) A minim.

HALB-TON (*Ger.*) Half-tone, semitone.

HALF-CADENCE. An imperfect cadence; a close on the dominant.

HALF-NOTE. A minim.

HÄLFTE (*Ger.*) A half.

HALL / **HALLE** (*Ger.*) Sound, clangour, clang.

HALL-DROMMETE (*Ger.*) A powerful trumpet.

HALLELUJAH (*Heb.*) *Praise ye the Lord.* A song of thanksgiving.

HALLEN (*Ger.*) To sound, to clang.

HALLING. A Norwegian dance in $\frac{4}{4}$ time.

HALL-TROMPETE (*Ger.*) A powerful trumpet.

HALMPFEIFE (*Ger.*) A shepherd's pipe.

HALS (*Ger.*) Neck of a violin, viola, &c.

HALT (*Ger.*) A pause.

HAMMER. That part of the *action*, or mechanism, of a pianoforte, which strikes the strings, and thus produces the sound.

HANAISE (*Fr.*) / **HANÁCCA** (*It.*) / **HANAKISCH** (*Ger.*) A Moravian dance in $\frac{3}{4}$ time.

HANCHE (*Fr.*) See ANCHE.
HÄNDE (*Ger. pl.*) The hands.
HAND-GLOCKE (*Ger.*) Hand-bell.
HAND-GUIDE. See GUIDE-MAIN.
HAND-KLAPPER (*Ger.*) Castanet.
HAND-LEITER (*Ger.*) Hand-guide: see GUIDE-MAIN.
HANDLUNG (*Ger.*) Action, plot; a drama.
HAND-TASTEN (*Ger.*) The fingerboard of an instrument.
HAND-TROMMEL (*Ger.*) A tambourine.
HARDIMENT (*Fr.*) Boldly, firmly.
HARFE (*Ger.*) A harp.
HARFENER (*Ger.*) Harp player.
HARFENETT (*Ger.*) A little harp.
HARFENIST (*Ger.*) Harp player.
HARFEN-SAITE (*Ger.*) Harp string.
HARFEN-SPIELER (*Ger.*) Harp player.
HARMONIA ÆTHERIA. See HARMONICA-ÄTHERISCH.
HARMONICA. Musical glasses, sometimes globular, sometimes flat. They are by some supposed to have been invented in 1762 by Benjamin Franklin, but they are mentioned by Kircher (who died 1680), in his 'Musurgiæ.' The tome is produced by rubbing the edge of the globular glasses with a moistened finger; or striking the flat ones with small hammers. The name is also applied to an organ stop of a delicate tone, and somewhat resembling the *Hohl-flute*.
HARMONICA-ÄTHERISCH (*Ger.*) A mixture stop of very delicate scale, in German organs.
HARMONIC FLUTE. An open metal organ stop, of 8 or 4 feet pitch, blown by a heavy wind: the pipes are of double length, that is, 16, or 8 feet, and the bodies have a hole bored in them, midway between the foot and the top: the tone is exceedingly full, fluty, and powerful. This stop was invented by Cavaillé-Coll, of Paris.
HARMONICHORD. An instrument invented by Fr. Kaufmann, resembling a pianoforte, but with a tone something like that of the violin, produced by the friction of a wooden cylinder, covered with leather, upon pianoforte strings.
HARMÓNICI (*It. pl.*) Harmonics, in playing the violin, harp, guitar, &c.
HARMONICON. A small instrument held in the hand, the sounds being produced from small metal springs, set in motion by blowing from the mouth. This little instrument as the precursor of the Harmonium.

Harmonics — Harp

HARMONICS. Certain faint sounds, which may be distinguished, by listening attentively to the vibrations of any deep-toned musical note. Harmonics are also artificially produced from the harp, violin, &c., by lightly touching the strings at certain points.

HARMONIE (*Fr. & Ger.*) Harmony.

HARMONIE-MUSIK (*Ger.*) Music for wind-instruments only.

HARMONIE-REGELN (*Ger.*) The rules, or laws, of harmony.

HARMONIEUSEMENT (*Fr.*) Harmoniously.

HARMIONIE-VERSTÄNDIGER (*Ger.*) Harmonist: one versed in harmony.

HARMONIEUX (*Fr.*) Harmonious.

HARMONIPHON. A small instrument, with a key-board like a pianoforte, invented in 1837, and intended to supply the place of the hautboys in an orchestra. The sounds are produced from small metal tongues, acted upon by wind, through a flexible tube.

HARMONIQUE (*Fr.*) Harmonical: the relation of sounds to each other: applied also to organ pipes of double length: *see* **HARMONIC FLUTE**.

HARMONIQUEMENT (*Fr.*) Harmonically.

HARMONIREN (*Ger.*) To harmonise, to be in unison.

HARMONISCH (*Ger.*) Harmonious: harmoniously: harmonical.

HARMONISCHE THEILUNG (*Ger.*) Harmonical division.

HARMONIST. One acquainted with the laws, and science, of harmony.

HARMONIUM. An instrument with keys like the pianoforte, and furnished with bellows. The sounds are produced by the wind acting upon small metal tongues, or vibrators. The harmonium possesses great power and volume of sound, and is capable of much delicacy of expression.

HARMONOMÈTRE (*Fr.*) An instrument to measure the proportion of sounds, a species of monochord.

HARMONY. Music in parts: sounds heard at the same time: the art of combining sounds, so as to form chords, and of treating these chords according to certain rules.

HARP. Like the term *lyre*, a harp is an old poetical term for a stringed instrument, struck with the fingers. The shape of the ancient harp differed from the modern one, in having no fore-pillar. Dante speaks of the harp being imported into Italy from Ireland. Vincentio Galilei, in the sixteenth century, alludes to the continued excellence of the Irish in making and playing on the harp, and also ascribes the invention of the triangular harp to the Irish, and, from a figure upon a coin of Cunobeline, it is supposed to have been in use at least twenty-four years before the Christian era. The Welsh and Irish harps appear to have been similar, and strung with three strings, either of gut or wire. The modern double-action harp has one string

HARPE (*Fr.*) A harp.

HARPÉGGIO (*It.*) *See* ARPÉGGIO.

HARPICÓRDO (*It.*) *See* ARPICÓRDO.

HARPIST. A harp player.

HARP-LUTE. A stringed instrument of modern invention, something between the harp and the guitar: it has frets, and twelve strings, the tone is said to be agreeable, though not powerful.

HARPO-LYRE (*Fr.*) A species of large guitar, with 21 strings, and three necks.

HARPSECOL. *See* HARPSICHORD.

HARPSICHORD. An instrument much used before the invention of the pianoforte, to which it was very inferior in power and expression. In shape it was similar to the grand pianoforte, and had sometimes two rows of keys: the strings were of thin brass or steel wire, and the sound was produced by a *plectrum*, or little piece of quill, fixed in a wooden 'jack,' which was raised by the end of the key: the quill moved the wire, and made it sound. The compass was about four octaves, and the keys were very sensitive to the slightest touch: however lightly the key was put down, it would produce a sound, but the sound was always the same, whether the touch was light or heavy; the various shades of loud and soft could only be obtained by changing from one set of keys to the other, or by moving certain stops, as in an organ. The *single* harpsichord had two unison strings: the *double* harpsichord had two unisons, and an octave.

HARTE (*Ger.*) Major, in respect to intervals and scales.

HART-KLINGEND (*Ger.*) Hard-sounding: of a harsh sound.

HARZ (*Ger.*) Resin; rosin.

HASUR (*Heb.*) An ancient instrument, with ten strings.

HÂTE (*Fr.*) Haste, speed.

HAUBOIS (*Fr.*) *See* HAUTBOIS.

HAUPT (*Ger.*) Head, chief, principal.

HAUPT-ACCENT (*Ger.*) The most important *accent*, of any measure.

HAUPT-KIRCHE (*Ger.*) Cathedral; metropolitan church.

HAUPT-MANUAL (*Ger.*) The great, or principal manual: the great organ.

HAUPT-NOTE (*Ger.*) The principal note, in a shake or turn: that note over which the ∞ , or *tr* the is placed.

HAUPT-PERIOD (*Ger.*) Capital period: the principal period in a musical phrase.

HAUPT-SÄNGERIN (Ger.) *Prima dona.*

Haupt-satz (*Ger.*) Principal theme, or subject: the *mottvo*, or leading idea.

Haupt-schluss (*Ger.*) Final cadence: perfect close in the original key.

Haupt-schüssel (*Ger.*) Principal key of a composition.

Haupt-septime (*Ger.*) The dominant seventh.

Haupt-stimme (*Ger.*) Principal voice: principal part.

Haupt-ton (*Ger.*) Fundamental, or principal tone: keynote: the tonic.

Haupt-werk (*Ger.*) Chief-work, or manual: the great organ.

Hausse (*Fr.*) The *nut* of a violin, or other bow.

Hausser (*Fr.*) To raise, or sharpen, the pitch.

Haut (*Fr.*) Acute, high shrill.

Hautbois (*Fr.*) The *oboè*, or hautboy.

Hautbois d'amour (*Fr.*) A species of the hautboy, with a pleasing tone, but difficult to play perfectly in tune: it is now very rare: also, an organ stop.

Hautboy. A treble wind-instrument of wood, of French invention, played with a *double reed*: the tone is penetrating, and slightly nasal, and capable of wonderful expression; it has a pastoral character, full of tenderness. The name is also given to an 8 feet organ reed stop, the tone of which is of a thin, penetrating, and wailing character, like that of the hautboy, which it is, of course intended to imitate.

Hautboy-clarion. See OCTAVE HAUTBOY.

Haute-contre (*Fr.*) Counter-tenor, high tenor.

Haute-dessus (*Fr.*) First treble, high treble.

Hautement (*Fr.*) Haughtily, dignified: briskly, boldly.

Haute-taille (*Fr.*) Upper tenor, high tenor.

Havanaise (*Fr.*) See HABANERA.

H dur (*Ger.*) The key of B major.

Heer-horn (*Ger.*) A military trumpet.

Heer-pauke (*Ger.*) A military drum; large kettle-drum.

Heer-pauker (*Ger.*) Kettle-drummer: military drummer.

Heftig (*Ger.*) Vehement, boisterous, impetuous.

Heftigkeit (*Ger.*) Vehemence; impetuosity.

Hehrmesse (*Ger.*) High mass.

Heimlich (*Ger.*) Mysterious, stealthy; homely.

Heiss (*Ger.*) Hot, ardent.

Heiter (*Ger.*) Cheerful, serene, bright.

Heldendichter (*Ger.*) An epic poet.

Helden-lied (*Ger.*) Heroic song.

Hendenmässig (*Ger.*) Heroic; in a heroic style.

Helikon — Hinsterbend

HELIKON (*Gr.*) Helicon, an ancient instrument, or diagram, invented by Ptolemy, for demonstrating, or measuring, consonances, or sounds.
HELL (*Ger.*) Bright, clear, sonrous.
HEMIDIAPENTE (*Gr.*) Diminished, or imperfect, fifth.
HEMIDITONOS (*Gr.*) Lesser, or minor, third.
HEMIOPE (*Gr.*) A small fife, or flute, with three holes: an ancient flute.
HEMITONIUM (*Gr.*) A semitone, half-tone.
HEPTACHORD (*Gr.*) A scale, or system, of seven sounds.
HEPTACHORDON (*Gr.*) The major seventh.
HERABSTRICH (*Ger.*) A down-bow.
HERAUFGEHEN (*Ger.*) To ascend.
HERSINGEN (*Ger.*) To sing, to recite in a singing manner.
HERSTRICH
HERUNTERSTRICH } (*Ger.*) A down-bow.
HERVORGEHOBEN
HERVORHEBEND
HERVORTRETEND } (*Ger.*) Play the notes very prominently and distinctly.
HERZHAFT (*Ger.*) Brace, bold, courageous.
HERZLICH (*Ger.*) Tenderly: delicate expression.
HERZIG (*Ger.*) Heartily and ingenuously; tenderly; charming, dear.
HEXACHORD (*Gr.*) A scale, or system, of six sounds.
HEXACHORDON (*Gr.*) A major sixth.
HEXACORDE (*Fr.*) A *Hexachord*: see that word.
HEXAMERON (*Gr.*) Set of six musical pieces, or songs.
HIALEMOS (*Gr.*) An elegy, a lament.
HIATUS (*Lat.*) A gap: imperfect harmony.
HIDDEN CONSECUTIVES. Certain apparent consecutive fifths, or octaves, which occur in harmony, in passing, by similar motion, to a perfect concord.
HIEF-HORN (*Ger.*) Bugle horn, hunting horn.
HIEF
HIEF-STOSS } (*Ger.*) Sound given by the bugle, or hunting horn.
HIEROPHON (*Gr.*) A singer of sacred music.
HIFT-HORN (*Ger.*) A wooden hunting horn.
HILFS (*Ger.*) Helping, auxiliary.
HIMMLISCH (*Ger.*) Heavenly, celestial, ethereal.
HINAUFSTRICH
HINSTRICH } (*Ger.*) An up-bow.
HINSTERBEND (*Ger.*) Dying away.

Hinstrich (*Ger.*) The up-bow in violoncello playing.
Hinter der Scene (*Ger.*) Behind the scenes.
Hinunterziehen (*Ger.*) A downward *portamento*.
Hirten-Flöte (*Ger.*) Shepherd's flute.
Hirten-Gedicht (*Ger.*) Pastoral poem, eclogue, idyl.
Hirten-Lied (*Ger.*) Pastoral song.
Hirten-Pfeife (*Ger.*) Rural pipe, pastoral pipe.
Hirtlich (Ger.) Rural, pastoral.
His (*Ger.*) The note B-sharp.
H moll (*Ger.*) The key of B minor.
Hoboe (*Ger.*) *Oboè*, hautboy.
Hoboen (*Ger. pl.*) *Oboè*, hautboys.
Hoboist (*Ger.*) Hautboy player.
Hoboy (*Ger.*) *Oboè*, hautboy.
Hoch-Amt (*Ger.*) High Mass.
Hochfeierlich (*Ger.*) Exceedingly solemn.
Hoch-Gesang (*Ger.*) Ode, hymn.
Hoch-Horn (*Ger.*) Hautboy.
Hoch-Horn-Bläser (*Ger.*) Player on the hautboy.
Hoch-Lied (*Ger.*) Ode, hymn.
Hoch-Messe (*Ger.*) High Mass.
Hochmuth (*Ger.*) Dignity, loftiness.
Höchsten (*Ger.*) Highest: *die höchsten und tiefsten Noten mit Nachdruck abgestossen*, the highest and the lowest notes to be struck off with energy.
Höchst-Lebhaft (*Ger.*) Very lively.
Hochzeit-Gedicht | (*Ger.*) Epithalamium, nuptial poem, wedding
Hochzeit-Lied | song.
Hochzeit-Marsch (*Ger.*) Wedding march, festival march.
Hocket. An old musical term: the interruption of a voice part, by rests, to produce a broken effect.
Hof-Capelle (*Ger.*) Court chapel.
Hof-Concert (*Ger.*) Court concert.
Hof-Dichter (*Ger.*) Poet laureate.
Hof-Kapelle (*Ger.*) Court band and singers.
Hof-Kapellmeister (*Ger.*) The director of a court orchestra.
Hof-Kirche (*Ger.*) Court church.
Höflich
Höflichkeit | (*Ger.*) In a pleasing and graceful style.
Hof-Musikant (*Ger.*) Court musician.

Hof-organist — Hüft

Hof-organist (*Ger.*) Court organist.

Höhe (*Ger.*) Acuteness, high.

Hohe-lied (*Ger.*) The Song of Solomon.

Hohen (*Ger.*) High, upper: *die hohen Noten der rechten Hand mit einigem Nachdruck*, the upper notes of the right hand with emphasis.

Hohl-flöte (*Ger.*) *Hollow-toned flute*: an organ stop producing a thick and powerful hollow tone, sometimes like the *Clarabella*, but stronger and fuller: each pipe has two holes in it, near to the top, and opposite to each other.

Hohl-quinte (*Ger.*) A *quint* stop of the *Hohl-flöte* species.

Höhnend (*Ger.*) Sneering, scoffing.

Hold (*Ger.*) Pleasing, agreeable, graceful.

Holzbasser (*Ger.*) A wind-wind player.

Holzernes Gelächter (*Ger.*) A xylophone.

Holzflöte (*Ger.*) *Wood-flute*: an organ stop.

Holzharmonica (*Ger.*) A xylophone.

Holzschlägel (*Ger.*) A wooden beater, or drum stick.

Homophonie (*Fr.*) | Unison: two or more voices singing in
Homophony (*Eng.*) | unison.

Hopser (*Ger.*) A German dance, a lively waltz.

Hops-tanz (*Ger.*) Hop-dance.

Hops-walzer (*Ger.*) Quick waltzes.

Horæ | (*Lat.*) *Hours*: chants, sung at prescribed hours,
Horæ regulares | in convents and monasteries.

Horn. Commonly called the French horn: an orchestral instrument of brass, or silver; of a circular form, and blown through a mouth-piece of the same material. The horn is a noble and melancholy instrument, with a sonorous, and expressive tone. Also, an 8 feet organ reed stop, of a smooth, full tone. The horn stop was invented by Byfield, a celebrated organ-builder of the eighteenth century.

Hörner (*Ger. pl.*) The horns.

Hornpipe. An old dance, in triple time, peculiar to the English nation. Modern hornpipes are usually in common time. The old hornpipe appears to have been a slow dance, modern ones are of a lively character. Also, the name of an old wind-instrument: *see* **Pibcorn**.

Hoasanna (*Lat.*) Part of the *Sanctus*, in a Mass.

Hreol (*Dan.*) A Danish peasant dance, very similar to the Reel.

Hübsch (*Ger.*) Charming, dainty.

Huchet (*Fr.*) A huntsman's, or postboy's, horn.

Huehuetl. A large drum used by the central American ancients.

Hüft-horn (*Ger.*) Bugle horn.

Huitième — Hyper

HUITIÈME DE SOUPIR (*Fr.*) A demisemiquaver rest.

HULDIGUNGSMARSCH (*Ger.*) Homage march.

HÜLFS-NOTE
HÜLFS-TON (*Ger.*) Auxiliary note, accessory note, a note standing one degree above, or below, the principal note.

HUMMEL (*Ger.*) A sort of bagpipes.

HUMORESKE (*Ger.*)
HUMORESQUE. A humorous or whimsical composition.

HUMSEN (*Ger.*) To hum, buzz, drone.

HUNTING HORN. A bugle, a horn used to cheer the hounds.

HÜPFEND (*Ger.*) Springing, skipping.

HURDY-GURDY. An old instrument, formerly called a *Rote*, or *Vielle*. It consists of four strings, which are acted upon by a wheel rubbed with resin powder, and which does the office of a bow. Two of the strings are affected by certain keys which stop them at different lengths, and produce the *tune*, while the others act as a drone bass.

HURTIG (*Ger.*) Quickly, swiftly: of the same meaning as the word *allégro*.

HURTIGKEIT (*Ger.*) Swiftness, quickness, agility.

HYDRAULON (*Gr.*) An organ blown by the action of water.

HYMENAION (*Gr.*) A wedding song.

HYMENEAL
HYMENEAN A marriage song.

HYMN. A song of praise, or adoration to the Deity. The first hymns, which were formed on the Hebrew model, were not metrical, but they took this form at an early period.

HYMNE (*Fr.* & *Ger.*)
HYMNUS (*Lat.*) Hymn: sacred song: an anthem: song of praise and adoration.

HYMNUS AMBROSIANUS (*Lat.*) The Ambrosian chant.

HYPATE (*Gr.*) The first, or most grave, string of the lyre. It seems to have been the practice of the ancients to give the more grave tones the uppermost place in the scale, contrary to the modern practice.

HYPATHOIDES (*Gr.*) The lower sounds, in the ancient Greek musical scale.

HYPER (*Gr.*) *Above*: this word is often prefixed to technical terms derived from the Greek.

HYPER-ÆOLIAN (*Gr.*) The *Authentic* Æolian mode.

HYPER-DIAPASON (*Gr.*) The upper octave.

HYPER-DITONOS (*Gr.*) The third above.

HYPER-DORIAN (*Gr.*) The *Authentic* Dorian mode.

HYPER-IONIAN (*Gr.*) The *Authentic* Ionian mode.

HYPER-LYDIAN (*Gr.*) The *Authentic* Lydian mode.

HYPER-MIXO-LYDIAN (*Gr.*) The *Authentic* Mixo-Lydian mode.
HYPER-PHRYGIAN (*Gr.*) The *Authentic* Phrygian mode.
HYPO (*Gr.*) *Below*: often prefixed to technical terms, derived from the Greek.
HYPO-ÆOLIAN (*Gr.*) The *plagal* Æolian mode.
HYPO-DIAPASON (*Gr.*) The lower octave.
HYPO-DIAPENTE (*Gr.*) The fifth below.
HYPO-DITONOS (*Gr.*) The third below.
HYPO-DORIAN (*Gr.*) The *Authentic* Dorian mode.
HYPO-IONIAN (*Gr.*) The *Authentic* Ionian mode.
HYPO-LYDIAN (*Gr.*) The *Authentic* Lydian mode.
HYPO-MIXO-LYDIAN (*Gr.*) The *Authentic* Mixo-Lydian mode.
HYPO-PHRYGIAN (*Gr.*) The *Authentic* Phrygian mode.
HYPORCHEMA. A dance accompanied with singing.

I

IAMBE (*Fr.*) Iambus.

IAMBIC. Verses composed of a short and long syllable alternately.

IAMBUS (*Lat.*) A poetical, and musical foot, consisting of one short unaccented, and one long accented note, or syllable.

IASTIAN (*Gr.*) *See* GREEK MODES.

ICTUS. Accent, stress, emphasis.

IDÍLLIO (*It.*)
IDYL (*Eng.*) } A short poem, in a pastoral style; an eclogue.
IDYLLE (*Fr. & Ger.*)

IL (*It.*) The: *il fláuto*, the flute.

ILARITÀ (*It.*) Hilarity, cheerfulness, mirth.

IL CÁNTO (*It.*) The melody.

IL DÍTO GRÓSSO (*It.*) The thumb.

IL DÓPPIO MOVIMÉNTO (*It.*) Double movement, that is, as fast again.

IL FAUT (*Fr.*) It is necessary.

IL FÍNE (*It.*) The end.

IL PIÙ (*It.*) The most.

IL PIÙ FÓRTE POSSÍBILE (*It.*) As loud as possible.

IL PIÙ PIÁNO POSSÍBILE (*It.*) As soft as possible.

IL PONTICÉLLO (*It.*) The old name for the break between the *natural* and *falsétto* voices.

IL TÉMPO CRESCÉNDO (*It.*) Increasing, or accelerating the time.

IL TÉRZO DÍTO À TÚTTE LE NÓTE DI BÁSSO (*It.*) The third finger on all the notes in the bass.

IL VIOLÍNO (*It.*) The violin.

IM (*Ger.*) In; in the.

IM ANFANG NICHT ZU RASCH (*Ger.*) Not too fast at the beginning.

IMBOCCATÚRA (*It.*) Mouth-piece, *embouchure*.

IMBRÓGLIO (*It.*) Confusion, want of distinct ideas.

IM GEMESSENEN SCHRITT (*Ger.*) In strict time, or *tempo*.

IMITÁNDO (*It.*) Imitating: *imitándo la vóce*, imitating the inflections of the voice.

IMITATIO (*Lat.*) Imitation, in counterpoint.

Imitation — Impetuosaménte

IMITATION. A species of fugue, in which the parts imitate each other, though not in the same intervals, or according to the strict laws, of a fugue, or canon.

IMITAZIÉNTE (*It.*) Impatient, hurried.

IM KLAGENDEN TON (*Ger.*) In a sorrowful tone.

IM LANGSAMER MARSCHTAKT (*Ger.*) In a slow march tempo.

IM LEBHAFTESTEN ZEITMASSE (*Ger.*) As fast as possible.

IM MÄSSIGEN TEMPO (*Ger.*) In a moderate time.

IMMER (*Ger.*) Always, continually.

IMMER BEWEGTER BIS ZUM ENDE (*Ger.*) With increasing emotion until the end.

IMMER GLEICHMÄSSIG LEICHT (*Ger.*) Light throughout.

IMMER LANGSAM (*Ger.*) Always slow.

IMMER LANGSAMER (*Ger.*) Continually slower; *rallentándo*.

IMMER LEBENDIGER (*Ger.*) See STRINGÉNDO.

IMMER STÄRKER WERDEND (*Ger.*) Continually louder; *crescéndo*.

IMMER SCHWÄCHER (*Ger.*) Becoming softer and softer.

IMMUTABILIS (*Lat.*) See ACCENT.

IMPARSAIT (*Fr.*) Imperfect.

IMPAZIÉNTE (*It.*) Impatient, restless.

IMPAZIENTEMÉNTE (*It.*) Impatiently, hurriedly.

IMPERFECT. Not perfect, less than perfect, in speaking of intervals, or chords.

IMPERFECT CADENCE. A cadence which ends on the triad of the dominant: the preceding chord may be either that of the tonic, or the sub-dominant: or, in minor keys, the sixth of the scale: the triad of the dominant always being *major*.

IMPERFECT CONSONANCES. The major, and minor, triad: and the major, and minor, sixth.

IMPERFECT INTERVALS. Those which include one semitone less than the perfect interval of the same note: as, perfect fifth, *seven* semitones; imperfect fifth, *six* semitones.

IMPERFECT MEASURE. An old term for time of only two in a bar: called also *Binary measure*.

IMPERFÉTTO (*It.*) Imperfect.

IMPERIOSAMÉNTE (*It.*) Imperiously, pompously, stately.

IMPERIOSITÀ (*It.*) Stateliness, pomposity.

IMPERIÓSO (*It.*) Imperious, pompous.

IMPERTURBÁBILE (*It.*) Quietly, easily.

ÍMPETO (*It.*) Impetuosity, vehemence.

IMPETUOSAMÉNTE (*It.*) Impetuously.

Impetuosità — Inchoatio

IMPETUOSITÀ (*It.*) Impetuosity, vehemence.

IMPETUÓSO (*It.*) Impetuous, vehement, boisterous.

IMPONÉNTE (*It.*) Imposingly, haughtily, emphatic.

IMPONIEREND (*Ger.*) Imposing, majestic.

IMPRESÁRIO (*It.*) The manager of an operatic establishment.

IMPRÓMPTU (*Fr.*) Extempore, unpremeditated.

IMPROPERIA (*Lat.*) The *reproaches* sung in the Roman Catholic service.

IMPROVISATEUR (*Fr.*) ⎫
IMPROVISATOR (*Ger.*) ⎭ *See* IMPROVVISATÓRE.

IMPROVISATRICE (*Fr.*) A poetess: a female *improvvisatóre*.

IMPROVISER (*Fr.*) To compose, or sing, extemporaneously.

IMPROVISÉ (*Fr.*) Extemporaneous.

IMPROVVISAMÉNTE (*It.*) Suddenly, extemporaneously.

IMPROVVISÁRE (*It.*) To perform, or sing, extemporaneously.

IMPROVVISÁTA (*It.*) An extempore composition.

IMPROVVÍSO (*It.*) Sudden, extemporaneous.

IMPROVVISSATÓRE (*It.*) One who sings, or declaims, in verse, extemporaneously.

IM RUHIGEN TEMPO (*Ger.*) In tranquil time.

IM STUDENTENTON (*Ger.*) In the style of the pupil, instead of the teacher.

IM TACT ⎫
IM TAKT ⎭ (*Ger.*) In time.

IM VOLKSTON (*Ger.*) In the style of a folk-song.

IM ZEITMASS (*Ger.*) In time.

IN (*It.*) In, into, in the: *in témpo*, in time.

IN ABWECHSELNDEN CHÖREN (*Ger.*) For alternate choirs; antiphonally.

INACUTÍRE (*It.*) To sharpen, to make sharp.

IN ALT (*It.*) The notes from G above the treble stave, to the F above, inclusive, are said to be *in alt*, which means, *high*.

IN ALTÍSSIMO (*It.*) The treble notes commencing at G, on the fourth ledger line, and all those notes above it, are said to be *in altíssimo*, which means, the *highest* notes.

IN BATTÚTA (*It.*) In strict time.

INBRUNST (*Ger.*) Ardour, fervour, warmth of passion.

INBRÜNSTIG (*Ger.*) Ardent, fervent: passionately.

INCALCÁNDO ⎫
INCALZÁNDO ⎭ (*It.*) Increasing the speed; *stringéndo*.

INCANTAZIÓNE (*It.*) Songs of incantation.

INCHOATIO (*Lat.*) The introductory notes, in plain-chant.

INCISÓRE DI NÓTE (*It.*) An engraver of notes, or music.

INCOMINCIÁNDO (*It.*) Commencing.

INCONSOLÁTO (*It.*) In a mournful style.

INCORDAMÉNTO (*It.*) Tension of the strings of an instrument.

INCORDÁRE (*It.*) To string an instrument.

INCROCIAMÉNTO (*It.*) Crossing; becoming close.

INDECÍSO (*It.*) Undecided, wavering, hesitating: slight changes of time, and a somewhat capricious value of the notes.

INDEGNATAMÉNTE
INDEGNÁTO } (*It.*) Angrily, furiously, passionately.

INDEX (*Fr.*) The fore-finger.

INDIFFERÉNTE
INDIFFERENTEMÉNTE } (*It.*) Coldly, with indifference: in a capricious manner.

INDIFFERÉNZA (*It.*) Indifference, coldly, irresolutely.

IN DISTÁNZA (*It.*) At a distance.

INFANTÍLE (*It.*) *Childlike, infantine*: the thin quality of tone in the upper notes of some female voices.

INFERIOR (*Lat.*) Lower.

INFERNÁLE (*It.*) Infernal, diabolic.

INFERVORÁTO (*It.*) Fervent, impassioned, vehement.

INFIAMMATAMÉNTE (*It.*) Ardently, impetuously.

INFINITE CANON. Called also *circular*, or *endless* canon: when the parts are so arranged that we may return from the end to the commencement, without stopping.

INFLATILE. Wind-instruments, as, flutes, hautboys, &c.

INFLATILIA. See INFLATILE.

INFLECTION. Modulation of the voice: change, or variation of sound: bonding, or turning of the tone: modification of the tone, or pitch of the voice.

INFRA (*Lat.*) Beneath, below.

INFRABASS (*Ger.*) Sub-bass, an organ stop of 16 feet tone.

IN FRÉTTA (*It.*) In haste, hastily.

INFURIÁNTE
INFURIÁTO } (*It.*) Furious, raging.

INGÁNNI (*It. pl.*) See INGÁNNO.

INGÁNNO (*It.*) A deception: applied to a deceptive, or interrupted, cadence: also, to any unusual resolution of a discord, or, an unexpected modulation.

INGÉGNO (*It.*) Art, skill, wit, discretion.

In gehender — Instruménto

IN GEHENDER BEWEGUNG (*Ger.*) At a walking pace; *andánte*.

INGENUAMÉNTE (*It.*) Naturally, ingenuously.

IN GLEICHER STÄRKEN, OHNE ANSCHWELLEN (*Ger.*) With a constant force; without *crescéndo*.

INHALT (*Ger.*) Contents.

IN HÖCHSTER ANGST (*Ger.*) In deepest anguish.

IN LONTANÁNZA (*It.*) At a distance.

ÍNNO (*It.*) Hymn, ode.

INNOCÉNTE
INNOCENTEMÉNTE (*It.*) Innocently, in an artless and simple style.

INNOCÉNZA (*It.*) Innocence, simplicity, artlessness.

IN NOMINE (*Lat.*) *In the name*; a 16th century, free fugue.

ÍNO (*It.*) An Italian final diminutive, the same as *étto*: thus, *fláuto*, a flute; *flattíno*, a little flute: *córno*, a horn; *cornétto*, a little horn: *andánte*, advancing, going easily; *andantíno*, advancing less, a little slower than *andánte*.

IN ÓRGANO (*It.*) An old term for music in *more than two parts*.

IN PÁLCO (*It.*) Applied to musical performances *on a stage*.

IN PARTICO (*It.*) In score.

INQUIÉTO (*It.*) Restless, uneasy, agitated.

INSEGNAMÉNTO (*It.*) Instruction, lesson, teaching.

INSEGNATÓRE (*It.*) Teacher, instructor.

INSENSÍBILE
INSENSIBILMÉNTE (*It.*) Insensibly, imperceptibly, by degrees, by little and little.

INSIEME (*It.*) Ensemble.

INSISTÉNDO (*It.*) Insistently, urgently.

INSTÄNDIG (*Ger.*)
INSTÁNTE (*It.*) Instant; urgent, at once.

INSTANTEMÉNTE (*It.*) Vehemently, earnestly.

INSTRUMENT À ARCHET (*Fr.*) Instrument played with a bow.

INSTRUMENT À CORDES (*Fr.*) A stringed instrument.

INSTRUMENTÁLE (*It.*) Instrumental.

INSTRUMENTATION. The art of writing for an orchestra, with a practical knowledge of each instrument, and the power of combining them effectively.

INSTRUMENT À VENT (*Fr.*) A wind-instrument.

INSTRUMENTAZIÓNE (*It.*) Instrumentation.

INSTRUMENTIREN
INSTRUMENTIRUNG (*Ger.*) *See* INSTRUMENTATION.

INSTRUMENT-MACHER (*Ger.*) An instrument-maker.

INSTRUMÉNTO (*It.*) An instrument.

Instruménto — Intimíssimo

INSTRUMÉNTO À CAMPANÉLLA (*It.*) A small case, containing one, two, or more octaves of small bells, tuned diatonically, and played with a key-board, like a pianoforte.

INSTRUMÉNTO À CÓRDA (*It.*) A stringed instrument.

INSTRUMÉNTO DA FIÁTO (*It.*) A wind-instrument.

INSTRUMÉNTO DA PÉNNA (*It.*) *Instrument with the quill*: an old name for the spinet.

INTAVOLÁRE (*It.*) To write notes, to copy music.

INTAVOLATÚRA (*It.*) Music book, tablature.

IN TÉMPO (*It.*) In time.

INTENDANT (*Fr.*) | Much the same as *Impresário*.
INTENDÉTE (*It.*) |

INTENZIONÁTO (*It.*) With emphasis.

INTERCALÁRE (*It.*) A verse interlaced, or often repeated: the burden of a song.

INTERLIGNE (*Fr.*) The space between the staff lines.

INTERLUDE. An intermediate strain, or movement, played or sung between the lines, or verse, of a hymn, &c.: or between the acts of a drama.

INTERLUDIUM (*Lat.*) | An interlude; intermediate: placed between
INTERMÉDE (*Fr.*) | two others; detached pieces introduced
INTERMÉDIO (*It.*) | between the acts of an opera; musical farce,
INTERMÉZZO (*It.*) | usually performed between the acts of a serious piece.

INTERMEDIÉTTO (*It.*) A short interlude, or *intermézzo*.

INTERMÉZZI (*It. pl.*) Interludes; detached pieces, or dances.

INTERRÓTTO (*It.*) Interrupted; broken; speaking of cadence, accent, or rhythm.

INTERRUPTED CADENCE. A cadence in which the triad of the dominant is followed by some chord which changes the progression of the harmony: *see* **FALSE CADENCE.**

INTERRUZIÓNE (*It.*) Interruption: *sénza interruzióne*, without interruption; make no pause.

INTERVAL. The distance, or difference of pitch, between two notes, or sounds.

INTERVALL (*Ger.*) |
INTERVALLE (*Fr.*) | An interval, space, distance: *see* **INTERVAL.**
INTERVÁLLO (*It.*) |
INTERVALLUM (*Lat.*) |

INTERVALLE (*Ger. pl.*) Intervals.

INTIME (*Fr.*) *See* **ÍNTIMO.**

INTIMÍSSIMO (*It.*) Very expressive, with much feeling.

ÍNTIMO (*It.*) Inward feeling; expressive.

INTONÁRE (*It.*) To sing, or tune; to sing in tune; to begin; to
INTUONÁRE intonate.

INTONATION. Producing, or emitting, musical sounds, perfectly in tune.

INTONÁTO (*It.*) To set to music; tuned.

INTONATÓRE (*It.*) Male singer.

INTONATRÍCE (*It.*) Female singer.

INTONATÚRA
INTONAZIÓNE (*It.*) Intonation, manner of producing tone.

INTONIREN (*Ger.*) To intone, to sound.

INTRÁDA (*It.*)
INDRADE (*Ger.*) A short prelude, or introductory movement: also, an obsolete phrase in old trumpet music.
INTRÁTA (*It.*)

INTRÉCCIO (*It.*) Intrigue; a short stage piece.

INTREPIDAMÉNTE (*It.*) Boldly, with intrepidity.

INTREPIDEZZA (*It.*) Intrepidity, boldness, resolution.

INTRÉPIDO (*It.*) Intrepid, bold, energetic.

IN TRÍPLO (*It.*) An old term, meaning, music in *three parts*.

INTRODUCIMÉNTO
INTRODÚZIONE (*It.*) Introduction, introductory movement, short overture.

INTROIT (*Eng.*)
INTROÏT (*Fr.*) *Entrance*: an hymn, or anthem, sung while the
INTRÓITO (*It.*) priest enters within the rails at the communion
INTROITUS (*Lat.*) table: also, the commencement of the Mass.

INTUONATÓRE (*It.*) Male singer.

INTUONATRÍCE (*It.*) Female singer.

INVENTION (*Fr.*) An old name for a species of prelude, exercise, or short fantasia.

INVENZIÓNE (*It.*) Invention, contrivance.

INVERSIO (*Lat.*) Inversion: see that word.

INVERSIO CANCRIZANS (*Lat.*) *Retrograde*, or *crab-like* inversion, or imitation; because it goes backwards.

INVERSION. A *change of position*, with respect to intervals, and chords; the lower notes being placed above, and the upper notes below.

INVERSIÓNE (*It.*) Inversion, an artifice in counterpoint: see
INVÉRSO INVERSION.

INVERTED. Changed in position: *see* INVERSION.

INVERTED TURN. A turn which commences with the lowest note, instead of the highest.

INVITATORIUM (*Lat.*) The name applied to the *antiphone*, or response, to the psalm 'Venite exultemus.'
INVOCATIO (*Lat.*)
INVOCÁTO (*It.*) — An invocation, or prayer: a solemn appeal.
INVOCAZIÓNE (*It.*)
IN ZWEI ABTEILUNGEN (*Ger.*) In two parts.
IO BACCHE (*Lat.*) A joyous burden, in ancient lyric poetry.
IONIAN
IONIC (*Gr.*) *See* GREEK MODES.
IO TRIUMPHE (*Lat.*) A phrase of exultation, often found in the lyric poetry of the ancient Romans.
ÍRA (*It.*) Anger, wrath, rage.
IRÁTA
IRATAMÉNTE (*It.*) Angrily, passionately.
IRÁTO
IRISH HARP. *See* HARP.
IRLANDAIS (*Fr.*)
IRLÄNDISCH (*Ger.*) — An air, or dance tune, in the Irish style.
IRONICAMÉNTE (*It.*) Ironically.
IRÓNICO (*It.*) Ironical.
IRRESOLÚTO (*It.*) Irresolute, wavering, hesitating.
ISOCHRONOUS. Performed in equal times.
ISON (*Gr.*) The key-note of a chant.
ISONTONIC (*Gr.*) *Equal toned*; equal temperament.
ISTÉSSO (*It.*) The same: *l' istésso témpo*, the same time as before.
ISTÉSSO VALÓRE, MA UN PÓCO PIÙ LÉNTO (*It.*) The notes to have the same value, but a little more slowly.
ISTRIÓNICA (*It.*) The theatrical art: histrionic.
ISTRUMENTÁLE (*It.*) Instrumental.
ISTRUMENTAZIÓNE (*It.*) Instrumentation.
ISTRUMÉNTO (*It.*) An instrument.
ITALIAN SIXTH. A name sometimes given to a chord composed of a major third, and an augmented sixth:

ITALIÁNO (*It.*)
ITALIENISCH (*Ger.*) — Italian: *à l'Italienne*, in the Italian style.
ITALIENNE (*Fr.*)
ITA MISSA EST (*Lat.*) The termination of the Mass: sung by the priest to Gregorian music.

J

JACH (*Ger.*) Precipitate, hasty.

JACK. A small piece of mechanism, in the harpsichord, spinet, &c., which was pushed up by the end of the key: in this, the *plectrum*, (a piece of crow-quill, or hard leather,) was inserted, which put the string into vibration.

JAGD-HIEF (*Ger.*) Sound of the bugle, or hunting horn.

JAGD-HORN | (*Ger.*) Hunting horn, bugle horn.
JAGD-ZINK |

JAGDRUF (*Ger.*) The sound of the horn.

JAGDSTÜCK (*Ger.*) Hunting piece.

JÄGER-CHOR (*Ger.*) Hunting chorus.

JÄGER-HORN (*Ger.*) Hunting horn, bugle horn.

JÄH (*Ger.*) Precipitate, hasty.

JALÉO (*Sp.*) A national Spanish dance.

JALOUSIESCHWELLER (*Ger.*) A *venetian-blind* swell, in an organ.

JAMBE (*Fr.*) *See* LAMBUS.

JÄMMERLICH (*Ger.*) Lamentable, deplorable.

JAMMERND (*Ger.*) Wailing, lamenting.

JANITSCHAREN-MUSIK (*Ger.*) Janizary music, Turkish music, with a band composed of the great drum, cymbals, triangle, crescent, and the usual brass instruments.

JARÁBE. A Spanish dance.

JAUCHZEND (*Ger.*) Shouting, joyful.

JEDOCH (*Ger.*) Yet; however; nevertheless.

JEU (*Fr.*) Play: the style of playing on an instrument: also, a register, or stop, in an organ, or harmonium: *grand jeu*, full organ, all the stops.

JEU À BOUCHE (*Fr.*) A *stopped* flue stop.

JEU CÉLESTE (*Fr.*) The name of a soft stop in an harmonium: also, an organ stop, of French invention, formed of two dulciana pipes; one being slightly raised in pitch, gives to the tone a waving, undulating character.

JEU D'ANCHES (*Fr.*) A reed stop, in an organ.

JEU D'ANGES (*Fr.*) Soft stops; as, dulciana, &c.

JEU D'ÉCHOS (*Fr.*) Echo stop.

JEU DE FLÛTES (*Fr.*) Flute stop.

Jeu d'orgues — Justiniáne

JEU D'ORGUES (*Fr.*) Register, or row of pipes, in an organ.

JEUX (*Fr. pl.*) *Stops*, or *registers*, in an organ, or harmonium.

JEUX FORTS (*Fr.*) Loud stops: *forte* stops.

JEW'S HARP. A small instrument, of brass or steel, and shaped somewhat like a *lyre*: when played, it is placed between the teeth, and struck with the fore-finger.

JEW'S TRUMP. A Jew's harp.

JIG. A brisk, lively air: an old species of dance, in $\frac{6}{8}$ or $\frac{12}{8}$ time: the name is supposed to have been derived from *Geig*, a fiddle.

JOCOSUS (*Lat.*) Merry, jocose.

JODELN (*Ger.*) A style of singing peculiar to the Tyrolese peasants, the natural voice and the falsetto being used alternately.

JOIE (*Fr.*) Delight, gladness.

JONCTION (*Fr.*) The blending or *junction* of two registers.

JONGLEOURS \
JONGLEURS (*Fr. pl.*) An old term for the itinerant musicians, of the tenth and following centuries.

JÓTA. A Spanish national dance.

JOUER (*Fr.*) To play upon an instrument.

JOUEUR DE CORNEMUSE (*Fr.*) A performer on the bagpipes.

JOVIALISCH (*Ger.*) Jovial, joyous, merry.

JOYEUSEMENT (*Fr.*) Joyously.

JUBEL-FLÖTE (*Ger.*) An organ stop of the flute species.

JUBEL-GESANG \
JUBEL-LIED (*Ger.*) Song of jubilee.

JUBELHORN (*Ger.*) A key-bugle.

JUBELND (*Ger.*) Rejoicing, jubilation.

JUBILÓSO. See GIUBBILÓSO.

JUNGFERNREGAL \
JUNGFERNSTIMME (*Ger.*) The *Vox Angelica*.

JUNK. An Arabian harp.

JUSQU'À (*Fr.*) Until, up to.

JUSTE (*Fr.*) Perfect, true, accurate, exact, as to intonation, and intervals.

JUSTESSE (*Fr.*) Exactness, correctness, or purity, of intonation.

JUSTESSE DE LA VOIX (*Fr.*) Purity of voice.

JUSTESSE DE L'OREILLE (*Fr.*) Correctness of ear.

JUSTINIÁNA (*It.*) \
JUSTINIÁNE (*It. pl.*) A rude, and loose, kind of song, now obsolete.

K

KABARO. A small drum, used in Egypt and Abyssinia.
KADENZ (*Ger.*) *See* CADENCE.
KAISERMARSCH (*Ger.*) An imperial march.
KALAMAIKA. A lively Hungarian dance.
KALKANT (*Ger.*) Bellows-treader.
KALLINIKOS. A Grecian dance, accompanied with singing.
KAMMER (*Ger.*) Chamber.
KAMMER-CONCERT (*Ger.*) Chamber concert: small concert.
KAMMER-KOMPONIST (*Ger.*) Court composer.
KAMMER-MUSIK (*Ger.*) Chamber music: music for private performance.
KAMMER-MUSIKUS (*Ger.*) Chamber musician: member of a prince's private band.
KAMMER-SPIEL (*Ger.*) *See* KAMMER-MUSIK.
KAMMER-STYL (*Ger.*) Style of chamber music, as opposed to the ecclesiastical and theatrical styles.
KAMMER-TON (*Ger.*) The *pitch*, or lower *tuning*, of the instruments, in chamber music; opposed to the higher tuning of the organ, in church music.
KANDELE. A stringed instrument, used in England.
KANON (*Ger.*) A canon.
KANZEL-LIED (*Ger.*) Hymn before the sermon.
KANZONE (*Ger.*) *See* CANZÓNA.
KAPELLE (*Ger.*) A chapel.
KAPELL-MEISTER (*Ger.*) *See* CAPELL-MEISTER.
KAPODASTER (*Ger.*) *See* CAPOTÁSTO.
KARFREITAG (*Ger.*) Good Friday; *see* CHARFREITAG.
KATACHRESIS (*Gr.*) The use of a discord, when not allowed by the old pedantic rules.
KASTAGNETTEN (*Ger.*) *See* CASTANETS.
KASTEN (*Ger.*) A case for an instrument.
KATALEKTISCH (*Ger.*) *Catalectic*; wanting a syllable at the end.
KATHEDRALE
KATHEDRAL-KIRCHE } (*Ger.*) Cathedral: *see* DOMKIRCHE.
KAUM (*Ger.*) Hardly, scarcely.

Kavatine — Key

KAVATINE (*Ger.*) *See* CAVATINA.

KECK (*Ger.*) Bold, confident.

KECKHEIT (*Ger.*) Boldness, vigour: *mit Keckheit vorgetragem*, with a vigorous style of performance.

KEENERS. Singers engaged by the Irish, to sing lamentation over the dead: this was performed at night, and generally accompanied with a harp.

KEHLE (*Ger.*) The voice, the throat.

KEHLKOPF (*Ger.*) The larynx.

KEHLLAUT (*Ger.*) Guttural, throaty sound.

KEHRAUS (*Ger.*) *Sweep-dance:* a peculiar kind of dance, practised at the conclusion of an entertainment.

KEIFEND (*Ger.*) Nagging, scolding, bickering.

KEINESWEGS SCHNELL (*Ger.*) By no means fast.

KEMAN. A Turkish violin, with three strings.

KENET. An Abyssinian trumpet.

KENNER (*Ger.*) A connoisseur.

KENNER IN DER MUSIK (*Ger.*) Professor of music.

KENT BUGLE (*Ger.*) A keyed bugle.

KERANA. A Persian horn sounded at sunset and midnight.

KERANIM. The sacred trumpet of the ancient Hebrews.

KERAS (*Gr.*) A horn.

KERAULOPHON (*Gr.*) An 8 feet organ stop, of a reedy and pleasing quality of tone: its peculiar character being produced by a small round hole being bored in the pipe, near to the top. It was invented by Messrs. Gray & Davison.

KEREN (*Heb.*) A Hebrew trumpet, originally made with a ram's horn.

KERN (*Ger.*) The languid, or langward, in organ pipes.

KERNIG (*Ger.*) With decision, firmness; *decíso*.

KEROPHONE. A free-reed organ stop, with a horn-like tone.

KERRENA. *See* KERANA.

KERRENA. An Indian trumpet.

KESSEL (*Ger.*) *Kettle*; the mouthpiece of a brass wind-instrument.

KESSELPAUKE (*Ger.*) A kettle-drum.

KETTEN-TRILLER (*Ger.*) Chain of shakes.

KETTLE-DRUM. A brass drum, of a cup-like shape, over which the parchment head is stretched.

KEY. The lever by which the sounds of a pianoforte, organ, or harmonium, are produced. Flutes, hautboys, and other wind-instruments, have also keys, by which certain holes are opened, or closed. A key also means, a scale, or series of notes, progressing diatonically, in a certain order of tones and semitones, the first note of the scale being called the *Key-note*, or *Tonic*.

KEY-BOARD. The row of keys, in a pianoforte, organ, or harmonium.

KEYED HARMONICA. An instrument with keys, the hammers striking upon plates of glass.

KEY-NOTE. The tonic, or first note of every scale.

KHALIL (*Heb.*) A flute or oboe.

KIELEN (*Ger.*) To *quill* the 'jacks' of the harpsichord, &c.

KIELFLÜGEL (*Ger.*) A wing-shaped harpsichord.

KINK-HORN (*Ger.*) Cornet, clarion: *see* ZINKE.

KINK-HÖRNER (*Ger. pl.*) Cornets, clarions: *see* ZINKEN.

KINNHALTER (*Ger.*) The chin rest of a violin.

KIRCHEN-COMPONIST (*Ger.*) Composer of church music.

KIRCHEN-DIENST (*Ger.*) Church-service: form of prayer.

KIRCHEN-FEST (*Ger.*) Church festival.

KIRCHEN-GESANG / **KIRCHEN-LIED** (*Ger.*) Spiritual song, plain song, canticle, psalm or hymn.

KIRCHEN-MUSIK (*Ger.*) Church music.

KIRCHEN-STÜCK (*Ger.*) Church-piece, or composition.

KIRCHEN-STYL (*Ger.*) Church style, ecclesiastical style.

KIRCHEN-TON (*Ger.*) Church mode, or tone: *see also* KAMMER-TON.

KIRCHEN-TRIO (*Ger.*) An obsolete species of composition, for two violins and bass.

KISSAR. A five stringed Nubian lyre.

KIT. A small pocket violin, used by teachers of dancing.

KITAR / **KITRA** An Arabian guitar.

KITHARA (*Gr.*) An instrument of the lyre species, used by the ancient Greeks.

KLAGE (*Ger.*) Lamentation.

KLAGE-GEDICHT / **KLAGE-LIED** (*Ger.*) Elegy, lamentation, mournful song.

KLAGE-TON (*Ger.*) Plaintive tune, or melody.

KLANG (*Ger.*) Sound: tune.

KLANGBODEN (*Ger.*) A sound-board.

KLÄNGE (*Ger. pl.*) Sounds: melodies.

KLANGFOLGE (*Ger.*) The tonality of a chord progression.

KLANG-GEDICHT / **KLANG-LIED** (*Ger.*) Sonnet.

KLANG-GESCHLECHT (*Ger.*) Genus, mode, scale.

KLANGLEHRE (*Ger.*) Acoustics.

Klanglos — Komponiren

KLANGLOS (*Ger.*) Soundless, mute.
KLANGSAAL (*Ger.*) Concert room, music room.
KLAPPE (*Ger.*) Key of any wind-instrument: a valve.
KLAPPEN-FLÜGELHORN (*Ger.*) Keyed bugle.
KLAPPEN-HORN (*Ger.*) A keyed trumpet.
KLAR (*Ger.*) Clear, bright; *klare Stimme*, a clear voice.
KLARHEIT (*Ger.*) Clearness, plainness, distinctness.
KLARINETTE (*Ger.*) A clarinet.
KLÄRLICH (*Ger.*) Clearly, distinctly.
KLASSISCH (*Ger.*) Classical.
KLAUSEL (*Ger.*) A close: a regular section of a strain, or movement.
KLAVIER (*Ger.*) See **CLAVIER**.
KLEIN (*Ger.*) Minor: speaking of intervals.
KLEIN-BASS
KLEIN-BASS-GEIGE } (*Ger.*) Violincello.
KLEINE FLÖTE (*Ger.*) A piccolo.
KLEIN-GEDACT (*Ger.*) A small covered stop, in an organ: a stopped flute.
KINGBAR (*Ger.*) Resonant, sonorous.
KLINGEL (*Ger.*) A bell.
KLINGEN
KLINGEND } (*Ger.*) Sounding, resonant, ringing, sonorous.
KLING-GEDICHT (*Ger.*) Sonnet.
KNABENSTIMME (*Ger.*) A boy's voice; a counter-tenor.
KNARRE (*Ger.*) A rattle.
KNEIFEND (*Ger.*) Plucking; *pizzicáto*.
KNIE-GEIGE (*Ger.*) *Viol da gámba*, violoncello.
KNIE-RÖHRE (*Ger.*) A pipe, or tube, bent as a knee.
KNOPF-REGAL (*Ger.*) See **APFEL-REGAL**.
KOBSA. A primitive Russian lute.
KOKETT (*Ger.*) Coquettish.
KOLLECTIVZUG (*Ger.*) A composition pedal, on an organ.
KOLLERN (*Ger.*) To sing in a thin, reedy voice.
KOLLO. A Japanese instrument, of the harp species.
KOMISCH (*Ger.*) Comical.
KOMMA (*Gr.* & *Ger.*) Comma: a musical section, or division.
KOMÖDIANT (*Ger.*) Comedian, actor, player.
KOMÖDIANTINN (*Ger.*) Am actress.
KOMÖDIE (*Ger.*) Comedy, play.
KOMPONIREN (*Ger.*) To compose.

KOMPONIST (*Ger.*) A composer.
KOMPOSITION (*Ger.*) A composition.
KONSERVATORIUM (*Ger.*) A conservatory.
KONTRA (*Ger.*) See **CONTRA**.
KONZERT-MEISTER (*Ger.*) See **CONCERT-MEISTER**.
KOPF-STIMME (*Ger.*) Falsetto, head-voice, *vóce di tésta*.
KOPPEL (*Ger.*) Coupler: coupling stop, or movement, in an organ: *see also* **COPPEL**.
KOR (*Ger.*) \
KÖRE (*Ger. pl.*) } See **CHOR**.
KORNETT (*Ger.*) A *cornet à pistons*.
KORYPHÆUS (*Gr.*) Chief, leader, of the dancers.
KOS. An Hungarian dance.
KOSAKE. A nation dance of the Cossacks.
KOTO. A Japanese harp, with thirteen silk strings.
KRÄCHZEN (*Ger.*) To croak; to sing in a croaking voice.
KRAFT (*Ger.*) Vigour, power, energy.
KRÄFTIG \
KRÄFTIGLICH } (*Ger.*) Powerful, vigorous, energetical: *kräftig und kurz*, loud and detached.
KRAKOVIAK \
KRAKOVIENNE } The Cracovienne, a Polish dance in $\frac{2}{4}$ time.
KRÄUSEL (*Ger.*) A mordent.
KREBSGÄNGIG (*Ger.*) Backward, retrograde.
KREIS (*Ger.*) A circle, a round.
KREISCHEND (*Ger.*) Shrieking, harsh, strident.
KREIS-TANZ (*Ger.*) Dance in a circle.
KREOL. A Danish reel.
KREUZ (*Ger.*) The character called a *sharp*.

KREUZ-DOPPELTES (*Ger.*) The mark called a *double sharp* ×, or ✖.

KRIEGERISCH (*Ger.*) Martial, warlike.
KRIEGS-GESANG \
KRIEGS-LIED } (*Ger.*) Warlike song, military song.
KRIEGS-SPIELER (*Ger.*) A military musician.
KROME. See **CRÓMA**.
KRUMM (*Ger.*) Crooked, curved, bent.
KRUMM-BOGEN (*Ger.*) The crook of a horn or trumpet.
KRUMM-HORN (*Ger.*) *Crooked horn*, or small cornet. This name is given to an 8 feet reed stop, in an organ, the tone of which formerly resembled that of a small cornet, but now the stop is generally called

Cremorna, *Clarionet*, or *Cormorne*, and the tone is estimated in proportion as it approximates that of a clarinet.

KRUSTISCHE INSTRUMENTE (*Ger.*) Instruments of percussion as, the drum, triangle, cymbals, &c.

KUH-HORN (*Ger.*) Cow-horn: Swiss, or Alpine horn.

KUHN (*Ger.*) Dashing, audacious, bold.

KUHREIGEN
KUHREIHEN } (*Ger.*) *See* RANZ DES VACHES.

KUJAWIAK. A Polish dance, similar to the *Mazurka*.

KUNST (*Ger.*) Art, skill; knowledge.

KÜNSTKENNER (*Ger.*) A connoisseur.

KÜSNSTLER (*Ger.*) An artist.

KUPPEL (*Ger.*) *See* KOPPEL.

KURZ (*Ger.*) Short, brief, detached, *staccáto*: *kurz und rein*, distinct and clear.

KUSSIR (*Fr.*) A Turkish musical instrument.

KUSTOS (*Gr.*) A cue; a direct.

KÜTZIAL-FLÖTE (*Ger.*) An organ stop, of the flute species.

KYRIE ELEISON (*Gr.*) *Lord have mercy upon us.* The first movement of a Mass.

KYRIELLE (*Fr.*) A Litany.

L

LA. A syllable, applied, in *solfaing*, to the note A: the sixth note in the scale of Guido d'Arezzo.

LA (*It. & Fr.*) The.

LA BÉMOL (*Fr.*) The note A-flat.

LA BÉMOL MAJEUR (*Fr.*) The key of A-flat major.

LA BÉMOL MINEUR (*Fr.*) The key of A-flat minor.

LABIAL. Organ pipes with *lips*, called also *flue* pipes.

LABIAL-STIMMEN (*Ger.*) Stops belonging to the *flue* work, not *reed* stops.

LABIEN (*Ger.*) Pipes.

LABIUM (*Lat.*) The *lip*, of an organ pipe.

LA CHASSE (*Fr.*) In the hunting style.

LACRIMÁNDO / **LACRIMÓSO** (*It.*) Sadly; in a mournful, pathetic style.

LADE (*Ger.*) Wind-chest, in an organ.

LA DÉSTRA (*It.*) The right hand.

LA DIÈSE (*Fr.*) The note A-sharp.

LÆVA (*Lat.*) The left: the left hand.

LAGE (*Ger.*) Position.

LAGENWECHSEL (*Ger.*) Shifting position, in violin playing.

LAGNÉVOLE / **LAGNÓSO** (*It.*) Dolorous, mournful.

LAGRIMÁNDO / **LAGRIMÓSO** (*It.*) Complaining: sadly; in a mournful style.

LAI (*Fr.*) Lay, ditty, short plaintive song.

LAISSER (*Fr.*) To allow; to let.

LA MAJEUR (*Fr.*) The key of A major.

L'ÂME (*Fr.*) *Sound-post*, of a violin, viola, &c.

LA MELODÍA BEN MARCÁTA (*It.*) The melody to be well marked.

LAMENT. An old name for harp music of the pathetic kind: applied also to the pathetic tunes of the Scotch.

LAMENTÁBILE (*It.*) Lamentable, mournful.

LAMENTABILMÉNTE (*It.*) Lamentably, dolefully.

LAMENTÁNDO (*It.*) Lamenting, mourning.

LAMENTAZIÓNE (*It.*) Lamentation, dirge.

Lamentévole — Largeur

LAMENTÉVOLE (*It.*) Lamentable, mournful, plaintive.
LAMENTEVOLMÉNTE (*It.*) Mournfully, plaintively.
LAMENTÓSO (*It.*) Lamentable, mournful.
LA MINEUR (*Fr.*) The key of A minor.
LAMPENFIEBER (*Ger.*) Stage fright.
LAMPO (*It.*) A flash of lightning.
LAMPONS (*Fr.*) Drinking songs.

LÄNDERER
LÄNDLER (*Ger.*) A species of slow, rustic waltz, in $\frac{3}{8}$ or $\frac{3}{4}$ time: some of the Styrian dances, of this kind, are charming melodies.

LAND-LIED (*Ger.*) Rural song, rustic song.
LANDU. *See* LUNDU.
LANG (*Ger.*) Long.

LANGE FERMATA
LANGE HALTEN (*Ger.*) A long pause.
LANGE PAUSE

LANGES SCHWEIGEN (*Ger.*) A long silence.
LANGSAM (*Ger.*) Slowly: equivalent to *Lárgo*.
LANGSAMER (*Ger.*) Slower.

LANGUAGE
LANGUID In an organ flue-pipe, this is, the flat piece of metal, or wood, placed horizontally at the top of the foot, just inside the mouth.

LANGUEMÉNTE (*It.*) Languishing, languidly.

LANGUÉNDO
LANGUÉNTE (*It.*) Languishing, feeble: with languor.
LÁNGUIDO

LANGUETTES (*Fr.*) The brass tongues, belonging to the reed pipes, in an organ.
LANGUÓRE (*It.*) Languor.
LANTUM. A species of large hurdy-gurdy.
LA PRÍMA VÓLTA FÓRTE, LA SECÓNDA PIÁNO (*It.*) The first time loud, the second time soft.

LARGAMÉNTE
LARGAMÉNTO (*It.*) Largely, fully: in a broad, large style of performance.

LARGÁNDO (*It.*) Getting slower and more impressive: *see* LÁRGO.
LARGE. The longest note formerly in use, in ancient music, shaped thus, ▐▌ : it is equal to eight semibreves.

LARGEMENT (*Fr.*) *See* LARGAMÉNTE.
LARGEUR (*Fr.*) Breadth.

LARGHÉTTO (*It.*) Slow, and measured, time: but not so slow as *Lárgo*: see ÉTTO.
LARGHÉZZA (*It.*) Breadth, largeness, freedom.
LARGHÍSSIMO (*It.*) Extremely slow: the superlative of *Lárgo*.
LÁRGO (*It.*) Slow, broad, solemn.
LÁRGO ANDÁNTE (*It.*) Slow and measured.
LÁRGO ASSÁI | (*It.*) Very slow.
LÁRGO DI MÓLTO |
LÁRGO MA NON TRÓPPO (*It.*) Slow, but not too much so: not dragging.
LÁRGO UN PÓCO (*It.*) Rather slow.
LARIGOT (*Fr.*) *Shepherd's flute*, or *pipe*: an acute organ stop, tuned an octave above the twelfth.
LARINGE (*It.*) The larynx.
LARMOYANT (*Fr.*) Weeping; tearfully.
LA SECÓNDA PÁRTE ÚNA VÓLTA (*It.*) The second part only once.
LASCIÁTE SUONÁRE (*It.*) *Undamped*, in playing the drums or cymbals.
LAÚD (*Sp.*) A lute.
LÁUDA (*It.*) Laud, praise: hymn of praise.
LAUDAMUS TE (*Lat.*) *We praise Thee*: part of the Gloria.
LAUDES (*Lat.*) | Canticles, or hymns of praise, that follow the early
LÁUDI (*It. pl.*) | Mass.
LAUDISTI (*Lat.*) Psalm singers, hymn singers.
LAUF (*Ger.*) That part of a violin, &c., into which the pegs are inserted: see also LÄUFE.
LÄUFE (*Ger. pl.*) Rapid divisions of notes: a flight, or run, of rapid notes.
LAUFTANZ (*Ger.*) A *courante*.
LAUNENSTÜCK (*Ger.*) A voluntary.
LAUNIG (*Ger.*) Lightly, gaily; humorous.
LAUT (*Ger.*) Loud: also, sound.
LAUTE (*Ger.*) The lute.
LÄUTEN (*Ger.*) To ring, to toll, to sound.
LAUTEN-FUTTER | (*Ger.*) Lute-case.
LAUTEN-KASTEN |
LAUTENIST (*Ger.*) Lute-player, lutanist.
LAUTEN-MACHER (*Ger.*) Lute-maker.
LAUTEN-SCHLÄGER | (*Ger.*) Lute-player, lutanist.
LAUTEN-SPIELER |
LAUTENZUG (*Ger.*) Lute-register.
LA VÓCE (*It.*) The voice.

La vôlta — Leggiadraménte

LA VÔLTA (*It.*) An old dance, in which was much turning and much capering.

LAVORÁRE (*It.*) To work, to labour.

LAY. A short, light, song or air.

LAY-CLERK. A vocalist in a choir, who is not in holy orders.

LE (*It. pl.*) The: *le vóci*, the voice.

LEADER. The first, or principal violin, in an orchestra.

LEADING NOTE. The major seventh of any scale: the semitone below the key-note: the major third of the dominant.

LEANING NOTE. *See* APPOGGIATÚRA.

LEBEN (*Ger.*) Life, vivacity.

LEBEWOHL (*Ger.*) Farewell.

LEBHAFT (*Ger.*) Lively, quick, vivacious, brisk.

LEBHAFT, ABER NICHT ZU SEHR (*Ger.*) Quick, but not too much so.

LEBHAFT BEWEGT (*Ger.*) With lively animation.

LEBHAFTER (*Ger.*) Move lively, quicker.

LEBHAFTESTEN (*Ger.*) Very quick.

LEBHAFTIGKEIT (*Ger.*) Liveliness, vivacity.

LEÇON (*Fr.*) A lesson, an exercise.

LEDGER LINES / **LEGER LINES** The short, extra, or additional lines, drawn above or below the stave.

LEER (*Ger.*) Empty, hollow; open.

LEGÁBILE / **LEGÁNDO** (*It.*) *See* Legáto.

LEGÁRE (*It.*) To slur, or bind.

LEGÁRE LE NÓTE (*It.*) Exceedingly smooth, and connected.

LEGÁTO (*It.*) Slurred: in a smooth and connected manner: a close, gliding, style of performance.

LEGATÚRA (*It.*) A slur, a ligature.

LÉGEND (*Fr.*) / **LÉGENDE** (*Fr. & Ger.*) A piece in a narrative or romantic style.

LÉGER (*It.*) / **LÉGÈRE** (*Fr.*) Light, nimble.

LÉGÈREMENT (*Fr.*) Lightly, nimbly, gaily.

LÉGÈRETÉ (*Fr.*) Lightness, agility.

LEGGATÍSSIMO. *See* LEGATÍSSIMO.

LEGGÉNDA (*It.*) A legend, a tale.

LEGGERAMÉNTE (*It.*) Lightly, easily.

LEGGERÉZZA (*It.*) Lightness, agility.

LEGGIADRAMÉNTE (*It.*) Gracefully, elegantly.

Leggiádro — Leitereigen

LEGGIÁDRO (*It.*) Graceful, elegant.
LEGGIÁRDO (*It.*) Lightly, delicately.
LEGGIERAMÉNTE
LEGGIÉRE } (*It.*) Easily, lightly, swiftly, delicately.
LEGGIERÉZZA (*It.*) Lightness, agility, delicacy.
LEGGIERÍSSIMO (*It.*) The utmost lightness, and facility.
LEGGIERMÉNTE (*It.*) Lightly, easily, delicately.
LEGGIÉRO (*It.*) Light, swift, delicate.
LEGGIERÚCOLO (*It.*) Rather light and delicate.
LEGGIÓ (*It.*) A chorister's desk, in a church choir.
LÉGNO (*It.*) Wood: *see* COL LÉGNO.
LEHRE (*Ger.*) A text book, system of learning.
LEHRER (*Ger.*) A teacher.
LEHR-GEDICHT (*Ger.*) Didactic poem.
LEHR-ODE (*Ger.*) Didactic ode.
LEIB-STÜCKCHEN (*Ger.*) Favourite air, or tune.
LEICHEN-GEDICHT (*Ger.*) Funeral poem, elegy.
LEICHEN-GESANG (*Ger.*) Dirge: funeral song.
LEICHEN-MUSIK (*Ger.*) Funeral music.
LEICHT (*Ger.*) Light, easy, facile: lightly.
LEICHTFERTIG (*Ger.*) Light, careless, playful.
LEICHT GESTOSSEN (*Ger.*) Lightly detached.
LEICHTHEIT
LEICHTIGKEIT } (*Ger.*) Lightness, facility, easiness.
LEICHTLICH (*Ger.*) Lightly, easily.
LEIDENSCHAFT (*Ger.*) Fervency, passion.
LEIDENSCHAFTLICH (*Ger.*) Passionately.
LEIER (*Ger.*) A lyre.
LEIERER (*Ger.*) A player on the lyre.
LEIERN (*Ger.*) To play on the lyre.
LEIERSPIELER (*Ger.*) A player on the lyre.
LEINE (*Ger.*) A staff line.
LEISE (*Ger.*) Low, soft, gentle: lightly.
LEISTUNG (*Ger.*) Performance, rendering.
LEIT-ACCORD (*Ger.*) A chord, or harmony, leading instinctively to another, as the chord of the dominant, leading to the tonic.
LEITEN (*Ger.*) To lead, guide.
LEITER (*Ger.*) Leader: also, the scale of any key.
LEITEREIGEN (*Ger.*) Such tones as belong to the scale of any key: the notes forming the scale.

LEITER-FREMD (*Ger.*) Accidental sharps, or flats, which do not belong to the key.

LEITMOTIF
LEITMOTIV (*Ger.*) Leading motive, or theme.

LEIT-TON (*Ger.*) The leading tone, the leading note.

LENÉZZA
LÉNO (*It.*) Weak, feeble; faintly: not vigorous.

LENT (*Fr.*) Slow, lingering, leisurely.

LENTAMÉNTE (*It.*) Slowly.

LENTÁNDO (*It.*) Slackening the time: going slower.

LENTEMENT (*Fr.*)
LENTEMÉNTE (*It.*) Slowly, leisurely.

LENTEUR (*Fr.*)
LENTÉZZA (*It.*) Slowness, delay: *avec lenteur*, with slowness, at a sedate pace.

LENTISSIMAMÉNTE
LENTÍSSIMO (*It.*) Extremely slow.

LÉNTO (*It.*) Slow, lingering.

LÉNTO ASSÁI
LÉNTO DI MÓLTO (*It.*) Very slow.
LÉNTO LÉNTO

LE PLUS DOUX POSSIBLE (*Fr.*) As soft as possible.

LE PLUS FORT POSSIBLE (*Fr.*) As loud as possible.

LEPSIS (*Gr.*) The ascending scale.

LES (*Fr. pl.*) The.

LESSER BARBITON. A name formerly given to the kit, or small violin used by dancing masters.

LESSER SIXTH. A minor sixth.

LESSER THIRD. A minor third.

LESSON. Formerly applied to exercises, or pieces consisting of two or three movements, for the harpsichord, and pianoforte.

LESTAMÉNTE (*It.*) Quickly, lively, brisk.

LESTÉZZA (*It.*) Agility, quickness.

LESTISSIMAMÉNTE (*It.*) Very quickly.

LESTÍSSIMO (*It.*) Very quick: extremely quick.

LÉSTO (*It.*) Quick, lively, nimble.

LETANE. See LITANIA.

L'ÉTÉ (*Fr.*) One of the movements in a quadrille.

LETTERÁLE
LETTERALMÉNTE (*It.*) Literally, exactly as written.

LETTÚRA (*It.*) A reading, lecture: an instruction given by a master to his scholars.

LETTÚRA DI MÚSICA (*It.*) A musical lecture.
LEUTÉSSA (*It.*) A bad lute.
LEÚTO (*It.*) A lute.
LEVÁRE (*It.*) To raise, lift, remove.
LEVÉ (*Fr.*) The up-stroke of the *bâton*.
LEVEZ (*Fr.*) Raise, take off.
LEVÉZZA (*It.*) Lightness.
LEVIER PNEUMATIQUE (*Fr.*) The pneumatic lever: a series of small bellows, or levers, placed on the wind-chest of an organ, containing air at a high pressure; by means of this the touch of a large organ may be made as light as that of a pianoforte.
LIAISON (*Fr.*) Smoothness: also, a *slur*, or a *bind*.
LIAISON DE CHANT (*Fr.*) The *sostenúto* style of singing.
LIBERAMÉNTE (*It.*) Freely, easily, plainly.
LIBERTÀ (*It.*) Liberty, freedom.
LIBITUM (*Lat.*) Pleasure.
LIBREMENT (*Fr.*) Freely, easily, plainly.
LIBRÉTTO (*It.*) The poem, or words, of an opera: a book of words, or poem, to be set to music.
LICÉNZA POÉTICA (*It.*) Poetic licence: alterations, or deviations from common rules.
LICÉO (*It.*) Academy, lyceum.
LICHANOS (*Gr.*) One of the strings on a lyre.
LIÉ (*Fr.*) Smoothly: the same as LEGÁTO.
LIEBES-LIED (*Ger.*) Love-song.
LIEBLICH (*Ger.*) Lovely, charming, sweet, delicious.
LIEBLICH-GEDACT (*Ger.*) A stopped-diapason organ register, of slender scale, and sweet tone.
LIED (*Ger.*) A song, air, ballad: a short poem set to music.
LIEDCHEN (*Ger.*) Short song, or melody.
LIEDER-BUCH (*Ger.*) Song book, hymn book.
LIEDER-DICHTER (*Ger.*) Lyrical poet, writer of songs.
LIEDER-SAMMLUNG (*Ger.*) Collection of songs.
LIEDER-SÄNGER (*Ger.*) Singer, ballad-singer, minstrel.
LEIDER-SPIEL (*Ger.*) An operetta, in which dialogue and music are equally employed; the music being of a light, vivacious character.
LIEDER-TAFEL (*Ger.*) A song-table: German glee club: vocalists who meet together to sing part-songs, generally such as are composed for male voices alone.
LIEDER-TANZ (*Ger.*) A song combined with dancing.

Lied ohne — Líscio

LIED OHNE WORTE (*Ger.*) Song without words: a short, *cantábile* composition, for the pianoforte, with a clearly defined melody.

LIEGEND (*Ger.*) Lying, horizontal.

LIER (*Dutch.*) The *lyre*.

LIÉTO (*It.*) Blithe, joyous, merry.

LIÉVE (*It.*) Light, easy.

LIGATO. See LEGÁTO.

LIGATUR (*Ger.*) See LIGATURE.

LIGATURA. See LEGATÚRA.

LIGATURE. An old name for a *tie*, of *bind*: *see also* SYNCOPATTION.

LIGNE (*Fr.*) A line of the stave.

LIGNEAM PSALTERIUM (*Lat.*) The wooden dulcimer, called in Germany, the straw fiddle. Gusikow, a Polish Jew, played upon this instrument, with astonishing skill, in 1836, and excited much admiration.

LIGNES ADDITIONNELLES (*Fr.*) See LEDGER LINES.

LIMMA. The ancient Greek name for a semitone.

LÍNEA (*It.*) A line of the stave.

LINÉZZA (*It.*) See LENÉZZA.

LÍNGUA (*It.*) The tongue, in organ reed stops.

LINGUALPFEIFE (*Ger.*) A reed-pipe, in an organ.

LINIE (*Ger.*) A line of the stave.

LINIEN-SYSTEM (*Ger.*) A scale: the lines of the stave.

LINK (*Ger.*) Left: *linke Hand*, the left hand.

LINON (*Gr.*) A string.

LINOS (*Gr.*) A rustic air.

LIPPE (*Ger.*) Lip.

LÍRA (*It.*) A lyre.

LÍRA DA BRÁCCIO (*It.*) The Italian lyre, an obsolete instrument with seven strings.

LÍRA DA GÁMBA (*It.*) An instrument similar to the *Líra da bráccio*, but held between the knees, and with twelve or sixteen strings.

LÍRA RÚSTICA (*It.*) A species of lyre, formerly in use among the Italian peasants.

LÍRA TEDÉSCA (*It.*) The German lyre.

LIRE LA MUSIQUE (*Fr.*) To read music.

LIRÉSSA (*It.*) A bad lyre, or harp.

LÍRICA / **LÍRICO** (*It.*) Lyric; lyric poetry; poetry adapted for music.

LIRÓNE (*It.*) A large lyre, or harp.

LÍSCIO (*It.*) Simple, unadorned, smooth.

LISPELND (*Ger.*) Lisping, whispering.
LISTÉSSO (*It.*) The same.
L'ISTÉSSO MOVIMÉNTO \
L'ISTÉSSO TÉMPO } (*It.*) In the same time as the previous movement.
LITANIA (*Lat.*) \
LITANIE (*Fr.*) } A litany.
LITANEI (*Ger.*) /
LITURGÍA (*It.*) Liturgy: sometimes accompanied with music.
LIUTÁJO (*It.*) A lute maker.
LIÚTO (*It.*) A lute.
LIVRE (*Fr.*) A book.
LIVRET (*Fr.*) A libretto.
LOB-GESANG \
LOB-LIED } (*Ger.*) Hymn, or song, of praise.
LOB-SINGEN (*Ger.*) To sing praises.
LÓCO (*It.*) *Place*: in its proper place: the passage is to be played precisely as written.
LOGEUM (*Lat.*) The stage of a Greek theatre.
LOGIERIAN SYSTEM. A system of musical instruction, introduced by John Bernard Logier, which, with instruction on the pianoforte, combines simultaneous performance in classes, and also, the study of harmony, modulation, &c.
LOMBÁRDA (*It.*) A species of dance, used in Lombardy.
LONG. A note ▬ formerly in use, equal to four semibreves, or half the length of the *Large*.
LONG DRUM. The large drum used in military bands, carried horizontally before the performer, and struck at both ends.
LONGUE PAUSE (*Fr.*) Make a long rest, or pause.
LONTÁNO (*It.*) Distant, remote, a great way off: *da lontáno*, at a distance.
LOURDE (*Fr.*) Heavy.
LOURE (*Fr.*) To unite the notes: also, the name of an old, slow, and dignified French dance, generally in $\frac{6}{8}$ time, or in common time, with the peculiarity of the second crotchet of every bar being dotted.
LOURRÉ (*Fr.*) Smoothly, connectedly: the same meaning as *Legáto*.
LOUVRE (*Fr.*) A name applied to a French air called '*L'amiable Vainqueur*', of which Louis XIV was extremely fond, and to which the French dancing-masters composed a dance.

Ludi — Lyra

LUDI MAGISTER / **LUDI MODERATOR** (*Lat.*) Theatrical manager, or director.

LUDI SPIRITUALES (*Lat.*) A species of ancient dramatic oratorio, acted on the stage.

LUDUS (*Lat.*) A play.

LUFTIG (*Ger.*) Light, airy, vaporous.

LUGÚBRE (*It.*) Lugubrious, mournful.

LULLEN (*Ger.*) To lull to sleep, a lullaby.

LUNDU. A Portuguese dance in $\frac{7}{4}$ or $\frac{2}{2}$ time.

LÚNGA PÁUSA (*It.*) A *long pause*, or rest, to be made.

LUÓGO (*It.*) See **LÓCO**.

LUSINGÁNDO / **LUSINGÁNTE** / **LUSINGÁTO** (*It.*) Soothing, coaxing; persuasively; in a playful, persuasive style.

LUSINGHEVOLMÉNTE (*It.*) Soothingly, persuasively.

LUSINGHIÉRE / **LUSINGHIÉRO** (*It.*) Flattering, fawning, coaxing, soothing.

LUSTIG (*Ger.*) Merrily, cheerfully, gaily.

LUSTLIED (*Ger.*) A gay, merry song.

LUTE (*Eng.*) / **LUT** (*Fr.*) / **LUTH** (*Fr.*) An instrument of very ancient origin, and common in the fourteenth century: it had many strings of gut, some of which were duplicates in pitch, and which were played by the hand. Vincentio Galilei ascribes its invention to the English, and says that in England lutes were made in great perfection. It was formerly much esteemed, and in shape bore some resemblance to the guitar: *see* **TABLATURE**.

LUTHIER (*Fr.*) A maker of lutes.

LUTINA. A small lute, or mandolin.

LUTTO (*It.*) Grief, sorrow, mourning.

LUTTUOSAMÉNTE (*It.*) Sadly, sorrowfully.

LUTTUÓSO (*It.*) Sorrowful, mournful.

LYCHANOS (*Gr.*) The third string of the lyre: *see* **HYPATR**.

LYDIAN. See **GREEK MODES**.

LYRA (*Gr.*) The lyre: which see.

LYRA HEXACHORDIS (*Gr.*) A lyre with six strings.

LYRA MENDICORUM (*Lat.*) The hurdy-gurdy.

LYRA-VIOL. An old instrument of the lyre, or harp, species: it had six strings, and seven frets.

LYRE. The most ancient stringed instrument, mythologically ascribed to Mercury, and said to have been invented about the year 2000 A.M., and formed with the shell of the tortoise: a species of harp.

LYRIC
LYRICAL
Poetry adapted for singing, and intended to be sung to a lyre or harp: formerly, the voice was always accompanied with the lyre or harp. A lyrical composition is the opposite to a dramatic one.

LYRICHORD. An old instrument of the lyre species.

LYRIKER
LYRISCH
(*Ger.*) Lyric, lyrical.

LYRIST. One who plays upon the harp or lyre.

LYRODI (*Gr.*) Ancient vocalists, who accompanied themselves on the lyre.

M

MA (*It.*) But: *Allégro ma non troppo*, quick but not too much so.

MACHALATH. A duet, the two voices singing alternately.

MACHÊTE. A small Portuguese guitar.

MACHICOT (*Fr.*) Leader of the choir, in a church.

MACHOL. An ancient Hebrew instrument.

MACH-WERK (*Ger.*) *Made-work*: music made up, or fabricated; merely the result of labour and study.

MADRIÁLE (*It.*) A madrigal: see MAGRIGÁLE.

MADRIALÉTTO (*It.*) A short madrigal.

MADRIGAL. A pastoral song: an elegant and elaborate composition, for three, four, five, or more voices, without accompaniment, in strict, or ancient style, with imitation and fugue: requiring ample knowledge of part-writing, and counterpoint: the parts, or melodies, moving in that conversational manner peculiar to the period of the sixteenth and seventeenth centuries.

The madrigal differs from the glee, in that the musical phrases, or portions of melody, complete in themselves, seldom coincided, or went together, in the different voice parts; one phrase being begun before the other was ended, so that they overlapped each other, as it were, and the composition was not a succession of different, though connected, musical phrases, but a repetition, under different circumstances, of the same phrase. The madrigal is generally sung in chorus, but the glee by single voices.

MADRIGÁLE (*It.*) A madrigal.

MADRIGALEGGIÁRE (*It.*) To compose madrigals.

MADRIGALÉSCO (*It.*) Of, or belonging to, a madrigal.

MADRIGALÉSSA (*It.*) A long madrigal.

MADRIGALÉTTO
MADRIGALÍNO } (*It.*) A short madrigal.

MAESTÀ
MAESTÁDE } (*It.*) Majesty, dignity: majestical: grandeur.
MAESTÁTE

MAESTÉVOLE (*It.*) Majestic: majestical.

MAESTEVOLÍSSIMO (*It.*) Most majestically.

MAESTEVOLMÉNTE \
MAESTOSAMÉNTE (*It.*) Majestically, stately, nobly.

MAESTOSÍSSIMO (*It.*) Exceedingly majestic.

MAESTÓSO (*It.*) Majestical, stately, dignified.

MAÉSTRA (*It.*) An *artiste*, female performer.

MAESTRÁLE (*It.*) Masterly.

MAESTRÉVOLE (*It.*) Masterly, highly finished.

MAESTRÍA (*It.*) Mastery, skill, art, ability, perfect command.

MAÉSTRI SECOLÁRI (*It.*) Teachers of secular, or instrumental music: teachers of the instruments at a *conservatório*.

MAÉSTRO (*It.*) Master: composer: an experienced, skilful artist.

MAÉSTRO DEL CÓRO (*It.*) Master of the choir, or chorus.

MAÉSTRO DI CAPPÉLLA (*It.*) Chapel-master: composer: director of the musical performances in a church or chapel.

MAGAS (*Gr.*) The bridge, of stringed instruments.

MAGGIOLÁTA (*It.*) A hymn, or song, in praise of the month of May.

MAGGIÓRE (*It.*) Greater, major: the major key.

MAGISCÓRO (*It.*) The chief of a choir.

MAGISTRÁLE (*It.*) See MAESTRÁLE.

MAGNIFICAT (*Lat.*) The canticle, or hymn, sung by the Virgin Mary in the house of Zacharias; and introduced into the Vespers, or evening service, of the Church.

MÁGNO (*It.*) Grand, great.

MAIN (*Fr.*) Hand: *main droite*, the right hand: *main gauche*, the left hand.

MAIS (*Fr.*) But.

MAÎTRE DE CHAPELLE (*Fr.*) Chapel-master: director of the choir.

MAÎTRE DE MUSIQUE (*Fr.*) Musical director.

MAJESTÀ (*It.*) \
MAJESTÄT (*Ger.*) Majesty, dignity, stateliness. \
MAJESTÉ (*Fr.*)

MAJEUR (*Fr.*) Major: major key.

MAJOR. *Greater*, in respect to intervals, scales, &c.

MAJOR CADENCE. A closing on the major chord.

MAJOR KEY \
MAJOR MODE That mode, or scale, in which the third from the tonic is major.

MAJOR-MODUS (*Lat.*) See MAJOR MODE.

MAJOR SEMITONE. A semitone which *changes* its place, or *letter*, on the staff: thus, C - D-flat, A - B-flat, &c.: see CÓMMA.

MAJOR THIRD. A diatonic interval containing two whole tones.

MAJOSIS. A jovial dance, of the Polish Jews.

MALAGUEÑA (*Sp.*) A *fandango*.

MALANCONÍA
MALENCÓNICO (*It.*) Melancholy, sadness.
MALINCÓLICO
MALINCONÍA

MALINCONICAMÉNTE
MALINCÓNICO
MALINCONIÓSO (*It.*) In a melancholy style.
MALINCONÓSO

MALSONNANT (*Fr.*) Ill sounding, bad toned.

MÁNCA (*It.*) The left.

MANCÁNDO
MANCÁNTE (*It.*) Decreasing, dying away.

MANCHE (*Fr.*) The neck, of a violin, &c.

MANDÓLA (*It.*) A cithern, or mandoline, of the size of a large lute.

MANDOLINE. An instrument with frets, of the guitar species, smaller than the *Mandora*. There are several kinds of mandolins. The strings, which are of gut and wire, are eight in number, of which four are duplicates; they are tuned like the violin, and are put in vibration with a quill, or plectrum.

MANDOLINÁTA (*It.*) The imitation of the *mandoline*, in pianoforte playing; a quite piece for *mandoline*.

MANDOLÍNO (*It.*) A mandolin.

MANDORA
MANDORE A small kind of lute, or guitar; with frets, and seven gut strings, three of which are duplicates.

MÁNI (*It. pl.*) The hands.

MÁNICA (*It.*) Fingering.

MÁNICO (*It.*) The neck, of the violin, guitar, &c.

MANICHORD
MANICORDE A species of spinet, or harpsichord: *see* **CLARICHORD**.

MANICORDIENDRAHT (*Ger.*) Wire for the *Manichord*, or *Clavichord*.

MANICHORDION (*Fr.*)
MANICHORDIUM (*Lat.*) *See* **MANICHORD**.

MANIÉRA (*It.*) Manner, style.

MANIÉRA AFFETTÁTA (*It.*) An affected style, or delivery.

MANIÉRA LÁNGUIDA (*It.*) A languid, sleepy style.

MANIÈRE (*Fr.*) Manner, style.

MANIÈRE D'ATTAQUE (*Fr.*) Touch, manner, or style, of playing the pianoforte, &c.

MANIEREN (*Ger. pl.*) Graces, embellishments, ornaments.

MÄNNERCHOR (*Ger.*) A male choir.

MÄNNERGESANG-VEREIN (*Ger.*) Men's vocal society.

MANNERISM. Peculiarity of style: the constant use of an over-recurring set of phrases: one unvaried manner, either of composition, or performance.

MÄNNLICHE STIMME (*Ger.*) A manly voice.

MÁNO (*It.*) The hand: *máno déstra*, or *máno drítta*, the right hand: *máno sinístra*, the left hand.

MANRÍTA (*It.*) The right hand.

MANUEL (*Eng. & Ger.*) | The *keys*, the *key-board*: in organ music this word means, that the passage is to be played by the hands alone, without using the pedals.
MANUÁLE (*Lat. & It.*) |

MANUALITER (*Ger.*) Organ pieces to be played by the fingers alone, without pedals.

MANUAL-KOPPEL (*Ger.*) A coupler between the manuals of an organ.

MANUALMÉNTE (*It.*) With the hands.

MANUAL-UNTERSATZ (*Ger.*) See SUB-BOURDON.

MANÚBRIO (*It.*) | The handle, or knob, by which a stop is drawn, in an organ.
MANUBRIUM (*Lat.*) |

MANUDUCTOR. A guide for the hand: one who beats time with his hand.

MARCÁNDO | (*It.*) Marked, strongly accented: well pronounced: with much emphasis.
MARCÁTO |

MARCATÍSSIMO (*It.*) Very strongly marked: as much as possible.

MARCÁTO IL PÓLLICE (*It.*) Mark, or accent strongly, the note played by the thumb.

MARCHE (*Fr.*) A march: in harmony, this means, a symmetrical sequence of chords.

MARCHE HARMONIQUE (*Fr.*) A harmonic progression.

MARCHE REDOUBLÉE (*Fr.*) A double-quick march.

MARCHE TRIOMPHALE (*Fr.*) A triumphal march.

MÄRCHEN (*Ger.*) Tale, legend, fable.

MÁRCIA | (*It.*) A march.
MARCIÁTA |

MARCIÁLE. See MARZIÁLE.

MARKIG (*Ger.*) Sturdy, vigorous; with much emphasis.

MARKIREN (*Ger.*) | To mark: to distinguish the tone by accented, or emphatic notes.
MARQUER (*Fr.*) |

MARQUÉ (*Fr.*) Marked, accented, emphasised.

MARQUEZ UN PEU LA MÉLODIE (*Fr.*) The melody to be slightly marked, or accented.

Marsch — Master

MARSCH (*Ger.*) A march.
MARSCHARTIG (*Ger.*) In the style of a march.
MÄRSCHE (*Ger. pl.*) Marches.
MARSCH-TAKT | (*Ger.*) March time.
MARSCH-ZEITMASS |
MARSEILLAISE (*Fr.*) The Marseilles hymn: a French national air.
MARTEAU (*Fr.*) The hammer of a pianoforte key; a tuning hammer.
MARTELÉ (*Fr.*) | *Hammering, hammered,* beaten: strongly
MARTELLÁNDO (*It.*) | marking the notes, as if hammered.
MARTELLÁRE (*It.*) To hammer: to strike the notes forcibly, like a hammer.
MARTELLÁTO (*It.*) *Hammered,* forcibly marked.
MARTELLEMENT (*Fr.*) The *acciaccatúra* in harp playing; a mordent in old music.
MARTRÁZA. A Spanish dance.
MARZIÁLE (*It.*) Martial: in the style of a march.
MASCHERÁTA (*It.*) |
MASK (*Eng.*) | A species of musical drama, or operetta,
MASKE (*Ger.*) | including singing and dancing, performed by characters in masks.
MASQUE (*Fr.*) |
MASRAKITHA. A wind-instrument, of the ancient Hebrews: it consisted of pipes of various sizes, fitted into a kind of wooden chest, into which wind was conveyed from the lips, by means of a pipe, and the sounds were produced by the fingers acting upon the apertures at the top.
MASS. A vocal composition, performed during the celebration of High Mass, in the Roman Catholic Church, and generally accompanied by instruments. It consists of five principal movements, the *Kyrie, Gloria, Credo, Sanctus,* and *Agnus Dei,* which are sometimes composed as solos, duets, &c; and sometimes in chorus, or fugue.
MASS (*Ger.*) Measure, time.
MÄSSIG (*Ger.*) Moderate: moderately.
MÄSSIG BEWEGT (*Ger.*) Moderately quick.
MÄSSIG LANGSAM (*Ger.*) Moderately slow.
MÄSSIG LEBHAFT (*Ger.*) Moderately lively.
MÄSSIGEN (Ger.) To diminish in speed and loudness.
MÁSSIMA (*It.*) A semibreve.
MASTER OF MUSIC. In the sixteenth century this appellation was given to eminent practical composers, &c., such as Okenheim, Iodocus, Pratensis, &c.

MASTER OF SONG. In the sixteenth century, this was applied to that member of the royal household, whose duty it was to teach the children of the Chapel Royal to sing.

MASURE
MASURECK
MASUREK
MASURKA
(*Ger.*) A lively Polish dance, of a sentimental character, in $\frac{3}{8}$, or $\frac{3}{4}$ time, of a peculiar rhythmic construction. It is quicker than the Polonaise, and has an emphasis on one of the unaccented parts of the bar.

MATALAN. A small Indian flute, used to accompany the Bayadere dances.

MATELOTTE (*Fr.*) A French sailor's dance, in $\frac{3}{4}$ time.

MATINÁRE (*It.*) To sing matins.

MATINÁTA (*It.*) A morning song; an *aubade*.

MATINÉE (*Fr.*) Morning concert.

MATINES (*Fr.*) *See* MATINS.

MATINS. Morning service: early morning service.

MATTHERZIG (*Ger.*) Faint-hearted, spiritless.

MATTINÁTA (*It.*) Morning song: morning music, played under a lady's window, early in the morning.

MATTINATÓRE (*It.*) He who sings or plays at sunrising, under the window of his lady.

MAUL-TROMMEL (*Ger.*) A Jew's harp.

MAXIMA (*Lat.*) The name of the longest note used in the fourteenth and fifteenth centuries: *see* LARGE.

MAZOURK
MAZOURKA
MAZUR
MAZURCA
MAZURKA
MAZURKE
(*Ger.*) A lively Polish dance, of a sentimental character, in $\frac{3}{8}$, or $\frac{3}{4}$ time, of a peculiar rhythmic construction, quicker than the *Polácca*: *see* MASURKA.

MEAN. The name formerly given to the *tenor* part of a composition.

MEASURE. The time: also, the music contained in each bar.

MÉCANISME (*Fr.*)
MECCANÍMO (*It.*)
Mechanical dexterity; technique.

MECHANIK (*Ger.*) Mechanism; the action of a pianoforte, or organ.

MECKERN (*Ger.*) To bleat, to tremolo.

MEDÉSIMO
MEDÉSMO
(*It.*) The same: *medésimo móto*, or, *medésimo témpo*, in the same time, or movement, as before.

MEDIANT (*Lat.*)
MÉDIANTE (*Fr.*)
The third note of the scale: the *middle note* between the tonic, and the dominant.

Medius — Melodisch

Medius (*Lat.*) The *mean* or tenor part; a ecclesiastical accent.
Meer-trompete | (*Ger.*) Sea trumpet.
Meer-horn
Mehr (*Ger.*) More than one; several.
Mehr-chörig (*Ger.*) For several voices.
Mehr-faches Intervall (*Ger.*) A compound interval.
Mehr-faches Stimme (*Ger.*) A compound or mixture stop on an organ.
Mehr-stimmig (*Ger.*) In several, or many, parts: for several voices.
Mehr-stimmiger Gesang (*Ger.*) A glee, or part-song.
Meister (*Ger.*) Master, teacher.7
Meister-gesang (*Ger.*) Master's song, minstrel's song.
Meister-sänger (*Ger.*) Minstrel's, master-singer.
Meister-spieler (*Ger.*) A virtuoso.
Melancolía (*It.*) | Melancholy, in a mournful style.
Mélancolie (*Fr.*)
Mélange (*Fr.*) A medley, a composition founded upon several popular, or favourite, airs.
Melisma (*Gr.*) A vocal grace, or embellishment: several notes sung to one syllable.
Melismatik (*Gr.*) Florid vocalisation: *see also* **Melisma**.
Melismatisch (*Ger.*) Florid, ornamented: *see* **Melisma**.
Melódie (*It.*) Melody, tune: *see* **Melodía**.
Melodestik (*Ger.*) The rules, or science, of melody.
Melodía (*It.*) Melody, tune; also, an organ stop of the *clarabella* species.
Melodica. A small pipe organ invented by Stein, Augsburg, 1770.
Melódico | (*It.*) Melodious, tuneful.
Melolicóso
Melodicon. An instrument invented by Riffel, in Copenhagen, the tones of which are produced from bent metal bars.
Mélodie (*Fr.*) Melody, tune.
Mélodie bien sentie (*Fr.*) The melody to be well expressed, or accented.
Melodik (*Ger.*) Melodious, tuneful.
Melodian. The name given to instruments of the *free-read* species.
Mélodieusement (*Fr.*) | Melodiously, sweetly.
Melodiosaménte (*It.*)
Melodióso (*It.*) Melodious, tuneful, musical.
Melodiosíssimo (*It.*) Extremely melodious.
Melodisch (*Ger.*) Melodious: melodiously.

MELODÍSTA (*It.*) | A melodist; one who writes good melodies.
MÉLODISTE (*Fr.*) |

MELODIUM. A variety of the harmonium.

MELODRAM (*Ger.*) | A species of pantomimic drama, or poem, of
MELODRAMA (*Eng.*) | French origin, with music interspersed,
MELODRAME (*Fr.*) | both vocal and instrument, the latter of
MELODRÁMMA (*It.*) | which is descriptive, and upon it much of
                        | the interest depends.

MELODRAMMÁTICO (*It.*) Melodramatic.

MELODY. A progression of single sounds, producing an agreeable effect upon the ear.

MELOGRAPH. A machine to write down in notes whatever is extemporised upon the pianoforte; but the invention was not quite perfect.

MELÓLOGO (*It.*) *See* MELOLOGUE.

MELOLOGUE. A recitation, accompanied with music.

MELOMAN (*Gr.*) A fanatical lover of music.

MELOMANTE. An intense passion for music.

MELOPÉA (*It.*) | Poetical, or rhetorical, melody: words and music
MÉLOPÉE (*Fr.*) | combined: the vocal declamation, or chant, of
                     | the drama.

MELOPHARE. A lantern, inside of which music paper, previously soaked in oil, is placed, so that the notes can be read when a light is placed inside: used for serenades at night.

MELOPIANO. A stringed instrument, invented in 1870, by Signor Caldera, of Turin, combining tones resembling those of the pianoforte and organ; the effect being obtained by a system of double and rapid percussion.

MELOPOEIA (*Gr.*) *See* MELOPÉA.

MELOPOMENOS (*Gr.*) A vocal melody.

MELOS (*Gr.*) Tune, song, melody.

MELOTHESIA (*Gr.*) The invention of a melody.

MELOTHETA (*Gr.*) Composer, musician.

MELOTYPE (*Gr.*) The art of printing notes, by types.

MÊME (*Fr.*) The same.

MÊME MOUVEMENT (*Fr.*) In the same time.

MÊME MOUVEMENT QUE PRÉCÉDEMMENT (*Fr.*) In the same time as the preceding.

MÉN (*It.*) Less: *mén présto*, less quick.

MENE. The name formerly given to the *tenor* part of a composition.

MENEER LE BRANLE (*Fr.*) To lead the dance.

MÉNÉSTRELS (*Fr.*) Minstrels.

MÉNÉTRIER (*Fr.*) Fiddler, rustic musician.

Méno — Metallophone

MÉNO (*It.*) Less: *méno fórte*, less loud: *méno mósso*, less movement, slower: *méno piáno*, not so softly: *méno vívo*, not so quick.

MENSCHEN-STIMME (*Ger.*) Human voice.

MENSUR (*Ger.*) Time, tune: correct measurement of intervals: also, the diameter, or scale, of organ pipes.

MENSURA (*Lat.*) Measure, time.

MENSURAL-GESANG (*Ger.*) Florid vocalisation.

MENSURAL-NOTEN (*Ger.*) Musical notation.

MÉNTE (*It.*) Mind, memory.

MENUET (*Fr.*)
MENUETT (*Ger.*) } A minuet, a slow dance, in $\frac{3}{4}$ time.
MENUETTO (*It.*)

MESCOLÁNZA (*It.*) A medley, a mixture of discordant sounds, bad harmony.

MESE (*Gr.*) The middle string of the lyre: *see* **HYPATE**.

MÉSSA (*It.*)
MESSE (*Fr. & Ger.*) } A Mass: *Masses*, Masses.

MÉSSA BÁSSA (*It.*) A silent Mass, whispered by the priest during a musical performance.

MÉSSA CONCERTÁTA (*It.*)
MESSE CONCERTANTE (*Fr.*) } A Mass consisting of concerted music.

MÉSSA DI VÓCE (*It.*) The gradual swelling, and diminishing of the voice.

MESSÁNZO. *See* **MESCOLÁNZA**.

MESSINGINSTRUMENTE (*Ger.*) Brass instruments.

MÉSTO (*It.*) Sad, melancholy, mournful.

MESTÓSO (*It.*) Sadly, mournfully, pensively.

MESURE (*Fr.*) The bar, or measure: the species of time.

MESURE À DEUX TEMPS (*Fr.*) Common time of *two* beats in a bar.

MESURE À TROIS TEMPS (*Fr.*) Triple time of *three* beat in a bar.

METAL. The material of which some organ pipes are made, composed of a mixture of tin and lead, in certain proportions; pipes made of pure tin give a clear, piercing tone; those of metal give a softer tone; if too much lead is mixed with the tin, the pipes are bad.

METÁLLICO (*It.*) Metallic: of a metallic quality.

METÁLLO (*It.*) Metallic: clear in tone: *bel metállo di vóce*, means, a voice clear, full, and brilliant.

METALLOPHONE. A species of pianoforte, with steel bars instead of strings; also, a species of xylophone, with metal bars.

MÉTHODE (*Fr.*) \
MÉTODO (*It.*) A method, system, style, school: treatise or book of instruction.

METRISCH (*Ger.*) Metrical.

METRONOM (*Ger.*) \
METRONOME (*Gr.*) An ingenious little machine for measuring the time, or the duration of notes, by means of a graduated scale and pendulum, which may be shortened or lengthened at pleasure.

METRUM (*Ger.*) Measure, time.

METTE (*Ger.*) Matins, morning service.

METTÉRE IN MÚSICA (*It.*) To set words to music.

METTÉTE (*It.*) To put, place, set.

METTEZ (*Fr.*) To *draw* or add a stop, in organ playing.

METTRE D'ACCORD (*Fr.*) To tune an instrument.

METTRE EN MUSIQUE (*Fr.*) To set to music.

METZILLOTH. Ancient Hebrew cymbals.

MÉZZA (*It.*) Half, medium, middle, moiety: moderate.

MÉZZA BRAVÚRA (*It.*) A song of medium, or moderate difficulty, as to execution.

MÉZZA MÁNICA (*It.*) The *half-shift*, in playing the violin, &c.

MEZZÁNA (*It.*) The middle string of a lute.

MÉZZA ORCHÈSTRA (*It.*) Half the orchestra.

MÉZZA VÓCE (*It.*) Half the power of the voice: a moderate, subdued tone, rather soft than loud.

MÉZZO (*It.*) Half, medium, middle, moiety: moderate.

MÉZZO CARÁTTERE (*It.*) A moderate degree of expression, and execution: music of a medium character.

MÉZZO FÓRTE (*It.*) Rather loud, moderately loud.

MÉZZO FÓRTE PIÁNO (*It.*) Rather loud, then soft.

MÉZZO PIÁNO (*It.*) Rather soft.

MÉZZO SOPRÁNO (*It.*) A low soprano, or second-treble voice: a female voice of lower pitch than the soprano, or treble, but higher than the contralto. The general compass is from G under the lines, to A above them. For this voice the C clef used to be placed on the second line of the stave.

MÉZZO STACCÁTO (*It.*) A little detached.

MÉZZO TENORE (*It.*) A half-tenor voice, nearly the same as a baryton.

MI (*It.*) This syllable, in *solfaing*, is applied to the note E.

MI BÉMOL (*Fr.*) The note E-flat.

MI BÉMOL MAJEUR (*Fr.*) The key of E-flat major.

MI BÉMOL MINEUR (*Fr.*) The key of E-flat minor.

Mi contra — Minuétto

MI CONTRA FA (*Lat.*) An expression used by old theorists, meaning, a *false relation*.

MIDDLE C. That C which is between the bass and treble staves.

MI DIÈSE (*Fr.*) The note E-sharp.

MILIEU (*Fr.*) Middle.

MILITAIREMENT (*Fr.*)
MILITÁRE (*It.*)
MILITARMÉNTE (*It.*) } Military: in a warlike, martial style.

MILOTE (*Sp.*) An Indian dance.

MI MAJEUR (*Fr.*) The key of E major.

MIMES. Mimic actors.

MI MINEUR (*Fr.*) The key of E minor.

MIMODRAME (*Fr.*) A pantomime.

MINACCEVOLMÉNTE (*It.*) In a threatening, menacing, manner.

MINACCIÁNDO (*It.*)
MINACCIÉVOLE } Threatening, menacing: in a boastful manner.

MINACCIOSAMÉNTE (*It.*) In a menacing manner.

MINACCIÓSO (*It.*) Threatening, menacing.

MINEUR (*Fr.*) Minor.

MINIM. A note equal to one-half of a semibreve.

MÍNIMA (*Lat. & It.*) A minim: literally, the *least*, because formerly a minim was the shortest note.

MINIM REST. A mark of silence, equal, in duration, to a minim: made thus, ▬.

MINNEDICHTER
MINNESÄNGER
MINNESINGER } (*Ger.*) Amatory, or erotic poets, who flourished in Germany from 1138 to 1347: they were succeeded from 1347 to 1519 by the *Meistersänger*, who formed a kind of corporation.

MINOR. Less, smaller, in speaking of intervals, &c.

MINÓRE (*It.*) Minor.

MINOR MODE. One of the modern modes, or scales, in which the third note is a *minor* third from the tonic.

MINOR SEMITONE. A semitone which *retains* its place, or *letter*, on the staff: thus: C, C-sharp; A, A-sharp; &c.: see COMMA.

MINOR THIRD. A diatonic interval containing three semitones.

MINSTRELS. The wandering poet-musicians of the tenth and following centuries.

MINUET (*Eng.*)
MINUETT (*Ger.*)
MINUÉTTO (*It.*) } An ancient slow and stately dance in two strains, in triple time of $\frac{3}{4}$, and supposed to be of French origin: modern movements of this name are generally quicker.

MINUETTÍNA (*It.*) A little minuet.
MINÚGE (*It.*) The strings of instruments; cat-gut.
MISCELLA (*Lat.*) The mixture: an organ stop.
MISE DE VOIX (*Fr.*) See MÉZZA VÓCE.
MISE EN SCÈNE (*Fr.*) The stage setting of a play, opera, &c.
MISERERE (*Lat.*) *Have mercy*: a psalm of supplication.
MISERICORDIA (*Lat.*) A *miserere*.
MISSA (*Lat.*) A Mass: see that word.
MISSA BREVIS (*Lat.*) A short mass.
MISSAL. The Mass book.
MISSA PRO DEFUNCTIS (*Lat.*) A Requiem: a Mass for departed souls.
MISSA SOLENNIS (*Lat.*) A solemn Mass, for high festivals.
MISSHÄLLIG (*Ger.*) Dissonant, discordant.
MISSHÄLLIGKEIT (*Ger.*) Dissonance, discordance.
MISSHELLIG (*Ger.*) See MISSHÄLLIG.
MISSKLANG (*Ger.*) Dissonance, discordance.
MISSKLÄNGE (*Ger. pl.*) Discordant sounds.
MISSLAUT (*Ger.*) Dissonance.
MISSLAUTEND (*Ger.*) Dissonant, discordant.
MISS-STIMMUNG | **MISS-TON** (*Ger.*) Discord, dissonance.
MISS-TÖNE (*Ger. pl.*) Discords, dissonances.
MISTÉRIO (*It.*) Mystery.
MISTERIOSAMÉNTE | **MISTERIÓSO** (*It.*) Mysteriously: in a mysterious manner.
MÍSTO (*It.*) Mixed.
MISÚRA (*It.*) A bar, a measure: time.
MISURÁTO (*It.*) Measured: in strict, measured, time.
MIT (*Ger.*) With, by.
MIT ALLER KRAST (*Ger.*) See TÚTTA FÓRZA.
MIT ÄUSSERST STARKER EMPFINDUNG (*Ger.*) With very strong emotion.
MITAUTER (*Ger.*) Concord, consonance.
MIT BEGLEITUNG (*Ger.*) With an accompaniment.
MIT BEWWGUNG (*Ger.*) Synonymous with *con móto*.
MIT DEN BOGEN GESCHLAGEN (*Ger.*) Struck with the back of the bow, in violin playing.
MIT GANZ SCHWACHEN REGISTERN (*Ger.*) With very soft stops.
MIT GROSSEM AUSDRUCK (*Ger.*) With great expression.
MIT HOLZSCHLÄGEL (*Ger.*) With a wooden beater, or drumstick.

Mit Keckheit — Modérno

MIT KECKHEIT (*Ger.*) With vigour and boldness: in the *bravúra*, or dashing style.

MIT KECKHEIT VORGETRAGEN (*Ger.*) In a bold, and vigorous, style of performance.

MITKLANG (*Ger.*) Resonance.

MITLAUT (*Ger.*) Concord, consonance.

MITLEIDIG | (*Ger.*) Compassionate.
MITLEIDSVOLL |

MITOS (*Gr.*) Thread: musical strings woven from flax.

MIT SANFTEN STIMMEN (*Ger.*) With soft stops.

MIT STARKEN STIMMEN (*Ger.*) With loud, or strong, stops.

MITTEL (*Ger.*) Middle; half.

MITTELAUT (*Ger.*) Mediant.

MITTEL-CADENZ (*Ger.*) A half, or imperfect, cadence.

MITTEL-STIMME (*Ger.*) The *mean*, or middle-voice, or part: the tenor.

MITTEL-STIMMEN (*Ger. pl.*) The middle parts, or voices.

MITTEL-STÜCK (*Ger.*) An interlude.

MITTEL-TON (*Ger.*) The Mediant: see that word.

MIT VOLLER ORGEL (*Ger.*) With full organ.

MIXED CADENCE. An old name for a cadence composed of the triad on the sub-dominant, followed by that upon the dominant.

MIXOLYDIAN. See **GREEK MODES**.

MIXTURA ACUTA (*Lat.*) An acute mixture stop: *see* **CYMBEL**.

MIXTURE. An organ stop, of a shrill and piercing quality, consisting of two, or more, ranks of pipes.

MÓBILE (*It.*) Moveable.

MOCIGÁNGA (*Sp.*) A musical interlude, common in Spain.

MODE. A scale: a certain arrangement of tones and semitones: *see* **MAJOR MODE**, *and* **MINOR MODE**.

MODERATAMÉNTE | (*It.*) Moderately, in moderate time: moderately
MODERÁTO | quick.

MODERÁTO ASSÁI CON MÓLTO SENTIMÉNTO (*It.*) A very moderate degree of quickness, with much expression.

MODERATÍSSIMO (*It.*) In a very moderate time.

MODERAZIÓNE (*It.*) Moderation, as to time, &c.

MODÉRÉ (*Fr.*) Moderate.

MODÉRÉMENT ANIMÉ (*Ger.*) Moderately fast.

MODÉRÉMENT LENT (*Ger.*) Moderately slow.

MODERN (*Eng.*) | Not in the ancient style.
MODÉRNO (*It.*) |

MODESTAMÉNTE \
MODÉSTO — (*It.*) Modestly, quietly, moderately.

MODIFICAZIÓNI (*It. pl.*) Modifications, light and shade of intonation, slight alterations.

MÓDO (*It.*) A mode, a scale: *módo maggióre*, the major mode: *módo minóre*, the minor mode.

MODOLÁRE \
MODULÁRE — (*It.*) To modulate: to accommodate the voice, or instrument, to a certain intonation: *see* MODULATION.

MODULÁNTE (*It.*) Modulating.

MODULATION. A change of key: going from one key to another, whether near, or remote, by a certain succession of chords, either in a natural and flowing manner, agreeable to the ear; or, sometimes, in a rapid and unexpected manner. As applied to the voice, modulation means, to accommodate the tone to a certain degree of intensity, or light and shade.

MODULAZIÓNE (*It.*) *See* MODULATION.

MODULIREN (*Ger.*) To modulate: *see* MODULATION.

MODUS (*Lat.*) A key, mode, scale: *modus major*, major scale: *modus minor*, minor scale.

MÖGLICH (*Ger.*) Possible.

MOHINDA. A short Portuguese love song.

MOHRENTANZ (*Ger.*) Morisco, morris-dance.

MOINS (*Fr.*) Less; *moins vite*, less quick.

MOITIÉ (*Fr.*) Half.

MOLL (*Ger.*) Minor.

MÓLLA (*It.*) A key of the flute, &c.: for raising or lowering a note.

MOLLE (*Fr.*) Soft, mellow, delicate.

MOLLEMÉNTE (*It.*) Faintly, softly, gently.

MOLLIS (*Lat.*) Soft.

MOLL-TONART (*Ger.*) Minor key, or scale.

MOLOSSUS (*Gr.*) A music foot of tree long sylables.

MÓLTA \
MÓLTO — (*It.*) Much, very much, extremely, a great deal.

MOLTISONÁNTE (*It.*) Resounding: very sonorous.

MÓLTO ADÁGIO (*It.*) Extremely slow.

MÓLTO ALLÉGRO (*It.*) Very quick.

MÓLTO MÓSSO (*It.*) Much movement: much motion.

MÓLTO SLARGÁNDO (*It.*) *Much extended*: much motion.

MÓLTO SOSTENÚTO (*It.*) Very sustained: very *legáto*.

MÓLTO VIVÁCE (*It.*) Very quick and lively.

Momentulum — Mormoraménto

MOMENTULUM (*Lat.*) A semiquaver rest.

MOMENTUM (*Lat.*) A quaver rest.

MONAULOS (*Gr.*) An ancient flute, played through the mouthpiece at the end, like the flageolet.

MONFERÍNA (It.) A lively Italian dance in $\frac{6}{8}$ time.

MONACÓRDO (*It.*)
MÓNOCHORD (*Eng.*)
 An instrument with one string, for measuring musical intervals, or sounds.

MONOCORDE (*Fr.*)
MONOCÓRDO (*It.*)
 On one string only: *see also* MONOCHORD.

MONODÍA (*It.*)
MONODIE (*Fr.*)
MONODY (*Eng.*)
 A melody intended to be performed by a single voice: also, an elegy, or lament.

MONODIC. For *one* voice: a solo.

MONODRAMA. A short drama, for a single actor, or actress, sometimes interspersed with music.

MONOPHONIC (*Gr.*) In *one* part only.

MONOTONE. Uniformly of sound: one and the same sound.

MONOTONIE (*Fr.*) Monotony, sameness of sound.

MONTANT (*Fr.*) Ascending.

MONTRÉ (*Fr.*) *Mounted*: in *front*: a term applied to the organ pipes which are placed in front of the case.

MONTEZ (*Fr.*) Raise.

MORBIDO (*It.*) Morbidly; softly, tenderly.

MORCEAU (*Fr.*) A musical piece, or composition.

MORDANT (*Fr.*)
MORDÉNTE (*It.*)
 Transient shake, or beat: an embellishment formed by two, or more, notes, preceding the principal note.

MORDENTEN UND DOPPEL-SCHLÄGER (*Ger.*) Beats, and turns.

MORÉNDO
MORIÉNTE
 (*It.*) Dying away, expiring; gradually diminishing the tone, and the time.

MORÉSCA (*It.*)
MORESQUE (*Fr.*)
 Moorish: morris-dance, in which bells are jingled, at the ancles; and swords, or staves, clashed, &c.

MORGEN-GESANG
MORGEN-LIED
 (*Ger.*) Morning song, morning psalm, or hymn.

MORGEN-STÄNDCHEN (*Ger.*) Morning music: *see* AUBADE.

MORÍSCO (*It.*) In the Moorish style: *see* MORÉSCA.

MORMORAMÉNTO (*It.*) A murmur.

Mormorándo
Mormorévole — (*It.*) With a gentle, murmuring, whispering, sound.
Moromoróso

Mósso (*It.*) Moved, movement, motion: *più mósso*, more motion, quicker: *méno mósso*, slower, less motion.

Móstra (*It.*) A direct.

Motett (*Eng.*)
Motette (*Ger.*) — A sacred composition of the anthem species, for several voices; but the words are not taken from the Holy Scriptures.
Motétto (*It.*)

Motívo (*It.*) Theme, subject, leading idea.

Móto (*It.*) Motion, movement; moving: *con móto*, with motion, rather quick.

Móto contrário (*It.*) Contrary motion: which see.

Móto obblíquo (*It.*) Oblique motion.

Móto precedénte (*It.*) The same time as the preceding movement.

Móto prímo (*It.*) The same time as the first.

Móto rétto (*It.*) Direct, or similar, motion.

Motteggiándo (*It.*) Jeeringly, mockingly, jocosely.

Mottétto (*It.*) A motet: which see.

Motus (*Lat.*) Motion, movement.

Motus contrarius (*Lat.*) Contrary motion.

Motus obliquus (*Lat.*) Oblique motion.

Motus rectus (*Lat.*) Direct, or similar, motion.

Mounted-cornet. An organ stop, usually consisting of five ranks of pipes, of large scale, and loudly voiced, placed upon a raised sound-board of their own (hence the name). It is only to be met with in old organs.

Mouth-piece. That part of a trumpet, horn, &c., which is applied to the lips.

Mouvement (*Fr.*)
Moviménto (*It.*) — Motion, movement, impulse: the time of a piece.

Muance (*Fr.*) A change or variation of notes; a *division*.

Mucksen (*Ger.*) To mutter, to utter a faint sound.

Mühelos (*Ger.*) Easily; without effort.

Mund (*Ger.*) The mouth.

Mund-harmonika (*Ger.*) The Jew's harp.

Mund-loch (*Ger.*) The mouth of an organ pipe.

Mund-stück (*Ger.*) Mouth-piece.

Münster (*Ger.*) Minster, cathedral.

Munter (*Ger.*) Lively, sprightly, briskly.

Munterkeit (*Ger.*) Briskness, liveliness, vivacity.

Murmeln — Musik-zimmer

MURMELN (*Ger.*) To murmur, whisper.
MURMURÁNDO (*It.*) See MORMORÁNDO.
MUSA (*Lat.*) A song: *see also* CORNAMÚSA.
MUSARS. The singers of songs, and ballads, in the tenth and following centuries.
MUSÉTTA (*It.*) See MUSETTE.
MUSETTE (*Fr.*) A species of small bagpipe much used in some parts of France, and inflated by means of bellows placed under the arm of the performer: also, an air, or rustic dance, of a sweet and pastoral character, composed for the instrument: also, an organ stop, of thin and delicate tone.
MUSIC. The language, or science, of sounds.
MÚSICA (*It.*) Music.
MÚSICA ARRABBIÁTA \
MÚSICA DI GÁTTI (*It.*) Burlesque music: caterwauling.
MUSICA COLORATA \
MUSICA FICTA (*Lat.*) An old name for music which deviated from the church modes.
MÚSICA DA CÁMERA (*It.*) Music for the chamber.
MÚSICA DA CHIÉSA (*It.*) Music for the church.
MÚSICA DA TEÁTRO (*It.*) Dramatic music.
MUSICÁLE (*It.*) Musical, belonging to music.
MUSICAL GLASSES. See HARMONICA.
MUSICALMÉNTE (*It.*) Musically.
MUSICA MELOPOETICA (Lat.) The art of making melody.
MUSICA ORGANICA (*Lat.*) Music for instruments.
MUSICÁRE (*It.*) To sing, or play, music.
MUSICHÉTTO (*It.*) A little musician.
MUSICHÉVOLE (*It.*) Musical.
MUSICHÍNO (*It.*) A little musician.
MÚSICO (*It.*) A musician; a professor, or practitioner, of music. The name was also applied to those male vocalists, who formerly snag soprano parts.
MUSICÓNE (*It.*) A great musician, or composer.
MUSICUS (*Ger.*) A musician.
MUSIK-FEST (*Ger.*) A music festival.
MUSIKINO (*Ger.*) A little musician.
MUSIK-LEHRER (*Ger.*) Teacher of music.
MUSIK-SAAL (*Ger.*) Music hall, music room.
MUSIKUS (*Ger.*) A member of an orchestra.
MUSIK-ZEITUNG (*Ger.*) A musical journal.
MUSIK-ZIMMER (*Ger.*) Music hall, music room.

MUSIQUE D'ÉGLISE (*Fr.*) Church music.

MÚTA (*It.*) *Change*: in horn, and trumpet, music, it means, to change the crooks: in drum parts it means, that the tuning of the drum is to be altered.

MUTATION (*Eng. & Fr.*)
MUTAZIÓNE (*It.*) The change of the voice, in adolescence: on the organ, *mutation*, or *filling-up* stops, are those which do not give a sound corresponding to the key pressed down; such as the quint, tierce, twelfth, &c.

MUTE. A small instrument of brass, ivory, or wood, sometimes placed on the bridge of a violin, viola, or violoncello, to diminish the tone of the instrument, by damping, or checking, its vibrations.

MUTED VIOL. *See* **VIOLE SOURDINE**.

MUTHWILLIG (*Ger.*) Lively, mischievous.

MUTIREN (*Ger.*) To change the voice, from soprano, to tenor, barytone, or bass.

MYKTEROPHONIE (*Gr. & Ger.*) To sing nasally; to sing through the nose.

MYSTÈRES (*Fr.*) Mysteries: a species of sacred drama, with music, which was practised in many of the European churches, before the Reformation.

N

NABLA / **NABLIUM**   A ten stringed instrument, used by the ancient Hebrews.

NACAIRE (*Fr.*) A bass drum, with a loud metallic tone, formerly much used.

NACCARA (*It.*) / **NACCARE** (*It. pl.*)   A large species of castanet.

NÁCCHERA (*It.*) Kettle-drums.

NOCCHERÉTTA (*It.*) A small kettle-drum.

NACCHERÍNO (*It.*) A kettle-drummer.

NACCHERÓNE (*It.*) A large pair of kettle-drums.

NACH (*Ger.*) After; following; agreeably to; in imitation of; to.

NACHAHMUNG (*Ger.*) Imitation.

NACHDRUCK (*Ger.*) Energy, emphasis, accent, expressiveness.

NACHDRÜCKLICH / **NACHDRÜCKSAM**   (*Ger.*) Energetic, emphatic, forcible, expressive.

NACHFOLGE (*Ger.*) Imitation.

NACHGEBEND (*Ger.*) *Rallentándo*.

NACHHALL (*Ger.*) Reverberation, echo.

NACHKLANG (*Ger.*) Resonance, echo.

NACHKLINGEN / **NACHSCHALLEN**   (*Ger.*) To ring, to resound, to echo.

NACHSATZ (*Ger.*) A response to a theme.

NACHSCHLAG (*Ger.*) Additional, or after-note.

NACHSINGEN (*Ger.*) To repeat a song: to sing after.

NACHSPIEL (*Ger.*) *After-play*: a postlude, or concluding piece.

NÄCHSTVERWANDTE TÖNE (*Ger.*) The nearest relative keys.

NACHT (*Ger.*) Night.

NACHT-GLOCKE (*Ger.*) Curfew, night-bell.

NACHT-HORN (*Ger.*) *Night-horn*: an organ stop of 8 feet tone, nearly identical with the *Quintaton*, but of larger scale, and more horn like in tone.

NACHTIGALL (*Ger.*) Nightingale.

NACHT-MUSIK (*Ger.*) *Night-music*, serenade.

NACHT-SCHLÄGER (*Ger.*) Nightingale.

NACHT-STÜCK (*Ger.*) A *nocturne*.

NACH UND NACH (*Ger.*) By little and little, by degrees.
NACH UND NACH IMMER RASCHER, SCHNELLER (*Ger.*) By degrees, continually increasing in rapidity.
NÆNIA (*Gr.*) A dirge.
NAFIRL. An Indian trumpet.
NAGÂRAH. A Moorish drum.
NAGAREET.
NAGARET. An Abyssinian drum.

NAGELGEIGE
NAGELHARMONIKA (*Ger.*) A *nail-fiddle*, an instrument with metal pins set into vibration with a bow.

NAHE (*Ger.*) Near.
NAÏF (*Fr.*)
NAIV (*Ger.*) Simple, artless, natural.
NAÏVE (*Fr.*)
NAÏVEMENT (*Fr.*) Plainly, naturally.
NAÏVETÉ (*Fr.*) Simplicity, artlessness.
NAKER. An obsolete name for the kettledrum.
NANGA. A negro harp.
NÄNIEN (*Ger.*) Dirges.
NARQUOIS (*Fr.*) Crafty, cunning.
NARRÀNTE (*It.*) In a narrative tone, or manner, as if reciting.
NARRENTANZ (*Ger.*) A fool's dance.
NASALLANT (*Ger.*) Nasal sound, or tone.
NASAL TONE. That thick, reedy tone, produced by the voice when it passes too much through the nostrils.
NASARD.
NASAT. An old name for an organ stop, tuned a twelfth above the diapasons.
NASSAT.

NASÉTTO (*It.*) The point of a bow.
NASON. A very quiet, and sweet toned, flute stop, of 4 feet tone, sometimes found in old organs, and producing a most lovely effect when combined with the diapasons.

NATIONAL AIR
NATIONAL MUSIC An air or melody is national, when it naturally expresses the feelings and sentiments of the people, and when it has been commonly sung through several generations.

NATUR (*Ger.*) Nature.
NATURAL. A character marked ♮, used to contradict a sharp, or flat.
NATURÁLE (*It.*) Natural, easy, free.
NATURALIST (*Ger.*) A self-taught musician.
NATURALISTISCH (*Ger.*) Amateurish; untrained.

NATURAL KEYS. Those which have no sharp or flat at the signature: as, C major, and A minor.

NATURALMÉNTE (*It.*) Naturally, easily, simply.

NATURAL MODULATION. That which is confined to the key of the piece, and its relatives.

NATÜRLICH (*Ger.*) Natural; unaffected.

NAUFRÁGIO (*It.*) A shipwreck; *fiásco*.

NAY. An Egyptian flute.

NAZARD. *See* NASARD.

NEAPOLITAN sixth. A chord composed of a minor third, and minor sixth, and occurring on the sub-dominant, or fourth degree of the scale. In the key of C (major, or minor), this chord is being really the first inversion of the triad of D-flat.

NEBEN-GEDANKEN (*Ger.*) Accessory, and subordinate ideas.

NEBEN-LINIE (*Ger.*) A *leger* line.

NEBEN-NOTE (*Ger.*) Auxiliary note.

NEBEN-REGISTER (*Ger.*) Secondary, or accessory stops in an organ, such as couplers, tremulant, bells, &c.

NEBEN-SATZ (*Ger.*) An auxiliary phrase.

NEBEN-STIMMEN (*Ger.*) Subordinate harmonic parts: also, secondary or mutation stops, such as the quint, twelfth, &c: *see also* **NEBEN-REGISTER.**

NEBEN-TONART (*Ger.*) A relative key.

NEBEN-ZÜGE (*Ger.*) *See* NEBEN-REGISTER.

NECESSÁRIO (*It.*) Necessary; *obbligáto*.

NEFER. An Egyptian guitar.

NEGHINOTH
NEGINOTH (*Heb.*) A term prefixed to certain psalms, and supposed to indicate, that they were to be sung to certain tunes, or accompanied by certain instruments, or to be sung in some peculiar manner.

NEGLI (*It. pl.*) In the, at the; *see* NEI.

NEGLIGÉNTE (*It.*) Negligent, unconstrained.

NEGLIGENTEMÉNTE (*It.*) Negligently, without exactness.

NEGLIGÉNZA (*It.*) Negligence, carelessness.

NEHMEN (*Ger.*) Take; take up; resume.

NEI (*It. pl.*)
NEL (*It.*)
NELLA (*It.*)
NELLE (*It. pl.*)
NELLO (*It.*)
NELL' (*It.*)
In the, at the: *nel báttere*, in the *down-beat*, or accented part of the bar: *nel témpo*, in time, in the previous time.

NEL STILO ANTÍCO (*It.*) In the ancient style.
NENIA (*Lat.*) A dirge.
NÉRO (*It.*) A crotchet.
NET (*Fr.*) Neatly, clearly, plainly.
NETE (*Gr.*) The last, or most acute string, of the lyre: *see* HYPATE.
NETT (*Ger.*)
NETTAMÉNTE (*It.*)
NETTE (*Fr.*)
Neatly, clearly, plainly.

NETTETÉ (*Fr.*)
NETTHEIT (*Ger.*)
NETTIGKEIT (*Ger.*)
Neatness, clearness, plainness.

NÉTTO (*It.*) Neat, clear: quick, nimble.
NEU (*Ger.*) New.
NEUMÆ (*Lat.*) An old name for *divisions*: which see.
NEUN (*Ger.*) Nine.
NEUNTE (*Ger.*) A ninth.
NEUVIÈME (*Fr.*) The interval of a ninth.
NEXUS (*Gr.*) An old term for a phrase, or a sequence.
NEXUS ANACAMPTOS (*Gr.*) Descending.
NEXUS CIRCUMSTANS (*Gr.*) Descending and ascending.
NEXUS RECTUS (*Gr.*) Ascending.
NICHT (*Ger.*) Not.
NICHT ANSCHWELLEN LASSEN (*Ger.*) Without swelling on the note.
NICHT EILEN (*Ger.*) Without hurrying.
NICHT SCHLEPPEN (*Ger.*) Without dragging.
NICHT SCHREIENDE STIMMEN (*Ger.*) *Not shrill stops*, in organ playing.
NICHT ZU GESCHWIND (*Ger.*) Not too quick.
NÍCOLO (*It.*) A forerunner of the bassoon.
NIEDER (*Ger.*) Down; low.
NIEDER-SCHLAG (*Ger.*) The down-beat, or accented part of the bar.
NIEDRIG (*Ger.*) Low or deep voice.
NIÉNTE (*It.*) Nothing.
NIMMT (*Ger.*) Takes; takes up.

Nineteenth — Nóta cambiáta

NINETEENTH. An interval comprising two octaves and a fifth: also, an organ stop, tuned a nineteenth above the diapasons: *see* **LARIGOT**.

NÍNNA-NÁNNA (*It.*) A cradle song; a lullaby.

NINTH. One note more than an octave.

NÓBILE (*It.*) Noble, grand, impressive.

NOBILITÀ (*It.*) Nobility, dignity, grandeur.

NOBILMÉNTE (*It.*) \
NOBLEMENT (*Fr.*) Nobly, grandly, impressively.

NOCH (*Ger.*) Still, yet; in addition.

NOCTURNE (*Fr.*) *See* NOTTÚRNO.

NODUS (*Lat.*) An enigmatical canon.

NOËL (*Fr.*) A Christmas carol, or hymn.

NŒUD (*Fr.*) A node; a turn.

NOIRE (*Fr.*) *Blank note*: a crotchet.

NOM DE PLUME (*Fr.*) A *pen-name*.

NOMOS (*Gr.*) \
NOMUS (*Lat.*) A tune, melody: a melodic sequence.

NON (*It.*) Not, no: *non mólto*, not much, not very much.

NÓNA (*It.*) A ninth.

NONCHALAMMENT (*Fr.*) Carelessly, drowsily.

NONE (*Ger.*) A ninth.

NONÉTTO (*It.*) A composition for nine voices, or instruments.

NON MÓLTO ALLÉGRO (*It.*) Not very quick.

NONNENGEIGE (*Ger.*) A nun's fiddle.

NONOLE (*Ger.*) A group of nine note, played in the time of eight.

NON TÁNTO (*It.*) Not so much, moderately, not too much.

NON TÁNTO ALLÉGRO (*It.*) Not so quick, not too quick.

NON TRÓPPO (*It.*) Not too much, moderately.

NON TRÓPPO PRÉSTO (*It.*) Not too quick.

NONUPLET. A group of nine note, played in the time of eight.

NORMAL-TON (*Ger.*) The normal tone, the note A, the sound to which instruments are tuned in an orchestra.

NORMAL-TONLEITER (*Ger.*) The natural scale, the scale of C, the open key.

NÓTA (*It.*) A note.

NOTA ABJECTA (*Lat.*) \
NÓTA ABBIÉTTA (*It.*) A useless, cancelled note.

NÓTA BIÁNCA (*It.*) A minim.

NÓTA BUÓNA (*It.*) A strong, or accented, note.

NÓTA CAMBIÁTA (*It.*) A changed, or irregularly transient note, a passing note.

NÓTA CARATTERÍSTICA (*It.*) A characteristic, or leading note.
NÓTA CATTÍVA (*It.*) A weak, or unaccented, note.
NOTA CONTRA NOTAM (*Lat.*) Note against note: *see* COUNTERPOINT.
NÓTA D'ABBELLIMÉNTO (*It.*) A note of embellishment, an ornamental note.
NÓTA DI PASSÁGGIO (*It.*) A passing note, a note of regular transition.
NÓTA DI PLACÉRE (*It.*) An optional grace note, an *ad libitum* embellishment.
NÓTA MARTELLÁTA (*It.*) A hammered note.
NÓTA SENSÍBILE (*It.*)
NOTA SENSIBILIS (*Lat.*) } The sensible, or leading note of the scale.
NÓTA SOSTENÚTA (*It.*) A sustained note.
NOTATION. The art of writing music in notes: representing musical sounds, and their various modifications, by notes, signs, &c.
NOTAZIONE MUSICÁLE (*It.*) Musical notation.
NOTE D'AGRÉMENT (*Fr.*) *See* NÓTA D'ABBELLIMÉNTO.
NOTE DE PASSAGE (*Fr.*) *See* NÓTA DI PASSÁGGIO.
NOTE DIÉSÉE (*Fr.*) Note marked with a sharp.
NOTEN-BUCH (*Ger.*) Music book, note book.
NOTEN-GESTELL (*Ger.*) Music stand.
NOTEN-PAPIER (*Ger.*) Music paper.
NOTEN-PLAN (*Ger.*) The stave: the scale.
NOTEN-PULT (*Ger.*) Music desk.
NOTEN-SCHREIBER (*Ger.*) Music copyist.
NOTES DE GOÛT (*Fr.*) Notes of embellishment.
NOTE SENSIBLE (*Fr.*) *See* NÓTA SENSÍBILE.
NOTEUR (*Fr.*) Music copyist.
NOTOGRAPH. *See* MELOGRAPH.
NOTTÚRNO (*It.*) A vocal, or instrumental, composition, of a light and elegant character, suitable for evening recreation: also, a piece resembling a serenade, to be played at night, in the open air.
NOURRIR LE SON (*Fr.*) To commence, or attack, a note, in singing, forcibly, and sustain it.
NÓVA (*It.*) A species of small flute, or pipe.
NOVEMOLE. A group of nine notes, to be performed in the same time as six of equal value.
NOWELL. *See* NOEL.
NUANCES (*Fr. pl.*) Lights and shades of expression, variety of intonation.
NUMERUS (*Lat.*) *Number*, used to denote musical time, rhythm, harmony.

Nuóvo (*It.*) New: *di nuóvo*, newly, again.
Nur (*Ger.*) Only.
Nutríto (*It.*) Fed, nourished.

O

O (*It.*) Or, as, either: fláuto o violíno, flute or violin.

OBBLIGÁTI (*It. pl.*)
OBBLIGÁTO (*It.*)
    Indispensable: necessary: cannot be spared: a part, or parts, which cannot be omitted, being indispensably necessary to a proper performance.

OBBLÍQUO (*It.*) Oblique: *see* OBLIQUE MOTION.

OBER (*Ger.*) Upper, higher: *Ober-Manual*, the upper manual.

OBER-LABIUM (*Ger.*) The upper lip of an organ pipe.

OBER-STIMME (*Ger.*) Treble, upper voice part.

OBER-TASTE (*Ger.*) The *black* keys of the pianoforte or organ keyboard.

OBER-THEIL (*Ger.*) The upper part.

OBER-TÖNE (*Ger.*) Overtones, harmonics, upper partials.

OBER-WERK (*Ger.*) Upper work, highest row of keys.

OBLIGÉ (*Fr.*)
OBLIGAT (*Ger.*)
    See OBBLIGÁTI.

OBLIQUE MOTION. When one part ascends or descends, whilst the other remains stationary.

OBLÍQUO (*It.*)
OBLIQUUS (*Lat.*)
    Oblique: *see* OBLIQUE MOTION.

OBOE (*Ger.*)
OBOÈ (*It. sing. & pl.*)
    A hautboy: also, the name of an organ stop: see Hautboy.

OBOÈ D'AMÓRE
OBOÈ LÚNGO
    (*It.*) This was longer than the ordinary oboè, with a thinner bore, and a smaller bell, and the pitch was a third lower. The tone was finer, and perhaps sweeter, though more plaintive: see also HAUTBOY D'AMOUR.

OBOÈ DA CÁCCIA (*It.*) Much larger than the above, and the music was written in the alto clef. The instrument is perhaps fairly represented by the *Córno inglése,* or *Cor anglais*.

OBOÈ LÚNGHI. *See* OBOÈ LÚNGO.

OBOEN (*Ger. pl.*) Hautboys.

OBOE-FLUTE. An organ stop of small 4 feet tone; the tone is very delicate and reedy.

OBOER (*Ger.*) A performer on the *oboè*.

OBOI. Hautboys: *see* OBOÈ.

Oboist — Odeum

OBOIST (*Eng.*)
OBOÍSTA (*It.*) } A performer on the *oboè*.

OCARÍNA (*It.*) A small wind-instrument, of the flute species, made from terracotta.

OCTAVA (*Lat.*) Octave: applied to 4 feet organ stops.

OCTAVE. An interval of eight diatonic sounds, or degrees: also the name of an organ stop: *see* PRINCIPAL.

OCTAVE-CLARION. A 2 feet reed stop in an organ.

OCTAVE FIFTEENTH. An organ stop of bright, sharp tone, sounding an octave above the fifteenth.

OCTAVE-GANG (*Ger.*) See RULE OF THE OCATVE.

OCTAVE HAUTBOY. A 4 feet organ reed stop: the pipes are of the hautboy species.

OCTAVE TWELFTH. See LARIGOT.

OCTAV-FLÖTE (*Ger.*) Flageolet, octave flute: also, an organ stop of 4 feet tone.

OCTAVIANTE (*Fr.*) Octave, applied to organ stops.

OCTAVIN (*Fr.*) An organ stop of 2 feet tone.

OCTAVINE (*Fr.*) The small spinet.

OCTET (*Eng.*)
OCTETT (*Ger.*)
OCTETTE (*Fr.*) } See OCTUOR.
OCTÉTTO (*It.*)

OCTIPHONIUM (*Lat.*) A vocal composition in eight real parts.

OCTO-BASS. An instrument invented by M. Vuillaume, of Paris: it is of colossal size, with three strings; and for the left hand there are moveable keys, by which the string is pressed on the frets placed upon the finger-board, with seven other pedal keys for the foot of the player. The sounds are full and strong, of great power without roughness.

OCTOCHORD (*Lat.*) An instrument like a lute, with eight strings.

OCTUOR (*Fr.*) A piece in eight parts, of, for weight voices or instruments.

OCTUPLET. A group of eight notes, played in the time of six.

OD (*It.*) Or, either.

ODE. A lyrical composition, much the same as a cantata: the Greek odes, or songs, gave passionate expression to the feelings.

ODEM (*Ger.*) The breath: *see* ATHEM.

ODÉON (*Gr.*)
ODEION (*Ger.*) } A circular building, in which the ancient Greeks and Romans held festivals: a concert room, or hall for musical performance.
ODEUM (*Lat.*)

ODER (*Ger.*) Or, or else: *für ein oder zwei Claviere*, for one or two manuals.

ODE-SYMPHONIE (*Fr.*) A symphony with a vocal chorus.

ODISCHE MUSIK (*Ger.*) Vocal music.

ŒUVRE (*Fr.*) Work, composition, piece: as *œuvre premier*, the first work, or composition.

OFFEN (*Ger.*) Open.

OFFENBAR (*Ger.*) open, evident, manifest.

OFFEN-FLÖTE (*Ger.*) An open flute, organ stop: *see also* **CLARABELLA**.

OFFERTOIRE (*Fr.*)
OFFERTÓTIO (*It.*)
OFFERTORIUM (*Lat.*)
OFFERTORY (*Eng.*) } A hymn, prayer, anthem, or, instrumental piece, sung or played, during the collection of the offertory.

OFFICIUM (*Lat.*) The Mass.

OFFICIUM DEFUNCTORUM (*Lat.*) A Requiem, or Mass for the dead.

OFFICIUM DIURNUM (*Lat.*) The *Horæ*, the day-service.

OFFICIUM DIVINUM (*Lat.*) High Mass.

OFFICIUM MATUTINUM (*Lat.*) Early Mass.

OFFICIUM NOCTURNUM (*Lat.*) The *Horæ*, sung at night.

OFFICIUM vespertinum (*Lat.*) Vespers, evening service.

OFICLEIDA. *See* **OPHICLEIDE**.

OHNE (*Ger.*) Without: *ohne Begleitungen*, without accompaniments.

OHNE PEDALE (*Ger.*) Without the pedals.

OHNE SORDINE (*Ger.*) Without the mute.

OKTAVE (*Ger.*) *See* **OCTAVE**.

OKTAVIN (*Ger.*) *See* **OCTAVIN**.

OLIVETTES (*Fr.*) The dances of the peasants, in Provence, after the olives are gathered.

OLLA-PODRIDA (*Sp.*) A medley.

OMBI. A west African harp.

OMBRA (*It.*) Shade.

OMNES
OMNIA } (*Lat.*) *See* **TÚTTI**.

ONCE MARKED OCTAVE. The name given in Germany to the notes between [musical notation] inclusive; those notes are expressed by small letters with one short stroke, $\bar{c}$ or c^1.

Ondeggiaménto — Opern-komponist

ONDEGGIAMÉNTO (*It.*) *Waving*: an undulating, or tremulous motion of the sound: also, a *close shake*, on the violin, &c.

ONDEGGIÁNTE (*It.*) | Waving, undulating, floating, trembling.
ONDULÉ (*Fr.*) |

ONDULATION (*Fr.*) Undulation, waving.

ONDULÉ (*Fr.*) Undulating; *see* ONDEGGIAMÉNTO.

ONDULIREN (*Ger.*) A tremulous tone in singing, or in playing the violin, &c.

ONGARSE | Hungarian.
ONGHERESE |

ONGLEUR (*Fr.*) An old term for a performer on the lyre, harp, &c.

ONZIÈME (*Fr.*) An interval of an eleventh.

OOD. An Egyptian guitar.

OPEN DIAPASON. An organ stop, generally made of metal, and thus called because the pipes are open at the top: it is tuned to the same pitch as the pianoforte, &c., and is the most important stop in the instrument.

OPEN HARMONY. *See* DISPERSED HARMONY.

OPEN NOTE. A note on the open string of a violin, &c.

OPEN PEDAL. The loud pedal, on a pianoforte.

OPEN SCORE. A score with each part on a separate stave.

OPEN STRING. The string of a violin, &c., when not pressed by the finger.

OPER (*Ger.*) | A drama set to music, for voices and instruments,
ÓPERA (*It.*) | with recitative, airs, choruses, &c., and with scenery, decorations, and action. The term is also applied to any *work*, or publication of a composer: *see also* OPUS.

ÓPERA BÚFFA (*It.*) A comic opera.

OPÉRA COMIQUE (*Fr.*) An opera with spoken dialogue.

ÓPERA DI CÁMERA (*It.*) A short opera, to be performed in a room.

OPÉRA HÉROÏQUE (*Fr.*) An heroic opera.

ÓPERA SÉMI-SÉRIA (*It.*) A semi-serious opera, of a romantic cast, neither tragic or comic.

ÓPERA SÉRIA (*It.*) | A serious, or tragic opera.
OPÉRA SÉRIEUX (*Fr.*) |

OPERÉTTA (*It.*) | A short opera, sometimes interspersed
OPÉRETTE (*Fr. & Ger.*) | with dialogue.

OPERIST (*Ger.*) An opera singer.

OPER-MÄDCHEN (*Ger.*) Opera girl, opera singer.

OPERN-HAUS (*Ger.*) Opera house.

OPERN-KOMPONIST (*Ger.*) A composer of operas.

OPERN-SÄNGER (*Ger.*) Opera singer.

OPHICLEIDE. A large bass wind-instrument of brass, or wood and brass, of modern invention, sometimes used in large orchestras, but chiefly in military music: the tone is loud, and of a deep pitch, though neither so powerful nor imposing as that of the trombones: *see also* BASSE D'HARMONIE.

It is also one of the most powerful known manual reed stop of 8 or 4 feet tone, in an organ, and is usually placed upon a separate sound-board, &c., with a great pressure of wind. The ophicleide was first introduced by W. Hill, into the organ in the Birmingham Town Hall; *see also* TUBA.

OPPÚRE (*It.*) See OSSÍA.

OPUS (*Lat. & Ger.*) Work, composition: as, *Op. 1*, the first work, or publication, of a composer.

OPUSCULUM (*Lat.*) A short, or little, work.

OPUS POSTUMUM (*Lat.*) A posthumous work, published after the death of the composer.

ORAGE (*Fr.*) A *storm*: the name of an organ stop, intended to imitate the noise of a storm.

ORA PRO NOBIS (*Lat.*) *Pray for us*: a part of the Roman Catholic mass.

ORATÓRIO (*It.*)
ORATORIUM (*Lat. & Ger.*) A sacred drama, founded upon some Scriptural story, set to music for voices and instruments, and performed without the aid of scenery and action: it derived its name from San Filippo Neri, who, about 1580, had sacred music sung in his oratory, after sermons and other devotions.

ORCHÉSOGRAPHIE (*Fr.*) The art of scientific dancing for the ballet.

ORCHESTER (*Ger.*)
ORCHÉSTRA (*It.*)
ORCHESTRE (*Fr.*) An orchestra: the place in a theatre, or concert room, where the musicians play: the term is also applied to the performers themselves collectively: as, a full orchestra, a small orchestra, &c.

ORCHESTER-VEREIN (*Ger.*) An orchestral society: instrumental association.

ORCHESTRAL FLUTE. An organ flute stop, of 8 feet pitch, in imitation of the orchestral version, made of harmonic pipes; *see* HARMONIC FLUTE.

ORCHESTRAL OBOE. An organ stop of 8 feet pitch, in imitation of the orchestral version.

ORCHESTRIK (*Ger.*) The art of scientific dancing for the ballet.

ORCHESTIQUE (*Fr.*) An old term, meaning, the art of dancing, belonging to dancing.

Orchestrion — Organ point

ORCHESTRION. An instrument invented by F. F. Kaufmann, of Dresden, imitating the sounds of a full orchestra, with *crescéndo* and *diminuéndo*.

ORDINAIRE (*Fr.*) | Ordinary, usual, common: *à témpo ordinário*, in
ORDINÁRIO (*It.*) | the usual time.

ORDINES (*Lat.*) The registers, or stops, in an organ.

ORDRE (*Fr.*) A suite.

ORÉCCHIA
ORÉCCHIO | (*It.*) The ear: *orécchia musicále*, a musical ear.

ORÉCCHI
ORÉCCHIE | (*It. pl.*) The ears.

OREILLE MUSICALE (*Fr.*) A musical ear.

ORGAN. A well-known musical instrument, of very ancient origin, used in churches, and other places of Divine worship: and also in large concert halls, &c. The earliest instrument of the organ species appears to have been the *masrakitha*, mentioned by Kircher, in his 'Musurgiæ': see MASRAKITHA.

ORGANE (*Fr.*) An organ.

ORGANÉTTO (*It.*) A small organ.

ORGANICEN (*Lat.*) An organist.

ORGANICAL (*Eng.*) | Relating to the organ.
ORGANIQUE (*Fr.*) |

ORGANISCHE MUSIK (*Ger.*) Organ music.

ORGANÍSTA (*It.*) An organist.

ORGANISTRUM (*Lat.*) An old form of the hurdy-gurdy.

ÓRGANI VOCÁLI (*It. pl.*) The vocal organs.

ORGAN LOFT. The part of the building, in which the organ is placed.

ÓRGANO (*It.*) An organ.

ÓRGANO DI CAMPÁNA (*It.*) An organ with bells.

ÓRGANO DI LÉGNO (*It.*) A xylophone; also, the flute work of an organ.

ORGANOGRAPHIE (*Lat.*) A description of an organ, and all its various stops.

ORGANOLOGIE (*Lat.*) Instructions for using all the various organ stops.

ÓRGANO PIÉNO (*It.*) | The full organ, with all the stops drawn.
ORGANO PLÉNO (*Lat.*) |

ÓRGANO PORTÁTILE (*It.*) A portable organ.

ORGAN POINT. A long pedal note, or stationary bass, upon which is formed a series of chords, or harmonic progressions.

ORGANO SIMPLEX (*Lat.*) This term occurs frequently in the writings of the musical monks, and seems to mean, the unisonous accompaniment of the tenor or other single voice in the versicles of the service.

ORGANUM (*Lat.*) This word was used in various senses by the ancient composers. Sometimes it meant, the organ itself; at other times it signified, that kind of choral accompaniment which comprehended the whole harmony then known.

ORGANUM PNEUMATICUM (*Lat.*) An organ.

ORGANÚTO (*It.*) Organical.

ORGEL (*Ger.*) Organ.

ORGEL-BÄLGE (*Ger.*) Organ bellows.

ORGEL-BAUER (*Ger.*) Organ builder.

ORGEL-CHOR (*Ger.*) Organ loft.

ORGEL-GEHÄUSE (*Ger.*) Organ case.

ORGEL-PFEIFE (*Ger.*) Organ pipe.

ORGEL-PLATZ (*Ger.*) Organ loft.

ORGEL-PUNKT (*Ger.*) *See* ORGAN-POINT.

ORGEL-SCHULE (*Ger.*) School, or method, for the organ.

ORGEL-STIMME (*Ger.*) A rank of organ pipes; a stop.

ORGEL-STÜCKE (*Ger.*) Pieces for the organ.

ORGEL-TRETER (*Ger.*) Organ treader, bellows treader, or bellows blower.

ORGEL-VIRTUOSE (*Ger.*) An accomplished organ player.

ORGEL-WOLF (*Ger.*) A cipher.

ORGEL-ZUG (*Ger.*) Organ stop, or row of pipes.

ORGUE (*Fr.*) An organ.

ORGUE À PERCUSSION (*Fr.*) An harmonium, with a percussion attachment.

ORGUE DE SALON
ORGUE EXPRESSIF | (*Fr.*) The harmonium.

ORGUE PLEIN (*Fr.*) Full organ: all the stops drawn.

ORGUE PORTATIF (*Fr.*) A portable organ.

ORGUE POSITIF (*Fr.*) A *fixed* organ: *see also* POSITIVE.

ORGUETTE (*Fr.*) An ancient portable organ.

ORGUINETTE (*Fr.*) A species of reed organ, played by perforated card.

ORICALCHI (*It.*) Brass instruments.

ORIFÍCIO
ORIFÍZIO | (*It.*) The orifice of organ pipes, in front, and at the top.

ORIGINALITÄT (*Ger.*) Originality, in composition.

ORIGINELL (*Ger.*) Original, newly invented, not borrowed from another.

Ornaménti — Ouïe

ORNAMÉNTI (*It. pl.*) | Ornaments, graces, embellishments, as, the
ORNEMENTS (*Fr. pl.*) | *appoggiatúra*, turn, shake, &c.

ORNATAMÉNTE
ORNÁTO | (*It.*) Ornamented, adorned, embellished.

ORNÉ (*Fr.*) See ORNATAMÉNTE.

ORPHARION. An old instrument of the lute species, with more strings and frets than the lute: the strings were of wire.

ORPHÉON | (*Fr.*) Species of musical instrument, of which
ORPHÉORON | nothing is known.

ORTHISCH (*Gr. &. Ger.*) High, acute.

ORTHOËPIK (*Gr. & Ger.*) The art of correct verbal declamation, in singing.

ORTHOTONIE (*Gr. & Ger.*) Correct accentuation in singing.

OSÁNNA (*It.*) Hosanna.

OSCILLATION. The vibration of tones in organ tuning, &c.

OSCÚRO (*It.*) Obscure; dull.

OSSERVÁNZA (*It.*) Observance, attention, strictness in keeping the time.

O SÍA (*It.*) See OSSÍA.

OSSERVÁNZA (*It.*) Care, observation, attention.

OSSÍA (*It.*) Or, otherwise, or else: *ossía più fácile*, or else in this more easy manner.

OSTERLIED (*Ger.*) Easter hymn.

OSTINÁTO (*It.*) Obstinate, continuous, unceasing: adhering to some peculiar melodial figure, or group of notes.

ÔTEZ (*Fr.*) *Off*: remove.

ÔTEZ LES ANCHES (*Fr.*) Remove, or push in, the reeds.

OTHEM (*Ger.*) The breath.

OTTÁVA (*It.*) An octave, an eighth.

OTTÁVA ÁLTA (*It.*) The octave above, an octave higher: marked thus, 8va.

OTTÁVA BÁSSA (*It.*) The octave below, an octave lower: marked thus, 8va *bássa*.

OTTAVÍNA (*It.*) The higher octave.

OTTAVÍNO (*It.*) The *fláuto píccolo*, or small octave flute.

OTTEMOLE. A group of eight notes, marked with the figure 8.

OTTÉTTO (*It.*) A composition in eight parts, of for eight voices or instruments.

OTTÓNE (*It.*) Brass.

OUÏE (*Fr.*) The hearing: *l'ouïe d'un instrument*, the sound-hole of an instrument.

OUVERTURE (*Fr.*)
OVERTÚRA (*It.*)
OVERTURE (*Eng. & Ger.*)
An instrumental composition, played as an introduction to an oratorio, or opera: also, as an independent piece, in which case it is called a *concert overture*.

OVERTÚRA DI BÁLLO (*It.*) An overture composed upon, or introducing, dance melodies.

OVVERO (*It.*) Or: *see* OSSÍA.

P

PAAR (*Ger.*) A pair, of instruments, &c.

PACATAMÉNTE (*It.*) Peacefully, tranquilly, calmly, quietly.

PACÁTO (*It.*) Quiet, tranquil, placid.

PADIGLIÓNE (*It.*) The bell of an instrument.

PADOANA. A slow, dignified species of dance.

PADOUÁNA
PADOVÁNA (*It.*) *See* PAVAN.
PADUÁNA

PÆAN (*Gr.*) A hymn: io pæan! huzza!

PÆON (*Gr.*) A musical foot, comprising one long, and three short notes or syllable, accented and marked thus, —◡◡◡, or ◡—◡◡.

PÁLCO (*It.*) The stage of a theatre.

PALESTRINASTIL (*Ger.*) In the style of Palestrina.

PALLET. The part of an organ, which, when pulled down, lets the wind into the pipes, making them speak.

PALETTES (*Fr.*) The white keys of a pianoforte, or organ.

PAMBE. A small Indian drum.

PAMULA (*Lat.*) An old name for the manual keys of an organ, &c.

PANAYLON (*Gr.*) The G flute, a new species with fifteen keys, invented by Professor Bayr, the compass of which extends from Fiddle G to c in altíssimo. The inventor succeeded in producing from it double notes, as thirds, fourths, sixths, &c., which, especially in the softer keys of E-flat, A-flat, D-flat, sound like musical glasses.

PANDEAN PIPES. One of the most ancient and simple of musical instruments: a shepherd's pipe, made of reeds or tubes of different lengths, stopped at the bottom, and fastened together, and blown into by the mouth, at the top.

PANDÓRA (*It.*)
PANDORE (*Ger.*) An old species of guitar, with wire strings: a small Polish lute, a Bandóre, or species of lute: *see* BANDÓRA.
PANDÚRA (*It.*)

PANFLÖTE (*Ger.*) *See* PANDEAN PIPES.

PANMELODION. A keyboard instrument, in which the tone was produced with metal bars, which are set into vibration, with the friction produced by a rotating wheel.

PANORGUE (*Fr.*) A small harmonium, which is attached to a pianoforte.

PAN'S PIPES. See PANDEAN PIPES.

PANTALEONE. An old instrument invented by Hebenstreit, and much celebrated in the beginning of the eighteenth century. It was more than 9 feet long, nearly 4 feet wide, and had 186 strings of gut, which were played on with two small sticks, like a dulcimer.

PANTALON (*Fr.*) One of the movements of the quadrille: also, the name of an old instrument of the dulcimer, species but larger, and played in the same manner: see PANTALEONE.

PAPAGENO-FLÖTE (*Ger.*) Pan's pipe, mouth organ.

PAPILLONS (*Fr.*) *Butterflies*; light, grace pieces for pianoforte.

PARALLEL MOTION. When the parts continue on the same degree, and only repeat the same sounds: also, two parts continuing their course and still remaining at exactly the same distance from each other.

PARAMESE (*Gr.*) The fifth string of the lyre: see HYPATE.

PARANETE (*Gr.*) The sixth string of the lyre: see HYPATE.

PARAPHRASE. An arrangement or transcription of a composition, generally of the florid kind.

PARFAIT (*Fr.*) Perfect, as to intervals, &c.

PARHYPATE (*Gr.*) The second string on the lyre: see HYPATE.

PÁRI (*It.*) Equal.

PARLÁNDO
PARLÁNTE (*It.*) Accented, speaking, singing in a whisper, talking; played as if with words: in a declamatory manner.

PARODÍA (*It.*) A parody: music or words slightly altered, and adapted to some new purpose.

PARODOS. The commencement of an ancient Greet chorus, in which the whole chorus used to join.

PAROLES (*Fr.*) Words for setting to music.

PAROLIER (*Fr.*) A writer of words which to be set to music.

PART. The music for each separate voice, or instrument.

PÁRTE (*It.*) A part, or portion, of a composition; a part, or *rôle*, in an opera.

PÁRTE CANTÁNTE (*It.*) The singing, or vocal, part; the principal vocal part, having the melody.

PARTERRE (*Fr.*) The pit of a theatre.

PARTHENIA (*Gr.*) Songs of the virgins.

PARTIE (*Fr.*) See PÁRTE.

PARTIE DU VIOLON (*Fr.*) A violin part.

PARTIMÉNTI (*It. pl.*) Exercises for the study of harmony and accompaniment.

PARTIMÉNTO (*It.*) An exercise, figured bass: see PARTIMÉNTI.

Partíta — Passing

PARTÍTA (*It.*) An old term synonymous with *variation*.
PARTITION (*Fr.*) ⎫
PARTITUR (*Ger.*) ⎬ A *score*, a *full score*, or entire draft, of a composition for voices or instruments, or both.
PARTITÚRA (*It.*) ⎭
PARTÍTO (*It.*) Scored, divided into parts.
PARTITUR-SPIEL (*Ger.*) Playing from the score.
PART SONGS. Songs for voices, in parts, introduced in Germany in the present century [19th].
PARTIZÓNE (*It.*) *See* PARTITION.
PAS (*Fr.*) A dance, a step: *pas courant*, the courant step.
PAS DE BOURRÉE (*Fr.*) The bouree step.
PAS DE CHARGE (*Fr.*) A double quick march.
PAS DE DANSE (*Fr.*) A step, in dancing.
PAS DE DEUX (*Fr.*) A dance by two performers.
PAS DE GAILLARDE (*Fr.*) The galliard step.
PAS DE HACHE (*Fr.*) Axe, or hatchet, step: a warlike dance.
PAS DE MENUET (*Fr.*) The minuet step.
PAS DE QUATRE (*Fr.*) A dance by four performers.
PAS DE TROIS (*Fr.*) A dance by three performers.
PAS GRAVE (*Fr.*) The courant step.
PASPY. *See* PASSEPIED.
PAS REDOUBLÉ (Fr.) A quick step; an increased, or redoubled step.
PASSACÁGLIA (*It.*) ⎫
PASSACÁGLIO (*It.*) ⎪ A species of chacone, a slow dance with divisions on a ground bass, in $\frac{3}{4}$ time, and
PASSACAILLE (*Fr.*) ⎬ always in a minor key; the chacone being
PASSACALLE (*Sp.*) ⎪ always in a major key.
PASSAGÁLLO (*It.*) ⎭
PASSÁGGIO (*It.*) A passage, or series of notes.
PASSAMÉSO (*It.*) A species of pastoral Italian song or melody.
PASSAMÉZZO (*It.*) An old slow dance, little differing from the action of walking.
PASSEND (*Ger.*) Suitable, convenient; fit.
PASSEPEID (*Fr.*) A sort of jig; a lively old French dance in $\frac{3}{4}$, $\frac{3}{8}$, or $\frac{6}{8}$ time; a kind of quick minuet, with three, or more, strains or reprises, the first consisting of eight bars.
PASSE-RUE (*Fr.*) *See* PASSACÁGLIA.
PAS SEUL (*Fr.*) A dance by one performer.
PASSING NOTES. Notes which do not belong to the harmony, but which serve to connect those which are essential, and carry the ear more smoothly from one harmony to another.

PASSIONÁTA (*It.*) Passionate, with fervour.
PASSIONATAMÉNTE (*It.*) In an impassioned manner.
PASSIONÁTE (*It.*) Passionate, impassioned, with fervour and
PASSIONÁTO pathos.
PASSIÓNE (*It.*) Passion, feeling.
PASSIÓNE (*It.*) The *Passion*, or seven last words of the Saviour on the Cross, set to solemn, and devotional, music.
PASSIONS-MUSIK (*Ger.*) An oratorio upon the subject of the passion and death of the Saviour.
PÁSSO (*It.*) A step.
PÁSSO-MÉZZO (*It.*) *See* PASSAMÉZZO.
PASSÚNA (*It.*) *See* POSAUNE.
PASTETE (*Ger.*) A medley, an opera made up of songs, &c., by
PASTÍCCIO (*It.*) various composers: the poetry being written to
PASTICHE (*Fr.*) the music, instead of the music to the poetry.
PASTORÁLE (*It.*) Pastoral, rural, belonging to a shepherd: a soft
PASTORELLE (*Fr.*) movement in a pastoral and rural style.
PASTORÍTA (*It.*) A shepherd's pipe; *see also* NACHTHORN.
PASTÓSO (*It.*) Mellow, soft.
PASTOURELLE (*Fr.*) One of the movements of a quadrille.
PATÉTICA (*It.*) Pathetic, pathetical.
PATETICAMÉNTE (*It.*) Pathetically.
PATÉTICO (*It.*)
PATHÉTIQUE (*Fr.*) Pathetic, pathetical.
PATHETISCH (*Ger.*)
PATIMÉNTO (*It.*) Affliction, grief, suffering.
PATOUILLE (*Fr.*) A xylophone.
PAUKE (*Ger.*) Kettle-drum.
PAUKEN (*Ger. pl.*) The kettle-drums.
PAUKEN-KLANG (*Ger.*) The sound of a kettle-drum.
PAUKEN-KLÖPFEL
PAUKEN-SCHLÄGEL (*Ger.*) Kettle-drum stick.
PAUKEN-STOCK
PAUKEN-SCHLÄGER (*Ger.*) Kettle-drummer.
PAUKER
PAÚRA (*It.*) Dismay, fear.
PÁUSA (*It.*) A rest, pause, stop.
PÁUSA GENERÁLE (*It.*) A pause, or rest, for *all* the performers.
PAUSE GÉNÉRALE (*Fr.*)

Pause — Pedáli

PAUSE (*Fr.*) A semibreve rest: also, a whole bar's rest in any species of time.

PAUSE (*Ger.*) A rest.

PAUSE (*Eng.*) A character consisting of a dot placed under a curve, ⌒, and which lengthens the duration of the note, or rest, beyond its natural value. When placed over a double bar it shows the termination of the movement, or the piece.

PAUSER (*Fr.*) | To pause, to rest, to keep silence.
PAUSIREN (*Ger.*) |

PAVAN (*Eng.*) | From *Pavo*, a peacock. An old dance of a serious
PAVÁNA (*It.*) | cast in $\frac{3}{4}$ time, generally in three strains, each of
PAVANE (*Fr.*) | which was repeated. It was grave and majestic, and performed with such dignity and stateliness as to show the propriety of the appellation. It was famous at the courts of Henry VIII. and Francis I. The *Pavan* was generally followed by the *Galliard*, a lighter kind of air, and made out of the *Pavan*.

PAVENTÁTO | (*It.*) Fearful, timorous: with an expression of horror
PAVENTÓSO | and anxiety.

PAVILLON (*Fr.*) The bole of a horn, or other wind-instrument.

PAVILLON CHINOIS (*Fr.*) An instrument with numerous little bells, which impart brilliancy to lively pieces, and pompous military marches.

PAVILLON EN L'AIR (*Fr.*) In horn playing, to turn the bells upwards.

PEÁNA (*It.*) A hymn, or song of praise.

PEDAL-CLAVES | (*Ger.*) The pedal key-board, in an organ.
PEDAL-CLAVIATUR |

PEDÁLE (*It.*) A pedal bass, or a stationary bass: see **PEDAL POINT**. In pianoforte music, this word means, that the pedal which takes off the dampers must be pressed down.

PEDALE (*Ger. pl.*) The pedals, or that set of keys in an organ, which are played on by the feet: in organ music it means that the notes, or passage, must be played by the feet.

PEDÁLE À ÓGNI BATTÚTA (*It.*) Use the pedal at each beat or division of the time.

PEDALE DOPPELT (*Ger.*) | Double pedals, in organ playing; playing
PEDÁLE DÓPPIO (*It.*) | the pedals with both feet at once.

PEDÁLE D'ÓRGANO (*It.*) The pedals of an organ.

PÉDALES (*Fr. pl.*) The pedals.

PEDAL-HARFE (*Ger.*) | A harp with pedals, to produce the semitones:
PEDAL-HARP (*Eng.*) | see HARP.

PEDÁLI (*It. pl.*) The pedals.

Pedaliéra — Percussióne

PEDALIÉRA (*It.*) The pedal keys of an organ.

PEDAL-POINT. A sustained bass, or pedal note, held on, or sustained, for several bars, whilst a variety of chords are introduced.

PEKKUS. A Greek lute or dulcimer.

PELLITÓNE (*It.*) A species of *bombardon*.

PENAYLON. *See* PANAYLON.

PENILLION (*Welsh*). A peculiar method of singing, practised by the Welsh: *see* WELSH SINGING.

PENNA (*It.*) A *feather*; a quill, a plectrum.

PENNANT. The hook of a quaver.

PENORÇON (*Fr.*) | An ancient instrument, resembling a *Ghittern*.
PENORKON (*Gr.*) |

PENSIERÓSO (*It.*) |
PENSIF (*Fr.*) | Pensively, mournfully.
PENSÓSO (*It.*) |

PENTACHONIUM (*Gr.*) A composition in five parts.

PENTACHORD (*Gr.*) An instrument with *five* strings: a scale or system of *five* diatonic sounds.

PENTAMÉTRO (*It.*) In poetry, a line which has five *feet*.

PENTATONIC SCALE. A scale of five notes, sometimes called the Scotch scale, and similar to the modern diatonic major scale, with the fourth and seventh degrees omitted. It is supposed to be the scale of the ancient Egyptians, Assyrians, and other Orientals, and is now in use amongst the Eastern nations, particularly the Chinese; a proof of its antiquity. It is also clearly traceable in the most ancient Irish music, but rarely appears in old Welsh or English tunes, except those composed in imitation of Scotch music. To this scale may be traced the instruments of *five* strings, and of *ten*, when the compass included the repetition of the scale in two octaves; often mentioned in the Bible.

PENTATONON (*Gr.*) An interval of five whole tones, more generally called the *augmented*, or *extreme*, sixth.

PENTE (*Gr.*) Five; a *quint*.

PER (*It.*) For, by, through, in: *per il fláuto sólo*, for the flute alone: *per il violíno*, for the violin.

PER ARSIN ET THESIN (*Lat.*) By reversal of accents.

PER BISCANTUM (*Lat.*) An old term for music in two parts.

PERCUSSION (*Eng.*) | Striking, as applied to instruments, notes, or
PERCUSSIÓNE (*It.*) | chords; or the touch on the pianoforte.

Perdéndo — Pézze

PERDÉNDO
PERDENDÓSI (*It.*) Gradually decreasing both the tone, and the time; dying away, becoming extinct.

PERFECT. A term applied to certain intervals and chords.

PERFECT CADENCE. A close upon the key-note, preceded by the dominant: it was not recognised before the seventeenth century, when it was used and brought into favour by Carissimi.

PERFECT CONCORDS
PERFECT CONSONANCES These are, the unison, the perfect fourth, perfect fifth, and the octave.

PERFÉTTO (*It.*) Perfect, complete.

PERIGOURDINE. A French dance in $\frac{3}{4}$ time.

PERIOD (*Eng.*)
PÉRIODE (*Fr.*)
PERIÓDO (*It.*) A complete, and perfect, musical sentence, containing several phrases, and bringing the ear to a perfect conclusion, or state of rest.

PERIODENBAU (*Ger.*) Composition: the construction of musical periods.

PERLÉ (*Fr.*)
PERLEND (*Ger.*) Pearled, brilliant: *cadence perlée*, brilliant cadence: *voix perlée*, pearly voice.

PERPÉTUO (*It.*) Perpetual, infinite, for ever.

PER RECTE ET RETRO (*Lat.*) Forward, then backward: the melody, or subject, reversed, note for note.

PES (*Lat.*) Foot, metre, species of verse: rhythm, time: also, a kind of ground, or burden, the basis for the harmony, in old English music: see also FOOT, &c.

PESAMMENT (*Fr.*)
PESÁNTE (*It.*) Heavy, ponderous; with importance and weight; forcibly, impressively.

PESANTEMÉNTE (*It.*) Heavily, ponderously.

PETÁCCHA (*It.*) A plectrum.

PETITE CHŒUR (*Fr.*) A small choir.

PETITE DÉTACHÉ (*Fr.*) Lightly *staccáto*; bowing with the point of the bow.

PETITE FLÛTE-À-BEC (*Fr.*) A flageolet.

PETITE MESURE À DEUX TEMPS (*Fr.*) Two-crotchet time, marked $\frac{2}{4}$.

PETITES FLÛTES (*Fr.*) The small flutes; the octave, or piccolo, flutes.

PETITE NOTES (*Fr.*) Grace notes.

PETITE RIENS (*Fr.*) Light, trifling pieces.

PÉTTO (*It.*) The chest, the breast: *vóce di pétto*, the chest voice.

PEU (*Fr.*) Little, a little.

PEU À PEU (*Fr.*) By degrees, little by little.

PÉZZE (*It. pl.*) Fragments, scraps: select, detached, pieces of music.

PÉZZI CONCERTÁNTI (*It. pl.*) Concertante pieces, in which each instrument has occasional solos.

PÉZZI DI BRAVÚRA (*It.*) Compositions for the display of dexterity, or rapid execution.

PÉZZO (*It.*) A piece of music.

PÉZZO D'INSIÉME (*It.*) An *ensemble* piece.

PFEIFE (*Ger.*) Pipe, fife, flute.

PFEIFEN-DECKEL (*Ger.*) The stopper, or covering, of an organ pipe.

PFEIFER (*Ger.*) A fifer, a piper.

PFIFFIG (*Ger.*) Artful, sly, cunning.

PHANTASIE (*Ger.*) See FANTASÍA.

PHANTASIREN (*Ger.*) To improvise.

PHILHARMONIC (*Gr.*) Music-loving.

PHILOMELA (*Lat.*) The nightingale.

PHILOMOUSOS (*Gr.*) A lover of music.

PHONAGOGOS (*Gr.*) The leading voice, or subject, in a fugue.

PHONASKIE (*Gr.*) Practice in vocalisation.

PHONASKOS (*Gr.*) | Cherisher of the voice, teacher of singing and
PHONASCUS (*Lat.*) | declamation.

PHONE (*Gr.*) The voice; a sound, or tone.

PHONETIK (*Gr.*) System of singing, or of harmony.

PHONICS (*Lat.*) The art of treating musical sounds, either singly, or in combination.

PHORMINX. An ancient Greek lyre.

PHRASE. A short musical sentence: a musical thought, or idea.

PHRASING. Dividing the musical sentences into rhythmical sections.

PHRYGIAN. One of the ancient modes: *see* GREEK MODES.

PHRYGISCHE TONART (*Ger.*) The Phrygian mode.

PHYSHARMONICA (*Gr.*) An instrument, the tone of which resembles that of the reed pipes in an organ, and is produced by the vibration of thin metal tongues, of a similar construction to those of the harmonium: the name is also applied to a stop in an organ, with *free reeds*, and with tubes of half the usual length.

PIACÉRE (*It.*) Pleasure, inclination, fancy, humour: *à piacére*, or *al piacér*, at pleasure, relaxing the strict regularity of the time.

PIACEVOLÉZZA (*It.*) Pleasing, graceful, agreeable.

PIACEVOLMÉNTE (*It.*) Pleasantly, gracefully.

PIACIMÉNTO (*It.*) See PIACÉRE.

PIAGÉNDO (*It.*) See PIANGÉNDO.

PIAGNÉVOLE (*It.*) Mournful, doleful, lamentable.

Pianaménte — Pibroch

PIANAMÉNTE
PIANÉNTE | (*It.*) Softly, gently, quietly.

PIANETTE (*Fr.*) A small pianoforte.

PIANÉTTO (*It.*) Very low, very soft.

PIANGÉNDO (*It.*) Plaintively, sorrowfully.

PIANGÉVOLE (*It.*) Lamentable, doleful.

PIANGEVOLMÉNTE (*It.*) Lamentably, mournfully.

PIANÍNO (*It.*) A small pianoforte.

PIANÍSSIMO (*It.*) Very soft, extremely soft.

PIANÍSSIMO QUÁNTO POSSÍBILE (*It.*) As soft as possible.

PIÁNO (*It.*) Soft, softly, gently.

PIANO À ARCHET (*Fr.*) A violin-piano.

PIANO À QUEUE (*Fr.*) A grand pianoforte.

PIANO CARRÉ (*Fr.*) A square pianoforte.

PIANO DROIT (*Fr.*) An upright pianoforte.

PIANO MUET (*Fr.*) A *dumb* pianoforte; practice pianoforte.

PIANOFORTE. An improvement upon the spinet, and harpsichord. The pianoforte was invented about 1746 by Christopher Gottlieb Schröter, who was born at Hohenstein, August 10, 1699. Improvements were afterwards introduced by Silberman, Spaeth, Stern, &c. The earliest form appears to have been that of the square pianoforte, and in Mozart's time the compass was only five octaves. The pianoforte was introduced into England in 1765.

PIANOFORTE SCHOOL. A copious and complete book of instruction for the pianoforte.

PIANOFORTE SCORE. The vocal parts of a composition in score, with a pianoforte arrangement of the instrumental parts. It is also called a vocal score.

PIANOGRAPHE. An ingenious machine, invented by M. Guérin, which, on being attached to the pianoforte, indicates, on paper prepared for the purpose, anything played by the pianist.

PIÁN PIÁNO Very softly, with a low voice.

PIÁN PIANÍSSIMO (*It.*) Exceedingly soft and gentle.

PIÁNTO (*It.*) Weeping, lamentation.

PIÁTTI (*It. pl.*) The cymbals.

PIB-CORN (*Welsh*). *Horn-pipe.* A wooden pipe formerly common in Wales, with holes at stated distances, and a horn at each end, the one to collect the wind blown into it by the mouth, and the other to carry off the sounds as modulated by the performer. It is supposed to have given the name to the air called the 'hornpipe'.

PIBROCH. A set of variations, played on a Scottish bag-pipe.

Picchettáto — Pitch-pipe

PICCHETTÁTO
PICCHIETTÁTO (*It.*) Scattered, detached: in violin playing it means, that sort of *staccáto* indicated by dots under a slur.

PÍCCIOLO
PICCOLÍNO
PÍCCOLO (*It.*) Small, little: *violíno pícciolo*, a small violin: *fláuto píccolo*, a small, or octave flute: the term *píccolo* is also applied to a small pianoforte.

PÍCCOLO. A 2 feet organ stop, of wood pipes, producing a bright and clear tone, in unison with the fifteenth.

PICCORN. A hornpipe.

PICKELFLÖTE (*Ger.*) The piccolo flute.

PIÈCE (*Fr.*) A composition, or piece, of music: an opera, or drama.

PIED (*Fr.*) A foot.

PIEDS (*Fr. pl.*) The feet: *avec les pieds*, with the feet, in organ playing.

PIÉNA
PIÉNO (*It.*) Full: *à piéna orchéstra*, for a full orchestra: *piéno córo*, the full chorus.

PIENAMÉNTE (*It.*) Fully: in a full and majestic style.

PIERCED GAMBA. An organ stop, of the Gamba species: *see* **KERAULOPHON**, *and* **HOHL-FLÜTE**.

PIETÀ
PIETOSAMÉNTE (*It.*) Piteously, tenderly, calmly; implying also, a rather slow, and sustained movement.
PIETÓSO

PÍFARA (*It.*) A fife.

PIFFERÁRE (*It.*) To play upon the fife: also, a piper, such as, in Italy, play pastoral airs in the streets at Christmas, one of which melodies forms the basis of Handel's *Pastoral Symphony*, in the 'Messiah'.

PIFFERÁRI (*It. pl.*) Pipers: *see* **PIFFERÁRE**.

PIFFERÍNA (*It.*) A little fife.

PIFFERO (*It.*) A fife, or small flute: also, an organ stop of 4 feet.

PIFFERÓNE (*It.*) A large fife.

PIKIREN (*Ger.*) *See* **PIQUÉ**.

PILEATA (*Lat.*) Capped; a stopped organ pipe.

PILGERCHOR (*Ger.*) *Pilgrims' Chorus*: an organ stop, on old German organs, a species of *Vox Humana*.

PINCÉ (*Fr.*) Pinched: *see* **PIZZICÁTO**.

PINCER (*Fr.*) To pluck.

PIQUÉ
PIQUER (*Fr.*) To play on the violin, &c., a series of notes a little staccáto, and with a light pressure of the bow to each note.

PITCH-PIPE. An instrument formerly used to sound the keynote of any vocal composition.

Più — Plaintivo

Più (*It.*) More: *più assái*, much more: *al più*, or *il più*, the most.
Più allégro (*It.*) Quicker, more lively.
Più fórte (*It.*) More loudly, louder.
Più lénto (*It.*) More slowly.
Più mosso (*It.*) Quicker.
Più piáno (*It.*) Softer, more softly.
Più présto (*It.*) Quicker, more rapidity.
Più sensibíle (*It.*) With a more prominent melody.
Più strétto (*It.*) Accelerating.
Più tósto (*It.*) *Rather*, inclined to: it also means, quicker, more rapid.
Più tósto allégro (*It.*) Rather quicker.
Più tósto lénto (*It.*) Rather slower.
Più vívo (*It.*) More animated, more lively.
Píva (*It.*) A pipe, a bagpipe.
Pizzicándo / **Pizzicáto** (*It.*) Pinched: meaning that the strings of the violin, &c., are not to be played with the bow, but pinched, or twitched, with the finger, producing a *staccáto* effect, in imitation of the guitar.
Placábile / **Placabilménte** (*It.*) Calmly, peacefully.
Placenteraménte (*It.*) Pleasingly; joyfully.
Placidaménte (*It.*) Calmly, placidly, tranquilly.
Placidézza (*It.*) Placidity, quietness.
Plácido (*It.*) Tranquil, quiet, calm.
Plácito (*It.*) Pleasure.
Plagal. Those ancient modes, in which the melody was confined within the limits of the dominant and its octave.
Plagal cadence. The triad on the sub-dominant, followed by the triad on the tonic, the latter being always *major*.
Plagalisch (*Ger.*) Plagal.
Plagiário (*It.*) / **Plagiat** (*Ger.*) A plagiarism: ideas borrowed, or imitated, from the works of another composer.
Plagiaulos (*Gr.*) A *fláuto travérso*.
Plain chant (*Fr.*) The plain song, or melody: *see* **Cánto férmo**.
Plainte (*Fr.*) A complaint, a lament.
Plaintif (*Fr.*) Plaintive, doleful.
Plaintívo (*It.*) Plaintively, expressively.
Plaisant (*Fr.*) Pleasing, merry, sportive.
Plaisanteries (*Fr.*) Amusing, light compositions.
Plaintivo. *See* **Plaintif**.

PLANCHETTE (*Fr.*) A mechanical pianoforte.
PLANXTY. Old harp music, of a lively, and tuneful, kind.
PLAQUÉ (*Fr.*) *Struck at once*, without any *arpéggio*, or embellishment.
PLAQUER (*Fr.*) To strike at once, in speaking of chords.
PLÄRREN (*Ger.*) To bleat, bawl, sing badly.
PLATÉA (*It.*) The pit, in a theatre.
PLAUDEREND (*Ger.*) Babbling, prattling.
PLEASANTRIES (*Eng.*) See **PLAISANTERIES**.
PLECTRUM (*Lat.*) A quill, or piece of ivory, or hard wood, used to twitch the strings of the *Mandoline*, &c.
PLEIN (*Fr.*) Full.
PLEIN JEU (*Fr.*) Full organ: the term is also applied to a mixture stop, of several ranks of pipes.
PLEIN JEU HARMONIQUE (*Fr.*) A mixture stop, in an organ.
PLENO ORGANO (*Lat.*) Full organ.
PLETTRO (*It.*) A bow, a fiddlestick; also, a plectrum.
PLINTÍVO (*It.*) See **PLAINTÍVO**.
PLOCK-FLÖTE (*Ger.*) See **BLOCKFLÖTE**.
PLÖTZLICH (*Ger.*) Suddenly; at once.
PLÖTZLICH WIEDER IM ZEITMASS (*Ger.*) Suddenly again, but in strict tempo.
PLUS (*Fr.*) More: *un peu plus lent*, a little more slowly: *à plus en plus vite*, more and more quicker.
PLUS ANIMÉ (*Fr.*) With more animation.
PLUS LENTEMENT (*Fr.*) Slower, more slowly.
PLUS VITE QU'AU DÉBUT (*Fr.*) More animated than at the beginning.
PNEUMATIC (*Gr.*) Relating to the air, or wind: a term applied to all wind-instruments, collectively.
PNEUMATIC ACTION / **PNEUMATIC LEVER** Mechanism intended to lighten the touch, &c., in large organs: see **LEVIER PNEUMATIQUE**.
POCETTA (*It.*) / **POCHE** (*Fr.*) / **POCHETTE** (*Fr.*) A kit, a small violin used by dancing masters.
POCHETTETTÍNO / **POCHÉTTO** / **POCHÍNO** (*It.*) A little: *rittard, un pochettíno*, a little slower.
POCHÍSSIMO (*It.*) A very little, as little as possible.
PÓCO (*It.*) Little: *póco allégro*, rather quick: *póco animáto*, rather animated, a little more animated.
PÓCO ALLERGRÉTTO E GRAZIÓSO (*It.*) Graceful and rather quick.
PÓCO ANIMÁTO (*It.*) Rather animated.

Póco — Poliphant

PÓCO À PÓCO (*It.*) By degrees, gradually.

PÓCO À PÓCO CRESCÉNDO (*It.*) Louder and louder by degrees.

PÓCO À PÓCO DIMINUÉNDO (*It.*) Softer and softer by degrees.

PÓCO À PÓCO, PIÙ DI FUÓCO (*It.*) With gradually increasing fire and animation.

PÓCO FÓRTE (*It.*) Moderately loud, rather loud.

PÓCO LENTO (*It.*) Moderately slow, a little slow.

PÓCO MÉNO (*It.*) A little less, somewhat less.

PÓCO PIÁNO (*It.*) Somewhat soft, rather soft.

PÓCO PIÙ (*It.*) A little more, somewhat more.

PÓCO PIÙ PIÁNO (*It.*) A little softer.

PÓCO PIÙ LÁRGO (*It.*) A little more slowly.

PÓCO PRÉSTO (*It.*) Rather quick.

PÓCO PRÉSTO ACCELERÁNDO (*It.*) Gradually accelerate the time.

POÈME SYMPHONIQUE (*Fr.*) A symphonic poem.

POETA (*Lat.*) A poet, writer.

POETICAL OVERTURE. A descriptive species of overture.

POGGIÁTO (*It.*) Dwelt upon, leaned upon.

PÓI (*It.*) Then, after, afterwards: *piáno pói fórte*, soft, then loud.

PÓI À PÓI (*It.*) By degrees: *pói à pói tútte le córde*, all the strings one after another.

POIGNET (*Fr.*) The wrist.

PÓI SÉGUE
PÓI SEGUÉNTE } (*It.*) Then follows, here follows.

POINT (*Fr.*) A dot.

POINT D'ARRÊT (*Fr.*) *See* CORÓNA.

POINT DE REPOS (*Fr.*) A pause.

POINT D'ORGUE (*Fr.*) *See* ORGAN POINT.

POINTÉE (*Fr.*) Dotted: *blanche pointée*, a dotted minim.

POINT FINAL (*Fr.*) A final, or concluding, cadence.

POITRINE (*Fr.*) The chest.

POLÁCCA (*It.*) A slow Polish dance of peculiar construction, in $\frac{3}{4}$ time, with six quaver-pulsations, the second bearing a strong emphasis, and the phrases usually terminating on the third crotchet of the bar.

POLCA (*It.*) *See* POLKA.

POLICHINELLE (*Fr.*) A clown dance.

POLIFÓNIO (*It.*) Polyphonic; more than one sound.

POLIPHANT. An instrument supposed to be a species of lute, or cither, strung with wire. Queen Elizabeth is said to have been a good performer upon it.

Polka — Portaménto

POLKA. A lively Bohemian or Polish dance in $\frac{2}{4}$ time, the first three quavers in each bar being accented, and the fourth quaver unaccented.

PÓLLICE (*It.*) The thumb: *marcáto il póllice*, mark the note played by the thumb.

POLNISCH (*Ger.*) In the Polish style.

POLNISCHER BOCK (*Ger.*) The bagpipe.

POLONAISE
POLONESE   *See* POLÁCCA.
POLONOISE

POLSKA. A Swedish dance in triple time.

POLYCHORD (*Gr.*) Any instrument with a great number of strings.

POLYHYMNIA (*Gr.*) The muse of song, or vocal music.

POLYMORPHOUS (*Gr.*) Of many forms, a term generally used in reference to canons.

POLYPHONIE
POLYPHONY   (*Gr.*) A composition in many parts, or for many voices.

POLYPHONIC
POLYPHONOUS   (*Gr.*) Full-voiced, for many voices.

POMMER (*Ger.*) A *bombard*.

POMPA (*It.*)
POMPE (*Fr.*)   Pomp; dignity.

POMPÖS (*Ger.*) Pompous, majestic.

POMPOSAMÉNTE (*It.*) Pompously, stately.

POMPÓSO (*It.*) Pompous, stately, grand.

PONCTUATION MUSICALE (*Fr.*) Musical punctuation; the art of phrasing.

PONDERÓSO (*It.*) Ponderously, massively, heavily.

PONTICÉLLO (*It.*) The *bridge* of the violin, &c.

PONT-NEUF (*Fr.*) A street ballad, a vulgar song.

POOFYE. An Hindoo noise flute.

POPOLÁRE (*It.*) Popular.

PORTAMÉNTO (*It.*) The original and legitimate meaning of the word is, - The production of a pure tone, neither nasal nor guttural; uniformity in the management of the voice; pressing the notes with firmness in order to bring out their tone distinctly; a medium between *staccáto* and *legáto*; the art of sustaining and conducting the voice; to have the voice free, yet firm and steady, keeping up the tone. The term is now applied to a gliding from higher to a lower, or from a lower to a higher note, but it does not produce a good effect in

English music, and very rarely in Italian, as it appears an affectation, rather than a just mode of heightening the expression.

PORTÁNDO LA VÓCE (*It.*) Sustaining the voice, holding it firmly on the notes.

PORTÁRE LA VÓCE (*It.*) To sustain the voice.

PORTÁR LA BATTÚTA (*It.*) To beat the time.

PORTÁTA (*It.*) The staff.

PORTATIVE. A *portable* organ.

PORTÁTO (*It.*) Sustained, drawn out.

PORTE DE VOIX (*Fr.*) An *appoggiatúra*, or beat.

PORTÉE (*Fr.*) The staff; also, *see* PORTAMÉNTO.

PORTEZ LA VOIX (*Fr.*) See PORTÁNDO LA VÓCE.

PORTUNAL-FLAUT (*Ger.*) An organ stop, of the clarabella species, the pipes of which are larger at the top than at the bottom, and produces a tone of clarionet quality.

PORTUNEN (*Ger.*) See BOURDON.

POSÁTO (*It.*) Quietly, steadily.

POSAUNE (*Ger.*) A trumpet: also, a trombone, a sackbut: also, an organ stop: *see* TROMBÓNE.

POSAUNEN-BLÄSSER / **POSAUNER** (*Ger.*) A trombone player, a trumpet player.

POSÉMENT (*Fr.*) Softly, gravely, gently.

POSER LA VOIX (*Fr.*) To attack cleanly, and with precision, in singing.

POSITIF (*Fr.*) The choir organ, or lowest row of keys, with soft-tones stops, in a large organ: also, a small *fixed* organ, thus named in opposition to a *portative* organ.

POSITION (*Fr.*) A position, or shift, on the violin, &c.

POSITIV (*Ger.*) See POSITIF.

POSIZIÓNE (*It.*) Position.

POSSÍBILE (*It.*) Possible: *il più fórte possíbile*, as loud as possible: *il più piáno possíbile*, as soft as possible.

POST-HORN (*Ger.*) A sort of bugle; also, an organ stop.

POSTHUME (*Fr.*) / **POSTHUMOUS** (*Eng.*) Published after the composer's death.

POSTLUDE / **POSTLUDIUM** (*Lat.*) After-piece; concluding voluntary.

POT-POURRI (*Fr.*) *Capríccio*, or *fantasia*, on favourite airs: a medley of various tunes.

POUCE (*Fr.*) The thumb.

POULE (*Fr.*) One of the movements of the quadrille.

POUR (*Fr.*) For: *pour la première fois*, for the first time, meaning, that on the repetition of the strain, this passage is to be omitted.

POUR FINIR (*Fr.*) *To finish*: indicating a chord, or bar which is to terminate the piece.

POUSSÉ (*Fr.*) Pushed: meaning, the *up-bow*.

PRÄCHTIG (*Ger.*) In a majestic, dignified style.

PRACHTVOLL (*Ger.*) In a very stately, dignified style.

PRÄCIS (*Ger.*) Exact, precise: *Sehr präcis im Rhythmus*, very exact in rhythm.

PRÆAMBULAM \
PRÆCENTIO (*Lat.*) A prelude.

PRÆCENTOR (*Lat.*) Precentor, leader of the choir.

PRÆFECTUS (*Lat.*) A president.

PRÆFECTUS CHORI (*Lat.*) Master of the choristers.

PRALL-TRILLER (*Ger.*) Transient, or passing, shake; an inverted *mordent*.

PRÄLUDIEN (*Ger. pl.*) Preludes.

PRÄLUDIREN (*Ger.*) To prelude, to play a prelude.

PRÄLUDIUM (*Lat. & Ger.*) A prelude, introduction.

PRÄSTANT (*Ger.*) See PRESTANT.

PRÄSTANTEN (*Ger.*) Pipes belonging to the *Prestant*, or open diapason, placed in the front of an organ case.

PRÁTICO \
PRATTÍCO (*It.*) Practical, skilful, experienced.

PRÄZIS (*Ger.*) Exact, precise.

PREAMBLE (*Eng.*) \
PRÉAMBULE (*Fr.*) An introductory voluntary; a prelude. \
PREAMBULUM (*Lat.*)

PRECENTOR. Leader and director of the choir in a cathedral, &c.

PRECETTÓRE DI MÚSICA (*It.*) A teacher of music.

PRÉCHANTRE (*Fr.*) See PRECENTOR.

PRECIPITAMÉNTE (*It.*) Precipitation, hurry, haste.

PRECIPITÁNDO (*It.*) Hurrying.

PRECIPITÁTO (*It.*) Precipitate, hurriedly.

PRECIPITAZIÓNE (*It.*) Precipitation, hurry, haste.

PRÉCIPITÉ (*Fr.*) Hurried, accelerated.

PRECIPITÓSO (*It.*) Hurrying, precipitous.

PRECISIÓNE (*It.*) Precision, exactness.

PRECÍSO (*It.*) Precise, exact: exactly.

PREFAZIÓNE (*It.*) Preface.

PREFECTUS CHORI (*Lat.*) See PRECENTOR.

Pregándo — Prímo

PREGÁNDO (*It.*) In a devotional, prayerful style

PREGHIÉRA (*It.*) Prayer, supplication.

PRELÚDIO (*It.*)
PRELUDIUM (*Lat.*) } Prelude, introductory movement.

PREMIER
PREMIÈRE } (*Fr.*) First.

PREMIÈRE DESSUS (*Fr.*) First treble, first soprano.

PREMIÈRE FOIS (*Fr.*) First time.

PREPARATION (*Eng.*)
PREPARAZIÓNE (*It.*) } A term relating to dissonances, in harmony. A discord is said to be prepared, when the note is heard in the preceding chord and in the same part, as a consonance.

PRÉPAREZ (*Fr.*) Prepare, get ready.

PRÉSA (*It.*) A sign showing the *entry* points in a canon or round.

PRÈS DE LA TABLE (*Fr.*) Near the sound-board.

PRESSÁNDO (*It.*)
PRESSANTE (*Fr.*) } Hurrying on, pressing on.

PRESSEZ (*Fr.*) *Accelerándo*, *stringéndo*.

PRESSIREN (*Ger.*) To hurry; *accelerándo*.

PRESTAMÉNTE (*It.*) Hurriedly, hastily.

PRESTANT (*Fr.*) The open diapason stop in an organ, of either 32, 16, 8, or 4 feet tone: see PRÄSTANTEN.

PRESTÉZZA (*It.*) Quickness, rapidity.

PRESTISSIMAMÉNTE
PRESTÍSSIMO } (*It.*) Very quickly; with the utmost rapidity; as fast as possible.

PRÉSTO (*It.*) Quickly, rapidly.

PRÉSTO ASSÁI (*It.*) See PRESTÍSSIMO.

PRIÈRE (*Fr.*) A prayer, supplication.

PRÍMA (*It.*) First, chief, principal: also, the tonic, or keynote, of any scale: *vióla príma*, the principal viola.

PRÍMA BÚFFA (*It.*) The principal female singer, in a comic opera.

PRÍMA DÓNNA (*It.*) Principal female singer, in a serious opera.

PRÍMA DÓNNA ASSOLÚTA (*It.*) First female singer in an operatic establishment: the only one who can claim that title.

PRÍMA OPÉRA (*It.*) First work.

PRÍMA PÁRTE (*It.*) First part.

PRÍMA VÍSTA (*It.*) First sight: at the first view.

PRÍMA VÓLTA (*It.*) First time.

PRIME (*Ger.*) First note, or tonic, of a scale.

PRIMGEIGER (*Ger.*) The leading or first violin; leader.

PRÍMO (*It.*) First, chief, principal: *violíno prímo*, first violin.

PRÍMO BÚFFO (*It.*) First male singer in a comic opera.
PRÍMO CÁNTO (*It.*) First treble.
PRÍMO MÚSICO (*It.*) Principal male singer.
PRÍMO TÉMPO (*It.*) The first, or original, time.
PRÍMO UÓMO (*It.*) The first tenor singer.
PRÍMO VIOLÍNO (*It.*) The first violin.
PRIM-TÖNE (*Ger. pl.*) Fundamental tones, or notes.
PRINCIPAL, *or* **OCTAVE.** An important organ stop, tuned an octave above the diapasons, and therefore of 4 feet pitch on the manual, and 8 feet on the pedals. In German organs the term *Principal* is also applied to all open diapasons of 32, 16, 8, and 4 feet.
PRINCIPAL BASS. An organ stop of the open diapason species, on the pedals: *see* PRINCIPAL.
PRINCIPÁLE (*It.*) Principal, chief: *violíno principále*, the principal violin: the term is also applied, in Handel's music, and in ancient church music, to a third trumpet, written in the C clef.
PRINCIPALMÉNTE (*It.*) Principally, chiefly.
PRINCIPAL OCTAVE. An organ stop: *see* PRINCIPAL.
PRINCÍPIO (*It.*) The beginning; the first time.
PRISE (*Fr.*) Entry, re-entry.
PROASMA. A short symphony; a prelude or introduction.
PROBE (*Ger.*) Proof, trial, rehearsal.
PROCÉLLA (*It.*) A storm, musical delineation of a tempest.
PROFÁNO (*It.*) Secular.
PROFESSEUR DE CHANT (*Fr.*) A singing master.
PROFESSEUR DE MUSIQUE (*Fr.*)
PROFESSÓRE DI MÚSICA (*It.*) Professor of music. In the Universities the professor of music enjoys academical rank, and the honourable office of examining for musical degrees.
PROGRAMM (*Ger.*)
PROGRÁMMA (*It.*)
PROGRAMME (*Fr.*) A programme; a list of pieces to be performed.
PROGRESSIO HARMONICA (*Lat.*) A mixture stop in German organs, commencing with two ranks at the bottom, and increasing to 3, 4, or 5 ranks, in the upper part of the manual.
PROGRESSION (*Eng.*)
PROGRESSIÓNE (*It.*) A succession of chords, a passage, a musical phrase.
PROGRESSIONS-SCHWELLER (*Ger.*) A species of crescéndo swell pedal, invented by Abbé Vogler.
PROIBÍTO (*It.*) Forbidden.
PROLATIO (*Lat.*) Adding a dot, to increase, or lengthen, the value of a note.

PROLOGUE. An introduction, a prelude.
PROLONGEMENT (*Fr.*) A *sostenúto* pianoforte pedal; the sustaining pedal.
PROMPTEMENT (*Fr.*) }
PRONTAMÉNTE (*It.*) } Readily, quickly, promptly.
PRÓNTO (*It.*) }
PRONUNZIÁRE (*It.*) To pronounce, to enunciate.
PRONUNZIÁTO (*It.*) Pronounced, clear, distinct, well-marked.
PROPÓSTA (*It.*) Subject, or theme, of a fugue.
PROSÆ SEQUENTIÆ (*Lat.*) Hymns sung at the festivals of Easter, and Pentecost.
PROSCÉNIO (*It.*) } The space *behind* the stage; the *stage front*, in
PROSCENIUM (*Lat.*) } front of the curtain.
PROSLAMBANOMENOS (*Gr.*) Additional, or supernumerary note: it corresponded with the note A above G gamut.
PROSODÍA (*It.*) } Prosody, correct accentuation in setting
PROSODIE (*Ger. & Fr.*) } words to music, and distinguishing long or short syllables.
PROSPEKT (*Ger.*) The front of an organ.
PRÓVA (*It.*) Proof, trial, rehearsal.
PROVENÇALES. Poets, or troubadours, in the eleventh century.
PSALLETTE (*Fr.*) Single-place, choir.
PSALLO (*Gr.*) To play on, or sing to, a stringed instrument.
PSALM. A sacred song, or hymn.
PSALM-BUCH (*Ger.*) A psalter, book of psalms.
PSALM-GESANG (*Ger.*) Psalmody.
PSALMISTÆ. A mediæval order of singing clergy.
PSALM-LIED (*Ger.*) Psalm, hymn.
PSALM-SÄNGER (*Ger.*) Psalmodist, psalm-singer.
PSALM-SINGEN (*Ger.*) Psalmody.
PSALTER (*Eng.*) The book of Psalms.
PSALTER (*Ger.*) Psaltery.
PSALTER-SPIEL (*Ger.*) Playing on the psaltery.
PSALTERION (*Fr.*) }
PSALTERIUM (*Lat.*) } An ancient Hebrew instrument, supposed to be a species of lyre, harp, or dulcimer.
PSALTERY (*Eng.*) }
PSALTES (*Gr.*) A player on, or singer to, a stringed instrument.
PSALTRIÆ (*Lat.*) Female singers, and players on the *psalterium*, who entertained the ancient Romans, at their banquets.
PSAUME (*Fr.*) A psalm.
PSAUTIER (*Fr.*) A psalter.

PUIS (*Fr.*) Then; afterwards.

PULPITUM (*Lat.*) The stage of an ancient Greek theatre.

PULSATILE. *Striking*: instruments of percussion, as the drum, tambourine, &c.

PULSARTOR ORGANORUM (*Lat.*) An *organ-beater*; organist.

PUNCTUM CONTRA PUNCTUM (*Lat.*)   Point against point: *see* **COUNTERPOINT**.

PUNCTUS (*Lat.*) | A dot, a point.
PUNKT (*Ger.*) |

PUNKTIRTE NOTEN (*Ger.*) Dotted notes.

PÚNTA (*It.*) The point, the top, the sharp end: also, a thrust, or push.

PÚNTA D'ÁRCO (*It.*) Point, or tip, of the bow.

PUNTÁTO (*It.*) Pointed, detached, marked.

PÚNTO (*It.*) A dot, a point.

PUPITRE (*Fr.*) A music desk.

PURFLING. The ornamental borders of violins.

PÚTTI (*It.*) Small boys; choir boys, &c.

PYKNON (*Gr.*) The *close note* in ancient Greek music; a mediæval semitone.

PYRAMIDAL FLUTE. An 8 feet organ stop, of wood.

PYRAMIDON (*Gr.*) An organ stop, of 16, or 32 feet tone, on the pedals, invented by the Rev. Sir F. A. G. Ouseley, Bart.: the pipes are of peculiar shape, being four times larger at the top than at the mouth, and, for the size, the tone is of remarkable gravity, resembling that of a stopped pipe in quality.

PYROPHONE. An instrument invented by Kastner, the tones of which are produced by gas-jets, being burnt under tuned resonators.

PYRRHIC (*Gr.*) An ancient Greek dance with lyre or flute accompaniment; also, a musical foot, containing two short syllables.

Q

QUADRAT (*Ger.*)
QUADRATE (*Eng.*) } The mark called a natural, ♮.
QUADRATUM (*Lat.*)

QUADRATUM (*Lat.*) A breve.

QUADRICINIUM
QUADRIPARTITE } (*Lat.*) A quartet, a composition in four parts.

QUADRILLE (*Fr.*) A French dance, or set of five consecutive dance movements, called *Le Pantalon*, *La Poule*, *L'Été*, *La Trenise* (or *La Pastourelle*), and *La Finale*.

QUÁDRO (*It.*)
QUADRUM (*Lat.*) } The mark called a natural, ♮.

QUADRUPLE COUNTERPOINT. Counterpoint in four parts, all of which may be inverted, and each of them taken as a bass, middle, or acute, part.

QUADRUPLE CROCHE (*Fr.*)
QUADRUPLE QUAVER (*Eng.*) } Four-hooked: a half-demisemiquaver, or semi-demisemiquaver.

QUÁDRUPLO (*It. & Lat.*) In four parts.

QUAL (*Ger.*) Agony, torment.

QUÁNTO (*It.*) As much as; as far as: *fórte quánto possíbile*, as loud as possible.

QUARREE (*Fr.*) The old name for a breve.

QUART (*Fr.*) A quarter.

QUÁRTA (*It.*) A fourth: also, the fourth voice, or instrumental, part.

QUARTA ABUNDANS (*Lat.*) An augmented fourth.

QUARTA DEFICIENS (*Lat.*)
QUÁRTA DIMINUÍTA (*It.*) } A diminished fourth.

QUÁRTA ECCEDÉNTE (*It.*) An augmented fourth.

QUÁRTA MÓNDI
QUÁRTA RÓNI } (*It.*) The sub-dominant, or fourth note of the scale.

QUART DE MESURE (*Fr.*) A crotchet rest.

QUART DE SON (*Fr.*) A quarter-tone.

QUART DE SOUPIR (*Fr.*) A semiquaver rest.

QUART DE TON (*Fr.*) A quarter-tone.

QUARTE (*Fr. & Ger.*) A fourth.

QUARTE AUGMENTÉE (*Fr.*) An augmented fourth.

QUARTE DE NAZARD (*Fr.*) *Fourth above the nazard*, an organ stop identical with the fifteenth.

QUARTE DIMINUÉE (*Fr.*) A diminished fourth.

QUARTE DU TON (*Fr.*) See QUÁRTA TÓNE.

QUARTER NOTE. A crotchet.

QUARTER TONE. A small interval: half a semitone: it may be described as something like that slight difference of pitch made on the violin, &c., between D-sharp and E-flat: G-sharp and A-flat: &c.

QUARTET (*Eng.*)
QUARTETT (*Ger.*)
QUARTETTE (*Fr.*)
QUARTETTO (*It.*)
  A composition for four voices or instruments.

QUARTETTÍNO (*It.*) A short quartet.

QUART-FAGOTT (*Ger.*)
QUART-FAGÓTTO (*It.*)
  An old sort of bassoon, formerly used as a tenor to the hautboy: called also, *Dulcíno*, and *Dulzain*.

QUART-FLÖTE (*Ger.*) A flute sounding a fourth above.

QUART-GEIGE (*Ger.*) A small fiddle.

QUARTÍNO (*It.*) A high clarinet in E-flat.

QUÁRTO (*It.*) See QUÁRTA.

QUÁRTO D'ASÉTTO (*It.*) A semiquaver rest.

QUÁRTO DI TUÓNO (*It.*) Quarter tone.

QUARTOLE (*Ger.*) A quadruplet: four notes played in the time of three.

QUART-POSAUNE (*Ger.*) A trombone, a fourth lower than normal.

QUARTSEXTAKKORD (*Ger.*) A six-four chord; a second inversion.

QUÁSI (*It.*) As if, like, almost, as it were.

QUÁSI AD LIB (*It.*) As if *ad lib*; almost at pleasure.

QUÁSI ALLEGRÉTTO (*It.*) Like a *Allegrétto*.

QUÁSI CADÉNZA (*It.*) In the style of a *cadénza*; *ad lib*.

QUÁSI PARLÁTO (*It.*) As if spoken.

QUÁSI TRÓMBE (*It.*) Like trumpets: bright, clear, ringing.

QUÁSI ÚNI FANTASÍA (*It.*) As if it were a fantasia.

QUATORZIÈME (*Fr.*) The interval of a fourteenth.

QUATRE (*Fr.*)
QUÁTTRO (*It.*)
  Four: *à quatre mains*, or *à quáttro máni*, for four hands, a pianoforte duet.

QUATRICINIUM (*Lat.*) A short piece for four horns, or trumpets.

QUATTRICRÓMA (*It.*) A demisemiquaver.

QUATUOR (*Lat. & Fr.*) A quartet.

QUAVER. A note equal to half a crotchet.

QUAVER REST. A mark of silence, equal in value to a quaver.

Quer — Quint-fágott

QUER (*Ger.*) Oblique, transverse, queer.

QUER-FLÖTE (*Ger.*) German flute: *see* FLÁUTO TRAVÉRSO.

QUER-PFEIFE (*Ger.*) A fife.

QUER-STAND (*Ger.*) False relation, in harmony.

QUER-STRICHE (*Ger.*) Ledger lines.

QUÉSTA
QUÉSTO } (*It.*) This.

QUEUE (*Fr.*) The tail, or stem, of a note: also, the tailpiece of a violin, &c.

QUETSCHUNG (*Ger.*) An *acciaccatúra*.

QUICK STEP. A lively march, generally in $\frac{2}{4}$ time

QUIÉTO (*It.*) Quiet, calm, serene.

QUILLISMA. A *neum*, or plainsong character, for a trembling voice, a sort of *mordent*.

QUINDÉCIMA (*It.*) *See* QUÍNTA DÉCIMA.

QUINT (*Lat.*)
QUÍNTA (*It.*) } A fifth: also, the name of an organ stop sounding a fifth (or twelfth) above the foundation stops.

QUINTABSATZ (*Ger.*)
QUINTABSCHLUSS (*Ger.*) } A half-cadence.

QUÍNTA DÉCIMA (*It.*) The fifth above the tenth, an organ stop identical with the fifteenth.

QUINTADENA
QUINTA-ED-UNA } *See* QUINTATON.

QUÍNTA MÓDI
QUÍNTA TÓNI } (*It.*) The dominant, or fifth from the tonic.

QUINTATON (*Ger.*) A manual organ stop of 8 feet tone; a stopped diapason of rather small scale, producing the twelfth, as well as the ground tone: it also occurs as a pedal stop of 32, and 16 feet tone.

QUINT-BASS. An organ pedal stop: *see* QUINT.

QUINTE (*Fr.* & *Ger.*) *See* QUINT.

QUINTE DE VIOLE (*Fr.*) The viola.

QUINTE OCTAVIANTE (*Fr.*) Octave quint; the twelfth.

QUINTER (*Fr.*) To sing in fifths.

QUINTERNE. An obsolete Italian instrument, resembling a lute.

QUINTET (*Eng.*)
QUINTETT (*Ger.*)
QUINTETTE (*Fr.*)
QUINTÉTTO (*It.*) } A composition for five voices, or instruments.

QUINT-FÁGOTT (*It.*) The small bassoon, or *fagottína*, sounding a fifth higher than the common bassoon.

QUINT-GEDACT (*Ger.*) An organ stop, of the stopped diapason species, sounding the fifth above.

QUÍNTO (*It.*) A fifth.

QUINTOLE (*Eng. & Ger.*) *See* QUINTUPLET.

QUINTOIRE. An old French term applied to *descant*.

QUINTOLE (*Lat.*) A group of five notes, having the same value as four of the same species.

QUINTON (*Fr.*) A five stringed viol.

QUINT-SAITE (*Ger.*) Treble string.

QUINTUOR (*Fr.*) *See* QUINTET.

QUINTUS DECIMUS (*Lat.*) *See* QUÍNTA DÉCIMA.

QUINTVIOLE (*Ger.*) The viola.

QUINTZIÈME (*Fr.*) The interval of a fifth.

QUIRE. A choir, body of singers: that part of a church where the choristers sit.

QUIRISTER. A chorister.

QUI TOLLIS (*Lat.*) A part of the *Gloria*.

QUODLIBET (*Lat.*) A melody of airs, &c., out of different works, or by various composers: a certain species of composition written in a comic style.

QUONIAM TU SOLUS (*Lat.*) Part of the *Gloria*.

R

RABANI \
RABANNA — A species of tambourine, used by the negroes.

RÁBBIA (*It.*) Rage, fury, madness.

RACCÓLTA (*It.*) A collection.

RACCONTÁNDO (*It.*) In the reciting or narrative style.

RACCÓNTO (*It.*) A tale, a story.

RACCOURCIR (*Fr.*) To abridge, shorten.

RACKETT (*Ger.*) An obsolete species of basson or bombard.

RACLER (*Fr.*) To saw, to scrape.

RADDOLCÉNDO \
RADDOLCÉNTE — (*It.*) With increasing softness; becoming softer by degrees.

RADDOPPIAMÉNTE (*It.*) Augmentation; reduplication; the doubling of an interval.

RADDOPPIÁNTE NÓTE (*It.*) Repeated, or reiterated, notes.

RADDOPPIÁTO (*It.*) Double, increased, augmented.

RADEL (*Ger.*) A solo with a choral refrain.

RADICAL BASS. The fundamental bass, the roots of the various chords.

RADLEIER (*Ger.*) A hurdy-gurdy.

RAFFRENÁNDO (*It.*) Checking the time; slightly *rallentándo*.

RAGGIÓNE (*It.*) Ratio, proportion.

RAGOKE. A small Russian horn.

RAKE. *See* RASTRUM.

RALENTIR (*Fr.*) To slacken the speed; to slow down.

RALLENTAMÉNTO \
RALLENTÁNDO — (*It.*) The time gradually slower, and the sound gradually softer. \
RALLENTÁTO

RANG (*Fr.*) A rank of organ pipes.

RANK. A set or row; a range.

RANKETT (*Ger.*) *See* RACKETT.

RANZ DES VACHES (*Fr.*) Pastoral airs played by the Swiss herdsmen, to assemble their cattle and keep them together on their return home.

RAPIDAMÉNTE (*It.*) \
RAPIDEMENT (*Fr.*) — Rapidly.

RAPIDITÀ (*It.*) \
RAPIDITÉ (*Fr.*) — Rapidity.

RÁPIDO (*It.*) Rapid.
RAPPEL. A noisy Egyptian instrument, something like a drum.
RAPPEL (*Fr.*) A military call.
RAPSODIE (*Fr.*) \
RAPSODY (*Old Eng.*) / A *capríccio*, a fragmentary piece, a wild, unconnected composition.
RASCH (*Ger.*) Quick, rapid; impetuous.
RASCHELN (*Ger.*) To rustle.
RASCHER (*Ger.*) Quicker.
RASCH WIE ZUVOR (*Ger.*) As quick as before.
RASE-GESANG \
RASE-LIED / (*Ger.*) A wild song, a dithyrambic.
RASEND (*Ger.*) Raging, blustering; mad.
RASGÁDO (*Sp.*) Drawing the thumb over the strings of the guitar, so as to produce an *arpéggio* effect.
RASSAGGIÁNDO (*It.*) With resignation.
RASTRAL \
RASTRUM / (*Lat.*) A little instrument for drawing music-lines, or staves.
RÄTHSELCANON \
RÄTSELKANON / (*Ger.*) A puzzle, or riddle canon.
RATTENÉNDO \
RATTENÚTO / (*It.*) Holding back, or restraining, the time.
RATTÉZZA (*It.*) Swiftness, quickness, rapidity.
RAUCEDÍNE (*It.*) Harshness.
RÁUCO (*It.*) \
RAUH (*Ger.*) / Hoarse, rough, harsh; rude, raw, coarse.
RAUSCHEN (*Ger.*) To rush, rustle, ripple, roar.
RAUSCHER (*Ger.*) The rapid repetition of a note.
RAUSCH-FLÖTE \
RAUSCH-PFEIFE \
RAUSCH-QUINT / (*Ger.*) Rustling-fifth: a mixture stop, in German organs, the 12th and 15th on one slide.
RAUSCH-WERK /
RÄUSPERN (*Ger.*) To clear the throat.
RAUQUE (*Fr.*) See **RÁUCO**.
RAVVIVÁNDO (*It.*) Reviving, quickening, reanimating.
RAVVIVÁNDO IL TÉMPO (*It.*) Accelerating the time.
RAVVIVÁRE (*It.*) To revive, to quicken the time.
RE. A syllable applied, in *solfaing*, to the note D.
REÁLE (*It.*) Real; distinct.

Rebab — Recitáto

REBAB
REBEB
REBEC
REBECCA
REBECK
REBED

A Moorish or Turkish instrument of the fiddle species, originally with only two strings, to which the Spaniards added a third. It was once very popular in England.

RE BÉMOL (*Fr.*) The note D-flat.

RE BÉMOL MAJEUR (*Fr.*) The key of D-flat major.

REBET. *See* REBAB.

REBIBE
REBIBLE (*Eng.*) *See* REBAB.

RÉCENSION (*Fr.*) An analytical criticism of a work; also, a critically revised edition.

RECESSIONAL. A hymn which is sung, as the choir and clergy leave the chancel, after a service.

RECHANGE (*Fr.*) Exchange.

RECHANTER (*Fr.*) To sing again.

RECHEAT (*Old Eng.*) Those sounds played on the horn, by huntsmen, to recall the hounds from a false scent.

RECHERCHÉ (*Fr.*) Sought out; rare; elegant: *see also* **RICERCÁTA**.

RECHT (*Ger.*) Right: *rechte Hand*, the right hand.

RÉCIT (*Fr.*) Recitative; a solo; a recital; also, one of the manuals on a French organ, equivalent to the English swell organ.

RECITÁNDO
RECITÁNTE (*It.*) Declamatory, in the style of recitative.

RÉCITANT (*Fr.*) A solo singer or player.

RECITATIF (*Fr.*) Musical declamation; speaking in music; without any very rhythmical, or decided, melody.

RECITATIF ACCOMPAGNÉ
RECITATIF OBLIGÉ (*Fr.*) An accompanied recitative.

RECITATIV (*Ger.*)
RECITATIVE (*Eng.*) *See* RECITATIF.
RECITATÍVO (*It.*)

RECITATÍVO ACCOMPAGNÁTO
RECITATÍVO OBBLIGÁTO (*It.*) An accompanied recitative.

RECITATÍVO PARLÁNTE
RECITATÍVO SÉCCO (*It.*) Unaccompanied recitative: also, when accompanied only by the violoncello and double bass, or the pianoforte, or organ.

RECITATÍVO STROMENTÁTO (*It.*) Recitative accompanied by the orchestra.

RECITÁTO (*It.*) *See* RECITÁNTE.

RÉCITER (*Fr.*) To perform a *récit*; to recite.
RECLAME (*Fr.*) Bird song.
RECLAMER (*Fr.*) To sing in imitation of a bird.
RECORDER. An old instrument, supposed to have been of the flute species; also, an organ stop, of 4, or 2 feet pitch.
RECTE (*Lat.*) Right, straight, forward.
RECTE ET RETRO (*Lat.*) Forward, then backward; the melody, or subject, reversed, note for note.
REDDÍTA (*It.*) Return to the subject; repetition of a melody.
REDEND (*Ger.*) Speaking; *see* PARLÁNDO.
RE DIÈSE (*Fr.*) The note D-sharp.
REDÍTA (*It.*) } *See* REDDÍTA.
REDITE (*Fr.*) }
REDONDILLA (*Sp.*) A *roundelay*.
REDOUBLEMENT (*Fr.*) *See* RADDOPPIAMÉNTO.
REDOWA }
REDOWAK } A Bohemian dance, in $\frac{2}{4}$ and $\frac{3}{4}$ time alternatively.
REDOWAZKA }
REDUBLICÁTO (*It.*) Doubled, in chords, intervals, &c.
REDUCIREN (*Ger.*) To reduce, or arrange, a full instrumental score, for a smaller band, or for the pianoforte, or organ.
REDUCTIO (*Lat.*) Reducing, or bringing back augmented intervals to their original value: *see also* REDUCIREN.
RÉDUCTION (*Fr.*) } A simplified, or condensed arrangement of a
REDUKTION (*Ger.*) } composition.
REDUZIÓNE (*It.*) }
REED. The flat piece of cane placed on the beak, or mouthpiece, of the clarinet, and basset-horn; this is called a *single* reed. The *double* reed is the mouth-piece of the hautboy, English horn, and bassoon, formed of two pieces of cane joined together in a particular manner. The term *Reed* is also applied to the small metal tube through which the wind passes, in some organ pipes: when the tongue strikes against the tube it is called a fixed, or *striking* reed; and when the tongue vibrates in the middle of the tube, without striking against the sides, it is called a *free* reed.
REED FIFTH } A stopped *Quint* register, in an organ, the stopper of
REED NASAT } which has a hole, or tube in it: *see* Rohr-Flöte.
REED STOPS. Those stops in an organ, the peculiar tone of which is produced by the wind having to pass through a *reed* placed at the bottom of the pipe, and putting the *tongue* into vibration.

Reel — Reminiscenz

REEL. A lively Scotch dance. Originally the term *Rhay*, or *Reel*, was applied to a very ancient English dance, called 'the Hay,' but now *Reel* means a lively Scotch melody of a particular kind: see RHAY.

REFRAIN (*Fr.*) The *burden* of a song; a ritornel; a repeat; a closing phrase: see BURDEN.

REFRET. See RITORNÉLLO.

REGAL (*Ger.*) \
RÉGALE (*Fr.*) A portable organ, used in former times, in religious processions.

REGEL (*Ger.*) A rule, principal; order.

REGENS CHORI (*Lat.*) The choir-master, in German churches.

REGINA CŒLI (*Lat.*) A hymn to the Virgin.

REGISTER (*Ger.*) The stops, or rows of pipes in an organ: also, applied to the high, low, or middle parts, or divisions, of the voice: also, the compass of a voice or instrument.

REGISTERING. The proper management of the stops, in an organ.

REGISTRE (*Fr.*) \
REGÍSTRO (*It.*) A stop knob, on an organ; *see also* REGISTER.

REGISTRIREN (*Ger.*) See REGISTERING.

RÈGLE (*Fr.*) \
RÉGOLA (*It.*) Rule, or precept, for composition, or performance.

RÈGLE DE L'OCTAVE (*Fr.*) See RULE OF THE OCTAVE.

REGULÆ (*Lat.*) The registers, or stops, in an organ.

REGULAR MOTION. Similar motion.

REHEARSAL. A trial, or practice, previous to a public performance.

REIFTANZ (*Ger.*) A circle dance; a shepherds' dance; a rustic dance.

REIHEN (*Ger.*) Song, dance.

REIHEN-TANZ (*Ger.*) Circular dance.

REIN (*Ger.*) Pure, perfect: *kurz und rein*, distinct and clear.

REINE STIMME (*Ger.*) Clear voice.

REISELIED (*Ger.*) A travelling song; a pilgrim's song.

RELATIO NON HARMONICA (*Lat.*) See QUER-STAND.

RELATIVE KEYS. Keys which only differ by having in their scales one sharp or flat more or less, or which have the very same signatures.

RELAZIÓNE (*It.*) Relation.

RELIGIEUX (*Fr.*) \
RELIGIÖS (*Ger.*) \
RELIGIOSAMÉNTE (*It.*) Religiously, solemnly, in a devout manner. \
RELIGIÓSO (*It.*)

RE MAJEUR (*Fr.*) The key of D major.

RE MINEUR (*Fr.*) The key of D minor.

REMINISCENZ (*Ger.*) Reminiscence: see PLAGIAT.

REMPLISSAGE (*Fr.*) Filling up; the middle parts.
RENTRÉE (*Fr.*) Re-entry of the subject, or theme.
RENVERSÉ (*Fr.*) Inverted.
RENVERSEMENT (*Fr.*) An inversion.
RENVERSER (*Fr.*) To invert.
RENVOI (*Fr.*) A repeat; the mark of repetition called a sign, 𝄋.
REOL (*Dan.*) A Danish peasant dance, very similar to the reel.
REPERCUSSIO (*Lat.*) The answer, in a fugue.
REPETATUR (*Lat.*) Let it be repeated.
RÉPÉTER (*Fr.*) To repeat.
REPETIMÉNTE (*It.*) Repetition.
RÉPÉTITEUR (*Fr.*) Private musical teacher.
RÉPÉTITION (*Fr.*) *See* **REPETIZIÓNE**.
REPETITOR (*Ger.*) } The director of a rehearsal.
REPETITÓRE (*It.*)
REPETIZIÓNE (*It.*) Rehearsal; repetition: *sénza repetiziónè*, without repeating.
RÉPLICA (*It.*) Reply, repetition: *see also* **REPERCUSSIO**.
REPLICÁTO (*It.*) Repeated.
REPLIQUE (*Fr.*) A repetition at another pitch.
RÉPONSE (*Fr.*) The answer, in a fugue.
REPOS (*Fr.*) A pause.
REPRISE (*Fr.*) The burden of a song; a repetition, or return, to some previous part: in old music, when a strain was repeated, it was called a *reprise*.
REPRISE D'UN OPÉRA (*Fr.*) The reproduction, or revival, of an opera.
REQUIEM (*Lat.*) A Mass, or musical service for the dead.
REQUINTO (*Sp.*) The small E-flat clarinet.
RÉSOLUMENT (*Fr.*) Resolutely.
RESOLUTIO (*Lat.*) } Resolving a discord into a concord; the discord being followed by such a concord as is according to rule.
RESOLUTION (*Eng.*)
RESOLÚTO (*It.*) Resolutely, boldly.
RESOLUZIÓNE (*It.*) Resolution, decision, firmness: also, the progression from a discord to a concord, in harmony.
RESONANCE. Sound, reverberation, echo.
RESONANZ-BODEN (*Ger.*) The sounding-board, of a pianoforte, &c.
RESONNER (*Fr.*) To resound, echo.

RESPIRATION (*Eng.*)
RESPIRAZIÓNE (*It.*) } Taking breath, in singing.
RESPÍRO (*It.*)
RESPÍRO (*It.*) A semiquaver rest.
RESPONSIÓNE (*It.*) See RESPÓNSO.
RESPONSÍVO (*It.*) Responsive.
RESPÓNSO
RESPONSORIEN } (*It.*) Response, or answer, of the choir: the answer, in a fugue.
RESPONSORIUM
RESPONSUM } (*Lat.*) See RESPONSIÓNE.
RESSERREMENT (*Fr.*) See STRÉTTO.
RESSORT (*Fr.*) The bass bar of a violin, &c.
RESTRICTIO (*Lat.*) The *Strétto*, in a fugue.
RESTEZ (*Fr.*) *Stay there*: to maintain a position on a string, in violin playing.
RESTS. The marks which indicate silence.
RESURREXIT (*Lat.*) Part of the *Credo* in a Mass.
RETARDATION. Slackening, or retarding, the time: also, a suspension, in harmony, producing some note of a previous chord, into succeeding ones.
RETENTIR (*Fr.*) To resound.
RETENU (*Fr.*) See RITENÚTO.
RETOUCHE (*Fr.*) To embellish a melody.
RETRAITE (*Fr.*) Retreat; tattoo, in military music.
RETRO (*Lat.*) Backwards, the melody reversed, note for note.
RETROGRADE. Going backwards.
RETROGRADE IMITATION. Where the answer, or imitating part, takes the subject backwards.
RETROGRÁDO (*It.*)
RETROGRADUS (*Lat.*) } Retrograde, going backwards.
RÉTTO (*It.*) Right, straight, direct.
RETUSA (*Lat.*) An old term for *stopped* organ pipes.
RÉVEILLE (*Fr.*) Awaking, the wake up, alarm, a military morning signal: also, horn music played early in the morning, to wake the hunters.
REVENEZ (*Fr.*) Return.
REVERBERIEREN (*Ger.*) To reverberate.
REVERIE. A quite contemplative piece.
REVERSE MOTION. Imitation by contrary motion, in which the ascending intervals are changed into descending intervals, and *visa versa*.

REVUE (*Fr.*) A musical medley with action and scenery, see, POTPOURI.
REZITATIV (*Ger.*) See RECITATIVE.
RHAPSODIE (*Ger.*) | See RAPSODIE.
RHAPSODY (*Eng.*) |
RHAY. An old Anglo-Saxon name for the dance called 'the Hay': see REEL.
RHYTHM. The division of musical ideas, or sentences, into regular metrical portions: musical accent and cadence, as applied to melody.
RHYTHMIQUE (*Fr.*) | Rhythmical.
RHYTHMISCH (*Ger.*) |
RHYTHMOPŒIA (*Gr.*) The regulation of quantity, in metrical verse.
RHYTHMUS (*Gr. &. Lat.*) | See RHYTHM.
RHYTHMUS (*Ger.*) |
RIBÁTTERE (*It.*) To reverberate.
RIBATTITÚRA | (*It.*) A beat, a passing note.
RIBATTÚTA |
RIBÉBA (*It.*) A Jew's harp.
RIBÉCA (*It.*) See REBEC.
RIBECCHÍNO (*It.*) A small *Rebec*.
RIBIBLE. An old instrument supposed to be of the ghittern, or fiddle species: see REBEC.
RICERCÁRE (*It.*) | *Sought after*: this term is applied to every kind
RICERCÁRI (*It. pl.*) | of composition wherein researches of
RICERCÁTA (*It.*) | musical design are employed. It is suitable
RICERCÁTO (*It.*) | to certain fugues, enriched by all the
artifices of counterpoint; but more especially to compositions of the nature of Madrigals, which, in addition to the artifices of design, possess also taste and expression. The term was formerly applied to *solféggi*, and also to instrumental exercises, when of considerable difficulty.
RICHIAMÁRE (*It.*) To sing with a shrill tone of voice: to warble, or whistle, in imitation of a bird.
RICHIÁMO (*It.*) A bird call.
RICHTIG (*Ger.*) Right, accurate, exact.
RICORDÁNZA (*It.*) Remembrance, recollection.
RIDDÓNE (*It.*) A *roundelay*.
RIDÉNDO | (*It.*) Laughing.
RIDÉNTE |
RIDEVOLMÉNTE (*It.*) Laughingly, pleasantly.
RIDICOLOSAMÉNTE (*It.*) Ridiculously.

Ridótto — Ringeltanz

RIDÓTTO (*It.*) *Reduced*: *arranged*, or *adapted*, from a full score: also, an entertainment consisting of singing and dancing, a species of opera.

RIDUZIÓNE (*It.*) A *reduction*; an arrangement.

RIESEN-HARFE (*Ger.*) Æolian harp.

RIESEN-STIMME (*Ger.*) Stentorian voice.

RIFACIMÉNTO (*It.*) Reconstruction of a work, in order to improve it.

RIFIORIMÉNTI (*It. pl.*) Ornaments, embellishments.

RÍGA (*It.*) A line of the staff.

RIGABÉLLO (*It.*) | A *regal*.
RIGABELLUM (*Lat.*) |

RIGADOON. A lively old French or Provençal dance, in triple time.

RIGÁTA (*It.*) The staff.

RIGAUDON (*Fr.*) See **ROGADOON**.

RIGOL. A *regal*.

RIGÓRE (*It.*) Rigour, strictness: *al rigóre di témpo*, with strictness of time.

RIGORÓSO (*It.*) Rigorous, exact, strict.

RIKK. A small Egyptian tambourine.

RILASCIÁNDO (*It.*) Relaxing the time, giving was a little.

RILASCIÁNTE (*It.*) Slower.

RILASSÁNDO (*It.*) Relaxing the time, giving was a little.

RILASSÁTO (*It.*) Slower.

RILEVÁTO (*It.*) Raised, elevated; noble.

RILCH. | A Russian lute.
RILKA. |

RÍMA (*It.*) Rhyme, verse, poem, song.

RIMEMBRÁNZA (*It.*) Memory, remembrance, souvenir.

RIMETTÉNDO
RIMETTÉNDOSI (*It.*) *Rallentándo*; also, returning, restoring.

RINFORZÁNDO
RINFORZÁRE
RINFORZÁTO
RINFÓRZO (*It.*) Strengthened, reinforced; a repeated reinforcement of tone or expression; indicating that *several* notes are to be played with energy and emphasis.

RING (*Ger.*) A ring; a circle.

RINGELGEDICHT (*Ger.*) A *roundelay*.

RINGELPAUKE (*Ger.*) A *Sistrum*.

RINGELREIM (*Ger.*) A refrain, chorus.

RINGELSTÜCK (*Ger.*) A round, a *rondo*.

RINGELTANZ (*Ger.*) A circle dance, round dance.

Ringen — Risvegliáto

RINGEN (*Ger.*) To ring, to sound.
RIPERCUSSIÓNE (*It.*) Repercussion.
RIPETÉRE (*It.*) To repeat; to rehearse.
RIPETITÚRA
RIPETIZIÓNE } (*It.*) Repetition; a refrain.
RIPIENIST. A player of the *ripiéno*, or *tútti* parts, in an orchestra.
RIPIÉNI (*It. pl.*)
RIPIÉNO (*It.*) } The *tútti*, or full parts which fill up and augment the effect of the full chorus of voices and instruments. In a large orchestra, all the violins, violas, and basses, except the principals, are sometimes called *ripiéni*.
RIPIÉNO DI CÍNQUE (*It.*) Mixture stop of five ranks, in Italian organs.
RIPIÉNO DI DUE (*It.*) Mixture stop of two ranks.
RIPIÉNO DI QUÁTTRO (*It.*) Mixture stop of four ranks.
RIPIÉNO DI TRE (*It.*) Mixture stop of three ranks.
RIPIENSTIMMEN (*Ger.*) *Ripiéno* parts.
RIPIEUR DI CÍNQUE (*It.*) See RIPIÉNO DI CÍNQUE.
RIPÍGLIO (*It.*) Repetition; reprise.
RIPOSATAMÉNTE (*It.*) With repose.
RIPÓSO (*It.*) Repose.
RIPÓSTA (*It.*) See RISPÓSTA.
RIPRÉNDERE (*It.*) To resume, to recommence.
RIPRÉSA
RIPRÉSE } (*It.*) Repetition, reiteration.
RISCALDÁNDO (*It.*) Becoming warmer; with more animation.
RISENTITAMÉNTE
RISENTÍTO } (*It.*) Marked, distinct, angrily, firmly.
RISOLUTAMÉNTE (*It.*) Resolutely, boldly, vigorously.
RISOLUTÉZZA (*It.*) Resolution, boldness, vigour.
RISOLUTÍSSIMO (*It.*) Very resolutely, as boldly as possible.
RISOLÚTO (*It.*) Resolved, resolute, bold.
RISOLUZIÓNE (*It.*) Resolution, determination: also, the resolution of a discord.
RISONÁNTE (*It.*) Resounding, ringing, sounding.
RISONÁNZA (*It.*) A sound, resonance.
RISONÁRE (*It.*) To resound, to ring, or echo.
RISPÓSTA (*It.*) The answer, in a fugue.
RISTRÉTTO (*It.*) The *Strétto*, the restriction, or contraction, of the subject, in a fugue.
RISVEGLIÁRE (*It.*) To wake up, to revive, to reanimate.
RISVEGLIÁTO (*It.*) Awaked, reanimated.

Ritardándo — Rôle

RITARDÁNDO (*It.*) Retarding, delaying the time, gradually.
RITARDÁNDO AL FÍNE (*It.*) Retarding the time, until the end.
RITARDÁRE (*It.*) To retard, slacken the pace.
RITARDÁTO (*It.*) Retarding, gradually retarding the time.
RITARDAZIÓNE (*It.*) Retardation; dragging.
RITÁRDO (*It.*) Retardation, gradual delay: in harmony, prolonging some note of a previous chord, into the succeeding one.
RITENÉNDO / **RITENÉNTE** (*It.*) Detaining, retaining: see **RITENÚTO**.
RITENÉNTO / **RITENÚTO** (*It.*) Detain, slower, kept back: the effect differs from *Ritandándo*, by being done at once, while the other is effected by degrees.
RITORNÉL (*It.*) / **RITORNÉLLO** (*It.*) / **RITOURNELLE** (*Fr.*) The burden of a song: also, a short symphony or introduction to an air: also, the symphonies between the repetitions of an air: also, the symphony which follows an air: it is also applied to *tútti* parts, introductory to, and between, or after, the solo passages in a concerto.
RITTERLICH (*Ger.*) Knightly, chivalrous.
RIVÉRSO / **RIVÉSCIO** (*It.*) See **Rovéscio**.
RIVOLGIMÉNTO (*It.*) Inversion of the parts, in double counterpoint.
ROBÚSTO (*It.*) Strong, powerful, robust.
RÓCHE (*It.*) Hoarse, rough-sounding, jarring.
ROCCOCO. Old-fashioned, odd.
RÓCO (*It.*) See **RÓCHE**.
ROCOCO. Old-fashioned, odd.
ROER-QUINT / **ROHR-QUINT** (*Ger.*) Reed-fifth: an organ stop, sounding the fifth above the diapasons: see **ROHR-FLÖTE**.
ROH (*Ger.*) Rough, coarse, rude.
ROHR (*Ger.*) Reed, pipe.
RÖHRE (*Ger. pl.*) Reeds.
ROHR-BLATT (*Ger.*) The reed of a clarinet, oboe, &c.
ROHR-FLÖTE (*Ger.*) *Reed-flute*, a stopped diapason, in an organ; the pipes are of wood, or metal, with reeds, tubes or chimneys at the top.
ROHR-NASAT (*Ger.*) See **REED-NASAT**.
ROHR-PFEIFE (*Ger.*) Reed-pipe.
ROHR-WERK (*Ger.*) Reed-work; the reed stops, in an organ.
ROLÁTA (*It.*) A *roulade*.
RÔLE (*Fr.*) A principal part in an opera or drama.

ROLLÁNDO (*It.*) Rolling on the drum, and tambourine.

ROLLE (*Ger.*) A run; a rapid succession of sequential figures or passages; *also see* RÔLE.

ROLLER. The *beard* of an organ pipe; also, part of the mechanism of an organ.

RÓLLO (*It.*) The roll on the drum, and tambourine.

ROMANCE (*Fr.*) A short lyric tale, set to music, not exactly like a song, and not necessarily with the same melody to every verse: a simple, graceful, and elegant melody, suitable for romantic poetry.

ROMANCE SANS PAROLES (*Fr.*) A story or song without words.

ROMANÉSCA (*It.*)
ROMANESQUE (*Fr.*) } A favourite Roman, or Italian, dance, of the sixteenth century, resembling the Galliard.

ROMANTIQUE (*Fr.*)
ROMANTISCH (*Ger.*) } Romantic, imaginative, fairy-like.

ROMÁNZA (*It.*)
ROMANZE (*Ger.*) } *See* ROMANCE.

ROMANZÉRO (*It.*) A suite of romantic pieces.

ROMANZESCO (*It.*) Romantic, imaginative, fairy-like.

ROMAUNT (*Old Eng.*) *See* ROMANCE.

ROMBÁNDO (*It.*) Humming, droning, murmuring, buzzing.

ROMERA. A Turkish dance.

RÖMISCH (*Ger.*) Roman.

RÖMISCHER GESANG (*Ger.*) Gregorian plain chant.

RÓNDA (*It.*) A round.

RONDE (*Fr.*) A semibreve.

RONDEAU (*Fr.*) A composition including several strains, in a cheerful and lively style; the first strain, which must terminate with a cadence on the tonic, is repeated several times in the course of the movement.

RONDILÉTTA
RONDINÉLLO
RONDINÉTTO
RONDÍNO } (*It.*) A short and easy rondo.

RONDEÑA (*Sp.*) *See* FANDANGO.

RÓNDO (*It.*) *See* RONDEAU.

RONDOLÉTTO (*It.*) A short and easy rondo.

RONZAMÉNTE (*It.*) Humming; crooning.

ROOT. The fundamental note of any chord.

ROSALIA (*Lat.*) The repetition of a passage several times over, each time on a different degree of the stave.

Rosin — Rückgang

ROSIN. The resin left after distillation of turpentine, used on the bows of violins, &c.

ROSSIGNOL (*Fr.*) The nightingale.

ROSTRAL (*Ger.*) A music pen.

RÓTA (*It.*) A wheel: applied to a canon, or a round.

ROTE. The old name of the hurdy-gurdy.

ROTÓNDO (*It.*) Round, full.

ROTRUENGES. Songs, resembling catches, of the ancient minstrels, or troubadours.

RÓTTE (*It.*) Broken, interrupted.

RÓTTO (*It.*) Broken, interrupted.

ROTULÆ (*Lat.*) Christmas roundelays.

ROTÚNDO (*It.*) Round.

ROULADE (*Fr.*) A florid vocal passage; a division, or rapid series of notes, using only one syllable.

ROULADES AUS FRAIS DE L'AUTEUR (*Fr.*) Roulades in bad taste, such as injure the melody of the composer.

ROULEMENT (*Fr.*) A roll, or shake, upon the drum, or tambourine: prolonged reiterations of one note, upon the guitar, &c.

ROUND. A species of canon in the unison or octave: also, a vocal composition in three or more parts, all written in the same clef, the performers singing each part in succession, as indicated by the figures at the beginning and the end of each line, the second voice beginning the first line, when the first voice begins the second, and so on. They are called *rounds*, because the performers follow one another in a circulatory motion.

ROUNDEL | Formerly, an ancient air appropriated to dancing:
ROUNDELAY | also, a species of antique rustic song or ballad
ROUNDLEY | common in the fourteenth century, in various parts
of which a return was made to the first verse or couplet, like the rondo: *see* **VIRELAY**.

ROVÉRSCIO | *See* **ROVÉSCIO**.
ROVÉRSIO |

ROVESCIAMÉNTO | (*It.*) Reverse motion, the subject backwards, in
ROVÉSCIO | double counterpoint.

RUANA. An Hindoo violin.

RUBÁTO (*It.*) *Robbed, stolen*; taking a portion of the duration from one note, an giving it to another: *see* **TÉMPO RUBÁTO**.

RUBÈBE (*Fr.*) A *rebec*.

RÜCK (*Ger.*) Back.

RÜCKBEWEGUNG (*Ger.*) A retrograde movement.

RÜCKGANG (*Ger.*) Return to repetition a previous theme.

RÜCKPOSITIV (*Ger.*) In German organs, that part which is placed behind the player, equivalent to the *choir* in English organs.

RÜCKUNG (*Ger.*) Syncopation.

RÜCKWEISER (*Ger.*) See SÉGNO.

RUDEMENT (*Fr.*) Roughly.

RUF (*Ger.*) A call, cry, summons; to voice; to sound a trumpet call.

RUH \
RUHE } (*Ger.*) Rest, repose; calm.

RUHEPUNCT \
RUHEPUNKT } (*Ger.*) Pause, point of rest, or repose: a cadence. \
RUHEZEIHEN

RUHIG (*Ger.*) Quiet, calm, gentle.

RUHIG BEWEGT (*Ger.*) Gently animated.

RÜHRUNG (*Ger.*) Emotion, feeling.

RÜHRTROMMEL (*Ger.*) The tenor drum.

RULE OF THE OCTAVE. The art of accompanying the scale, either ascending or descending, when taken in the bass, with the proper chords or harmony.

RULLÁNDO \
RULLÁNTE } (*It.*) Rolling on the drum, or tambourine.

RUND (*Ger.*) Round; smooth, flowing.

RUÓLO (*It.*) A roll; also, a species of Italian waltz.

RUSSE (*Fr.*) Russian: *à la Russe*, in the Russian style.

RUSSIAN BASSOON. A deep-tones instrument of the serpent species, sometimes used in military bands.

RUSSPFIEFE (*Ger.*) See RAUSCHQUINTE.

RUSTICÁNO \
RÚSTICO } (*It.*) Rural, rustic.

RUTSCHER (*Ger.*) A slider; also, the dance called a *Galopade*.

RÚVIDO (*It.*) Rough, coarse.

RYMOUR (*Old Eng.*) A rural poet.

RYTHME (*Fr.*) Rhythm.

RYTHMÉ (*Fr.*) Rhythmical.

RYTHMUS (*Ger.*) See RHYTHMUS.

S

SABBEKA
SABECA } (*Heb.*) A species of Hebrew harp.

SABOT (*Fr.*) An inferior violin.

SACCADE (*Fr.*) A firm pressure of the violin bow against the strings, enabling the player to produce two, three, or four notes at one stroke.

SACKBUT. An old bass wind-instrument, resembling a trombone.

SACK-GEIGE (*Ger.*) A pocket-fiddle, a *kit*.

SACK-PFEIFE (*Ger.*) A bagpipe: see CORNAMÚSA.

SACK-PFEIFER (*Ger.*) Player on the bagpipe.

SACK-PIPE. A bagpipe: see CORNAMÚSA.

SACQUE-BOUTE (*Fr.*) A sackbut.

SAENGERFEST (*Ger.*) A musical and social festival.

SAGA. An ancient Scandinavian tale, legend, or poem.

SAGBUT
SAGBUTT } See SACKBUT.

SÁGGIO (*It.*) An essay, a trial.

SAISON (*Fr.*) The musical season.

SAITE (*Ger.*) A string.

SAITEN-BÄNDIGER (*Ger.*) A musician.

SAITEN-BEZUG (*Ger.*) Set of strings.

SAITEN-FESSEL (*Ger.*) Tail-piece, of the violin, &c.

SAITEN-DRAHT (*Ger.*) Wire string.

SAITEN-HALTER (*Ger.*) Tail-piece, of the violin, &c.

SAITEN-INSTRUMENT (*Ger.*) String-instrument.

SAITEN-KLANG (*Ger.*) The sound made by a string.

SAITEN-ORGEL (*Ger.*) A string organ, invented by Gümbel.

SAITEN-SPIEL (*Ger.*) String-instrument, music of a string-instrument.

SAITEN-SPIELER (*Ger.*) Performer on a string-instrument.

SAITEN-SPIELERINN (*Ger.*) Female performer on a string-instrument.

SAITEN-TON (*Ger.*) The sound made by a string.

SALAMANIE. An Oriental flute.

SALAMINE. An echo *dulciana*, or *salicional*.

Salcional — Sanftmuth

SALCIONAL
SALICIONAL An 4, 8, or 16 feet organ stop, of small scale, and reedy tone.
SALICET

SALLE DE CONCERT (*Fr.*) A concert room.

SALLE DE MUSIQUE (*Fr.*) A music room.

SALM (*Ger.*)
SÁLMO (*It.*) } A psalm.

SALMI (*Fr.*) *See* QUODLIBET.

SALPINX. The ancient Greek trumpet.

SALTÁNDO (*It.*) Leaping, proceeding by skips, or jumps.

SALTÁRE (*It.*) To leap, dance, skip.

SALTARÉLLA (*It.*)
SALTARELLE (*Fr.*) } (*It.*) A Roman, or Italian dance, very quick, and in $\frac{2}{4}$ time.
SALTARÉLLO (*It.*)

SALTATÓRI (*It.*) Jumpers, or dances of very great agility.

SALTER (*Ger.*) *See* PSALTER.

SALTERELLA (*It.*) *See* SALTARÉLLA.

SALTERÉTTO (*It.*) A musical figure in $\frac{6}{8}$ time, the first and fourth quavers being dotted; very usual in movements *álla Siciliána*.

SALTERÍO
SALTÉRO } (*It.*) Psalter, book of psalms.

SALTÉRO (*It.*) Psaltery, instrument with ten strings.

SÁLTO (*It.*) A leap, or skip, from one note to a distant one: also, a dance.

SALVÁRE (*It.*) *To save*; to resolve.

SALVE REGINA (*Lat.*) *Hail Queen!* A hymn to the Virgin Mary.

SAMBÚCA
SAMBÚKA } (*It.*) An old instrument, supposed to be the same as the sackbut; made from the boughs of the elder-tree.

SAMBUCISTRIA (*Lat.*) A player on the *Sambúca*.

SAMMLUNG (*Ger.*) A collection, of airs, &c.

SÄMMTLICH (*Ger.*) All, all together; complete.

SAMPÓGNA
SAMPÓNIA } (*It.*) A species of pipe: *see* ZAMPÓGNA.

SANCHO. A negro guitar.

SANCTUS (*Lat.*) *Holy!* A part of the Mass.

SANFT (*Ger.*) Soft, mild, smooth: *mit sanften Stimmen*, with soft stops.

SANFT-FLÖTE (*Ger.*) Soft-toned flute.

SANFTHEIT (*Ger.*) Softness, smoothness, gentleness.

SÄNFTIG (*Ger.*) Soft, gentle.

SANFTMUTH (*Ger.*) Softness, gentleness.

Sanftmüthig — Sax-horns

SANFTMÜTHIG (*Ger.*) Softly, mildly, gently.
SANFTMÜTHIGKEIT (*Ger.*) Softness, mildness, gentleness.
SANG (*Ger.*) Song.
SANGBAR (*Ger.*) Singable; made singable.
SANGDICHTER (*Ger.*) A lyric poet.
SÄNGER (*Ger.*) A singer.
SÄNGERINN (*Ger.*) A female singer, a songstress.
SANGLOT (*Fr.*) An old form of *portaménto*.
SANG-MEISTER (*Ger.*) Singing-master.
SANGVOGEL (*Ger.*) A song-bird.
SANGWEISE (*Ger.*) Melody.
SANS (*Fr.*) Without.
SANS FRAPPÉ (*Fr.*) *Without striking*; play the notes without striking them hard, or forcibly.
SANS PÉDALES (*Fr.*) Without the pedals.
SAQUEBUTE (*Fr.*) The sackbut.
SARABAND (*Eng.*)
SARABÁNDA (*It.*)
SARABANDE (*Fr. & Ger.*) An old Spanish dance, of great antiquity, and of a serious and majestic kind: originally introduced by the Moors, and danced with castanets; it is in slow $\frac{3}{4}$ or $\frac{3}{2}$ time, and characterised by the second crotchet or minim, of the bar, being lengthened.
SARDÓNICO (*It.*) Sardonic, mocking.
SARTARÉLLA
SARTARÉLLO (*It.*) A Neapolitan dance: see **SALTARÉLLA**.
S'ATTÁCCA (*It.*) See **ATTÁCCA**.
SATTEL (*Ger.*) The nut of the finger-board of the violin, &c.
SATZ (*Ger.*) Musical passage, composition, theme, subject.
SÄUSELN (*Ger.*) To rustle, murmur, sigh, hum.
SAUT (*Fr.*) See **SÁLTO**.
SAUTEREAU (*Fr.*) The jack of the spinet.
SAUTEREI (*Old Eng.*) A dulcimer, or psaltery.
SAUTILLÉ (*Fr.*) With a *springing* bow, in violin playing.
SAUVEMENT (*Fr.*) The resolution of a dissonance.
SAUVER (*Fr.*) To resolve a dissonance.
SAVOŸARDE (*Fr.*) See **À LA SAVOŸARDE**.
SAX-HORNS. Brass instruments introduced by M. Sax, with a wide mouth-piece, and 3, 4, or 5 cylinders: the tone is round, pure, and full; and they comprise, the very high small sax-horn, the soprano, the alto, the tenor, baritone, bass, and double-bass.

SAXOPHONES. A new family of brass wind-instruments invented by M. Sax: their tones are soft and penetrating in the higher part, expressive in the middle, and full and rich in the lower part of their compass. The Saxophones are 6 in number, the high, the soprano, the alto, the tenor, the baritone, and the bass: they are played with a single reed, and a clarinet mouth-piece.

SAXOTROMBAS. Brass instruments introduced by M. Sax, with wide mouth-pieces, and 3, 4, or 5 cylinders: the tone is of a shrill character, partaking of the quality both of the trumpet and the bugle, and their number is the same as that of the sax-horns.

SAX-TUBAS. Brass instruments introduced by M. Sax, with wide mouth-pieces, and 3 cylinders: the tone is very sonorous.

SAYNETE (*Sp.*) Farces with music.

SBÁLZE (*It.*) Skip, or leap, in melody.

SBÁRRA (*It.*) A bar line.

SBÁRRA DÓPPIA (*It.*) A double bar.

SCAGNÉLLO (*It.*) The bridge, of the violin, &c.

SCÁLA (*It.*) A scale, or gamut.

SCALD. The ancient Scandinavian bards.

SCALEN-SCHULE (*Ger.*) School for scale-playing; exercises on the scales.

SCÁLE RÓTTE (*It. pl.*) Broken scales; imperfect, or unequal, scales.

SCANNÉLLO / **SCANNÉTTO** (*It.*) *See* SCAGNÉLLO.

SCARABILLÁRE UN VIOLÍNO (*It.*) To scrape a fiddle.

SCÉLTA (*It.*) Choice, selection.

SCEMÁNDO (*It.*) Diminishing, decreasing in force.

SCÉNA (*It.*) / **SCENE** (*Eng.*) Part of an act, portion of an opera: an act generally comprises several scenes.

SCENÁRII (*It.*) Side scenes.

SCENÁRIO (*It.*) The plot of a work; also, a play-bill.

SCHABLONE (*Ger.*) A pattern, or stencil.

SCHABLONENMUSIK (*Ger.*) Music without inspiration.

SCHÄFER (*Ger.*) A shepherd, or swain.

SCHÄFER-GEDICHT (*Ger.*) Idyl, eclogue, pastoral.

SCHÄFER-LIED (*Ger.*) Pastoral song, shepherd-song.

SCHÄFER-MÄSSIG (*Ger.*) A pastoral.

SCHÄFER-PFEIFE (*Ger.*) Shepherd's pipe.

SCHÄFFLERTANZ (*Ger.*) An ancient festival dance of the Coopers' Guild of Munich.

SCHAFORGEL (*Ger.*) A species of bag-pipe.

Schalkhaft — Scherzlich

SCHALKHAFT (*Ger.*) Roughish, sportive, playful, waggish.
SCHALL (*Ger.*) Sound.
SCHALL-BECHER (*Ger.*) The bell of an instrument.
SCHALL-BECKEN (*Ger.*) Cymbal.
SCHALL-BODEN (*Ger.*) A sound-board.
SCHALL-BRET (*Ger.*) Sound-board, or wind-chest of an organ.
SCHÄLLE (*Ger. pl.*) Sounds.
SCHALLEN (*Ger.*) To sound, to echo.
SCHALL-GLAS (*Ger.*) A musical glass.
SCHALL-HORN (*Ger.*) Horn, cornet, trumpet.
SCHALL-LEHRE (*Ger.*) Acoustics.
SCHALL-LOCH (*Ger.*) Sound-hole.
SCHALL-ROHR (*Ger.*) Speaking-trumpet.
SCHALL-STAB (*Ger.*) Triangle.
SCHALMAY / **SCHALMEIE** (*Ger.*) A shawm: also, an 8 feet reed organ stop; the tone resembles that of the cremona, or clarinet: *see also* **CHALUMEAU**.
SCHANZUNE (*Ger.*) A *chanson*.
SCHARF (*Ger.*) Sharp, acute; a shrill mixture stop, of several ranks of pipes.
SCHATTENHAFT (*Ger.*) Shadowy.
SCHAURIG (*Ger.*) Weird, ghastly, horrible.
SCHAUSPIEL (*Ger.*) Drama, dramatic piece.
SCHAUSPIELER (*Ger.*) Actor, player.
SCHAUSPIELERINN (*Ger.*) Actress.
SCHAUSPIELHAUS (*Ger.*) A theatre.
SCHEITHOLT (*Ger.*) A *tromba mariana*.
SCHELLEN (*Ger.*) Bells, jingles; sleigh-bells.
SCHELMISCH (*Ger.*) Roguish, knavish.
SCHERZ (*Ger.*) Jest, joke, fun, raillery; *also, see* **SCHÉRZO**.
SCHERZANDÍSSIMO (*It.*) Exceedingly playful, and lively.
SCHERZÁNDO (*It.*) / **SCHERZÁNTE** (*It.*) / **SCHERZÉVOLE** (*It.*) Playful, lively, sportive, merry.
SCHERZEVOLMÉNTE (*It.*) Playfully, merrily, lively.
SCHERZGEDICHT (*Ger.*) A comic poem.
SCHERZHAFTIGKEIT (*Ger.*) Playfulness, sportiveness.
SCHERZHAFT (*Ger.*) Playful, lively, sportive, merry.
SCHERZÍNO (*It.*) A short *schérzo*.
SCHERZLICH (*Ger.*) Merrily, playfully, sportively.

SCHÉRZO (*It.*) Play, sport, a jest: a piece of a lively, sportive character, and marked, animated rhythm: also, one of the movements in a modern symphony.

SCHERZOSAMÉNTE (*It.*) Merrily, playfully, sportively.

SCHERZÓSO (*It.*) Merry, playful, jocose.

SCHIEBER (*Ger.*) The slide of the violin bow.

SCHIETTAMÉNTE (*It.*) Simply, unadorned.

SCHIETTÉZZA (*It.*) Simplicity, plainness.

SCHIÉTTO (*It.*) Simple, plain, neat.

SCHISMA (*Ger.*) A very minute difference between the sound of intervals.

SCHLACHT (*Ger.*) Battle, fight.

SCHLACHT-HYMNE (*Ger.*) Battle hymn.

SCHLACHT-GESANG (*Ger.*) War song.

SCHLACHT-RUF (*Ger.*) War-cry; war signal.

SCHLAG (*Ger.*) Stroke, blow: a beat, as regards time.

SCHLÄGEL (*Ger.*) Hammer, mallet, drumstick.

SCHLAGEN (*Ger.*) To strike, to beat: to warble, or trill: *die Pauken schlagen*, to beat the kettle-drums: *den Takt schlagen*, to beat the time.

SCHLAGER (*Ger.*) A successful piece.

SCHLAGFEDER (*Ger.*) A plectrum.

SCHLAGZITHER (*Ger.*) The ordinary plectrum zither.

SCHLECHT (*Ger.*) Bad; weak.

SCHLEIFEN (*Ger.*) To slide, to glide.

SCHLEIFER (*Ger.*) Slurred note, gliding note.

SCHLEIFE-UNGSZEICHEN
SCHLEIFE-ZEICHEN (*Ger.*) A slur, a mark of the *legáto* style.

SCHLEPPEND (*Ger.*) Dragging, drawing.

SCHLICHT (*Ger.*) Smooth, simple, even.

SCHLUMMERLIED (*Ger.*) A slumber song.

SCHLUSS (*Ger.*) The end, conclusion.

SCHLÜSSEL (*Ger.*) A clef.

SCHLÜSSELFIEDEL (*Ger.*) A nail fiddle.

SCHLUSS-FALL (*Ger.*) A cadence.

SCHLUSS-KADENZ (*Ger.*) A final cadence.

SCHLUSS-REIM (*Ger.*) The *burden*, or refrain, of a song.

SCHLUSS-STRICHE (*Ger.*) A double bar.

SCHLUSS-STÜCK (*Ger.*) Concluding pieces, finale.

SCHLUSS-ZEICHEN (*Ger.*) A double bar; also a *pause*.

SCHMACHTEND (*Ger.*) Languishing.

Schmeichelnd — Schucplattltanz

SCHMEICHELND (*Ger.*) Caressing, flattering, coaxing.
SCHMELZEND (*Ger.*) Diminishing, dying away.
SCHMERZ (*Ger.*) Grief, sorrow.
SCHMERZHAFT (*Ger.*) Dolorous, sorrowful.
SCHMERZHAFTIGKEIT
SCHMERZLICH } (*Ger.*) In a dolorous style.
SCHMERZVOLL (*Ger.*) Full of grief; dolefully.
SCHMETTERND (*Ger.*) Ringing, clanging, brassy, shrill.
SCHNABEL (*Ger.*) The mouth-piece of a clarinet, flageolet, or saxophone.
SCHNARR (*Ger.*) Rattle; harsh, jarring sound.
SCHNARREN (*Ger.*) To rattle; also, to sing *falsétto*.
SCHNARR-LAUT (*Get.*) A harsh, rattling sound.
SCHNARR-PFEIFEN
SCHNARR-WERK } (*Ger.*) Reed pipes; reed work, or stops, in an organ.
SCHNARR-TROMMEL (*Ger.*) A side drum.
SCHNEIDIG (*Ger.*) Piercing, cutting, energetic.
SCHNELL (*Ger.*) Quickly, rapidly: *etwas bewegter schnell*, a little quicker.
SCHNELLE (*Ger.*) Quickness, swiftness, rapidity.
SCHNELLER (*Ger.*) Quicker, faster; also, an inverted *mordent*.
SCHNELLIGKEIT (*Ger.*) *See* **SCHNELLE**.
SCHNELL-WALTZER (*Ger.*) Quick waltzes.
SCHNELL WIE ZUERST (*Ger.*) As quick as at the beginning; *témpo prímo*.
SCHNELZER (*Ger.*) An inverted *mordent*.
SCHNURREN (*Ger.*) To hum, buzz, rattle.
SCHÖN (*Ger.*) Beautiful, handsome; lofty.
SCHOTTISCHE (*Ger.*) A modern dance, rather slow, in $\frac{2}{4}$ time.
SCHRÄG (*Ger.*) Oblique, slanting.
SCHREIBART (*Ger.*) Style, manner of composing, or writing.
SCHREIBER (*Ger.*) A music copyist.
SCHREIEND (*Ger.*) Acute, shrill, screaming.
SCHREIWERK (*Ger.*) *Shrill-work*; acute, or mixture stops.
SCHRITTMÄSSIG (*Ger.*) Slow; *andánte*.
SCHUB (*Ger.*) The slide of a violin bow.
SCHUCHTERN (*Ger.*) Modest, shy, retiring.
SCHUH (*Ger.*) A shoe.
SCHUCPLATTLTANZ (*Ger.*) A clog dance.

SCHULE (*Ger.*) A School, or method for learning any instrument: also, a peculiar style of composition; the manner, or method, of an eminent composer, performer, or teacher.

SCHÜLER (*Ger.*) A pupil.

SCHÜLERHAFT (*Ger.*) *Pupil-like*; clumsy; the opposite to scholarly.

SCHULGERECHT (*Ger.*) Regular, in due form; written correctly, in accordance with the rules and principles of musical science.

SCHULTER (*Ger.*) Shoulder.

SCHUSTERFLECK (*Ger.*) See ROSÁLIA.

SCHWACH (*Ger.*) *Piáno*, soft, weak, feeble.

SCHWÄCHEN (*Ger.*) To die away; *calándo*.

SCHWÄCHER (*Ger.*) Fainter, softer, more *piáno*.

SCHWÄCHER WERDEND (*Ger.*) Softer by degrees.

SCHWANKEND (*Ger.*) Faltering; wavering.

SCHWARM (*Ger.*) A swarm, flock, crowd.

SCHWEBUNG (*Ger.*) *Waving*; a lighter species of *tremulant*, for the more delicate stops, such as the vox humana, &c., to produce a very gentle oscillation in imitation of the wavering tone of a complaining human voice, in slow pathetic passages.

SCHWEGEL (*Ger.*) A wind instrument; also, an organ flue pipe.

SCHWEGELPFEIFE (*Ger.*) An organ stop with slightly tapering flue pipes, see also SPILLFLÖTE.

SCHWEIF (*Ger.*) A tail; a coda.

SCHWEIGE (*Ger.*) A rest.

SCHWEIGEN (*Ger.*) Silence; being silent.

SCHWEIGT (*Ger.*) See TACET.

SCHWEINSKOPF (*Ger.*) An old name for a grand-pianoforte.

SCHWEIZER (*Ger.*) Swiss.

SCHWEIZER-FLÖTE
SCHWEIZER-PFEIFE (*Ger.*) Swiss flute or pipe.

SCHWELLEN (*Ger.*) To increase in loudness; to swell.

SCHWELLER (*Ger.*) The *swell* of an organ.

SCHWER (*Ger.*) Heavily, ponderously.

SCHWERMÜTHIG (*Ger.*) In a pensive, melancholy style.

SCHWIEGEL (*Ger.*) An organ stop, of the flute species, and of metal, pointed at the top.

SCHWINDEND (*Ger.*) Dying away; *moréndo*.

SCHWINGEN (*Ger.*) To swing.

SCHWINGUNG (*Ger.*) Vibration of a string, &c.

SCHWUNGVOLL (*Ger.*) With swing, passion, and enthusiasm; sublime.

SCIÁLUMO (*It.*) See CHALUMEAU.

SCILLA (*Lat.*) Small bells, formerly used to hang upon the tail of the ermine, upon royal ermine robes; an heraldic term.

SCINTILLÁNTE (*It. & Fr.*) Sparkling, brilliant.

SCIÓLTA (*It.*) Free.

SCIOLTAMÉNTE (*It.*) With freedom, agility; easily; the notes being rather detached than *legáto*.

SCIOLTÉZZA (*It.*) Freedom, ease, lightness.

SCIÓLTO (*It.*) Free, light: *see* SCIOLTAMÉNTE.

SCIVOLÁNDO (*It.*) *See* GLISSÁNDO.

SCOLIA. Ancient Greek festive songs.

SCOLÁRDO (*It.*) Scholar, accomplished pupil.

SCORDÁTO (*It.*) Out of tune, false, untuned.

SCORDATÚRA (*It.*) Tubing a violin differently, for the more easily performing certain peculiar passages.

SCORE. The whole instrumental and vocal parts of a composition, written on separate staves, placed under each other.

SCORRÉNDO (*It.*) Gliding from one sound into another.

SCOTCH SCALE. *See* PENTATONIC SCALE.

SCOTCH SNAP. A peculiarity in Scotch tunes, and those written in imitation of the supposed Scotch character: it is the lengthening the tome of a second one, at the cost of the one before it, placing a semiquaver before a dotted quaver; it gives emphasis and spirit to dance tunes, and when well applied has a lively effect. It does not occur in the ancient tunes, and appears to have been introduced into Scotland by the gypsy fiddlers who migrated there from Hungary and Bohemia, and in whose music the snap was a peculiar feature.

SCOZZÉSE (*It.*) Scotch; in the Scotch style.

SCRÍVA (*It.*) *Written: si scríva*, as it is written, without any alteration or embellishment.

SCUCÍTO (*It.*) Disconnected.

SDEGNÁNTE (*It.*) Angry, passionate.

SDÉGNO (*It.*) Anger, wrath, passion.

SDEGNOSAMÉNTE (*It.*) Scornfully, disdainfully.

SDEGNÓSO (*It.*) Furious, passionate, fiery.

SDRUCCIOLÁNDO (*It.*) Sliding, slipping.

SDRUCCIOLÁRE (*It.*) To slip, to slide the hand, by turning the fingernails towards the keys of the pianoforte, and drawing the hand lightly, and rapidly, up or down.

SDRUCCIOLAMÉNTO | (*It.*) Sliding the fingers along the strings, or
SDRUCCIOLÁTO | keys, of an instrument.

SE (*It.*) If, in case, provided, as, so, &c.

SE BISÓGNA (*It.*) If necessary, if required.

SEC (*Fr.*) See SÉCCO.

SECCARÁRA (*It.*) A Neapolitan dance.

SÉCCO (*It.*) \
SÈCHE (*Fr.*) Dry, unornamented, coldly; the note, or chord, to be struck plainly, without ornament or *arpéggio*.

SÉCHERESSE (*It.*) Dryness; aridity.

SECHS (*Ger.*) Six.

SECHS-ACHTELTACT (*Ger.*) Time or measure of $\frac{6}{8}$.

SECHS-SAITIG (*Ger.*) Instrument with six strings.

SECHTE (*Ger.*) A sixth.

SECHS-THEILIG (*Ger.*) In six parts.

SECHS-ZEHN (*Ger.*) Sixteen.

SECHS-ZEHNFÜSSIG (*Ger.*) A 16 feet organ pipe.

SECHZEHNTHEIL-NOTE (*Ger.*) A semiquaver.

SECÓNDA (*It.*) Second, a second.

SECONDAIRE (*Fr.*) Secondary.

SECONDÁNDO (*It.*) Following, supporting.

SECÓNDA VÓLTA (*It.*) The second time.

SECOND-DESSUS (*Fr.*) The second treble.

SECONDE (*Fr.*) Second, a second.

SECONDE FOIS (*Fr.*) The second time.

SECÓNDO (*It.*) Second, a second.

SECÓNDO PARTÍTO (*It.*) The second part, or voice.

SECTIO CANONIS (*Lat.*) An aliquot division of a monochord, to produce the required harmonic.

SECUNDE (*Ger.*) Second, a second.

SECUNDIREN (*Ger.*) To play the second part.

SECUNDUM ARTEM (*Lat.*) According to art or rule.

SEDECIMA (*Lat.*) A German organ stop; when of 2 feet tone it is identical with the English fifteenth; and when of 1 feet, it sounds the twenty-second, or an octave above the fifteenth.

SEELE (*Ger.*) Soul, feeling; also, the sound-post of a violin.

SEELEN-AMT \
SEELEN-MESSE (*Ger.*) Requiem, or Mass for departed souls.

SEER. A bard or rhapsodist.

SÉGNO (*It.*) A *sign*, 𝄋 : *al ségno*, return to the sign: *dal ségno*, repeat from the sign.

SÉGNO D'ASPÉTTO (*It.*) A rest, pause.

Segue — Semi-cróma

SEGUE (*It.*) Follows, now follows, as follows: it also means, **go on**, *in a similar*, or *like manner*, showing that a passage is to be played like that which precedes it.

SEGUE CÓRO
SEGUE IL CÓRO | (*It.*) The chorus follows, go on to the chorus.

SEGUE IL DUÉTTO (*It.*) The duet follows.

SEGUE IL MENUÉTTO (*It.*) The minuet follows.

SEGUE LA FINÁLE (*It.*) The finale now follows.

SEGUÉNDO
SEGUÉNTE | (*It.*) Following, next: *non si fa úna cadénza, ma s'attácca súbito il seguénte*, begin the next movement immediately, without a cadence.

SEGUÉNZA (*It.*) A sequence.

SEGUE SÉNZA INTERRUZIÓNE (*It.*) Go on without stopping.

SEGUE SÚBITO SÉNZA CAMBIÁRE IL TÉMPO (*It.*) Go on immediately without changing the time.

SEGUIDÍLLA (*Sp.*) A favourite Spanish dance in $\frac{3}{4}$ time.

SEGUÍTE (*It. pl.*) See SEGUE.

SEGUÍTO (*It.*) A suite; see also SEGUE.

SEHNEN (*Ger.*) To long for, to desire passionately.

SEHNSUCHT (*Ger.*) Desire, longing: ardour, fervour.

SEHR (*Ger.*) Very, much, extremely.

SEHR LEBHAFT (*Ger.*) Very lively; extremely animated and vivacious.

SÉI (*It.*) Six.

SEITEN-BEWEGUNG (*Ger.*) Oblique motion.

SEITENSATZ (*Ger.*) An episode, secondary subject.

SEIZIÈME (*Fr.*) Sixteenth.

SEIZIÈME DE SOUPIR (*Fr.*) Semi-demisemiquaver rest, 𝄿.

SEKUNDE (*Ger.*) Second, a second.

SEMEIOGRAPHIE (*Gr.*) See SEMIOGRAPHIE.

SEMI (*Lat.*) Half: *semi-tone*, half a tone.

SEMIBISCRÓMA (*It.*) A demisemiquaver.

SEMIBRÉVE (*It. & Eng.*)
SEMIBREVIS (*Lat.*) | Half a breve: the longest note now in general use, 𝅝.

SEMIBREVE REST. A rest, ▬ equal in duration to a semibreve.

SEMI-CHORUS. A chorus to be sung by half, or only a few of the voices.

SEMI-CRÓMA (*It.*) A semiquaver, 𝅘𝅥𝅯.

SEMI-DEMISEMIQUAVER. A half-demisemiquaver, 𝅘𝅥𝅲 : 64 of them being equal to a semibreve.
SEMI-DIAPENTE (*Lat.*) Diminished, or imperfect, fifth.
SEMI-DIATESSARON (*Lat.*) Diminished fourth.
SEMI-DITONO (*Lat.*) A minor third.
SEMI-FUSA (*Lat.*) A semiquaver.
SEMI-MÍNIMA (*It.*) A *half-minim*, a crotchet.
SEMIOGRAPHIE (*Gr.*) The art of notation, or writing music in notes.
SEMIQUAVER. A note equal to half a quaver, 𝅘𝅥𝅯 .
SEMIQUAVER REST. A rest equal in duration to a semiquaver, 𝄿 .
SEMI-SÉRIO (*It.*) A serious opera, with comic scenes.
SEMITONE (*Eng.*) A half-tone.
SEMI-TONIQUE (*Fr.*) Chromatic.
SEMITONIUM (*Lat.*) A half-tone.
SEMITONIUM MODI (*Lat.*) The leading note, or major seventh.
SEMI-TRÍLLO (*It.*) An inverted *mordent*.
SEMITUÓSO (*It.*) A semitone.
SÉMPLICE (*It.*) Simple, pure, plain.
SEMPLICEMÉNTE (*It.*) Simply, plainly, without ornament.
SEMPLICÍSIMO (*It.*) With the utmost simplicity.
SEMPLICITÀ (It.) Simplicity, plainness.
SÉMPRE (*It.*) Always, evermore, continually.
SÉMPRE CON GRAN DOLCÉZZA E GRÁZIA (*It.*) Always with great sweetness and grace.
SÉMPRE FÓRTE (*It.*) Always loud, loud throughout.
SÉMPRE LEGÁTO (*It.*) Always smooth, smooth throughout.
SÉMPRE PIÁNO (*It.*) Always soft, soft throughout.
SÉMPRE PIÙ AFFRETTÁNDO IL TÉMPO (*It.*) Continually increasing the time.
SÉMPRE PIÙ DI FUÓCO (*It.*) Always with more spirit.
SÉMPRE PIÙ FÓRTE (*It.*) Continually increasing the force.
SÉMPRE PIÙ PRÉSTO (*It.*) Continually quicker.
SÉMPRE RINFORZÁNDO (*It.*) Always emphasising the phrases.
SÉMPRE RITARDÁNDO (*It.*) Always slower, slower and slower.
SÉMPRE STACCÁTO (*It.*) Always detached, *staccáto* throughout.
SENSÍBILE (*It.*) Sensible, expressive, with feeling.
SENSIBILITÀ (*It.*) Sensibility, feeling, expression.
SENSIBILMÉNTE (*It.*) Sensibly, expressively, in a feeling manner.

Sensible — Septuplet

SENSIBLE (*Fr.*) The leading note, or major seventh of the scale.

SENTIE (*Fr.*) Felt, expressed: *mélodie bien sentie*, the melody well expressed or accented.

SENTIMENTÁLE | (*It.*) Feeling, sentiment, judgement, delicate
SENTIMÉNTO | expression.

SÉNZA (*It.*) Without.

SÉNZA ACCOMPAGNAMÉNTO (*It.*) Without accompaniment.

SÉNZA BÁSSI (*It.*) Without the basses.

SÉNZA BATTÚTA (*It.*) Not in strict time.

SÉNZA FIÓRI (*It.*) Without ornaments, without embellishments.

SÉNZA INTERRUZIÓNE (*It.*) Without interruption, play on without stopping.

SÉNZA MISÚRA (*It.*) Not in strict time.

SÉNZA OBOÈ (*It.*) Without the hautboy.

SÉNZA ORNAMÉNTI (*It.*) Without ornaments, without embellishments.

SÉNZA ÓRGANO (*It.*) Without the organ.

SÉNZA PEDÁLE (*It.*) Without the pedals.

SÉNZA REPETIZIÓNE | (*It.*) Without repetition.
SÉNZA RÉPLICA |

SÉNZA RIGÓRE (*It.*) Without regard to the exact time.

SÉNZA SORDÍNI (*It.*) Without the dampers, in pianoforte playing, meaning that the dampers are to be raised from the strings.

SÉNZA SORDÍNO (*It.*) Without the mute, in violin playing, &c.

SÉNZA TÉMPO (*It.*) Without regard to the time; in no definite time.

SE PIÁCE (*It.*) At will, at pleasure.

SEPTADECIMA (*Lat.*) A seventeenth.

SEPTAKKORD (*Ger.*) A cord of the seventh.

SEPTAVE. A scale of seven notes.

SEPTDEZIME (*Ger.*) A seventeenth.

SEPTET (*Eng.*) |
SEPTETT (*Ger.*) | A composition for seven voices, or instruments.
SEPTÉTTO (*It.*) |

SEPTIÈME (*Fr.*) | The interval of a seventh; also an organ stop,
SEPTIME (*Ger.*) | speaking a flat 21st above the diapasons.

SEPTIMEN-ACCORD (*Ger.*) A chord in which the seventh is an important sound: the chord of the seventh, comprising the root, the 3rd, 5th, and 7th.

SEPTIMOLE | (*Lat.*) A group of seven notes, having the value, and
SEPTOLE | to be played in the time of four, of the same species.

SEPTUOR (*Fr.*) A composition for seven voices, or instruments.

SEPTUPLET. See SEPTIMOLE.

SÉQUENCE (*Fr. & Eng.*) A series, or progression, of similar chords, or intervals, in succession.

SEQUÉNTE (*It.*) *See* SEGUÉNTE.

SEQUENZ (*Ger.*) | *See* SÉQUENCE.
SEQUÉNZA (*It.*) |

SERAPHINE. A species of harmonium.

SERBÁNO (*It.*) The serpent: see that word.

SERÉNA (*It.*) *Evening*; an evening song of the troubadours.

SÉRÉNADE (*Fr. Eng. & Ger.*) | Night-music; songs at night; an evening concert in the open air:
SERENÁTA (*It.*) | also, a musical composition on an amorous subject; or a light, pleasing, instrumental composition, comprising several movements.

SERENATÉLLA (*It.*) A little serenade.

SERÉNO (*It.*) Serene, calm, cheerful.

SÉRIA (*It.*) Serious, grave, tragic: in a serious style.

SERIEUSE (*Fr.*) Serious, grave.

SÉRIEUSEMENT (*Fr.*) Seriously, gravely, earnestly.

SERIEUX (*Fr.*) Serious, grave.

SERINETTE (*Fr.*) A bird organ.

SÉRIO (*It.*) Serious, grave, tragic: in a serious style.

SERIÓSO (*It.*) *See* SÉRIA.

SERPEGGIÁNDO (*It.*) Gentle winding, and creeping onwards.

SERPENT (*Eng.*) | A wind-instrument somewhat resembling a
SERPÉNTE (*It.*) | serpent in form, and of a deep, coarse tone;
SERPENTÓNO (*It.*) | chiefly used in military bands, though nearly superseded by the ophicleide: the name is sometimes given to a reed stop in an organ.

SERRÁNDO (*It.*) Becoming faster.

SERRÁTA (*It.*) A concluding performance.

SERRÁTO (*It.*) | Becoming faster.
SERRÉ (*Fr.*) |

SERREZ (*Fr.*) Press on; *accelerándo*.

SERVICE. Certain portions of the Church of England *matins*, and *evensong*, set to music.

SESQUI (*Lat.*) One and a half.

SESQUIALTERA (*Lat.*) An organ stop, comprising of two, or more, ranks of pipes, of acute pitch, and normally containing a tierce.

SESQUINONA (*Lat.*) The minor tone.

SESQUIOCTAVA (*Lat.*) The major tone.

SESQUIQUARTA (*Lat.*) The major third.

Sesquiquinta — Sfogáto

SESQUIQUINTA (*Lat.*) The minor third.
SESQUITERTIA (*Lat.*) The perfect fourth.
SESQUITONE (*Lat.*) An interval of 1½ octaves.
SÉSTA / **SÉSTO** (*It.*) The interval of a sixth: *see also* SEXTE.
SESTET (*Eng.*) / **SESTÉTTO** (*It.*) A composition for six voices or instruments.
SESTÍNA (*It.*) A sextuplet; also a stanza of six lines.
SESTOLE / **SESTOLET** A sextuplet.
SÉTTE (*It.*) Seven.
SÉTTIMA / **SÉTTIMO** (*It.*) The interval of a seventh.
SETZ-ART (*Ger.*) Style, or manner, of composition.
SETZEN (*Ger.*) To compose.
SETZER (*Ger.*) A composer.
SETZ-KUNST (*Ger.*) The art of musical composition.
SEUFZEND (*Ger.*) Moaning, sighing.
SEUL (*Fr.*) Solo; alone; for a single voice.
SEVENTEENTH. An organ stop: *see* TIERCE.
SEVENTH. An interval containing seven diatonic degrees.
SEVERAMÉNTE (*It.*) Severely, strictly, rigorously.
SEVERITÀ (*It.*) Severity, strictness, rigour.
SEVÉRO (*It.*) Severe, strict, exact.
SEXQUIALTERA. *See* SESQUIALTERA.
SEXTA (*Lat.*) A sixth; also, an organ mixture stop.
SEXTAKKORD (*Ger.*) A chord of the sixth.
SEXTA TONI (*Lat.*) The sixth interval from the tonic.
SEXTE (*Ger.*) A sixth: also the name of an organ stop with two ranks of pipes, sounding the interval of a major sixth, a twelfth and tierce on one slide.
SEXTENFOLGEN (*Ger.*) A sequence of sixth.
SEXTETT (*Ger.*) A sestet.
SEXTETTO. *See* SESTÉTTO.
SEXTOLE / **SEXTOLET** / **SEXTUPLET** (*Lat.*) A group of six notes, having the value, and to be played in the time of four.
SEXTUOR (*Fr.*) A sestet.
SEXTUS (*Lat.*) A sixth part or voice.
SFOGÁTO (*It.*) Lightly sung or played.

SFOGGIÁNDO (*It.*) Extravagant, pompous.
SFÓRZA (*It.*) Forced, with force and energy.
SFORZÁNDO \
SFORZÁTO (*It.*) Forced: one particular chord, or note, is to be played with force and emphasis.
SFORZATAMÉNTE (*It.*) Impetuously, energetically.
SFÓRZO (*It.*) Force, stain.
SFUGGÍTO (*It.*) Avoided, shunned; rambling: *see* CADÉNZA.
SFUMÁTO (*It.*) Very lightly.
SFUMATÚRA (*It.*) A light delicate piece.
SGALLINACCIÁRE (*It.*) To crow; a bad method of singing.
SGAMBÁTO (*It.*) Tired, wearied.
SGRISCIÁRE (*It.*) To *quack* on reed instruments.
SHAKE. An ornament produced by the rapid alteration of two consecutive notes.
SHALLOT. The piece of brass or wood, on which the tongue, in an organ reed pipe, beats against.
SHALM. A character which raises a note one semitone, ♯.
SHAWM. A wind-instrument of the ancient Hebrews, supposed to be of the reed, or hautboy, species.
SHIFT. A change of position of the left hand, in playing the violin, &c.
SHIGIONOTH (*Heb.*) *According to variable tunes.*
SHOFAR (*Heb.*) A Hebrew trumpet.
SHORT OCTAVES. A term applied to the lower notes in old organs, where some of the notes were omitted.
SI. Applied in *solfaing* to the note B.
SI BÉMOL (*Fr.*) The note B-flat.
SI BÉMOL MAJEUR (*Fr.*) The key of B-flat major.
SI BÉMOL MINEUR (*Fr.*) The key of B-flat minor.
SIBILANTS. The hissing letters, such as *s* and *z*.
SIBILUS (*Lat.*) A little flute used to teach song-birds.
SICH VERLIEREND (*Ger.*) Vanishing, disappearing; dying away.
SICILIÁNA \
SICILIÁNO (*It.*) A dance of the Sicilian peasants, a graceful movement of a slow, soothing, pastoral character, in $\frac{6}{8}$ or $\frac{12}{8}$ time.
SI DIÈSE (*Fr.*) The note B-sharp.
SIDE-DRUM. A drum suspended at the side of the performer.
SIEB (*Ger.*) An organ sound-board.
SIEBEN (*Ger.*) Seven.
SIEBEN-KLANG (*Ger.*) Heptachord, a scale of seven notes.

Sieben — Simplement

SIEBEN-PFEIFE DES PAN (*Ger.*) *The seven pipes of pan*: pan-pipes.
SIEBENTE (*Ger.*) A seventh.
SIEBENZEHTE (*Ger.*) A seventeenth.
SIEGES-GESANG | (*Ger.*) A triumphal song.
SIEGES-LIED |
SIEGUE, correctly *Segue*, which see.
SIFF-FLÖTE (*Ger.*) See SIFFLÖT.
SIFFLER (*Fr.*) To whistle.
SIFFLET (*Fr.*) A whistle.
SIFFLET DE PAN (*Fr.*) Pan-pipes.
SIFFLÖT | (*Ger.*) *Whistle flute*: an organ stop of 2 or 1 foot tone,
SIFFLÖTE | of the *Hohl-flute* species.
SIGNALIST (*Ger.*) A military trumpet player.
SIGNATUR (*Ger.*) | The sharps or flats marked at the beginning of a
SIGNATURE (*Eng.*) | piece.
SIGNE (*Fr.*) The sign, 𝄋 : *see* SÉGNO.
SIGNES ACCIDENTELS (*Fr.*) Accidental sharps, flats, or naturals.
SIGNES DES SILENCES (*Fr.*) rests.
SIGNUM (*Lat.*) A sign.
SIGUIDÍLLA. See SEGUIDÍLLA.
SILBENDEHNUNG (*Ger.*) Sing more than one note to a syllable.
SILBERTON (*Ger.*) Silvery tone.
SILENCE (*Fr.*) | A rest.
SILÉNZIO (*It.*) |
SILÉNZIO PERFÉTTO (*It.*) Perfect silence, general rest.
SI LÉVA IL SORDÍNO (*It.*) Take off the mute.
SILHOUETTES (*Fr.*) *Shadows*; sketches, *souvenirs*; recollections.
SILLET (*Fr.*) A nut.
SI MAJEUR (*Fr.*) The key of B major.
SI MINEUR (*Fr.*) The key of B minor.
SIMICUM. An ancient Greek instrument, supposed to be of the lyre or harp species, with thirty-five strings.
SIMILAR MOTION. Two, or more, parts, always moving in the same direction.
SÍMILE (*It.*) | Like, alike, in like manner, similarly; meaning,
SÍMILI (*It.*) | the continuation of some form previous
SIMILITER (*Lat.*) | indicated.
SIMPLE INTERVALS. Those which do not exceed an octave.
SIMPLEMENT (*Fr.*) Simply, unaffected.

SIMPLE TIMES. Those which contain but one principal accent in a bar; as $\frac{2}{4}$, $\frac{3}{4}$, $\frac{3}{8}$, &c.

SÍN'. *See* SÍNO.

SÍN' AL FÍNE (*It.*) To the end, as far as the end.

SÍNCOPA | (*It.*) *See* SYNCOPÁTO.
SÍNCOPE |

SINFONÍA (*It.*) | *See* SYMPHONY.
SINFONIE (*Fr.*) |

SINFONÍCO (*It.*) Symphonic.

SING-AKADEMIE (*Ger.*) Vocal academy.

SING-ART (*Ger.*) Manner, or style, of singing.

SINGBAR (*Ger.*) That may be sung.

SING-CHOR (*Ger.*) Singing choir, quire.

SINGEN (*Ger.*) To sing, to chant: singing, chanting.

SINGEND (*Ger.*) *See* CANTÁBILE.

SING-GEDICHT (*Ger.*) Hymn, poem intended to be sung.

SINGHIOZZÁNDO (*It.*) Sobbingly.

SING-KUNST (*Ger.*) The art of singing.

SINGLE ACTION HARP. A harp with pedals, by which each string can be raised one semitone.

SINGLE CHANT. A simple harmonised melody, extending only to one verse of a psalm, as sung in cathedrals, &c.

SING-MÄHRCHEN (*Ger.*) Ballad.

SING-MEISTER (*Ger.*) Singing-master.

SING-PULT (*Ger.*) Singing-desk.

SING-SANG (*Ger.*) Sing-song.

SING-SCHAUSPIEL (*Ger.*) Singing-drama, a drama with songs, &c. interspersed.

SING-SCHULE (*Ger.*) Singing school: a school, or method, for the voice.

SING-SCHÜLER (*Ger.*) Singing-boy.

SING-SPIEL (*Ger.*) An opera, melodrama, a piece interspersed with songs.

SING-STIMME (*Ger.*) Singing voice: a vocal part.

SING-STIMMEN (*Ger. pl.*) The voices: the vocal parts.

SING-STÜCK (*Ger.*) Air, melody.

SING-STUNDE (*Ger.*) Singing-lesson.

SING-TANZ (*Ger.*) Dance, accompanied by singing.

SING-VEREIN (*Ger.*) A choral society.

SING-WEISE (*Ger.*) Melody, tune.

Sinístra — Sixth

SINÍSTRA (*It.*) The left hand.

SINÍSTRÆ (*Lat.*) Left-handed flutes: *see* **DEXTRÆ**.

SINÍSTRA MÁNO (*It.*)
SINISTRA MANU (*Lat.*) } The left hand.

SÍNO (*It.*) To, as far as, until: *con fuóco sín' al fíne*, with spirit to the end.

SÍNO AL FÍNE PIANÍSSIMO (*It.*) *Pianíssimo to the end.*

SI PIÁCE (*It.*) At pleasure, as you please.

SI RADDÓPPIA IL TÉMPO (*It.*) *Redouble the time*; as fast again.

SIREN (*Eng.*)
SIRÈNE (*Fr.*) } An instrument used to measure the frequency of a sound; also, a fog-horn.
SIRENE (*Ger.*)

SIRENEN-GESANG (*Ger.*) Siren-song; a soft, luscious, seductive melody.

SI RÉPLICA (*It.*) A repeat; to be repeated.

SI SCRÍVA (*It.*) As written, without any alteration, or embellishment.

SI SEGUE (*It.*) Go on.

SISTÉMA (*It.*) The staff.

SISTER (*Ger.*) An old German guitar with seven strings.

SÍSTRO (*It.*) A triangle.

SISTRUM (*Lat.*) An instrument of percussion of very great antiquity, supposed to have been invented by the Egyptians, and constructed of brass, shaped like the frame and handle of a racket; the head part had three, and sometimes four, horizontal bars, placed loosely on it, which were allowed to play freely, so that when the instrument was shaken, rattling sounds must have been produced.

Some writers have confounded the *Sistrum* with the *Cymbals*, though they could have had nothing in common except their harsh metallic sounds.

SI TÁCE (*It.*) Be silent.

SITAR. An Hindoo guitar.

SITOLE. A species of zither.

SITZ (*Ger.*) A position in violin palying.

SI VÓLGA (*It.*) Turn over.

SIXIÈME (*Fr.*) A sixth.

SIX POUR QUATRE (*Fr.*) A double triplet, or sextuplet: six notes to be played in the time of four.

SIXTE (*Fr.*) A sixth.

SIXTEENTH NOTE. A semiquaver, ♪.

SIXTH. An interval including six diatonic degrees.

SIXTINE (*Fr.*) A sextuplet.
SKALA (*Ger.*) Scale, gamut.
SKALDE (*Ger.*) A scald; ancient Scandinavian bard.
SKIZZEN (*Ger. pl.*) Sketches; short pieces.
SKOLIEN. A Swedish drinking song.
SLÁNCIO (*It.*) Vehemence, impetuosity.
SLARGÁNDO \
SLARGANDÓSI (*It.*) Extending, enlarging, widening; the time become gradually slower.
SLARGÁTO (*It.*) Slower.
SLEGÁTO (*It.*) Untied; disconnected; the opposite to *legáto*.
SLENTÁNDO \
SLENTÁNTO (*It.*) Relaxing the time, becoming gradually slower.
SLIDE. See **GLISSER**.
SLISSÁTO (*It.*) Slurred, gliding.
SLUR. A curved line over two or more notes, to show that they must be played smoothly.
SMALL OCTAVE. The name given in Germany to the notes between [music notation] inclusive: these notes are expressed by small letters, as, a, b, &c.
SMÁNIA (*It.*) Fury, madness; rage, frenzy.
SMANIÁNTE \
SMANIÁTO (*It.*) Furious, vehement, frantic; with rage.
SMANICÁRE (*It.*) To shift, or change the position of the hand, in playing the violin, guitar, &c.
SMANIÓSO (*It.*) See **SMANIÁNTE**.
SMINUÉNDO \
SMINUÍTO \
SMORÉNDO (*It.*) Diminishing, decreasing, gradually softer.
SMORFIÓSO (*It.*) Affected, coquettish, full of grimaces.
SMORZÁNDO \
SMORZÁTO (*It.*) Extinguished, put out, gradually dying away.
SNARES. Cords distended across the surface of a drum, to produce a rattling effect.
SNÉLLO (*It.*) Nimble, quick, brisk.
SOÁVE \
SOAVEMÉNTE (*It.*) Sweetly, agreeably, lightly, gently, softly, delicately.
SOCIETÀ DEL QUARTÉTTO (*It.*) A quartet society.
SOCIÉTÉ CHANTANTE (*Fr.*) A singing society.
SODÉZZA (*It.*) Firmness, decision.

Soffocándo — Solmizáre

SOFFOCÁNDO
SOFFOGÁNDO } (*It.*) Damping the strings of a harp, with the hand.

SOFORT (*Ger.*) At once, immediately.

SOGGÉTTO (*It.*) Subject, theme, motive.

SOGLEICH (*Ger.*) Immediately.

SOGNÁNDO (*It.*) Dreamy.

SOIRÉE MUSICÁLE (*Fr.*) A musical evening.

SOL. The note G.

SÓLA (*It.*) Alone: *see* SÓLO.

SOL BÉMOL (*Fr.*) The note G-flat.

SOL BÉMOL MAJEUR (*Fr.*) The key of G-flat major.

SOL BÉMOL MINEUR (*Fr.*) The key of G-flat minor.

SOL DIÈSE (*Fr.*) The note G-sharp.

SOL DIÈSE MINEUR (*Fr.*) The key of G-sharp minor.

SOLEMNIS (*Lat.*) Solemn.

SOLÉNNE (*It.*) Solemn, grave, splendid.

SOLENNEL
SOLENNELLE } (*Fr.*) Solemn.

SOLENNEMÉNTE (*It.*) Solemnly.

SOLENNIS (*Lat.*) Solemn.

SOLENNITÀ (*It.*) Solemnity, pomp.

SÓLFA (*It.*) The musical notes and characters: *see* SOLFÁING.

SOLFÁING. The practice of SOLFÉGGI: which see.

SOLFÈGE (*Fr.*)
SOLFÉGGI (*It. pl.*) } Exercises for the voice, in which the notes are called by their names, *do, re, mi, fa, sol, la, si*.
SOLFÉGGIO (*It.*)

SOLFEGGIAMÉNTI (*It.*) *Solféggi.*

SOLFEGGIÁRE (*It.*) To practice *Solféggi*.

SOLFEGGIEREN (*Ger.*)
SOLFIER (*Fr.*) } To sing *Solféggi*.

SÓLI (*It. pl.*) A particular passage played by principals only, one performer to each part.

SÓLITO (*It.*) *Accustomed*; in the usual manner.

SOLLÉCITO (*It.*) Careful, *solicitous*; meaning as attentive and careful style of execution.

SOL MAJEUR (*Fr.*) The key of G major.

SOL MINEUR (*Fr.*) The key of G minor.

SOLMISÁRE (*It.*)
SOLMISIREN (*Ger.*) } The practice of the scale, pronouncing the name of each note, do, re, mi, &c.: to this kind of vocal exercise the practice of Solféggi is added.
SOLMIZÁRE (*It.*)

SOLMIZATION. *See* SOLFÉGGI, *and* SOLMISÁRE.

SÓLO (*It. Fr. & Ger.*) Alone; music for *one* principal voice or instrument, either with, or without, accompaniment.

SOLOMANIE. A Turkish flute.

SOLO ORGAN. The name, in English organs, of the fourth row of keys, to which stops of a solo character are contained.

SOLO-SÄNGER (*Ger.*) A solo-player, principal singer.

SOLO-SPIELER (*Ger.*) Solo player.

SOLTÁNTO (*It.*) Alone, only.

SOMBRER (*Fr.*) To produce a veiled sombre tone.

SÓMMA (*It.*) Extreme, exceeding great: *sómma espressióne*, very great expression.

SOMMERLIED (*Ger.*) A summer song.

SOMMEROPHONE. A species of bombardon invented by Sommer, Weimar.

SOMMÉSSO (*It.*) Subdued.

SOMMIER (*Fr.*) A wind-chest in an organ.

SOMNOLENTO (*It.*) Dreamy, sleepy; subdued.

SON (*Fr.*) Sound, tone.

SONÁBILE (*It.*) Sounding, resonant.

SONAGLIÁRE (*It.*) To jingle, to ring a little bell.

SONÁGLIO (*It.*) A small, tinkling bell.

SONAMÉNTO (*It.*) Sounding, ringing, playing.

SONÁNTE (*It.*) Sounding, resonant.

SONÁRE (*It.*) To sound, to have a sound, to ring, to strike, to play upon.

SONÁRE ÁLLA MÉNTE (*It.*) To play extempore, to improvise.

SONÁRE IL VIOLÍNO (*It.*) To play upon the violin.

SONÁTA (*It.*)
SONATE (*Fr. & Ger.*) The sonata had its origin about the middle of the seventeenth century, and the name was applied to the *Sonáta di Chiésa*, which consisted of slow movements, intermixed with fugues; and the *Sonáta di Cámera*, consisting of a variety of airs, such as the *Allemande*, the *Courant*, and *Saraband*, &c. The *Sonáta* afterwards gradually assumed its present form towards the end of the eighteenth century, and now comprises several different movements, generally for one single instrument. The same form of composition, which is technically called *the Sonata* form, is also common to symphonies, trios, quartets, &c.: *see* SYMPHONY.

SONÁTA DA CHIÉSA (*It.*) A church sonata, an organ sonata.

SONÁTA DI BRAVÚRA (*It.*) A brilliant, showy sonata.

SONÁTA PER IL CÉMBALO (*It.*) A pianoforte sonata.

Sonáta — Sons éttouffés

SONÁTA QUÁSI ÚNA FANTASÍA (*It.*) A sonata in the style of fantasia, not strictly formal.

SONATÍLLA (*It.*)
SONATÍNA (*It.*) — A short, easy sonata.
SONATINE (*Fr.*)

SONATÓJO (*It.*) A sounding-board.

SONATÓR DI VIOLÍNO (*It.*) A fiddler, violin player.

SONATÓRE (*It.*) An instrumental performer.

SONATRÍCE (*It.*) A female performer.

SON BOUCHÉ (*Fr.*) A closed note on a horn.

SON CUIVRÉ (*Fr.*) A Brassy note.

SON DEUX (*Fr.*) A sweet sound.

SON ÉTOUFLÉ (*Fr.*) A stifled, veiled, or muted sound.

SONÉTTO (*It.*) A sonnet.

SONÉVOLE (*It.*) Sonorous, ringing, sounding.

SONG. A poem modulated to the voice: verse containing an expression of feeling or sentiment, without any narrative or dramatic interest. The Greek songs, or odes, gave passionate expression to the feelings inspired by love and wine.

SON HARMONIQUE (*Fr.*) An harmonic.

SONIFEROUS. Producing or conveying sound; sonorous.

SONNANTE (*Fr.*) An instrument consisting of steel bars, hit with a hammer, and used in military bands.

SON NATUREL (*Fr.*) An open note on a horn.

SONNER (*Fr.*) To sound.

SONNERIE (*Fr.*) A chime; also, a military signal.

SONNET. A short poem of fourteen lines.

SONNEUR (*Fr.*) A bell ringer.

SÓNO (*It.*) Sound, tone.

SONOMETER. An instrument for measuring intervals, or the vibrations of sounds.

SONORAMÉNTE (*It.*) Sonorously, harmoniously.

SONORE (*Fr.*) Sonorous, harmonious, resonant, full-tones, vibrating.

SONORIDAD (*Sp.*) Harmony, sound, sonorousness.

SONÓRO (*It.*) See SONORE.

SON ORDINAIRE (*Fr.*) An open note on a horn.

SONORITÀ (*It.*)
SONORITÉ (*Fr.*) — Harmony, sound, sonorousness.

SONOROPHONE. A species of bombardon.

SON PLEIN (*Fr.*) A full, round tone.

SONS ÉTTOUFFÉS (*Fr. pl.*) Stifled, or muffled, tones.

Sons harmoniques — Sospensivaménte

Sons harmoniques (*Fr. pl.*) Harmonic sounds.
Sons pleins (*Fr. pl.*) In flute music, this means, that the notes must be blown with a very full, round, tone.
Sonus (*Lat.*) Sound, tone.
Sópra (*It.*) Above, upon, over, before.
Soprálto (*It.*) A high contralto.
Sopráni (*It. pl.*) Treble voices.
Sopran (*Ger.*) | The treble, the highest kind of female voice: a
Sopráno (*It.*) | treble, or *sopráno*, singer.
Sopranino
Sopráno acúta | (*It.*) A high *sopráno*.
Sopráno concertáto (*It.*) The soprano solo part, the part for a solo treble voice, in a chorus.
Sopráno córda (*It.*) The E string of the violin.
Sopráno drammático (*It.*) A dramatic *sopráno* with a powerful voice.
Sopráno leggiéro (*It.*) A light *sopráno*.
Sopráno sfogáto (*It.*) A very high *sopráno*.
Sopran-schlüssel (*Ger.*) The *sopráno* clef.
Sopran-stimme (*Ger.*) A soprano voice.
Sópra úna córda (*It.*) On one string.
Sórda (*It.*) Muffled, veiled tone.
Sordaménte (*It.*) Softly, gently; also, damped, muffled.
Sordellína (*It.*) A species of bagpipe.
Sordíni (*It. pl.*) *Mutes*, in violin playing; and the *Dampers*, in pianoforte music: see CON SORDÍNI, and SÉNZA SORDÍNI.
Sordíno (*It.*) A mute, a small instrument of brass, wood, or ivory, placed on the bridge of a violin, &c., to muffle, or deaden the vibrations. A mute is sometimes applied to the clarinet, and horn.
Sórdo (*It.*) Muffled, veiled tone.
Sordone (*Fr.*) | An obsolete species of bassoon; also, an old organ
Sordóno (*It.*) | stop, of a muffled character.
Sordun (*Ger.*) A mute for a trumpet; also, *see* SORDÓNO.
Sorgfältig (*Ger.*) Carefully: *sorgfältig gebunden*, very smoothly.
Sorríso (*It.*) A smile.
Sortie (*Fr.*) A concluding voluntary; also, *see* SORTÍTA.
Sortíta (*It.*) The opening air in an operatic part, the entrance *ária*.
Sospensióne (*It.*) A suspension.
Sospensivaménte (*It.*) Irresolutely, waveringly.

SOSPIRÁNDO
SOSPIRÁNTE
SOSPIRÉVOLE
SOSPIRÓSO
   (*It.*) Sighing, very subdued, doleful.

SOSPÍRO (*It.*) A crotchet rest.

SOSTENÉNDO
SOSTENÚTO
   (*It.*) Sustaining the tone, keeping the notes down their full duration.

SÓTTO (*It.*) Under, below.

SÓTTO BÓCE
SÓTTO VÓCE
   (*It.*) Softly, in a low voice, in an undertone.

SOUBASSE (*Fr.*) An organ stop: see SUB-BASS.

SOUBRETTE (*Fr.*) A female singer for a subordinate part, in a comic opera.

SOUBRETTENROLLE (*Ger.*) A waiting-made.

SOU-CHANTRE (*Fr.*) A sub-chanter.

SOUFFLER (*Fr.*) To blow.

SOUFFLER L'ORGUE (*Fr.*) To blow the bellows of an organ.

SOUFFLERIE (*Fr.*) The machinery belonging to the bellows, in an organ.

SOUFFLETS (*Fr.*) The bellows of an organ.

SOUFFLEUR
SOUFFLEUSE
   (*Fr.*) Bellows-blower: also, a prompter in a theatre.

SOUFFLEUR D'ORGUES (*Fr.*) Bellows-blower of an organ.

SOUM. A Burmese harp.

SOUND-BOARD. The thin board over which the strings of the pianoforte, &c., are distended; also, the board on which the pipes, in an organ, are placed.

SOUPAPE (*Fr.*) A valve of a wind instrument.

SOUPIR (*Fr.*) A crotchet rest.

SOUPIR DE CROCHE (*Fr.*) See DEMI-SOUPIR.

SOUPIR DE DOUBLE CROCHE (*Fr.*) See QUART DE SOUPIR.

SOUPIR DE TRIPLE CROCHE (*Fr.*) See DEMI-QUART DE SOUPIR.

SOURDELINE (*Fr.*) An Italian bagpipe, or *musette*.

SOURDEMENT (*Fr.*) In a subdued manner.

SOURDINE (*Fr.*) The name of an harmonium stop: see also SORDÍNO.

SOUS (*Fr.*) Under, below, beneath.

SOUS-DOMINANTE (*Fr.*) The sub-dominant, or fourth of the scale.

SOUS-MÉDIANTE (*Fr.*) The sub-mediant, or sixth of the scale.

SOUS-TONIQUE (*Fr.*) The sub-tonic, the seventh of the scale, or note below the tonic.

SOUTENIR (*Fr.*) To sustain a sound.

SOUTENU (*Fr.*) *See* SOSTENÚTO.
SOUVENIR (*Fr.*) Recollection, reminiscence.
SPAGNOLÉSCO (*It.*) In the Spanish style.
SPAGNOLÉTTA / **SPAGNUÓLA** (*It.*) A Spanish dance, a species of minuet.
SPÁLLA (*It.*) The shoulder.
SPANDÉNDO (*It.*) Spreading, *crescéndo*.
SPANISCH (*Ger.*) *See* SPAGNOLÉSCO.
SPANISCHER REITER / **SPANISCHER KREUZ** (*Ger.*) A double-sharp.
SPART (*Ger.*) Scattered, divided; distributed.
SPÁRTA (*It.*) / **SPARTE** (*Ger.*) A full score.
SPARTÍRE (*It.*) / **SPARTIREN** (*Ger.*) To score; to arrange old scores in modern notation.
SPARTÍTA (*It.*) / **SPARTÍTO** (*It.*) A full score.
SPÁRTO (*It.*) Scattered, divided; distributed.
SPASSAPENSIÉRE (*It.*) The Jew's harp.
SPASSHAFT (*Ger.*) Sportively, playfully, merrily.
SPASSHAFTIGKEIT (*Ger.*) Sportiveness, playfulness.
SPASSHAFTLICH (*Ger.*) Sportively, merrily, playfully.
SPATIUM (*Lat.*) / **SPÁZIO** (*It.*) A space, of the stave: a distance, an interval.
SPEDIÉNDO (*It.*) Hastening, hurrying.
SPERDÉNDOSI (*It.*) Fading away.
SPERRVENTIL (*Ger.*) An organ which has ventils acting on certain stops.
SPEZZÁTO (*It.*) Divided; broken.
SPIANÁTO (*It.*) Smooth, even; *legáto*.
SPICCATAMÉNTE (*It.*) Brilliantly.
SPICCÁTO (*It.*) Separated, pointed, distinct, detached: in violin music it means that the notes are to be played with the point of the bow.
SPIEGÁNDO (*It.*) Extending; *crescéndo*.
SPIEGELKANON (*Ger.*) A canon to be read backwards.
SPIEL (*Ger.*) Playing; style of playing.
SPIELART (*Ger.*) Manner of playing, style of performance.
SPIELBAR (*Ger.*) Playable; suitable for playing.
SPIELEN (*Ger.*) To play on an instrument.
SPIELEND (*Ger.*) Playing; also, playful.

Spieler — Sprechendgesang

SPIELER (*Ger.*) Performer.

SPIELLEUTE (*Ger. pl.*) Musicians.

SPIELMANN (*Ger.*) A musician.

SPIGLIATÉZZA (*It.*) Agility, sprightliness.

SPILLFLÖTE (*Ger.*) A species of *Spitzflöte*, which see.

SPINÆ (*Lat.*) *Thorns*; a name formerly applied to the quills of the spinet.

SPINET (*Eng.*)
SPINETT (*Ger.*)
SPINÉTTA (*It.*)
An old instrument of the harpsichord or virginal species, of a small triangular shape, with one row of keys, and one string of thin brass or steel wire to each note. It bore the same relation to the harpsichord, as the square pianoforte does to the grand one of the present day. A spinet with two rows of keys, each fingerboard containing 4¾ octaves, was found amongst the lumber at Windsor Castle, with the inscription, 'Johannes Ruckers me fecit. Antverpiæ, 1612.' It is now in the state apartments.

SPINETT-DRAHT (*Ger.*) Virginal, or spinet wire.

SPINNEN DES TONS (*Ger.*) Drawing-out the toes.

SPIRÁNTE (*It.*) Expiring; dying away.

SPÍRITO (*It.*) Spirit, life, energy.

SPIRITOSAMÉNTE
SPIRITÓSO
(*It.*) Lively, animated, brisk, spirited, sprightly.

SPIRITUÁLE (*It.*)
SPIRITUEL (*Fr.*)
Sacred, spiritual.

SPIRITUELLE (*Fr.*) Ideal, ethereal; witty.

SPIRITUÓSO. See SPIRITÓSO.

SPITZ (*Ger.*) Pointed.

SPITZE (*Ger.*) The point of the bow; also, the toe in organ playing.

SPITZ-FLÖTE
SPITZ-FLUTE
(*Ger.*) *Pointed-flute*; an organ stop of a soft pleasing tone, the pipes of which are conical, and pointed, at the top.

SPITZ-HARFE (*Ger.*) A small pointed or triangular harp, to be set upon a table.

SPITZIG (*Ger.*) Pointed, cutting, biting.

SPITZ-QUINTE (*Ger.*) An organ stop, with pointed pipes, sounding a fifth above the foundation stops.

SPONDEE (*Lat.*)
SPÓNDEO (*It.*)
A musical foot consisting of two long notes or syllables, ———.

SPÖTTISCH (*Ger.*) Mocking, scoffing.

SPOTTLIED (*Ger.*) A satirical song.

SPRECHEND (*Ger.*) Speaking.

SPRECHENDGESANG (*Ger.*) Recitative.

SPRECHENDOPER (*Ger.*) An opera with spoken dialogue.
SPRESSIÓNE (*It.*) Expression.
SPRUCHGESANG (*Ger.*) An anthem.
SPRUNG (*Ger.*) A skip in melody.
SQUILLÁNTE (*It.*) Clear, plain, sounding, ringing.
STA (*It.*) This, as it stands; to be played as written.
STABAT MATER (*Lat.*) A hymn on the Crucifixion.
STÁBILE (*It.*) Firm.
STACCÁRE (*It.*) To detach, to separate each note.
STACCATÍSSIMO (*It.*) Very much detached, as *staccáto* as possible.
STACCÁTO (*It.*) Detached, distinct, separated from each other.
STADT (*Ger.*) Town, city.
STADT-MUSIKUS / **STADT-PFEIFER** (*Ger.*) Town musician.
STAGIÓNE (*It.*) The season, the musical season.
STAGIÓNE DI CARTÉLLO (*It.*) The operatic season.
STAHLHARMONIKA / **STAHLSPIEL** (*Ger.*) An instrument consisting of tuned steel bars, played with a hammer.
STAMENTIENPFEIFE (*Ger.*) *See* SCHWEGEL.
STAMM (*Ger.*) Stem, trunk; root.
STAMM-ACCORD (*Ger.*) A radical, or fundamental chord, from which others are formed.
STAMMENTIN-PIPE. An organ stop: *see* SCHWIEGEL.
STAMPÍTA (*It.*) An air, a tune, a song.
STANCE (*Fr.*) *See* STÁNZA.
STANCHÉZZA (*It.*) Weariness, lassitude.
STÁNCO (*It.*) Weary, fatigued.
STÄNDCHEN (*Ger.*) A serenade.
STANDHAFT (*Ger.*) Steadily, firmly, resolutely.
STANDHAFTIGKEIT (*Ger.*) Firmness, steadiness, resolution.
STANGHÉTTA (*It.*) A bar line, the thin bar line drawn across the stave.
STÁNZA (*It.*) / **STANZE** (*Ger.*) A verse of a song.
STARK (*Ger.*) Strong, loud, vigorous.
STÄRKE (*Ger.*) Vigour, force, energy, stress.
STARKER (*Ger.*) Louder.
STARKE STIMMEN (*Ger.*) Loud stops: *see* MIT STARKEN STIMMEN.
STAT (*Lat.*) This, as it stands.
STAVE. The five parallel lines on which the notes are placed.
STÉCCA (*It.*) A *stick*; a choked, strained voice.

STECHER (*Ger.*) An *sticker*, part of the mechanism, of an organ; also, an engraver.

STEG (*Ger.*) The bridge, of a violin, &c.

STEIGERND (*Ger.*) Intensifying, working up.

STELLUNG (*Ger.*) Position, in violin playing.

STEM. The thin stroke which is drawn from the head of a note.

STENTÁNDO (*It.*) Delaying, retarding.

STENTÁRE (*It.*) To delay; to work hard.

STENTATAMÉNTE (*It.*) Slow; laborious.

STENTÁTO (*It.*) Hard, forced, loud.

STENTORPHON (*Gr.*) A very large scale organ stop, of fluty tone.

STERBE-LIED (*Ger.*) Funeral hymn.

STERBEND (*Ger.*) Dying away; *moréndo*.

STERBEGESANG / **STERBELIED** (*Ger.*) A death song; a funeral hymn.

STÉSO (*It.*) Extended, diffused, large.

STÉSO MÓTO (*It.*) A slow movement.

STÉSSO (*It.*) The same: *l'istésso témpo*, in the same time.

STETS (*Ger.*) Always.

STHÉNOCHIRE. A machine for strengthening, and imparting flexibility to the fingers; being a compound of the *dactylion* and the *hand guide*.

STIBACCHIÁTO (*It.*) Relaxing, retarding, the time.

STICCÁDO / **STICCÁTO** (*It.*) A musical instrument; the sounds are produced by striking on little bars of wood, which are tuned to the notes of the scale, and stuck with a little ball at the end of a stick.

STICH (*Ger.*) A dot.

STICKER. Part of the mechanism, in an organ.

STIEFEL (*Ger.*) The boot of an organ reed-pipe.

STIEL (*Ger.*) A stem or neck.

STIERHORN (*Ger.*) A cow-horn giving only one note.

STIFT (*Ger.*) The *jack* of a spinet, &c.

STIL (*Ger.*) / **STÍLE** (*It.*) Style, manner of composition, or performance.

STILL (*Ger.*) Calmly, quietly.

STILL-GEDACT (*Ger.*) A stopped diapason, of a quiet tone.

STÍLO (*It.*) / **STILUS** (*Lat.*) Style, manner of composition, or performance.

STIMM-ANSATZ (*Ger.*) Vocal attack.

STIMM-BAR (*Ger.*) Tuneable, singable.

STIMM-DECKEL (*Ger.*) Sound-board.

STIMME (*Ger.*) The voice, sound: also, the sound-post in a violin, &c.: also, a part in vocal or instrumental music: also, an organ stop or register.

STIMMEN (*Ger. pl.*) Parts, or voices: also, organ stops.

STIMMER (*Ger.*) Tuner: also, a tuning hammer.

STIMM-GABEL (*Ger.*) Tuning fork.

STIMM-HAMMER (*Ger.*) Tuning key, tuning hammer.

STIMM-HORN (*Ger.*) A tuning cone, for organ tuning.

STIMMIG (*Ger.*) Having a sound.

STIMMLOS (*Ger.*) Voiceless.

STIMM-PFEIFE (*Ger.*) Wooden fife, pitch-pipe.

STIMM-STOCK (*Ger.*) The sound-post, of a violin, &c.

STIMMUNG (*Ger.*) Tuning, tune, tone.

STIMMUNG-HALTEN (*Ger.*) To keep in tune.

STIMMUNG-BILD (*Ger.*) A tone picture.

STIMM-ZUG (*Ger.*) A tuning slide.

STINGUÉNDO (*It.*) Dying away, becoming extinct.

STIRACCHIÁNDO
STIRACCHIÁTO
STIRÁNDO
STIRÁTO
(*It.*) Stretched, forced, retarded: *see* AL-LARGÁNDO.

STIVA (*Lat.*) A *neume*.

STOCK (*Ger.*) Stick, stem, stalk; a bundle of thirty strings.

STOCK-FAGOTT (*Ger.*) An obsolete species of double bassoon.

STOCK-FLÖTE (*Ger.*) A combined flute and walking stick.

STOCK-PFEIFE (*Ger.*) An old German flute.

STOCK-CHEN (*Ger.*) The heel of a violin.

STONÁNTE (*It.*) Discordant, out of tune.

STOCKEND (*Ger.*) Slackening, *rallentándo*.

STOLLEN (*Ger.*) *See* STROPHE.

STOLZ (*Ger.*) Proud.

STONÁNTE (*It.*) Dissonant.

STOP. A register, or row of pipes, in an organ: on the violin, &c., it means the pressure of the finger upon the string.

STOPFEN (*Ger.*) To stop; to place the hand into the bell of a horn.

STOPPED DIAPASON. An organ stop, thus named because the pipes are stopped, or covered, at the top: it is one of the most important stops, and of the same pitch as the Open Diapason, but much softer in tone, and the pipes are only half as long.

STÓRTA (*It.*) A *serpent*: see that word.

Stortína — Streng

STORTÍNA (*It.*) A small serpent.
STOSS (*Ger.*) A knock, a blow, a blast.
STOTTERN (*Ger.*) To stutter, stammer.
STRACANTÁRE (*It.*) To sing charmingly.
STRACCICALÁNDO (*It.*) Babbling, prattling.
STRACCINÁTO. See **STRASCINÁTO**.
STRAFF (*Ger.*) Strict.
STRAIN. A portion of music divided off by a double bar.
STRAMBÓTTO \
STRAMBÓTTOLO / (*It.*) A folk-song, a rustic love ditty.
STRAPPÁRE (*It.*) To throw off a note lightly, by a rapid turn of the wrist.
STRAPPÁNDO \
STRAPPÁTO / (*It.*) Thrown off; torn off.
STRASCICÁNDO (*It.*) *Dragging* the time, *trailing*, playing slowly.
STRASCICÁTO (*It.*) *Dragged*, *trailed*, played slowly.
STRASCINÁNDO (*It.*) *Dragging* the time, playing slowly.
STRASCINÁNDO L'ÁRCO (*It.*) Keeping the bow of the violin close to the strings, as in executing the *tremolándo*, so as to slur, or bind the notes, closely.
STRASCINÁTO (*It.*) *Dragged* along, played slowly.
STRASCINÍO (*It.*) *Dragging*, playing slowly.
STRASCÍNO (*It.*) A grace, or embellishment, chiefly vocal, and used in slow passages; it is a kind of drag, and consists of about 8 or 10 notes given in an unequal, and descending motion.
STRATHSEY. A lively Scotch dance, in common time.
STRAVAGÁNTE (*It.*) Fantastical, odd, capricious, extravagant.
STRAVAGÁNZA (*It.*) Extravagance, eccentricity, quaintness.
STRAZIÁNTE (*It.*) Mockingly.
STREICHEN (*Ger.*) To strike, to stretch, to touch in passing; to draw a bow across the strings; also, to cut out a portion of a work.
STREICHEND (*Ger.*) Stringy in tone.
STREICHENDE REGISTER (*Ger.*) String-toned organ stops.
STREICHER (*Ger.*) A player upon bowed instruments; also, string-toned organ stops.
STREICH-INSTRUMENT (*Ger.*) *Stroke-instrument*, a stringed instrument played with a bow, as the violin, viola, &c.
STREICH-ORCHESTER (*Ger.*) A string orchestra.
STREICH-QUARTETT (*Ger.*) See **STRING QUARTET**.
STREICH-ZITHER (*Ger.*) A zither played with a bow.
STRENG (*Ger.*) Strict, severe, rigid.

STRENGE GEBUNDEN (*Ger.*) Strictly *legáto*, exceedingly smooth.

STRENG IM TEMPO (*Ger.*) Strictly in time.

STRÉPITO (*It.*) Noise.

STREPITOSAMÉNTE (*It.*) With a great noise.

STREPITÓSO (*It.*) Noisy, boisterous.

STRETTA (*It.*) A concluding passage, coda, or finale, in an opera, taken in quicker time to enhance the effect.

STRÉTTO (*It.*) *Pressed, close, contracted*; that part of a fugue where the subject and answer succeed one another at a very short interval, both of them being united in one and the same harmony.

STRICCIÁNDO (*It.*) *See* STRASCICÁNDO.

STRICH (*Ger.*) *Stroke*, the manner of bowing.

STRICH-ART (*Ger.*) The art or manner of bowing.

STRICH-ARTEN (*Ger.*) Different ways of bowing.

STRIDÉNTE | (*It.*) Shrill, harsh, raucous, noisy, blatant.
STRIDÉVOLE |

STRIKING REED. That kind of reed pipe in an organ, in which the tongue strikes against the tube or *shallot*, in producing the tone: *see* REED.

STRILLÁRE (*It.*) To screech, scream, shriek.

STRÍLLO (*It.*) A loud, shrill cry, &c.

STRIMPELLÁTA (*It.*) Strumming, scraping.

STRINGÉNDO (*It.*) Pressing, accelerating the time.

STRÍNGERE (*It.*) To hasten.

STRING QUARTET. A composition for four instruments of the violin species, as, two violins, a viola, and violoncello.

STRISCIÁNDO | (*It.*) Gliding, slurring, sliding smoothly from one
STRISCIÁTO | note to another.

STRÓFA | (*It.*) A strophe, stanza.
STRÓFE |

STROH (*Ger.*) Straw.

STROHBASS (*Ger.*) The husky lower tones of some bass voices.

STROHFIEDEL (*Ger.*) A xylophone.

STROMBAZZÁTA | (*It.*) The sound of a trumpet.
STROMETTÁTA |

STROMBETTÁRE (*It.*) To sound, or play on, the trumpet.

STROMBETTIÉRE (*It.*) A trumpet player.

STROMENTÁTO (*It.*) Instrumental, scored for an orchestra.

STROMENTAZIÓNE (*It.*) Scoring; instrumental music.

STROMÉNTI (*It. pl.*) Musical instruments.

STROMÉNTI DA CÓRDA (*It. pl.*) String instruments.

Stroménti da fiáto — Suáve

STROMÉNTI DA FIÁTO (*It. pl.*) Wind-instruments.
STROMÉNTI D'ÁRCO (*It. pl.*) Bowed instruments.
STROMÉNTI DA TÁSTO (*It. pl.*) Keyboard instruments.
STROMÉNTI DI RINFÓRZA (*It. pl.*) Reinforcing instruments.
STROMÉNTI DI VÉNTO (*It. pl.*) Wind-instruments.
STROMÉNTI D'OTTÓNE (*It. pl.*) Brass instruments.
STROMÉNTO (*It.*) An instrument.
STROPHE. The first part of a Greek ode; also, a group of metrically arranged lines, to form a *stanza*..
STRUMENTÁLE (*It.*) Instrument.
STRUMÉNTO (*It.*) See STROMÉNTO.
STUBEN-ORGEL (*Ger.*) Small portable organ.
STÜCK (*Ger.*) Piece, air, tune: musical entertainment.
STÜCKEN (*Ger.*) Little air, or tune.
STUDIEN (*Ger. pl.*) Studies.
STÚDIO (*It.*) \
STUDIUM (*Ger.*) / A study, an exercise intended for the practice of some particular difficulty.
STUFE (*Ger.*) Step, degree.
STUFE DER TONLEITER (*Ger.*) A degree of the scale.
STUFENFOLGE \
STUFENGANG / (Ger.) A scale, a sequence.
STUMM (*Ger.*) Dumb.
STUMME PFEIFE (*Ger.*) A dummy pipe, on an organ.
STUMMES KLAVIER (*Ger.*) A dumb piano.
STUONÁNTE \
STUONÁTO / (*It.*) Dissonant, out of tune.
STUPÓRE (*It.*) Amazement, stupor.
STURM (*Ger.*) Storm, tumult, fury.
STÜRMEND \
STÜRMISCH / (*Ger.*) Impetuously, boisterously, furiously.
STÜRZE (*Ger.*) The bell of a horn.
STUTZFLÜGEL (*Ger.*) A small grand pianoforte.
STYL (*Ger.*) Style.
STYLE DÉCOUSU (*Fr.*) Loose, unconnected style.
STYRIENNE (*Fr.*) An air with *Jodelling* refrain.
SÙ (*It.*) Above, upon; up.
SUABE-FLUTE. An organ stop of clear, liquid tone, not so loud as the *wald-flute*: it was invented by William Hill, of London.
SUÁVE (*It. & Fr.*) Sweet, mild, agreeable, pleasant.

Suaveménte — **Súlla**

Suaveménte / **Suavità** (*It.*) Sweetness, delicacy, suavity.

Sub (*Lat.*) Under, below, beneath.

Sub-Bass (*Ger.*) Under-bass; an organ register in the pedals, usually a double-stopped bass of 32 or 16 feet tone, though sometimes open wood pipes of 16 feet, as at Haarlem.

Sub-Bourdon. An organ stop of 32 feet tone, with stopped pipes.

Sub-Chanter. The precentor's deputy, in a cathedral choir.

Sub-Diapente (*Lat.*) / **Sub-Dominant** (*Eng.*) The fourth note of any scale, or key.

Sub-Flöte (*Ger.*) See SIFFLÖTE.

Sub-Octave. An organ coupler, producing the octave below.

Subitaménte / **Súbito** (*It.*) Suddenly, immediately, at once.

Subject. A melody, or theme; a leading *motívo*.

Sub-Mediant. The sixth of the scale.

Sub-Principal. *Under principal*; that is, below the pedal diapason pitch: in German organs this is a double bass stop, of 32 feet tone.

Sub-Semifusa (*Lat.*) A demisemiquaver.

Sub-Semitone. The semitone below the key-note.

Sub-Semitonium Modi (*Lat.*) The leading note.

Sub-Tonic. The note a semitone below the key-note.

Sudden Modulation. Modulation to a distant key, without any intermediate chord to prepare the ear.

Sufflöte (*Ger.*) See SIFFLÖTE.

Suffocáto (*It.*) Muffled, choked, deadened.

Suffolaménto (*It.*) A hiss, whistle, murmur.

Suggétto (*It.*) Subject; theme, melody.

Súgli / **Súi** (*It.*) On the, upon, the; near the.

Suite (*Fr.*) A *series*, a succession: *une suite de pièces*, a series of lessons, or pieces.

Suivez (*Fr.*) Follow, attend, pursue; the accompaniment must be accompanied to the singer, or solo player.

Sujet (*Fr.*) A subject, melody, or theme.

Súl / **Súll'** / **Súlla** (*It.*) On, upon the: *súl G*, on the G string: *súl ponticéllo*, on, or close to, the bridge.

Súlla Mézzo Córda (*It.*) On the middle of the string.

Súlla Mézzo Mánico (*It.*) On the middle of the fingerboard.

Súlla Pedaliéra (*It.*) On the pedal-board.

Súlla — Surdeline

SÚLLA TASTIÉRA (*It.*) Upon the keys, upon the finger-board.
SÚL PONTICÉLLO (*It.*) Bow closed to the bridge.
SULTANA. A species of violin with wire strings in pairs.
SUMARA. A Turkish double-flute.
SUMMEN (*Ger.*) To hum.
SUMMEND (*Ger.*) Humming.
SUMSEN (*Ger.*) To hum; to buzz, to ring.
SÚNTO (*It.*) An extract.
SÚO LÓCO (*It.*) In its own, or usual, place.
SUONÁR SORDAMÉNTE (*It.*) To play softly.
SUONÁRE LE CAMPÁNE (*It.*) To ring the bells.
SUONÁTA (*It.*) A sonata.
SUONÁTE DI CHIÉSA (*It. pl.*) *See* SONÁTA DA CHIÉSA.
SUÓNI ALTERÁTI (*It.*) Notes altered with flats or sharps.
SUÓNI ARMÓNICHI (*It. pl.*) Harmonic sounds.
SUÓNI MUSICÁLI (*It. pl.*) Musical sounds.
SUÓNO (*It.*) Sound, tone, music; a song.
SUÓNO ARMONIÓSO (*It.*) Harmonious sound.
SUÓNO DÉLLE CAMPÁNE (*It.*) The sound of bells.
SUPER (*Lat.*) Above, over.
SUPÉRBO (*It.*) Superb; lofty, proud.
SUPER-DOMINANT (*Lat.*) The note in the scale, next above the dominant.
SUPERFLUOUS INTERVALS. Those which are one semitone more than the *perfect*, or *major*, intervals: *see* AUGMENTED INTERVALS.
SUPER-OCTAVE. An organ stop tuned two octave, or a fifteenth, above the diapasons: also, a coupler producing the octave above.
SUPER-TONIC (*Eng.*) | The note next above the tonic, or key note;
SUPERTONIQUE (*Fr.*) | the second note of the scale.
SUPPLICÁNDO
SUPPLICHÉVOLE | (*It.*) In a supplicatory manner.
SUPPLICHEVOLMÉNTE |
SÚR (*Fr. & It.*) On, upon, over.
SURABONDANT (*Fr.*) Superabundant; more than usual.
SURAIGU (*Fr.*) Over-acute; over-sharp.
SURDELINE. The old Italian bagpipe, a large, and rather complicated instrument, consisting of many pipes and conduits for the conveyance of the wind, with keys for the opening of the holes by the pressure of the fingers, and inflated by means of bellows, which the performer blows with his arm, at the same time that he fingers the pipe.

SUR LA QUATRIÈME CORDE (*Fr.*) On the fourth string.
SUR LA SECONDE CORDE (*Fr.*) Upon the second string.
SUR LA TOUCHE (*Fr.*) On the fingerboard.
SUR LE CHEVALET (*Fr.*) Near the bridge, in violin playing.
SUR ÚNA CÓRDA (*It.*) ⎫
SUR UNE CORDE (*Fr.*) ⎬ Upon one string.
SUS-DOMINANTE (*Fr.*) The subdominant.
SUSPENDED CADENCE. *See* **INTERRUPTED CADENCE**.
SUSPENSION. The retention of some note, or notes, of a cord, into the succeeding one.
SUSPIRIUM (*Lat.*) A crotchet rest.
SÜSS (*Ger.*) Sweetly.
SÜSSFLÖTE (*Ger.*) A soft flute stop on an organ.
SUSSURÁNDO ⎫
SUSSURÁNTE ⎬ (*It.*) Whispering, murmuring.
SUS-TONIQUE ⎫
SUTONIQUE ⎬ (*Fr.*) The supertonic.
SVEGLIÁNDO (*It.*) Arousing, awakening.
SVEGLIÁTO (*It.*) Brisk, lively, sprightly.
SVELTE (*Fr.*) ⎫
SVÉLTO (*It.*) ⎬ Free, light, easy.
SVILUPPAMÉNTO ⎫
SVILÚPPO ⎬ (*It.*) Unfolding, development.
SWELL. That part of an organ, which contains a number of pipes enclosed in a box, the front of which may be gradually opened or closed, by means of a pedal, and thus the tone made louder, or softer, by degrees.
SWISS FLUTE. An organ stop, of agreeable tone, something like that of the *gámba*.
SYLBE (*Ger.*) A syllable.
SYLLABIC SONG. A melody in which every syllable has its distinct note: of this species is recitative.
SYMPHONÉTA (*It.*) Polyphony.
SYMPHONÍA (*It.*) ⎫
SYMPHONIE (*Fr. & Ger.*) ⎬ *See* **SYMPHONY**.
SYMPHÓNICO (*It.*) Harmonious; pertaining to a *symphony*.
SYMPHONIKER (*Ger.*) A composer for full orchestra; a writer of symphonies.
SYMPHONION. An instrument invented by Fr. Kaufmann, resembling the orchestrion; and combining the tone of a pianoforte with that of the flute, clarinet, &c.

Symphonique — Szopelka

SYMPHONIQUE (*Fr.*) \
SYMPHONISCH (*Ger.*) — Harmonious; pertaining to a *symphony*.

SYMPHONISTE (*Fr.*)   A composer; a writer of symphonies; an orchestral player.

SYMPHONIOUS. Harmonious, agreeing in sound.

SYMPHONY. A grand composition, of several movements, for full orchestra. The symphony, in its present form, was introduced by Haydn, and generally consists of an *adágio*, *allégro*, *andánte*, *minuétto* (or *schérzo*), *trío*, and *finále*. The term is also applied to the introductory, and concluding, instrumental parts of a song, or other vocal composition.

SYNCOPÁTA \
SYNCOPÁTE \
SYNCOPÁTO (*It.*) Syncopated, bound together: contraction of a note by cutting off part of its value and giving it to the following note.

SYNCOPATIO (*Lat.*) \
SYNCOPATION (*Eng.*) \
SYNCOPE (*Fr.*) An unequal division of the time or notes: irregular accent: binding the last note of one bar to the first note of the next: accented notes occurring in the unaccented part of a bar: *see also* **SYNCOPÁTA**.

SYNCOPIREN (*Ger.*) To syncopate: *see* **SYNCOPATION**.

SYNKOPE (*Ger.*) *See* **SYNCOPATION**.

SYRINGA (*Lat.*) \
SYRINGE (*Fr.*) Pandian pipes.

SYSTÈME (*Fr.*) The whole range of musical tones; the compass of an instrument.

SYZYGIA (*Lat.*) A chord; a triad.

SZOPELKA. A Russian oboe.

T

TABÁLLO (*It.*) A kettle-drum.

TABLATÚRA (*It.*)
TABLATURE (*Fr. & Eng.*)
TABULATUR (*Ger.*) The method of notation used for the lute, and other instruments of the like kind; the strings being represented by a number of lines, on which were marked the letters a, b, c, &c., which letters referred to the frets on the neck of the instrument. Marks of a hooked form, thus, ♪♪♪ were placed over the letters to signify the time, or value of the notes. The Italians used figures, instead of letters.

TABLE D'HARMONIE (*Fr.*) A table, or diagram, of chords, intervals, &c.

TABLE D'INSTRUMENT (*Fr.*) The belly of an instrument.

TABOR
TABOURET A little drum used to accompany the pipes, in rustic dances.

TABOURIN (*Fr.*) *See* **TABOR**.

TABRET. An ancient Hebrew instrument, mentioned in Scripture.

TÁCE (*It.*)
TACET (*Lat.*)
TÁCI (*It.*)
TACLÁSI (*It.*) *Be silent*: meaning that certain instruments are not to play: *óboe tacet*, let the oboe be silent.

TACT (*Ger.*) Time, measure.

TACT-ACCENT (*Ger.*) A metrical accent; also, the primary accent of a measure or group.

TACT-ART (*Ger.*) Species of time: common, or triple.

TACT-BEZEICHNUNG (*Ger.*) The time signature.

TACT-ERSTICKUNG (*Ger.*) Syncopation.

TACTFEST (*Ger.*) Steadiness in keeping time.

TACT-FÜHRER (*Ger.*) The conductor; leader.

TACT-HALTEN (*Ger.*) To keep correct time.

TACT-LINIE
TACT-STRICH (*Ger.*) A bar-line, the lines which mark the bars.

TACHMÄSSIG (*Ger.*) Conformable to the time.

TACT-MESSER (*Ger.*) A metronome.

TACT-NOTE (*Ger.*) A semibreve.

Tact-schläger — Tampon

TACT-SCHLÄGER (*Ger.*) Time-beater.

TACT-STOCK (*Ger.*) A *bâton*, for beating time.

TACTUS (*Lat.*) A beat; a stroke with the hand in beating time.

TACT-ZEICHEN (*Ger.*) The figures, or signs, at the beginning of a piece, to show the time.

TAFELFÖRMIGES KLAVIER \
TAFELKLAVIER (*Ger.*) A table-shaped pianoforte.

TAFEL-MUSIK (*Ger.*) Table music, music sung at table; as, part-songs, glees, &c.

TAGLIED (*Ger.*) Morning song; *aubade*.

TÁGLIO (*It.*) To *cut*, or reduce the length of a work.

TAILLE (*Fr.*) The tenor part: the viola.

TAILLE DE VIOLON (*Fr.*) The viola, or tenor violin.

TAIL-PIECE. That piece of ebony to which the strings of the violin, viola, &c., are fastened.

TAKIGOTI. A Japanese dulcimer.

TAKT (*Ger.*) See TACT.

TALABALÁCCO (*It.*) A species of Moorish drum.

TALAN. Hindoo cymbals.

TALON (*Fr.*) The *heel* of the bow; that part nearest the nut; also, the heel in pedal playing.

TALLÓNE (*It.*) The heel of the bow.

TAMBOUR (*Fr.*) Drum: the great drum: also, a drummer.

TAMBOURA. A species of oriental guitar.

TAMBOUR DE BASQUE (*Fr.*) A tabour or tabor: a tambourine.

TAMBOURET (*Fr.*) \
TAMBOURINE (*Eng.*) A timbrel, a small instrument of percussion, like the head of a drum, with jingles placed round its rim to increase the noise.

TAMBOURIN (*Fr.*) A species of dance, accompanied by the tambourine: *see also* TAMBOURINE.

TAMBOURINEUR (*Fr.*) Drummer, tambourine player.

TAMBOUR MAJOR. *See* DRUM-MAJOR.

TAMBURÁCCIO (*It.*) A large old drum: a tabor.

TAMBURÉLLO \
TAMBURÉTTO (*It.*) A tambourine: a little drum.

TAMBURÍNO (*It.*) A little drum: also, a drummer.

TAMBÚRO (*It.*) A drum.

TAMBÚRO MILITÁRE (*It.*) A side drum.

TAMBÚRO RULIÁNTE (*It.*) A tenor drum.

TAMBURÓNE (*It.*) The great drum.

TAMPON (*Old Fr.*) A bass-drumstick with two heads.

Tam-tam — Tásto sólo

TAM-TAM. An Indian instrument of percussion, a species of drum, or tambourine.

TANBUR (*Ger.*) *See* TAMBÚRO.

TÄNDELND (*Ger.*) In a playful manner.

TANGENT (*Ger.*) The *jack* of a harpsichord.

TANTARA. An imitative work in hunting songs.

TANTÍNO (*It.*) A little; very little.

TÁNTO (*It.*) So much, as much: *allégro non tánto*, not so quick, not too quick.

TANTUM ERGO (*Lat.*) A hymn sung at the benediction in the Roman Catholic service.

TANZ (*Ger.*) A dance

TÄNZE (*Ger. pl.*) Dances.

TÄNZER (*Ger.*) A dancer.

TÄNZERINN (*Ger.*) A female dancer.

TANZ-KUNST (*Ger.*) The art of dancing.

TANZ-LIEDER (*Ger.*) Dance songs.

TARANTÉLLA (*It.*) A Neapolitan dance, in quick $\frac{6}{8}$ time, played to those who have been bitten by the tarantula, to make them dance violently, and produce perspiration, which is said to effect a cure.

TARAU. A Burmese fiddle with three silk strings.

TARDAMÉNTE (*It.*) Slowly.

TARDÁNDO (*It.*) Lingering, retarding the time.

TARDANTEMÉNTE (*It.*) Slowly.

TARDÁTO (*It.*) Lingering, retarding the time.

TÁRDO (*It.*) Tardy, lingering, slow, dragging.

TARENTELLÍNA (*It.*) A short *tarantélla*.

TASCHENGEIGE (*Ger.*) A pocket *fiddle* or *kit*.

TASTÁME (*It.*)
TASTATUR (*Ger.*) — The keys, or key-board, of a pianoforte, organ, &c.
TASTATÚRA (*It.*)
TASTIÉRA (*It.*)

TASTE (*Ger.*) A key of a pianoforte, &c.: also, the touch.

TASTEN-BRETT
TASTEN-LEITER — (*Ger.*) Key-board of a pianoforte, &c.

TASTEN-WERK (*Ger.*) A keyed instrument.

TÁSTO (*It.*) A key of a pianoforte, &c.: also, the touch.

TÁSTO SÓLO (*It.*) *One key alone*: in organ or pianoforte music, this means, a note without harmony, the note being sustained: it generally occurs at an 'organ-point.'

TÁTTO (*It.*) The touch.

TATTOO. The military drum signal for retiring at night.

TAUTOLOGY. A tiresome repetition of the same passage.

TCHANG. | A Chinese guitar.
TCHE.

TEÁTRO (*It.*) A theatre.

TEÁTRO DI GRAN CARTÉLLO (*It.*) Lyric theatre of the first rank.

TEÁTRO DIÚRNO (*It.*) A theatre in which performances take place by day.

TECHNICON. An apparatus for training the hands and fingers.

TECHNIK (*Ger.*) Technical terms.

TECHNIPHONE. An earlier name for the Virgil Clavier.

TECHNISCH (*Ger.*) Technical: this work is also applied to indicate mechanical proficiency, as regards execution.

TEDDÉO (*It.*) Te Deum.

TEDÉSCA | (*It.*) German: *álla Tedésca*, in the German style.
TEDÉSCO

TE DEUM (*It.*) *We praise Thee*: a canticle, or hymn of praise.

TEIL (*Ger.*) A part; a portion.

TEILTÖNE (*Ger.*) Partials.

TEILUNG (*Ger.*) A division, subdivision.

TÉMA (*It.*) A theme, or subject; a melody.

TEMPERAMENT (*Eng.*) A term used in the mathematical division of sounds: that equalisation of the intervals, in tuning, which brings their whole system more or less near that of the diatonic and chromatic scales: *see* EQUAL, *and* UNEQUAL TEMPORAMENT.

TEMPERÁNDO (*It.*) Moderating the speed.

TEMPERATAMÉNTE (*It.*) Moderately.

TEMPERATUR (*Ger.*) *See* TEMPERAMENT.

TEMPERIEREN (*Ger.*) To temper. Moderate, soften.

TEMPÉSTA (*It.*) | A tempest.
TEMPESTE (*Old Fr.*)

TEMPESTOSAMÉNTE (*It.*) Furiously, impetuously.

TEMPESTÓSO (*It.*)
TEMPESTUEUSE (*Fr.*) | Tempestuous, stormy, boisterous.
TEMPESTUEX (*Fr.*)

TEMPÊTE (*Fr.*) A boisterous dance in $\frac{2}{4}$ time.

TÉMPO (*It.*) Time, measure or duration: *à témpo*, in time.

TÉMPO CÓMODO (*It.*) Convenient time; an easy, moderate degree of movement.

TÉMPO DI BÁLLO (*It.*) In dance time; rather quick.

TÉMPO DI CAPPÉLLA (*It.*) In the *Church-time*; in the time of church music.

TÉMPO DI GAVÓTTA (*It.*) In the time of a gavot.

TÉMPO DI MENUÉTTO (*It.*) In the time of a minuet.

TÉMPO DI POLÁCCA (*It.*) In the time of a polácca.

TÉMPO DI PRÍMA PÁRTE (*It.*) In the same time as the first part.

TÉMPO DI VALSE (*It.*) In waltz time.

TÉMPO DÓPPIO (*It.*) Twice as fast.

TÉMPO FÓRTE (*It.*) A strong beat.

TÉMPO FRETTÉVOLE
TÉMPO FRETTOLÓSO (*It.*) In quicker time, hurrying, hastily.

TÉMPO GIÚSTO (*It.*) In exact, just, reasonable, time.

TÉMPO ORDINÁRIO (*It.*) Ordinary, or moderate time.

TÉMPO PERDÚTO (*It.*) Lost, interrupted, irregular time.

TÉMPO PRÍMO (*It.*) First, or original time; the same time as at the first.

TEMPORÁLE (*It.*) Time, season; also, a storm, tempest.

TEMPOREGGIÁTO (*It.*) The time is to be accompanied to the solo singer, or player.

TEMPORISER (*Fr.*) To accommodate the time of the accompaniment to the soloist.

TÉMPO RUBÁTO (*It.*) *Robbed*, or *stolen*, time; irregular time; meaning a slight deviation to give more expression, by retarding one note, and quickening another, but so that the time of each bar is not altered in the whole.

TEMPO WIE VORHER (*Ger.*) The time as before.

TEMPS (*Fr.*) Time: also, the various parts or division of a bar.

TEMPS FOIBLE (*Fr.*) The weak, or unaccented parts of a bar.

TEMPS FORT (*Fr.*) The strong, accented parts of bar.

TEMPS FRAPPÉ (*Fr.*) The down-beats, or accented parts.

TEMPS LEVÉ (*Fr.*) The up-beats, or unaccented parts.

TEMPUS BINARIUM (*Lat.*) Duple time.

TEMPUS IMPERFECTUM (*Lat.*) *Imperfect time*; a term used by old writers, meaning common time of *two* in a bar.

TEMPUS PERFECTUM (*Lat.*) *Perfect time*; a term used by old writers, meaning time of *three* in a bar.

TEMPUS TERNSRIUM (*Lat.*) Triple time.

TEMS (*Fr.*) Time: also, the various parts or division of a bar.

TENDREMENT (*Fr.*) Tenderly, delicately.

TENEBRÆ (*Lat.*) Darkness: a name given to the Roman Catholic evening service, during Holy Week.

Tenéndo — Teodía

TENÉNDO IL CÁNTO (*It.*) Sustain the melody.

TENERAMÉNTE (*It.*) Tenderly, delicately.

TENÉRE (*It. & Lat.*) To hold; to sustain.

TENERÉZZA (*It.*) Tenderness, softness, delicacy.

TÉNERO (*It.*) Tenderly, softly, delicately.

TENÉTE SÍNO ÁLLO FÍNE DEL SUÓNO (*It.*) Keep down the keys as long as the sound continues.

TENEUR (*Fr.*) The *cánto férmo* of a hymn-tune or choral.

TENIR (*Fr.*) To hold, a violin bow, &c.

TENOR. That species of male voice next above the baritone, and extending from the C upon the second space in the bass, to G on the second line in the treble.

TENOR C. The lowest C in the tenor voice: the lowest string of the violin, or tenor violin.

TENOR CLEF. The C clef, when placed upon the fourth line.

TENÓRE (*It.*) Tenor voice: a tenor singer: male voice: *see also* VIÓLA.

TENÓRE BÚFFO (*It.*) The second tenor singer of an opera company, for comic parts.

TENÓRE LEGGIÉRO (*It.*) A tenor voice of a light quality of tone.

TENÓRE ROBÚSTO (*It.*) A tenor singer with a full-tones voice.

TENORÍNO (*It.*) A falsétto tenor; a castráto.

TENORIST (*Ger.*) A tenor singer.

TENOROON. The old tenor hautboy, the compass of which extended downwards to tenor C. The name is sometimes applied to an organ stop, which does not, however, resemble the *Tenoroon* either in regard to pitch, or quality, but only as to compass, the pipes being of the double open diapason species, on the manuals, and terminating at tenor C; the octave of pipes below this being omitted.

TENOR POSAUNE (*Ger.*) The tenor trombone.

TENOR-SCHLÜSSEL (*Ger.*) The tenor clef.

TENOR-VIOLE (*Ger.*) \
TENOR-VIOLIN (*Eng.*) } The viola.

TENOR-ZEICHEN (*Ger.*) The tenor clef.

TENSILE. A term applied to all stringed instruments, on account of the tension of their strings.

TENTH. An interval comprising an octave and a third: also, an organ stop tuned a tenth above the diapasons, called also *decima*, and *double tierce*.

TENUE (*Fr.*) *See* TENÚTO.

TENÚTE \
TENÚTO } (*It.*) Held on, sustained, or kept down, the full time.

TEODÍA (*It.*) A song in praise of the Deity.

TÉORBE (*Fr.*) A *Theorbo*, which see.
TEORÉTICO (*It.*) Theoretical.
TEORÍA (*It.*) Theory.
TEORÍA D'ARMONÍA (*It.*) The theory of harmony.
TEORÍA DEL CÁNTO (*It.*) The theory, or art, of singing.
TEORÍCO (*It.*) Theoretical; a teach of theory.
TEPIDAMÉNTE (*It.*) Coldly, with indifference.
TEPIDITÀ (*It.*) Coldness, indifference.
TÉPIDO (*It.*) Lukewarm.
TER (*Lat.*) Thrice, three times.
TERCET (*Fr.*) A triplet.
TERMINAZIÓNE (*It.*) The turn at the end of a shake.
TERMINI TECHNICI (*Lat.*) Technical terms.
TERNARY MEASURE. Triple time.
TERPODION. An instrument invented by Buschmann, of Hamburg, resembling the harmonium in appearance, the tone being produced from sticks of wood: the name is also given to an organ stop of 8 feet tone.
TERTIA (*Lat.*) \
TERTIE (*Ger.*) Third, tierce: also an organ stop, sounding a third, or tenth, above the foundation stops.
TERTIAN (*Lat.*) An organ stop composed of to pipes, tierce and larigot, on one slide, sounding the interval of a minor third.
TER UNCA (*Lat.*) *Three-hooked*: the old name of the demisemiquaver.
TERZ (*Ger.*) \
TÉRZA (*It.*) A third, the interval of a third: also, an organ stop sounding a third above the fifteenth: *see* TIERCE.
TERZE (*Ger.*)
TERZADÉCIMA (*It.*) An interval of a thirteenth.
TERZ DECIMOLE (*Ger.*) A group of thirteen notes, having the value of eight similar ones.
TERZDEZIME (*Ger.*) An interval of a thirteenth.
TERZETTÍNO (*It.*) A short trio.
TERZÉTTO (*It.*) A short piece or trio for three voices.
TERZ-FLÖTE (*Ger.*) A flute sounding a minor third above: also, an organ stop.
TERZIE (*Ger.*) See TERZ.
TERZÍNA (*It.*) A triplet.
TÉRZO (*It.*) See TERZ.
TERZTÖNE (*Ger.*) Tierce-tones.
TESSITÚRA (*It.*) \
TESSITURE (*Eng.*) The general range or average pitch of a theme or song.
TÉSTA (*It.*) Head.

Tésto — Threnodie

TÉSTO (*It.*) Text: subject, theme, motive; also, the words of an opera, or song.

TÊTE (*Fr.*) The head of a note; also, the scroll of a violin.

TETRACHORD (*Gr.*)
TETRACÓRDO (*It.*)
TETRACORDE (*Fr.*)
  A fourth: also, a series, or scale, of four diatonic sounds.

TETRACHORDON. A small piano-like instrument, whose strings are set into vibration, with a rubber cylinder.

TEXTBUCH (*Ger.*) The *libretto*.

THEATER-KAPELLE (*Ger.*) The orchestra of a theatre.

THÉÂTRE DE LA NATION (*Fr.*) The Grand Opera House.

THÉÂTRE DE LA RÉPUBLIQUE (*Fr.*) Théâtre Français.

THÉÂTRE DE LA MONTANSIER (*Fr.*) Formerly the Palais Royal.

THEILE (*Ger. pl.*) Parts, divisions of the bar: also, strains, or component parts of a movement or piece.

THEMA (*Ger.*)
THÈME (*Fr.*)
  A theme, or subject.

THEMATISCHES VERZEICHNISS (*Ger.*) A thematic list of compositions, with a few bars of each principal theme.

THEORBE (*Ger.*)
THEORBO (*Eng.*)
  An ancient instrument of the lute species: *see* ARCH-LUTE.

THEORETIKER (*Ger.*)
THÉORICIEN (*Fr.*)
  A theoretical musicians, a theorist.

THRORIA (*Lat.*)
THÉORIE (*Fr.*)
THEORY (*Eng.*)
  The science of music: the principles of sound, as regards concords and discords: the system of harmonical and melodial arrangement.

THESIS (*Gr.*) Down-beat, the accented part of the bar.

THEYAOU. A Burmese fiddle with three silk strings.

THIRD. An interval comprising three diatonic degrees.

THIRD FLUTE. A flute sounding a minor third higher than the concert flute.

THIRTEENTH. An interval comprising an octave and a sixth, or thirteen diatonic degrees.

THIRTY-SECOND-NOTE. A demisemiquaver, ♪.

THOROUGH BASS. Figured bass: also, accompanying from a figured bass.

THRENODIE (*Gr.*) An elegy, funeral song.

THRICE MARKED OCTAVE. The name given in Germany to the notes between [notation] and [notation] inclusive; these notes are expressed by small letters, with three short strokes, thus, $\overline{\overline{\overline{c}}}$ or c^3.

THRO. A Burmese fiddle with three silk strings.

THÜRNER (*Ger.*) Town musician.

TIBIA (*Lat.*) The ancient name of all wind-instruments with holes, such as the flute, pipe, fife: originally the term was applied to the human leg-bone, made into a flute: also, an organ stop, of 8 feet tone, and of a very smooth tone.

TIBIA CLAUSA (*Lat.*) An organ stop, of the stopped diapason species, with a full tone, invented by Hope-Jones.

TIBIAE PARES (*Lat. pl.*) Two flutes, one for the right hand, and the other for the left, which were played on by the same performer.

TIBIA MAJOR (*Lat.*) An organ stop of 16 feet tone, the pipes of which are stopped or covered.

TIBIA MOLLIS (*Lat.*) An organ stop, of soft tone, invented by Hope-Jones.

TIBIA PLENA (*Lat.*) A powerfull organ flue stop, invented by Hope-Jones.

TIBIA UTRICULARIS (*Lat.*) An ancient bagpipe.

TIBICEN (*Lat.*) The ancient flute player, or piper.

TIBICINA (*Lat.*) A female flute player, or piper.

TIEF (*Ger.*) Deep, low, profound.

TIEFER (*Ger.*) Deeper, lower: *8ve tiefer*, octave below.

TIEFSTIMMIG (*Ger.*) Deep voiced.

TIEFTÖNEND (*Ger.*) Deep toned.

TIEPIDAMÉNTE (*It.*) Coldly; with indifference.

TIERCE (*Fr.*) A third: also, the name of an organ stop tuned a major third higher than the fifteenth.

TIERCE DE PICARDIE (*Fr.*) *Tierce of Picardy:* a term applied to a *major third*, when introduced in the last chord of a composition in a minor mode: the custom was supposed to have originated in Picardy.

TIERCE MAXIME (*Lat.*) *Augmented third*, containing five semitones: as, from F to A-sharp.

TIERCET. A triplet.

TIGE (*Fr.*) The stick of a bow.

Timbal — Tirant

Timbal (*Sp.*)
Timbale (*Fr.*) — A kettle-drum.
Timbállo (*It.*)

Timbalarion (*Fr.*) A set of tuned kettle-drums.

Timbalier (*Fr.*) A kettle-drummer.

Timballes (*Fr. pl.*) Kettle-drums.

Timbour chromatique (*Fr.*) A set of tuned kettle-drums.

Timbre (*Fr.*) *Quality* of tone, or sound.

Timbrel. An ancient Hebrew instrument, supposed to have been like a tambourine.

Tímbro (*It.*) *Quality* of tone, or sound.

Tímido (*It.*) Timid, fearful.

Timóre (*It.*) Timidity, fear.

Timorosaménte (*It.*) Timidly, with fear.

Timoróso (*It.*) Timorous, with hesitation.

Timpanétto (*It.*) A small drum, or timbrel.

Tímpani (*It. pl.*) The kettle-drums.

Timpanísta (*It.*) A performer on the kettle-drums.

Tímpano (*It.*) Drum, timbrel, tabor.

Tímpano copérto
Tímpano sórdo — (*It.*) A covered, or muffled drum.

Tintamarre (*Fr.*) Hubbub, noise.

Tintement (*Fr.*)
Tintínno (*It.*) — Tingling of a bell: vibration, or ringing sound.

Tintinnabulum (*Lat.*)
Tintinnábolo (*It.*) — A little bell.
Tintinnábulo (*It.*)

Tintinnaménto
Tintinnándo
Tintinnío — (*It.*) Tinkling.
Tintíno

Tínto (*It.*) Shade, tint, colour, in relation to tone.

Tiórba (*It.*) *See* **Theorbo**.

Tipping. *See* **Double-Tongueing**.

Tirade (*Fr.*) Slurring or sliding through an interval; also, a rapid run between tow melody notes.

Tiránna (*Sp.*) A Spanish national air or song, accompanied by the guitar.

Tirant (*Fr.*) A stop-knob on an organ; a button or piston; a drum-cord.

TIRÁRE (*It.*) To draw, drag, pull.

TIRASSE (*Fr.*) The pedals of an organ which act on the manual keys, by pulling, or drawing them down; a pedal coupler.

TIRÁRTO (*It.*) Drawn, pulled, stretched out: a down-bow: *see also* **TIRASSE**.

TÍRA TÚTTO (*It.*) A pedal, or mechanism in an organ, which, acting upon all the stops, enables the performer to obtain at once full power of the instrument.

TIRÉ (*Fr.*) *Drawn, pulled*: a down-bow.

TIROLÉSE (*It.*) *See* **TYROLIENNE**.

TISCHHARFE (*Ger.*) A *dish-harp*, a species of auto-harp.

TITTY. An Hindoo bagpipe.

TOBEND (*Ger.*) Blustering, violently.

TOCCÁTA (*It.*) Prelude, species of capriccio or fantasia: a piece requiring brilliant execution.

TOCCATÍNA (*It.*) A short *toccáta*.

TOCCÁTO (*It.*) An trumpet music, a fourth part for a bass-trumpet, instead of kettle-drums.

TOCSIN. An alarm bell.

TOD (*Ger.*) Death.

TODTEN-MARSCH (*Ger.*) Funeral march.

TODTEN-MUSIK (*Ger.*) Funeral music.

TON (*Fr. & Ger.*) Tone, tune, sound, voice, melody: also, accent, stress: also, the pitch of any note as to its acuteness or gravity: also, the key, or mode: *le ton d'ut*, the key of C: *see also* **TONE**.

TON-ABSTAND (*Ger.*) An interval.

TONADA (*Sp.*) A tune, a melody, a song.

TONADÍCA (*Sp.*) A song of a lively and cheerful character,
TONADÍLLA generally with guitar accompaniment.

TONALITÀ (*It.*) Key structure or relationship; also, the whole scheme of scales, chords.

TONÁNTE (*It.*) Thunderous; very loud.

TONARION
TONARIUM A Roman pitch pipe.

TONART (*Ger.*) Mode, scale, key.

TONARTENVERWANDSCHAFT (*Ger.*) Key relationship.

TONATÉLLA
TONATÍLLAS Spanish national airs, or dances: *see* **TONADÍLLA**.

TON-AUSWEICHUNG (*Ger.*) Modulation.

TON BAS (*Fr.*) A low, deep tone.

TON-BESTIMMUNG (*Ger.*) The mathematical determination of sounds.

TON-BILD (*Ger.*) Tone picture.

TON BOUCHÉ (*Fr.*) Stopped tone on an horn.

TON-BÜHNE (*Ger.*) An orchestra.

TON D'ÉGLISE (*Fr.*) A church mode.

TON DE LA TROMPETTE (*Fr.*) The crook of a trumpet.

TON-DICHTER (*Ger.*) Poet of sound, a composer of music.

TON-DICHTUNG (*Ger.*) Musical composition, of a high character.

TÓNDO (*It.*) Round, full in tone.

TONE. An interval containing two semitones.

TÖNE (*Ger. pl.*) *See* TON.

TONEND (*Ger.*) Sounding; resounding.

TON-FALL (*Ger.*) A cadence.

TON-FARBE (*Ger.*) Tone colour; *timbre*.

TON-FOLGE (*Ger.*) Tune, melody.

TON-FÜHRUNG (*Ger.*) Modulation: also, succession of melody or harmony.

TON-FÜLLE (*Ger.*) Volume; melodiousness.

TON-FUSS (*Ger.*) Metre.

TON-GANG (*Ger.*) Tune, melody.

TON-BEBUNG (*Ger.*) Intonation; tone production; tonality.

TON-GATTUNG
TON-GESCHLECHT (*Ger.*) The individuality of the two modes, the major and the minor: *Tongeschlecht* is the more correct term

TON GÉNÉRATEUR (*Fr.*) The ruling, or principal key, in which a piece is written.

TON HAUT (*Fr.*) A high, acute tone.

TON-HÖHE (*Ger.*) Pitch.

TONIC (*Eng.*)
TÓNICA (*It.*) The key-note of any scale: the chief, fundamental ground-tone, or first note, of the scale.
TONIQUE (*Fr.*)

TONIC SOL-FA. A system of writing and teaching music, in which letters of the alphabet, and other signs, are used, instead of the usual notation on the stave. In this system *do* is always applied to the tonic.

TONÍMETRO (*It.*) A tuning-folk.

TONISCH (*Ger.*) Pertaining to the tonic.

TONITRUONE. A thunder making machine.

TON-KUNDE (*Ger.*) The science of music.

TON-KUNST (*Ger.*) Music: the art and science of music.

TON-KÜNSTLER (*Ger.*) Musician.

TON-LAGE (*Ger.*) Pitch; register; compass.

TON-LEHRE (*Ger.*) Acoustics.

TON-LEITER (*Ger.*) Scale, gamut.

TON MAJEUR (*Fr.*) Major key.

TON-MALEREI (*Ger.*) Sound-painting, musical invention.

TON MINEUR (*Fr.*) Minor key.

TÓNO (*Sp.*) See TON.

TONOS (*Gr.*) A whole tone; also, a tone.

TONOTECHNIE (*Fr.*) The art of making the notes on the cylinder of a barrel organ.

TON-REICH (*Ger.*) Rich and full in *timbre*.

TON-REIHE (*Ger.*) A scale.

TON-REIN (*Ger.*) True intonation of fifths, on the violin &c.

TONS (*Fr. pl.*) See TON.

TON-SATZ (*Ger.*) A musical composition.

TON-SCHLUSS (*Ger.*) A cadence.

TON-SCHLÜSSEL (*Ger.*) The key; key note.

TON-SCHRIFT (*Ger.*) Musical notes.

TONS DE LA TROMPETTE / **TONS DU COR** (*Fr.*) The additional crooks of the trumpet and horn, for raising or lowering the pitch.

TONS DE L'ÉGLISE (*Fr.*) The church modes, or tones.

TON-SETZER (*Ger.*) Composer: a less flattering term than *Ton-dichter*.

TON-SETZER-KUNST (*Ger.*) The art of musical composition.

TON-SETZUNG / **TON-STÜCK** (*Ger.*) A musical piece, or composition.

TON-SPIEL (*Ger.*) Music, a concert.

TON-SPIELER (*Ger.*) Musical performer.

TON-SPRACHE (*Ger.*) The language of tones; music.

TON-STUFE (*Ger.*) A degree, or step, of the stave.

TON-SYLBE (*Ger.*) Accented syllables.

TON-SYSTEM (*Ger.*) System of tones or sound: the science of harmony: the systematic arrangement of musical tones of sounds in their regular order.

TON-UMFANG (*Ger.*) The compass of an instrument.

TONUS (*Lat.*) A whole tone; also, a tone.

TON-UNTERSCHIED (*Ger.*) An interval.

TON-VERÄNDERUNG (*Ger.*) Modulation, change of key.

TON-VERHALT (*Ger.*) Rhythm.

TON-VERZIEHUNG (*Ger.*) *Tempo rubáto*.

TON-WEITE (*Ger.*) The compass of a voice, or instrument.

TON-WERK (*Ger.*) A musical composition.

Ton-wissenschaft — Tracktür

TON-WISSENSCHAFT (*Ger.*) The science of music.

TON-ZEICHEN (*Ger.*) Accent: note, or musical character.

TÖNEN (*Ger.*) To tune, to sound: sounding, tuning.

TOOMOURAH. An Hindoo tambourine.

TOOROOREE. A Brahmin trumpet.

TOPH. A small Hebrew drum or timbrel.

TOQUET (*Fr.*) See TOCCATO.

TORCÉLLO (*It.*) The old name for an organ.

TORNÁNDO (*It.*) Returning.

TÓRVO (*It.*) Stern, grim, dogged.

TOSTAMÉNTE (*It.*) Quickly, rapidly.

TOSTÍSSIMAMÉNTE | (*It.*) Extremely quick, very promptly; with
TOSTÍSSIMO | great rapidity.

TÓSTO (*It.*) Quick, swift, rapid: *see also* PIÙ TÓSTO.

TOUCHE (*Fr.*) The *touch*: also, a key of the pianoforte, &c.

TOUCHES (*Fr. pl.*) The keys of a pianoforte, &c.

TOUCHETTE (*Fr.*) A fret.

TOUJOURS (*Fr.*) Always; *see* SÉMPRE.

TOURS DE FORCE (*Fr.*) *Bravúra* passages, roulades, divisions, &c.

TOUQUET (*Fr.*) See TOCCATO.

TRABATTÉRE (*It.*) To beat; to strike.

TRACHEA (*Lat.*) The wind-pipe.

TRACKERS. Part of the mechanism of an organ, used to convey the movement of the keys, to the sound-boards, thus making the pipes speak.

TRACTUS (*Lat.*) A species of anthem, in the Roman Catholic service.

TRADÓLCE (*It.*) Very sweet.

TRADÓTTO (*It.*) | Translated, arranged, adapted, fitted to.
TRADUIT (*Fr.*) |

TRADUZIÓNE (*It.*) An arrangement.

TRAGEN DER STIMME (*Ger.*) To carry the voice; *see* PORTE DE VOIX.

TRAGORGEL (*Ger.*) A portable organ.

TRAÎNÉ (*Fr.*) Slurred, bound: lingering, drawn along.

TRAIT (*Fr.*) Passage, run; a phrase.

TRAIT DE CHANT (*Fr.*) A melodic passage, or phrase.

TRAIT D'HARMONIE (*Fr.*) Succession of chords, a sequence.

TRAIT D'OCTAVE (*Fr.*) See RULE OF THE OCTAVE.

TRAITÉ (*Fr.*) A treatise on the practice, or the theory, of music.

TRACKTÜR (*Ger.*) The mechanism which connects the keys, of an organ, to the pallets: *see* TRACKERS.

TRÄLLERN (*Ger.*) To trill, to hum a tune.
TRANQUILLAMÉNTE (*It.*) Quietly, calmly, tranquilly.
TRANQUILLÉZZA
TRANQUILLITÀ | (*It.*) Tranquillity, calmness, quietness.
TRANQUÍLLO
TRANSCRIT (*Fr.*) Copied, transcribed.
TRANSIENT MODULATION. That modulation which is of very short duration; quitting the new key almost as soon as it is entered upon.
TRANSITIO (*Lat.*) | Passing suddenly out of one key into another, without preparation for, or hinting at, the new key; or without making use of chords common to both keys.
TRANSITION (*Eng.*) |
TRANSITUS (*Lat.*) A passing note.
TRANSITUS IRREGULARIS (*Lat.*) Irregular passing notes: *see* CHANGING NOTES.
TRANSITUS REGULARIS (*Lat.*) Passing notes placed on the *unaccented* parts of the bar.
TRANSPOSED. Removed, or changed, into another key.
TRANSPONIREN (*Ger.*) | To transpose a piece into another key.
TRANSPOSER (*Fr.*) |
TRANSPOSITEUR (*Fr.*) One who transposes; also, a transposing keyboard; also, a mechanism on a trumpet or horn, used to remove the need for *crooks*.
TRANSPOSITION. Change of key; removing a piece into another key.
TRAQUENARD (*Fr.*) A brisk sort of dance.
TRASCINÁNDO (*It.*) Dragging the time.
TRASCRÍTTO (*It.*) Copied, transcribed.
TRANSCRIZIÓNE (*It.*) A transcription.
TRANSPORTÁTO
TRANSPÓSTO | (*It.*) Transposed.
TRATTÁTO (*It.*) *See* TRAITÉ.
TRATTENÚTO (*It.*)
TRÁTTO (*It.*) Dragged, retarded.
TRAUER-GESANG (*Ger.*) Mourning song, dirge.
TRAUER-MARSCH (*Ger.*) Funeral march.
TRAUER-MUSIK (*Ger.*) Funeral music.
TRAURIG (*Ger.*) Heavily, sadly, mournfully, pensively.
TRAUM (*Ger.*) A dream, fancy, vision.
TRAUMEND (*Ger.*) Dreaming.
TRÄMERIE (*Ger.*) Dreaming; day dream; reverie.
TRÄMERISCH (*Ger.*) Dreamy.

Travailler — Très-vif

TRAVAILLER (*Fr.*) To work; to work hard.

TRAVERSFLÖTE (*Ger.*) A transverse flute; also, an organ flute stop of 4 feet pitch.

TRAVERSIÈRE (*Fr.*)
TRAVÉRSO (*It.*) Cross, across: applied to the transverse, or German flute, to distinguish it from the *flûte à bec*.

TRAVESTIE (*Ger.*) A travesty; a parody.

TRE (*It.*) Three: *à tre*, for three voices or instruments.

TREBLE. The upper part, the highest voice, the soprano, that which generally contains the melody.

TRE CÓRDE (*It.*) *Three strings*: in pianoforte music this means that the pedal which moves the keys or action, must no longer be pressed down.

TREDEZIME (*Ger.*) An interval of a thirteenth.

TREFFÜBUNG (*Ger.*) An exercise for *attack* or *entry*.

TREIBEND (*Ger.*) Hastening; *accelerándo*.

TREIZIÈME (*Fr.*) An interval of a thirteenth.

TREMÁNDO
TREMÁNTE (*It.*) See TREMOLÁNDO.

TREMBLANT (*Fr.*) Shaking: see TREMULANT.

TREMBLEMENT (*Fr.*) A trill; also a tremolo.

TREMÉNDO (*It.*) Terrible, dreadful.

TREMOLÁNDO
TREMOLÁTE
TRÉMOLO
TRÉMULO (*It.*) *Trembling, quivering*; a note, or chord, reiterated with great rapidity, producing a tremulous kind of effect.

TREMOLANT
TREMULANT An organ stop which gives to the tone a sorrowful, waving, trembling, or undulating effect, resembling the *vibráto* in singing, and the *tremolándo* in violin playing: also, an harmonium stop of the same kind.

TREMÓRE
TREMORÓSO (*It.*) Tremor, trembling: see also TREMOLÁNDO.

TRENCHMORE. An old dance, supposed to have been of a lively species.

TRENISE (*Fr.*) One of the movements in a quadrille.

TRENÓDIA (*It.*) See THRENODIE.

TRÈS (*Fr.*) Very, most.

TRÈS-ANIMÉ (*Fr.*) Very animated, very lively.

TRÉSCA (*It.*) A country dance.

TRESCÓNE (*It.*) A species of dance.

TRÈS-VIF (*Fr.*) Very, lively, very brisk.

TRETER (*Ger.*) *Treader*, of the bellows, in German organs.

TRIAD. A chord of three consonant notes, a common chord.

TRIAL (*Fr.*) A comic tenor; *tenóre búffo*.

TRIANGLE. A small three-sided steel frame, which is struck during a dance, or march, in imitation of the tone of a little bell.

TRIAS DEFICIENS (*Lat.*) The imperfect chord, or triad.

TRIAS HARMONICA (*Lat.*) *See* TRIAD.

TRIBRACH (*Lat.*) A trisyllabic musical foot, comprising three short notes, or syllables, ⌣⌣⌣.

TRICHORDON (*Lat.*) A *colachon* with three strings.

TRICHTER (*Ger.*) The tube or resonator of a reed pipe, on an organ; also, the bell of a brass instrument.

TRICÓRDE (*It.*) With three strings.

TRICINIUM (*Lat.*) A composition in three parts.

TRIGESIMA-PRIMA (*Lat.*) Thirty-first.

TRIGESIMA-SEXTA (*Lat.*) Thirty-sixth.

TRIGESIMA-TERTIA (*Lat.*) Thirty-third.

TRIGON / **TRIGONUM** An instrument of the lyre species, with three strings.

TRILLÁNDO (*It.*) A succession or chain of shakes, on different notes.

TRILLÁRE (*It.*) To shake, to trill.

TRILLE (*Fr.*) / **TRILLER** (*Ger.*) / **TRÍLLO** (*It.*) A shake, a trill.

TRILLER-KETTE (*Ger.*) A chain, or succession, of shakes.

TRILLERN (*Ger.*) To trill, to shake.

TRILLETTE (*Fr.*) / **TRILLÉTTO** (*It.*) A short trill, or shake.

TRILLETTÍNO (*It.*) A soft shake, a soft trilling.

TRÍLLO CAPRÍNO (*It.*) A false shake.

TRINK-GESANG / **TRINK-LIED** (*Ger.*) A Bacchanalian, or drinking song.

TRINONA. An organ stop, of open 8 feet tone, and pleasant gamba-like tone.

TRÍO (*It.*) A piece for three instruments in England the word is also applied to a piece for three voices, but incorrectly, *terzétto* being the proper appellation. A *trío* is also the second movement to a *menuétto*, march, waltz, &c., and is said to have been formerly played by three instruments only, two hautboys and a bassoon: the *trío* first appeared in the very early overtures, and afterwards in the symphony, and joined with the minuet: aster the *trío* the first, or principal movement, must always be played again.

TRIOLE (*Ger.*) \
TRIOLET (*Fr.*) A triplet, a group of three notes, to be played in the time of two.

TRIOMPHALE (*Fr.*) Triumphal.

TRIOMPHANT (*Fr.*) Triumphant.

TRIONFÁLE (*It.*) Triumphal.

TRIONFÁNTE (*It.*) Triumphant.

TRIPEL (*Ger.*) Triple.

TRIPEL-TAKT (*Ger.*) Triple time.

TRIPEL-ZUNGE (*Ger.*) Tipple tonguing.

TRIPHONY. Three sounds heard together.

TRÍPLA (*It.*) A triplet; also, triple time.

TRIPLE COUNTERPOINT. Counterpoint in three parts, invertible; that is, so contrived that each part will serve indifferently for either bass, middle, or upper part.

TRIPLE CROCHE (*Fr.*) A triple, or three-hooked note; a demisemiquaver.

TRIPLET. A group of three notes, played in the usual time of two similar ones.

TRIPLE TIMES. Such as have an *odd*, or *uneven* number of parts in a bar, as *three*, *nine*, &c.

TRIPLUM (*Lat.*) In mediæval music a *third* part added to the *cánto férmo*.

TRÍPOLA (*It.*) A triplet; also, triple time.

TRISAGION (*Gr.*) A hymn in which the word *Holy* is repeated three times in succession.

TRISEMITONIUM (*Lat.*) The lesser, or minor, third.

TRISTESSE (*Fr.*) Sadness, melancholy.

TRISTÉZZA (*It.*) Sadness, heaviness, pensiveness.

TRÍSTO (*It.*) Sad, melancholy; affliction.

TRITON (*Fr.*) \
TRITONE (*Eng.*) A superfluous, or augmented, fourth, containing three whole tones.

TRITONIKON (*Gr.*) A double-bassoon made of metal.

TRITÓNO (*It.*) \
TRITONUS (*Lat.*) *See* TRITON.

TRITT (*Ger.*) Step, tread, treadle.

TRITT-BRETT \
TRITT-HOLZ (*Ger.*) The board upon which the bellow-treader steps, in blowing an organ.

TRIYUS (*Lat.*) The Lydian, or third authentic mode.

TRIUMPH-LIED (*Ger.*) Triumphal song.

Triumph — Trommler

TRIUMPH-MARSCH (*Ger.*) Triumphal march.

TROCHERE (*Lat.*) A dissyllabic musical foot, containing one long and one short syllable, —‿.

TROIS (*Fr.*) Three.

TRÓMBA (*It.*) A trumpet: also, an 8 feet reed stop in an organ, of smooth tone.

TRÓMBA A CHIÁVI (*It.*) A keyed trumpet, or bugle.

TRÓMBA A PISTÓNI (*It.*) A trumpet with pistons.

TRÓMBA CROMÁTICA (*It.*) The modern valve trumpet, upon which semitone can be produced.

TRÓMBA DI BÁSSO (*It.*) The bass trumpet.

TROMBADÓRE (*It.*) A trumpeter.

TRÓMBA MARÍNA (*It.*) See TRUMPET MARINE.

TRÓMBA REÁLE (*It.*) Royal trumpet: an organ stop of 8 feet pitch

TRÓMBA SPEZZÁTA (*It.*) An obsolete name for the bass trombone.

TROMVATÓRE (*It.*) A trumpeter.

TRÓMBA VENTILE (*It.*) See TRÓMBA CROMÁTICA.

TROMBÉTTA (*It.*) A small trumpet; also, a trumpeter.

TROMBETTATÓRE | (*It.*) A trumpeter.
TROMBETTÍNO |

TROMBÓNE (*It. & Fr.*) A very powerful, rough-toned instrument, of the trumpet species, but much larger, and with a sliding tube: also, a very powerful, and full-toned reed stop in an organ, of 8 feet tone on the manual, and 16, or 32 feet on the pedal.

TROMBÓNE A CILÍNDRI (*It.*) A trombone with cylinders.

TROMBONE À COULISSE (*Fr.*) A slide trombone.

TROMBONE À PISTONS (*Fr.*) A trombone with pistons.

TROMBÓNE A TÍRO | (*It.*) A slide trombone.
TROMBÓNE DUTTILE |

TROMBÓNI (*It. pl.*) Trombones.

TROMMEL (*Ger.*) The military drum.

TROMMEL-KLÖPFEL (*Ger.*) Drumstick.

TROMMELN (*Ger.*) To drum; drumming, beating the drum.

TROMMEL-RUF (*Ger.*) A drum-call.

TROMMEL-SAITEN (*Ger.*) The *snare* of a side-drum.

TROMMEL-SCHLÄGEL (*Ger.*) Drumstick.

TROMMEL-SCHLÄGER (*Ger.*) Drummer.

TROMMEL-STÖCKE (*Ger. pl.*) Drumsticks

TROMMEL-STÜCK (*Ger.*) A tambourine, or tabor.

TROMMEL-WIRBEL (*Ger.*) A roll on a drum.

TROMMLER (*Ger.*) A drummer.

Trompa — Trug

TROMPA / **TROMPE** (*Fr.*) A trumpet: also, a hunting horn.

TROMPE À LAQUAIS / **TROMPE DE BÉARN** (*Fr.*) The Jew's harp.

TROMPE DE CHASSE (*Fr.*) A hunting horn.

TROMPE DES APLES (*Fr.*) An ancient Alpine horn made with the hollowed trunk of a tree.

TROMPETE (*Ger.*) A trumpet: also, a reed stop in an organ.

TROMPETEN-BÄSER (*Ger.*) A trumpeter.

TROMPETEN-GEIGE (*Ger.*) A *trómba marina*.

TROMPETEN-REGISTER / **TROMPETEN-ZUG** (*Ger.*) Trumpet stop or register, in an organ.

TROMPETEN-SCHALL (*Ger.*) Sound of the trumpet.

TROMPETEN-TUSCH (*Ger.*) A fanfare; a trumpet flourish.

TROMPETER (*Ger.*) A trumpeter.

TROMPETER-STÜCKCHEN (*Ger.*) Flourish of a trumpet, short piece of music played on the trumpet.

TROMPETTE (*Fr.*) A trumpet: also, a reed stop in an organ: also, a trumpeter.

TROMPETTE À CLEFS (*Fr.*) The keyed trumpet.

TROMPETTE À COULISSE (*Fr.*) A slide trumpet.

TROMPETTE À PISTONS (*Fr.*) The valve trumpet.

TROMPETTE D'HARMONIE (*Fr.*) An orchestral trumpet.

TROMPETTE HARMONIQUE (*Fr.*) Harmonic trumpet, a reed stop in an organ, of 8 or 16 feet: *see* **HARMONIC FLUTE**.

TROMPETTE MARINE (*Fr.*) See **TRUMPET MARINE**.

TRÓNCO (*It.*) Truncated; cut off.

TROOP. A quick march, a march in quick time.

TRÓPPO (*It.*) Too much: *non tróppo allégro*, not too quick.

TRÓPPO CARICÁTA (*It.*) Too much loaded, or *overburdened*: as, a melody with too much, or too heavy, an accompaniment, &c.

TROUBABOURS (*Fr. pl.*) The bards, and poet-musicians, of Provence, about the tenth century.

TROUBLÉ (*Fr.*) Troubled, grieved.

TROUPE (*Fr.*) A company of musicians, players, &c.

TROUVÈRES / **TROUVEURS** See **TROUBABOURS**.

TRÜB (*Ger.*) Gloomy, sad, melancholy.

TRUG-KADENZ / **TRUG-SCILUSS** / **TRUG-SCHLÜSSE** (*Ger.*) Interrupted, or deceptive, cadence: an unexpected, or interrupted resolution of a discord.

TRUMBSCHEIT (*Ger.*) See TRÓMBA MARINA.

TRUMMEL (*Ger.*) See TROMMEL.

TRUMM-SCHEIT (*Ger.*) A rude musical instrument. With one or more strings, played with a bow, and imitating the sound of a trumpet.

TRUMPET. A well-known brass wind-instrument: also, an 8 feet reed stop in an organ, both on the manuals and pedals; the tone is clear and penetrating, somewhat resembling that of a trumpet.

TRUMPET MARINE. An ancient species of monochord, played with a bow, and producing a sound resembling that of a trumpet.

TSCHÜNG (*Ger.*) A Chinese gong.

TUBA (*Lat.*) A trumpet: also, the name of a powerful reed stop in an organ: see OPHICLEIDE.

TUBA CLARION (*Lat.*) A 4 feet reed stop of the *tuba* species: see TUBA.

TUBA CURVA (*Lat.*) An old form of trumpet.

TUBA MAJOR
TUBA MIRABILIS (*Lat.*) An 8 feet reed stop, on a high pressure of wind, first introduced into the Birmingham Town Hall organ, and invented by William Hill: see OPHICLEIDE.

TUBASSON (*Fr.*) An organ pedal trombone stop.

TUBICEN (*Lat.*) A trumpet player.

TUBALFLÖTE (*Ger.*) See JUBALFLÖTE.

TUCKET (*Old Eng.*) A trumpet flourish.

TUIAU D'ORGUE (*Fr.*) See TUYAU D'ORGUE.

TUMULTUÓSO (*It.*) Tumultuous, agitated.

TUÓNI (*It.*) Tones, sounds, modes.

TUÓNI ECCLESIÁSTICI (*It. pl.*) See CHURCH MODES.

TUÓNO (*It.*) A tone, a sound: a tune; also, thunder.

TUÓNO MÉZZO (*It.*) A semitone.

TUORBE (*Fr.*) See THEORBO.

TURBINOSAMÉNTE
TURBINÓSO (*It.*) In a furious, stormy manner.

TÚRCA
TURCHÉSCO (*It.*) Turkish: *álla Túrca*, in the style of Turkish music: which see.
TÚRCO

TÜRKISCH (*Ger.*) See TÚRCA.

TURKISH MUSIC. See JANITSCHAREN-MUSIK.

TURLURETTE (*Fr.*) A species of guitar.

TURN. A group of notes consisting of the *principal* note, the note *above*, and the note *below* it.

TURR. A three stringed Burmese violin.

TUSCH (*Ger.*) A flourish; a triple flourish on trumpets and drums.

Tute — Tziti

Tute (*Ger.*) A cornet.

Tuthorn (*Ger.*) A cowherd's horn.

Tútta (*It.*) All, the whole: entirely, quite: *tútta árco*, with the whole length of the bow.

Tútta Pórza | (*It.*) The whole power as loud as possible with
Tútta la Fórza | the utmost force and vehemence.

Tútte (*It. pl.*) All, the entire band or chorus: in a solo or concerto it means, that the full orchestra is to come in.

Tútte córde (*It. pl.*) *All the strings*: in pianoforte music this means that the pedal which shifts the action or movement, must no longer be press down.

Tútti (*It. pl.*) See Tútte.

Tútti unísoni (*It. pl.*) All in unison.

Tútto (*It.*) See Tútta.

Tuyau à anche (*Fr.*) An organ reed-pipe.

Tuyau d'orgue (*Fr.*) An organ pipe.

Tuyan bouche (*Fr.*) A closed or stopped organ pipe.

Tuyau ouvert (*Fr.*) An open organ pipe.

Twelfth. An interval of twelve diatonic degrees: also, an organ stop tuned twelve notes above the diapasons.

Twenty-second. See Octave-fifteenth.

Twice marked octave. The name given, in Germany, to the notes between [musical notation] inclusive; these are expressed by small letters with two short strokes, thus, $\overline{\overline{c}}$ or c^2.

Tymbal. A species of kettle-drum.

Tymbale. See Timbale.

Tymbres. Little bells used to hang upon royal ermine robes: *see* Scilla.

Tympan. A timbrel, or drum.

Týmpani. See Tímpani.

Tympanísta. See Timpanísta.

Týmpano. See Tímpano.

Tympanon (*Fr.*) A dulcimer; also, a kettle-drum.

Tympanum (*Lat.*) Timbrel, tabor: old name for the drum.

Tyrolienne (*Fr.*) Songs, or dances, peculiar to the Tyrolese.

Tzetse. An Abyssinian guitar.

Tziti. An Hindoo bagpipe.

U

ÜBEL (*Ger.*) Bad.

ÜBEL-KLANG / ÜBEL-LAUT (*Ger.*) Cacophony, dissonance: a discord.

ÜBEN (*Ger.*) To practice.

ÜBER (*Ger.*) Over, above.

ÜBERBLASEN (*Ger.*) To blow a horn; also, to over-blow a wind instrument.

ÜBEREILT (*Ger.*) Over-hurried, precipitate.

ÜBEREINSTIMMUNG (*Ger.*) Consonance, harmony, accordance.

ÜBERGANG (*Ger.*) Transition, change of key; passing from one key to another.

ÜBERGEFÜHRTE STIMMEN (*Ger.*) Divided organ stops.

ÜBERGEHEND (*Ger.*) Proceeding to.

ÜBERGREIFEN (*Ger.*) To cross hands in pianoforte or organ playing; also, to lift the thumb from the neck, in violoncello playing.

ÜBERLAUT (*Ger.*) *Over loud*: too loud, noisy.

ÜBERMÄSSIG (*Ger.*) Augmented, superfluous.

ÜBERMÜTHIG (*Ger.*) Over merry; in wild spirits.

ÜBERSETZUNG (*Ger.*) A translation.

ÜBERSTÜRST (*Ger.*) Hurried.

ÜBUNG (*Ger.*) An exercise; a study for the practice of some peculiar difficulty.

ÜBUNGEN (*Ger. pl.*) Exercises: *see* ÜBUNG.

ÜBUNGSABEND (*Ger.*) A pupil's concert.

ÜBUNGSSTÜCK (*Ger.*) A practice piece; a study.

UDÍTA / UDÍTO (*It.*) Heard: the sense of hearing.

UDITÓRE (*It.*) An auditor, listener, hearer.

UGUÁLE (*It.*) Equal, like, similar.

UGUÁGLIANZA / UGUALITÀ Equality, evenness, uniformity.

UGUALMÉNRE (*It.*) Equally, alike.

ÚLTIMO (*It.*) The last.

UMÁNA / UMÁNO (*It.*) Human: *vóce umána*, the human voice.

Umfang — Unequal

UMFANG (*Ger.*) Compass, extent.

UMFANG DER STIMME (*Ger.*) Compass of the voice.

UMHEIMLICH (*Ger.*) Strange, uneasy, gloomy, sinister.

UMKEHRUNG (*Ger.*) Inversion.

UMÓRE (*It.*) Humour.

UMSCHLAGEN (*Ger.*) To break, to crack the voice; also, to over-blow a wind instrument.

UMSETZEN (*Ger.*) To compose.

UMSTELLEN (*Ger.*) To invert.

UMSTELLUNG (*Ger.*) Inversion.

UMSTIMMUNG (*Ger.*) A special tuning of a stringed instrument; *see also*, MÚTA.

UN (*It.*) A, an, one: *úna córda*, one string, on one string only: in
ÚNA pianoforte music it means that the soft pedal is to be used.

ÚNA VÓLTA (*It.*) Once.

UNBEDECKT (*Ger.*) Uncovered, open organ pipes.

UNBEZOGEN (*Ger.*) Unstrung, not furnished with strings.

UNCA (*Lat.*) The old name for a quaver.

UND (*Ger.*) And: *Arie und Chor*, air and chorus.

UNDA MARIS (*Lat.*) *Wave of the sea*: an organ stop tuned rather sharper than the others, and producing an undulating or waving effect, when drawn in conjunction with another stop: this oscillation effect is sometimes produced by means of a pipe with two mouths, the one a little higher than the other.

UNDECIMA (*Lat.*) The eleventh.

UNDECIMÓLE (*It.*) A group of eleven notes, played in the time of eight.

UNDECUPLET. See UNDECIMÓLE.

UNDER SONG. In very old English music this was a kind of ground, or drone accompaniment to a song, and which was sustained by another singer: called also *burden* and *foot*.

UNDEZIME (*Ger.*) An eleventh.

UNDULAZIÓNE (*It.*) Undulation, the expressive, tremulous tone produced by a peculiar pressure of the finger upon the strings of the violin.

UNEIGENTLICHE FUGA (*Ger.*) An irregular fugue.

UNENDLICH (*Ger.*) Infinite.

UNEQUAL TEMPERAMENT. That method of tuning the twelve sounds included in an octave, which renders some of the scales more in tune than the others: *see* EQUAL TEMPERAMENT.

UNEQUAL VOICES. Male and female voices both employed in the same piece: *see* EQUAL VOICES.

UNESSENTIAL NOTES. Those which do not form an essential part of the harmony: passing, auxiliary, or ornamental notes.

UNGAR
UNGARISCH (*Ger.*) Hungarian; in the Hungarian style.

UNGEBUNDEN (*Ger.*) Unconstrained; also, not tied or syncopated; also, in a free style.

UNGEDULDIG (*Ger.*) Impatient.

UNGEFÄUR (*Ger.*) About; approximately.

UNGERADE TAKT-ART (*Ger.*) Triple time, uneven time.

UNGESTÜM (*Ger.*) Impetuous, boisterous, wild.

UNGEZWUNGEN (*Ger.*) Easy, natural.

UNGLEICH (*Ger.*) Unlike; unequal.

UNHARMONISCH (*Ger.*) Inharmonious.

UNHARMONISCHER QUERSTAND
UNHARMONISCHER UMSTAND (*Ger.*) A false relation.

UNI (*Fr.*) United.

UNIÓNE (*It.*) A coupler on an organ.

UNISON. One sound, a single unvaried sound, a string that has the same sound with another.

UNISONANT. In unison, of the same pitch.

UNÍSONI (*It. pl.*) Unisons: two, three, or more parts are to play, or sing, in unison with each other; or, if this be not possible, they must play in octaves.

UNÍSONO (*It.*)
UNISONOUS (*Eng.*) A unison, in unison, two or more sounds having the same pitch.
UNISONUS (*Lat.*)

UNITAMÉNTE (*It.*) Together, jointly, unitedly.

UNÍTO (*It.*) United.

UNÍVOCO (*It.*) Consisting of *one* voice or sound.

UNMERKLICH (*Ger.*) By almost imperceptible degrees.

UNMERKLICH BELEBEND (*Ger.*) Increasing the speed very gradually.

ÚNO (*It.*) See **ÚNA**.

ÚNO À ÚNO (*It.*) One by one, one after another.

UN PEU ÉLARGI (*Fr.*) A little broadened.

UN PEU EN DEHORS (*Fr.*) Rather prominent.

UN PEU LARGEMENT (*Fr.*) Rather broadly.

UN PEU PLUS LENT (*Fr.*) A little more slowly.

UN PEU PLUS VITE (*Fr.*) A little more quickly.

UN POCHETTÍNO
UN POCHÍNA (*It.*) A little, a very little.

UN POCHÍNO PIÙ MÓSSO (*It.*) A very little more lively.

UN PÓCO (*It.*) A little.

UN PÓCO ALLÉGRO (*It.*) A little quick, rather quick.

UN PÓCO PIÙ (*It.*) A little more.

UN PÓCO RITENÚTO (*It.*) A little slower: *see* **RITENÚTO**.

UNREIN (*Ger.*) Imperfect; out of tune, false.

UNRUHIG (*Ger.*) Restless.

UNSCHULDIG (*Ger.*) Innocent.

UNSINGBAR (*Ger.*) Unmelodious.

UN STYLE AISÉ (*Fr.*) A free, easy style.

UNTER (*Ger.*) Under, beneath, below.

UNTER-BASS (*Ger.*) The double bass.

UNTER-BROCHEN (*Ger.*) Interrupted.

UNTERHALTUNGS-STÜCK (*Ger.*) Entertainment, a short play, a short piece of music.

UNTERRICHT (*Ger.*) Instruction, information.

UNTERSATZ (*Ger.*) Supporter, stay: a pedal register, double stopped bass of 32 feet tone, in German organs: *see* **SUB-BOURDON**.

UNTERSCHLAG (*Ger.*) A backfall.

UNTERSETZEN (*Ger.*) To pass the thumb under a finger, or one foot under the other

UNTERTASTE (*Ger.*) A white key.

UNTERWERK (*Ger.*) The lowest manual of an organ.

UNVERSIERT (*Ger.*) Unadorned, unembellished.

UNVOLLKOMMEN (*Ger.*) Imperfect, incomplete.

UÓMO (*It.*) Man.

URH-HEEN. A species of Chinese fiddle.

URSPRÜNGLICH (*Ger.*) First; original.

ÚSCIR DI TUÓNO (*It.*) To get out of tune.

USUS (*Lat.*) The rules of music.

UT. The note C: the syllable originally applied by Guido to the note C, or *do*.

UT BÉMOL (*Fr.*) The note C-flat.

UT DIÈSE (*Fr.*) The note C-sharp.

UT QUEANT LAXIS (*Lat.*) The commencing words of the hymn to St. John the Baptist, from which Guido is said to have taken the syllables, *ut, re, mi, fa, sol, la*, for his system of solmisation.

UT SUPRA (*Lat.*) As above, as before: *see* **CÓME SÓPRA**.

UTRICULARIÆ. *See* Tibia.

V

VÀ (*It.*) Go on: *và crescéndo*, go on increasing the tone.

VACETO (*It.*) Quick: (seldom used).

VACCILÁNDO (*It.*)
VACILLANT (*Fr.*) Wavering, uncertain, irregular in the time.
VACILLÁNTE (*It.*)

VAGANS (*Lat.*) Wandering.

VAGHÉZZA (*It.*) Grace, beauty, charm.

VÁGO (*It.*) Vague, rambling, uncertain, as to the time, or expression.

VÁLCE (*It.*)
VALSE (*Fr.*) A waltz, a dance, in ¾ time.

VALEUR (*Fr.*)
VALÓRE (*It.*) The value, length, or duration, of a note.

VALSE À DEUX TEMPS (*Fr.*) A modern waltz, in which the dancers make two steps in each measure.

VALSE CHANTÉE (*Fr.*) A waltz songs.

VALSE DE L'OISEAU (*Fr.*) A waltz in imitation of the warbling of a bird.

VAPOREUX (*Fr.*) Light, delicate.

VÀ RALLENTÁNDO (*It.*) Go on dragging the time, continue to drag the time.

VARIAMÉNTE (*It.*) In a varied, free style of performance, or
VARIAMÉNTO execution.

VARIANTE (*It. & Fr.*) A variant.

VARIATIONEN (*Ger. pl.*) A piece presented, as it were, in a new
VARIATIONS (*Eng.*) and varied aspect, and not as a different
VARIAZIÓNE (*It. pl.*) piece; the form, or outline, of the composition being preserved, but the parts, or sentences, more or less altered.

VARIÁTO (*It.*)
VARIÉ (*Fr.*) Varied, diversified, with variations.

VARIEREN (*Ger.*) To vary.

VARSOVIÁNA (*It.*) *Warsaw dance*: a dance in ¾ time, with the
VARSOVIENNE (*Fr.*) down beat of every second measure strongly accented.

VATERLÄNDISCHES LIED (*Ger.*) A patriotic song.

Vaudeville — Vergnügt

VAUDEVILLE (*Fr.*) A country ballad or song, a roundelay: also, a simple form of *operétta*: a comedy, or short drama, interspersed with songs.

VAUT (*Fr.*) Is equal to.

VEEMÉNTE (*It.*) Vehement, forcible.

VEEMÉNZA (*It.*) Vehemence, force.

VELÁTA | (*It.*) *Veiled*: a voice sounding as if it were covered with a veil.
VELÁTO |

VELLUTÁTA | (*It.*) In a velvety manner; in a soft, smooth, and velvety style.
VELLUTÁTO |

VELÓCE | (*It.*) Swiftly, quickly, in a rigid time.
VELOCEMÉNTE |

VELOCISSIMAMÉNTE | (*It.*) Very swiftly, with extreme rapidity.
VELOCÍSSIMO |

VELOCITÀ (*It.*) Swiftness, rapidity.

VELOUTÉ (*Fr.*) Smooth, velvety.

VENEZIÁNA (*It.*) Venetian, the Venetian style.

VENTAGES. Holes in wind instruments, which are covered by the fingers of keys.

VENTIL (*Ger.*) | Valve, in modern wind-instruments, for producing the semitones: also, a valve for shutting off the wind, in an organ.
VENTÍLE (*It.*) |

VENTILHORN (*Ger.*) A valve horn.

VENTILKORNETT (*Ger.*) A *cornet à pistons*.

VENTILPOSAUNE (*Ger.*) A valve trombone.

VENÚSTO (*It.*) Beautiful: sweetly, gracefully.

VÊPRES (*Fr.*) Vespers; evening prayers.

VERÄNDERUNGEN (*Ger. pl.*) Variations.

VERBINDUNG (*Ger.*) Combination, union, conjunction, connexion.

VERBINDUNGSAKKORD (*Ger.*) A connecting chord.

VERBINDUNGSZEICHEN (*Ger.*) A tie; a slur.

VERDECKT (*Ger.*) *Decked*; covered, concealed.

VERDOPPELT (*Ger.*) Doubled.

VERDOPPELUNG (*Ger.*) Doubling.

VEREIN (*Ger.*) Society, association.

VERENGUNG (*Ger.*) Diminution of a time-value or interval.

VERGELLEN (*Ger.*) To diminish gradually.

VERGÉTTE | (*It.*) The stem, or tail of a note.
VERGHÉTTA |

VERGLIEDERN (*Ger.*) To articulate.

VERGNÜGT (*Ger.*) Cheerful; pleasant.

VERGRÖSSERUNG (*Ger.*) Augmentation of a fugue subject &c.
VERHALLEND (*Ger.*) Dying away, sounding away.
VERHÄLTNISS (*Ger.*) Ratio, proportion of intervals &c.
VERILAY. Rustic ballad, a roundelay: *see* VAUDEVILLE, *and also* FREEMEN'S SONGS.
VERÍSMO (*It.*) Truth; naturalism.
VERISTISCH (*Ger.*) Naturalistic.
VERKEHRUNG (*Ger.*) Inverse imitation.
VERKLEINERUNG (*Ger.*) Diminution of a theme.
VERKLINGEND (*Ger.*) Dying away.
VERKÜRZUNG (*Ger.*) Drawing closer together; *strétto*.
VERLÄNGERUNGS-ZEICHEN (*Ger.*) The dot of prolongation, placed after a note.
VERLAUF (*Ger.*) Progress.
VERLIEBT (*Ger.*) Loving, tender.
VERLIEREND (*Ger.*) Dying away.
VERLÖSCHEND (*Ger.*) Dying away; extinguishing.
VERMINDERT (*Ger.*) Diminished; diminished interval.
VERMITTELUNGSSATZ (*Ger.*) A *middle piece*; an episode.
VERNEHMLICH (*Ger.*) Clear, distinct.
VERS (*Ger.*) Verse, strophe, stanza.
VERSCHALLEN (*Ger.*) To cease to sound; to die away.
VERSCHIEBUNG (*Ger.*) Delay: *mit Verschiebung*, with delay, lingering, retardation.
VERSCHIEDEN (*Ger.*) Various, several.
VERSCHMELZEN (*Ger.*) To blend.
VERSCHWINDEND (*Ger.*) Vanishing; dying away.
VERSE. That portion of an anthem, or service, intended to be sung by one singer to each part, and not by the full choir in chorus.
VERSE ANTHEM. An anthem which contains a solo, duet, &c., or one or more *verses*: *see* VERSE, *and* FULL ANTHEM.
VERSET (*Fr.*) | Short pieces for the organ, intended as preludes,
VERSETTE (*Ger.*) | interludes, or postludes.
VERSÉTTO (*It.*) A short, or little verse: a strophe.
VERSETZEN (*Ger.*) To transpose.
VERSETZUNG (*Ger.*) Transposition.
VERSETZUNGS-ZEICHEN (*Ger.*) The marks of transposing, the *sharp*, the *flat*, and the *natural*.
VERSIKEL (*Ger.*) A versicle.
VERSILÁRE (*It.*) To sing antiphonally.
VÉRSO ERÓICO (*It.*) Heroic verse.

Vérso — Vibrazióne

VÉRSO SCIÓLTO (*It.*) Blank verse.
VERSPÄTUNG (*Ger.*) Retardation, delay.
VERSTÄRKEN (*Ger.*) To reinforce; *rinforzándo*.
VERSTÄRKT (*Ger.*) *Sforzándo*.
VERTIMMEN (*Ger.*) To put out of tune.
VERSTIMMT (*Ger.*) Out of tune.
VERTATUR
VERTE (*Lat.*) Turn over.
VERTHEILT (*Ger.*) Divided, distributed.
VERTONEN (*Ger.*) To compose.
VERTÖNEN (*Ger.*) To die away.
VERTRÄUMT (*Ger.*) Dreamy.
VERVE (*Fr.*) Spirit, energy, animation.
VERWANDT (*Ger.*) Related, relative keys, &c.
VERWANDTSCHAFT (*Ger.*) Relationship; affinity.
VERWECHSELUNG (*Ger.*) Changing, mutation, as to key, tone, &c.
VERWEILEND (*Ger.*) Delaying, retarding the time.
VERWERFUNG (*Ger.*) Transposing.
VERZIERENDE VORSCHLAG (*Ger.*) An ornamental *appoggiatúra*.
VERZIERT (*Ger.*) Embellished, decorated.
VERZIERUNG (*Ger.*) Embellishment, ornament.
VERZIERUNGEN (*Ger. pl.*) Embellishments.
VERZIERUNGSNOTE (*Ger.*) A grace-note.
VERZÖGERUNG (*Ger.*) Retardation.
VERZWEIFELT (*Ger.*) Despairing, broken-hearted, despondent, desperate.
VESPER (*Ger.*)
VESPERÆ (*Lat.*)
VÉSPERO (*It.*) The evening service in the Roman Catholic Church.
VESPERS (*Eng.*)
VÉSPRO (*It.*)
VEZZOSAMÉNTE (*It.*) Tenderly, softly, gracefully.
VEZZÓSO (*It.*) Graceful, sweet, tender.
VIBRÁNTE (*It.*) Vibrating; a tremulous, quivering touch: full resonance of tone.
VIBTÁTE
VIBRÁTO (*It.*) A strong, vibrating, full quality of tone: resonant.
VIBRATION (*Fr.*) Vibration, tremulousness.
VIBRATÍSSIMO (*It.*) Extremely vibrating and tremulous.
VIBRAZIÓNE (*It.*) Vibration, tremulousness.

VIBRER (*Fr.*) \
VIBRIEREN (*Ger.*) — To vibrate.

VICÉNDA (*It.*) Alternation, change.

VICENDÉVOLE \
VICENDEVOLEMÉNTE (*It.*) Alternately, by turns.

VICÍNO (*It.*) Near, neighbouring.

VIDE (*Fr.*) \
VÍDO (*It.*) *See* **VUIDE**.

VIDEL (*Ger.*) Fiddle.

VIEL. An old name for instruments of the violin species.

VIEL (*Ger.*) Much, a great deal: *mit vielem Tone*, with much tone.

VIÉLE (*Fr.*) \
VIÉLLA (*It.*) The hurdy-gurdy. \
VIELLE (*Fr.*)

VIELLEUR (*Fr.*) Hurdy-gurdy player.

VIEL-STIMMIG (*Ger.*) For many voices.

VIER (*Ger.*) Four.

VIER-FACH (*Ger.*) Four-fold, of four ranks of pipes, &c.

VIER-FÜSSIG (*Ger.*) Four-foot, speaking of organ stops.

VIER-GESANG (*Ger.*) Song for four voices.

VIER-SPIEL (*Ger.*) Quartet; for four performers.

VIER-STIMMIG (*Ger.*) Four-voiced, in four parts, for four voices or instruments.

VIER-STÜCK (*Ger.*) Quartet; for four performers.

VIERTE (*Ger.*) A fourth.

VIERTEL (*Ger.*) Quarter.

VIERTEL-NOTE (*Ger.*) *Quarter-note*; a crotchet, the fourth part of a semibreve.

VIERTEL-TON (*Ger.*) A quarter-tone.

VIER-VIERTEL-TACT (*Ger.*) Common time of four crotchets.

VIERZEHN (*Ger.*) Fourteen.

VIER-ZWEITEL-TACT (*Ger.*) Time of four minims.

VIETÁTO (*It.*) Forbidden, prohibited.

VIF (*Fr.*) Lively, brisk, quick, sprightly.

VIGOROSAMÉNTE (*It.*) vigorously, with energy.

VIGORÓSO (*It.*) Vigorous, bold, energetic.

VIGÜÉLA (*Sp.*) A species of lute or guitar.

VIGUEUR (*Fr.*) Vigour.

VILLAGEOIS (*Fr.*) Rustic: *à la villageoise*, in a rustic style.

Villáncico — Viole sourdine

VILLÁNCICO
VILLÁNCIO } (*Sp.*) A species of pastoral poem or song.

VILLANÉLLA (*It.*)
VILLANELLE (*Fr.*) } An old rustic Italian dance, accompanied with singing.

VILLANÉSCO (*It.*) Rustic, rural.

VILLÁNICO. See VILLÁNCICO.

VILLÓTA (*It.*) A Venetian folk-song.

VILLÓTTE (*It.*) An old name for secular music in parts.

VINA. An ancient Hindoo viol

VINÁTE (*It.*) Drinking songs.

VINETTEN (*Ger.*) Vintage songs; drinking songs.

VINETTES. See VINÁTE.

VIOL. An old instrument somewhat resembling the violin: it had six strings, with frets, and was played with a bow.

VIÓLA (*It.*) The tenor violin.

VIÓLA DA BRÁCCIO (*It.*) The vióla; thus named because it rested on the arm.

VIÓLA D'AMÓRE (*It.*) A little larger than the *vióla*, and furnished with frets, and a greater number of strings, some above the finger-board, and some below: the tone was very pleasing. The name is also given to an organ stop of similar quality to the *gamba*, or *salcional*.

VIÓLA POMPÓSA (*It.*) Said to have been invented by J. S. Bach. An enlarged viol or *vióla*, of the same compass as the *violoncello*, but with the addition of a fifth string, sounding E, which facilitated the extended compass. It is now obsolete.

VIOLARS. Players on the viol, about the tenth and following centuries.

VIOL DA BRÁCCIO (*It.*) See VIÓLA DA BRÁCCIO.

VIOL DE GAMBA
VIOL DI GÁMBA } (*It.*) *Leg-viol*: an obsolete instrument, a little smaller than the violoncello, and furnished with frets, and five or six strings: it was held between the legs in playing, hence its name, and the tone was rather nasal. Also the name of an organ stop: *see* GÁMBA.

VIOLE (*Ger. & Fr.*) The *vióla*.

VIOLE D'AMOUR (*Fr.*) See VIÓLA D'AMÓRE.

VIOLE D'ORCHESTRE (*Fr.*) A very stringy organ stop.

VIOLENT (*Fr.*) Violent, impetuous.

VIOLENTEMÉNTE (*It.*) Violently, with force.

VIOLÉNTO (*It.*) Violent, vehement, boisterous.

VIOLÉNZA (*It.*) Violence, force, vehemence.

VIOLE SOURDINE (*Fr.*) An organ stop in imitation of the muted strings of the orchestra.

Violet — Virelay

VIOLET. A species of *viole d'armour*, with only six strings; the name is also applied to a gamba stop of 4 feet tone.

VIOLÉTTA (*It.*) A small viola.

VIOLIN. See VIOLÍNO.

VIOLINA. A string-toned organ stop, of 4 foot pitch.

VIOLINÁTA (*It.*) A piece for violin; also a piece, in imitation of the violin.

VIOLINBOGEN (*Ger.*) A violin bow.

VIOLIN DIAPASON. An open diapason on an organ, with a stringy tone.

VIOLINETTE. A kit; also, see VIOLÍNO PÍCCIOLO.

VIOLINE (*Ger.*) The violin: also, an organ stop of 8, 4, or 2 feet tone.

VILÍNO (*It.*) The violin: it attained its present shape, with four strings, in the sixteenth century.

VIOLÍNO PÍCCIOLO
VIOLÍNO PÍCCOLO (*It.*) A small violin.
VIOLÍNO POCHÉTTO

VIOLÍNO PRINCIPÁLE (*It.*) The first, or principal violin part, the leading violin, or *chef d'attaque*.

VIOLIN-PRINCIPAL. An 8 or 4 feet organ stop, with an agreeable, and violin-like tone.

VIOLIN-SAITE (*Ger.*) Violin string.

VIOLIN-SCHLÜSSEL
VIOLIN-ZEICHEN (*Ger.*) The treble clef, used for the violin, &c.

VIOLIN-STEG (*It.*) Violin-bridge.

VIOLÍSTA (*It.*)
VIOLISTE (*Fr.*) A player on a viol or viola.

VIOLON (*Fr.*) The French name for the violin.

VIOLON (*Ger.*) The double bass: see also VIOLÓNE.

VIOLONAR (*Fr.*) A double-bass.

VIOLONCELL (*Ger.*)
VIOLONCELLE (*Fr.*) The large, or bass violin: the name is also applied to an organ stop of small scale, and crisp tone.
VIOLONCÉLLO (*It.*)

VIOLÓNE
VIOLÓNO (*It.*) The double-bass: the name is also applied to an open wood stop, of much smaller scale than the diapason, on the pedals of an organ, the pipes of which are a little wider at the top than at the bottom, and furnished with ears and beard at the mouth: the tone is crisp, and resonant, like that of the double-bass, but the speech is a little slow.

VIOLONISTE (*Fr.*) A violinist.

VIRELAY. A rustic song or ballad, in the fourteenth century: nearly the same as the roundel, but with thus difference, the roundel begins and

Virginal — Vocalisation

ends with the same sentence, or strain, but the virelay is under no such restriction.

VIRGINAL. A small keyed instrument, much used about the time of Queen Elizabeth I, and placed upon a table, when played upon. It is supposed to have been the origin of the spinet, as the latter was of the harpsichord.

VIRTUOSE (*Ger.*) | A skilful performer upon some particular instrument.
VIRTUÓSO (*It.*) |

VIRTUOSE DE PUPÎTRE (*Fr.*) A virtuoso conductor.

VIRTUOSITÄT (*Ger.*) Remarkable proficiency, fine execution: applied both to singers and players.

VIS-À-VIS (*Fr.*) A harpsichord or pianoforte, with two keyboards, opposite each other.

VÍSTA (*It.*) Sight: *à príma vísta*, at first sight.

VISTAMÉNTE
VÍSTO (*It.*) quickly, swiftly, briskly, immediately.
VITAMÉNTE

VITE | (*Fr.*) Quickly, swiftly: un peu plus vite, a little more quickly.
VITEMENT |

VITESSE (*Fr.*) Swiftness, quickness.

VITULA (*Lat.*) A viol.

VIVÁCE
VIVACEMÉNTE (*It.*) Lively, briskly, sprightly, quickly.

VIVACÉTTO (*It.*) Rather lively.

VIVACÉZZA
VIVACITÀ (*It.*) Vivacity, liveliness.

VIVACISSIMAMÉNTE (*It.*) With the utmost life and rapidity.

VIVACÍSSIMO (*It.*) Very lively, extreme vivacity.

VIVAMÉNTE (*It.*) Briskly, lively, quickly.

VIVE (*Fr.*) Lively, brisk, sprightly.

VIVÉNTE (*It.*) Animated, lively.

VIVÉZZA (*It.*) Vivacity, liveliness.

VÍVIDO (*It.*) Lively, brisk.

VIVÍSSIMO (*It.*) Very spirited.

VÍVO (*It.*) Life, lively, alive, brisk.

VIVÓLA (*It.*) A viol: common in the fourteenth century.

VOCÁLE (*It.*) Vocal, belonging to the voice.

VOCALÉZZO (*It.*) A vocal exercise.

VOCALION. A species of harmonium.

VOCALISATION. Command of the voice, vocal execution: also, vocal writing or composition.

Vocalise — Vóglia

VOCALISE (*Eng.*)
VOCALIZZARE (*It.*) To practice vocal exercises, using the vowels; chiefly with the letter A sounded in the Italian manner.

VOCALÍZZI (*It. pl.*) Vocal exercises, to be sung on the vowels.

VOCAL SCORE. *See* **PIANOFORTE SCORE.**

VÓCE (*It.*) The voice.

VÓCE BUÓNA (*It.*) A good voice.

VÓCE DI CÁMERA (*It.*) Voice for the chamber: one suited for private, rather than for public, singing.

VÓCE CATTÍVA (*It.*) A bad voice.

VÓCE DI CÁMERA (*It.*) A *chamber voice*, one that is only suitable for chamber concerts.

VÓCE DI GÓLA (*It.*) The throat voice: also, a guttural voice.

VÓCE DI PÉTTO (*It.*) The natural, or chest voice, the lower register of the voice.

VÓCE DI TÉSTA (*It.*) The head voice, the *falsétto*, or feigned voice: the upper register of the voice.

VÓCE FLÉBILE (*It.*) A doleful voice.

VÓCE GRANÍTA (*It.*) A firm, massive voice, round and full.

VÓCE INTONÁTA (*It.*) A pure-toned voice.

VÓCE PASTÓSA (*It.*) A soft, plump, flexible voice.

VÓCE RÁUCA (*It.*) A hoarse, rough voice.

VOCERELLÍNA (*It.*) A pretty little voice.

VÓCE SÓLA (*It.*) The voice alone.

VÓCE SPIANÁTA (*It.*) *Drawn out*: an even, smooth, sustained voice.

VÓCE SPICCÁTA (*It.*) A clear, distinct voice, well articulated.

VÓCE UMÁNA (*It.*) The human voice.

VOCIÁCCIA (*It.*) A bad, disagreeable voice.

VOCÍNA (*It.*) A little, thin voice.

VOCÍNO (*It.*) A pleasing little voice.

VOCIOLÍNA (*It.*) A small, thin voice.

VOCIÓNE (*It.*) A strong, loud voice.

VOGEL (*Ger.*) A bird.

VOGEL-FLÖTE (*Ger.*) Bird-flute.

VOGEL-PFEIFE (*Ger.*) Bird-call, flageolet.

VOGEL-GESANG (*Ger.*) *Singing of birds*: an accessory stop in some very old German organs, producing a chirping effect, by some little pipes standing in a vessel with water, through which the wind passes to them.

VÓGLIA (*It.*) Desire, longing: ardour, fervour.

Voice — Vollkommen

VOICE. Sound emitted by the mouth: applied also to the tuning, and quality of tone, of organ pipes, the voicing being a most important part of the organ-builder's work, and a test of his skill, and correctness of ear. To voice, also means, writing the voice parts, regard being had to the nature and capabilities of each kind of voice.

VOICE PARTS. The vocal parts chorus parts.

VOIX (*Fr.*) The voice.

VOIX AIGRE (*Fr.*) A harsh shrill voice.

VOIX ARGENTINE (*Fr.*) A clear-toned voice.

VOIX CÉLESTES (*Fr.*) *Celestial voices*; an organ stop, of French invention, formed of two dulcianas, one of which has the pitch slightly raised, which gives to the stop a waving, undulating character: also, a soft stop on the harmonium: *see also* UNDA MARIS.

VOIX DE POITRINE (*Fr.*) Chest voice, natural voice.

VOIX DE TÊTE (*Fr.*) Head voice.

VOIX ÉCLATANTE (*Fr.*) Loud, piercing, voice.

VOIX GLAPOSSANTE (*Fr.*) A shrill voice.

VOIX GRÊLE (*Fr.*) A thin, sharp voice.

VOIX HUMAINE (*Fr.*) *See* VOX HUMANA.

VOIX PERLÉE (*Fr.*) A pearly voice.

VOIX VOILÉE (*Fr.*) A veiled voice.

VOKAL (*Ger.*) Vocal.

VOLÁNTE (*It.*) *Flying*: a light and rapid series of notes.

VOLÁNTE (*It.*) Swift, light.

VOLÁTA (*It.*) A flight, run, rapid series of notes, a *roulade*, or *division*.

VOLÁTE (*It. pl.*) *See* VOLÁTA.

VOLATÍNA (*It.*) A little flight, &c.: *see* VOLÁTA.

VOLATÍNE (*It. pl.*) Short runs, &c.: *see* VOLÁTA.

VOLÉE (*Fr.*) A *voláta*.

VOLKS-GESANG (*Ger.*) A folk song.

VOLKS-LIED
VOLKS-STÜCKCHEN | (*Ger.*) National song, popular air.

VOLL (*Ger.*) Full: *mit vollen Werke*, with full organ.

VOLLE ORGEL (*Ger.*) Full organ.

VOLLE WERK (*Ger.*) *See* VOLLES WERK.

VÖLLER (*Ger.*) Fuller, louder.

VOLLES WERK (*Ger.*) The full organ.

VOLL-GESANG (*Ger.*) Chorus.

VÖLLIG (*Ger.*) Perfect, complete; full.

VOLLKOMMEN (*Ger.*) Perfect, complete.

VOLL RÜHRUNG (*Ger.*) Full of emotion.
VOLL SEHNSICHT (*Ger.*) Full of yearning, longing.
VOLL-STIMMIG (*Ger.*) Full-toned, full-voiced.
VOLL-STIMMIGKEIT (*Ger.*) Fullness of tone.
VOLL-TÖNEND / **VOLL-TÖNIG** (*Ger.*) Full sounding, sonorous.
VOLONTÉ (*Fr.*) Will, pleasure: *à volonté*, at will.
VÓLTA (*It.*) / **VÓLTE** (*It. pl.*) Time: as *úna vólta*, once; *dúe vólte*, twice.
VÓLTA PRÍMA (*It.*) First time.
VOLTÁRE (*It.*) To turn, to turn over.
VÓLTA SECÓNDA (*It.*) The second time.
VÓLTE (*It. pl.*) An obsolete dance in ¾ time, resembling the *galliard*, and with a rising and leaping kind of motion.
VOLTEGGIÁNDO (*It.*) Crossing the hands, on the pianoforte.
VOLTEGGIÁRE (*It.*) To cross the hands, in playing.
VÓLTI (*It.*) Turn, turn over.
VÓLTI SÚBITO (*It.*) Turn over quickly.
VOLUBILITÀ / **VOLUBILMÉNTE** (*It.*) Volubility, freedom of performance, fluency in delivery.
VOLUME. Applied to a voice with a full, round tone.
VOLUNTARY. An organ piece, either extemporaneous, or otherwise, played after the Psalms, &c., in the Church of England service: also, a species of *toccáta*, generally in two or three movements, calculated to display the capabilities of the instrument, and the skill of the performer: the name is supposed to be derived from the extemporaneous, prompt, and ready development of a theme or subject, in a quicker succession of notes than is required in the accompaniment of choral harmony.
VOLÚTA (*It.*) / **VOLUTE** (*Fr.*) The scroll of a violin, &c.
VOM (*Ger.*) From the.
VOM ANFANG (*Ger.*) From the beginning; *Da cápo*.
VOM BLATTE (*Ger.*) At sight.
VOM ZEICHEN (*Ger.*) From the sign; *Dal ségno*.
VON (*Ger.*) By, of, from, on.
VOR (*Ger.*) Before, in front of; for; with; more than; above.
VORANGEHEND (*Ger.*) Foregoing, preceding.
VORAUSNAHME (*Ger.*) Anticipation.
VORBEREITUNG (*Ger.*) Preparation, of discords, &c.

Vorgreifung — Vuóto

VORGREIFUNG \
VORGRIFF (*Ger.*) Anticipation.

VORHALT (*Ger.*) A suspension, or syncopation.

VORHANDEN (*Ger.*) Occurring, appearing.

VORHER (*Ger.*) Before: *tempo wie vorher*, the time as before.

VORHERGEHEND (*Ger.*) Preceding, foregoing, previous.

VORIG (*Ger.*) Previous, before, preceding.

VORSCHLAG (*Ger.*) *Appoggiatúra*, beat.

VORSPIEL (*Ger.*) Prelude, introductory movement.

VORSPIELER (*Ger.*) Leader of the band: the principal, or prímo performer upon any orchestral instrument.

VORSTELLER (*Ger.*) Performer, player.

VORTRAG (*Ger.*) Execution, mode of executing a piece: delivery, elocution, diction: the act of uttering or pronouncing.

VORTRAGSBEZEICHNUNG \
VORTRAGSZEICHEN (*Ger.*) Musical signs, expression marks, *témpo* marks, &c.

VORTRAGSTÜCK (*Ger.*) A concert piece.

VORWÄRTS (*Ger.*) Forwards; *stringéndo*.

VORZEICHNUNG (*Ger.*) The signature: also, a sketch, or outline, of a composition.

VORZUTRAGEN (*Ger.*) Brought out, made prominent.

VÓTO (*It.*) See **VUÓTO**.

VOX (*Lat.*) The voice, sound, tone: accent.

VOX ACUTA (*Lat.*) A shrill, or acute, voice.

VOX ANGELICA (*Lat.*) *Angelic voice*: see **VOIX CÉLESTES**.

VOX GRAVIS (*Lat.*) A deep voice.

VOX HUMANA (*Lat.*) *Human voice*: an organ reed stop of 8 feet tone, intended to imitate the human voice, which it sometimes does, though very imperfectly.

VOX MYSTICA. An organ stop of 8 feet pitch, a species of vox humana.

VOX NASALIS (*Lat.*) A nasal voice.

VOX RETUSA (*Lat.*) An 8 feet organ stop.

VOX VIRGINEA (*Ger.*) A girlish voice; see **VOX ANGELICA**.

VUE (*Fr.*) Sight, view.

VUIDE (*Fr.*) Open: the note is to be played on the open string.

VUÓTO (*It.*) Open; empty.

W

WACHSEND (*Ger.*) *See* CRESCENDO.

WACHTEL (*Ger.*) A quail; also, a toy instrument imitating a quail.

WAITS. An old word meaning, hautboys: also, players on the hautboys: *see also* WAYGHTES.

WALD (*Ger.*) Forest, a wood.

WALD-FLÖTE (*Ger.*) *Forest-flute*, shepherd's flute: an organ stop with a full and powerful tone.

WALD-HORN (*Ger.*) *Forest-horn*: also, winding-horn, French horn, bugle horn: also, an 8 feet organ reed stop.

WALD-PFIEFE (*Ger.*) *See* WALD-FLÖTE.

WALD-QUINTE (*Ger.*) A Wald-flöte, but speaking a fifth higher.

WALNIKA. A Russian peasant bagpipe.

WALS (*Dutch*) | Waltz, national German dance.
WALZER (*Ger.*) |

WANKEND (*Ger.*) Hesitating, wavering.

WÄRME (*Ger.*) Warmth, fervour.

WASSER (*Ger.*) Water.

WAYGHTES. Persons who play hymn tunes, &c., in the streets, during the night, about Christmas: *see also* WAITS.

WAYTES. *See* WAITS.

WECHSEL (*Ger.*) Change, variation; exchange.

WECHSEL-GESANG (*Ger.*) Alternative, or antiphonal, song.

WECHSEL-NOTEN (*Ger.*) *Changing notes*: passing notes, notes of irregular transition, appoggiaturas.

WEHMUTH |
WEHMÜTHIGKEIT | (*Ger.*) Melancholy, sadness, sorrow.

WEIBERSTIMME (*Ger.*) A female voice.

WEICH (*Ger.*) Minor; also, tender, soft, mellow.

WEICHHEIT (*Ger.*) Tenderness, kindness.

WEIHNACHTS-LIED (*Ger.*) Christmas carol, song.

WEINEND (*Ger.*) Whining, weeping, wailing.

WEISE (*Ger.*) A tune; also, a manner, mood; fashion, style.

WEISS (*Ger.*) White.

WEISSE-NOTE (*Ger.*) *White note*, minim.

WEIT (*Ger.*) Broad, wide; open, extended.

WEITE HARMONIE (*Ger.*) Dispersed, or open, harmony.

WEITPFEIFE (*Ger.*) A flute stop on an organ, with a large scale.

WELLE (*Ger.*) A roller, part of the mechanism of an organ.

WELLENBRETT (*Ger.*) A roller-board, part of the mechanism of an organ, used to distribute the movement of the keys, to the sound-boards.

WELSH HARP. *See* HARP.

WELSH SINGING. A mode of singing in which the harper plays the melody, and the singer chants an accompanying part, chiefly on the dominant; both contriving to finish together.

WELTLICH (*Ger.*) Secular.

WENIG (*Ger.*) Little: *ein wenig stark*, a little strong, rather loud.

WENIGER (*Ger.*) Less.

WENIGER ABGEMESSEN (*Ger.*) *Less measured*: faster.

WERDEN (*Ger.*) To become, to grow.

WERK (*Ger.*) *Work*, movement, action: *see* HAUPTWERK.

WERTH (*Ger.*) Worth, value; especially *time-value* or duration.

WESENTLICH (*Ger.*) Essential.

WESENTLICHE DISSONANZ (*Ger.*) The essential dissonances or a chord, as opposed to passing notes, &c.

WESENTLICHE SEPTIME (*Ger.*) Dominant seventh.

WETTERHARFE (*Ger.*) An Æoline harp.

WHOLE NOTE. A semibreve.

WHOLE STEP. A step of a whole tone.

WIE (*Ger.*) As; as if.

WIEDER-ANFANGEN (*Ger.*) To begin again, to recommence.

WIEDER-GRABE (*Ger.*) Interpretation, reading, manner of performance.

WIEDER-HOLUNG (*Ger.*) Repeating, repetition.

WIEDER-HOLUNGSZEICHEN (*Ger.*) A repeat sign.

WIEDERKEHR (*Ger.*) The re-entry of a part.

WIEDER-KLANG / **WIEDER-SCHALL** (*Ger.*) Echo, resounding.

WIEDERUM (*Ger.*) Again.

WIEGENLIED (*Ger.*) A cradle song, lullaby; *berceuse*.

WIE TRÄUMEND (*Ger.*) As if in a dream; dreamily.

WILD (*Ger.*) Furious, wild, ferocious.

WIND COUPLER. A valve in the wind trunk of an organ, to shut off, or on, the wind, *see* VENTIL.

WIND-HARFE (*Ger.*) Æolian harp.

WIND-LADE (*Ger.*) Wind-chest, in an organ.

WIND-MESSER / **WIND-WAGE** (*Ger.*) Anemometer, wind-gauge.

WINSELIG (*Ger.*) Plaintive.

WINSELSTIMME (*Ger.*) A plaintive voice.

WIRBEL (*Ger.*) Peg of a violin, viola, &c.: the stopper in an organ pipe.

WIRBEL-KASTEN (*Ger.*) That part of the neck of a violin, &c., which contains the pegs.

WIRBEL-TANZ (*Ger.*) A circular or whirling dance.

WIRBEL-TROMMEL (*Ger.*) A tenor drum.

WIRBELN (*Ger.*) To *roll* on a drum.

WOGEND (*Ger.*) Waving, undulating.

WOHL (*Ger.*) Well.

WOHLGEFÄLLIG (*Ger.*) Agreeable, pleasing.

WOHLKLANG / **WOHLLAUT** (*Ger.*) Concord, harmony.

WOHLKINGEND (*Ger.*) Harmonious.

WOHLTEMPERIRT (*Ger.*) Well-tempered, as in pitch.

WOLF. An old name applied to an impure fifth, which occurs in pianofortes, or organs, tuned in unequal temperament.

WORT (*Ger.*) A word.

WORTE (*Ger. pl.*) Words.

WÖRTEBUCH (*Ger.*) A dictionary.

WRIST-GUIDE. A part of the chiroplast, invented by Logier, to assist young pianoforte players in keeping the wrist in a proper position.

WUCHTIG (*Ger.*) Weighty, weightily; ponderously, emphatically.

WÜRDE (*Ger.*) Dignity.

WUTH (*Ger.*) Rage, fury, madness.

WÜTHEND / **WÜTHIG** (*Ger.*) Furiously, frantically.

X

XÄNORPHIKA (*Ger.*) A species of pino-violin, invented by Röllig, Vienna, 1797.

XYLHARMONICON (*Gr.*) The wooden harmonica, invented in 1810 by Uthe, an organ-builder at Sangerhausen.

XYLOPHONE | A wooden dulcimer, with a compass of about two
XYLORGANUM | octaves, with tuned wooden bars.

XYLORGAND (*Fr.*) Some species of musical instrument.

XYLOSISTRON. An earlier form of the *Xylharmonicon*.

Y

YABAL (*Heb.*) A trumpet blast.
YANG KIN. A Chinese dulcimer with brass strings.
YO. The Indian flute.
YODEL. *See* **JODELN.**
YUE KIN. The *moon guitar* of the Chinese.

Z

ZA. Formerly applied in some countries to the note B-flat.

ZÄHLEN (*Ger.*) To count time.

ZALEO. A Spanish national dance.

ZAMACUCA. The national dance of Chili.

ZAMPÓGNA
ZAMPÚGNA | (*It.*) An ancient pipe, or bagpipe, now nearly extinct; with a reedy tone resembling, but much inferior to the clarinet: *see* **CORNAMUSA**, *and* **CHALUMEAU**.

ZAMPOGNÉTTA
ZAMPOGNÍNO | (*It.*) A small bagpipe.

ZANER. An Egyptian instrument of the bassoon species.

ZÄNKISCH (*Ger.*) Cantankerous, quarrelsome.

ZANZE. An African drum.

ZAPATEÁDO (*Sp.*) A Spanish national dance, in which a noise is made with the shoe.

ZAPFEN-STREICH (*Ger.*) The tattoo.

ZARABÁNDA (*Sp.*) *See* **SARABÁNDE**.

ZARAMÉLLA (*It.*) An Italian rustic pipe with a double reed; a species of *musette*.

ZARGE (*Ger.*) The *sides* of a violin, guitar, &c.

ZART
ZÄRTLICH | (*Ger.*) Tenderly, softly, delicately.

ZARTE STIMMEN (*Ger. pl.*) Delicate stops: *mit zarten Stimmen*, with delicate stops.

ZART-FLÖTE (*Ger.*) Soft-flute: an organ stop of the flute species.

ZARZUÉLA (*Sp.*) A short drama, with incidental music, something similar to the *vaudeville*.

ZAUBER (*Ger.*) Magic.

ZAUBERFLÖTE (*Ger.*) Magic flute: also, the name of an organ stop, consisting of stopped pipes overblown to produce the twelfth, *see also* **HARMONIC-FLUTE**.

ZAUBERLIED (*Ger.*) Magic song.

ZEFFIRÓSO (*It.*) Light, airy, delicate.

ZEHN (*Ger.*) Ten.

ZEICHEN (*Ger.*) A sign, note, character, &c.

ZEIT (*Ger.*) Time.

ZEIT-MASS (*Ger.*) Time, measure.

ZEITUNG (*Ger.*) Newspaper, periodical.

ZELÁNTE (*It.*) Zealous, ardent, fervent.

ZÈLE (*Fr.*) \
ZÉLO (*It.*) } Zeal, ardour, energy.

ZELOSAMÉNTE (*It.*) Zealously, ardently; with earnestness.

ZELÓSO (*It.*) Zealous, ardent, earnest.

ZENG. Persian cymbals.

ZERFLIESSEND (*Ger.*) Melting away.

ZERGLIEDURUNG (*Ger.*) Dissection; analysis.

ZERSTREUT (*Ger.*) Dispersed, spread, scattered.

ZIEHHARMONIKA (*Ger.*) An accordion.

ZIEMLICH (*Ger.*) Somewhat, rather; suitable.

ZIEMLICH LANGSAM (*Ger.*) Moderately slow.

ZIERATHEN (*Ger.*) Ornaments, embellishment.

ZIERLICH (*Ger.*) Neat, elegant, graceful.

ZIFFER (*Ger.*) A figure; numeral, cipher.

ZIFFERN (*Ger.*) To figure, as in *figured bass*.

ZIGEUNER (*Ger.*) A gypsy; a Bohemian.

ZIGEUNERARTIG (*Ger.*) Gypsy-like.

ZIGEUNERMUSIC (*Ger.*) Gypsy music.

ZIL. A Turkish instrument of some species.

ZÍLAFONE (*It.*) A xylophone.

ZÍLLO (*It.*) A chirp; chirping.

ZIMBALON. An improved dulcimer, used in Hungarian music.

ZIMBEL (*Ger.*) Cymbal.

ZIMBELSTERN (*Ger.*) An organ stop, consisting of a star positioned at the top of an organ, which contains tuned bells, when rotated it makes a tinkling sound, *see* CIMBEL-STERN.

ZINCKE (*Ger.*) *See* ZINKE.

ZINFONÍA (*It.*) A symphony.

ZÍNGANO (*It.*) A gypsy.

ZINGARÉSA (*It.*) In the style of gypsy music.

ZINGARÉSCA (*It.*) A song or dance in the style of the gypsies.

ZÍNGARO (*It.*) Gypsy, in the gypsy style.

ZINK-BLÄSER (*Ger.*) Cornet player.

ZINKE (*Ger.*) \
ZINKEN (*Ger. pl.*) } Small cornet, a species of horn or trumpet of very ancient date, now almost obsolete. It was made either of wood, or the small branches on the head of the deer. Also, the name of a treble stop, in German organs, which is sometimes a reed, and at others a mixture stop.

Zinkenist — Zurna

ZINKENIST (*Ger.*) A cornet player.

ZIRKEL (*Ger.*) A circle.

ZISCH (*Ger.*) A hiss.

ZITHER (*Ger.*) The guitar; a species of cithern, or cittern, having a number of strings distended over a resonance box.

ZITHERHARFE (*Ger.*) A species of auto-harp.

ZITHER-SCHLÄGER (*Ger.*) Guitar player.

ZÍTTERA (*It.*) A zither.

ZITTÍNO (*It.*) Silence.

ZÖGERND (*Ger.*) Lingering, retarding.

ZÖGERNDER (*Ger.*) A continual retarding of the time, slower and slower.

ZÓLFA (*It.*) See SÓLFA.

ZÓLFA DÉGLI ARMÉNI (*It.*) The church music used by the Armenians.

ZÓPPA | (*It.*) Lame, halting: see SYNCOPATION.
ZÓPPO |

ZORNIG (*Ger.*) Angry, scorning.

ZU (*Ger.*) To, unto; in addition to, along with; at, in, on, by, for; too.

ZUERST (*Ger.*) Firstly, at first.

ZUFÄLLIG (*Ger.*) Accidental sharp, flat, &c.

ZÚFFOLO | (*It.*) Flageolet, small flute, or whistle.
ZÚFOLO |

ZUFOLÓNE (*It.*) A flute, large whistle.

ZUG (*Ger.*) Draw-stop, or register, in an organ.

ZÜGE (*Ger.*) See ZUG.

ZÜGEGLÖCKCHEN (*Ger.*) The passing-bell; a knell.

ZUGPOSAUNE (*Ger.*) Slide trombone.

ZUGTROMPETE (*Ger.*) Slide trumpet.

ZUGWERK (*Ger.*) The tracker-action of an organ; mechanical parts of an organ.

ZUKLANG (*Ger.*) Unisons, harmony, concord.

ZUM (*Ger.*) To the, for the, &c.

ZUMMARAH. An Egyptian bassoon.

ZUNGE (*Ger.*) The tongue of a reed pipe.

ZUNGENPFEIFE (*Ger.*) A reed pipe.

ZUNGENSCHLAG (*Ger.*) *Tonguing* on wing instruments.

ZUNGENSTIMME (*Ger.*) A reed stop, on an organ.

ZUNGENWERK (*Ger.*) The *reed-work* on an organ.

ZUPFEND (*Ger.*) Plucking; *pizzicáto*.

ZURNA. A Turkish oboe.

Zurück — Zwischen

Zurück (*Ger.*) Back.
Zurück-haltend (*Ger.*) *Rallentándo*.
Zurück-haltung (*Ger.*) Retardation, keeping back.
Zusammen (*Ger.*) Together.
Zusammen-gesetzt (*Ger.*) Compound, condensed: compound time, &c.
Zusammen-klang | (*Ger.*) Harmony, consonance.
Zusammen-laut |
Zusammen-stimmig (*Ger.*) Harmonious, concordant.
Zusammen-stimmung (*Ger.*) Harmony, concord, consonance.
Zutraulich (*Ger.*) Confidently.
Zuvor (*Ger.*) Before.
Zwei (*Ger.*) Two.
Zwei-chörig (*Ger.*) For to voice, divided choir.
Zwei-fach | (*Ger.*) *Two-fold*, of two ranks, in organ pipes:
Zwei-fältig | *compound*, speaking of intervals, such as exceed the octave; as, the 9th, 10th, &c.
Zwei-füsser (*Ger.*) A two-foot pipe, in an organ.
Zwei-gesang (*Ger.*) For two voices, a duet.
Zwei-gestrichen (*Ger.*) *With two strokes*: applied to C on the third space in the treble and the six notes above: *see* TWICE MARKED OCTAVE.
Zweig-lied (*Ger.*) A sequence of two links or chords.
Zwei-klang (*Ger.*) A chord of two sounds.
Zwei-manuale (*Ger. pl.*) Two manuals.
Zwei-sang (*Ger.*) For two voices, a duet.
Zwei-stimmig (*Ger.*) For two voices, or parts, a duet.
Zweites Manual (*Ger.*) The second manual.
Zwei-und-dreissigstel-note (*Ger.*) A demisemiquaver.
Zwei-viertel-takt (*Ger.*) Time of two crotchets, $\frac{2}{4}$.
Zwei-zweitel-takt (*Ger.*) Time of two minims, $\frac{2}{2}$.
Zwerch-flöte (*Ger.*) *Transverse flute*, the German flute.
Zwerch-pfeife (*Ger.*) *Transverse pipe*, the fife.
Zwey (*Ger.*) *See* ZWEI.
Zwischen-gesang | (*Ger.*) An episode.
Zwischen-handlung |
Zwischen-räume (*Ger. pl.*) The spaces of the stave.
Zwischen-staz (*Ger.*) Intermezzo, parenthesis, episode.

ZWISCHEN-SPIEL (*Ger.*) Interlude, played between the lines, or verse, of a hymn.
ZWITSCHERHARFE (*Ger.*) *See* SPITZHARFE.
ZWITSCHERN (*Ger.*) To twitter, chirp, warble.
ZWÖLF (*Ger.*) Twelve.
ZYMBEL (*Ger.*) Cymbal.

A Bibliography of Organ Music
by WB Henshaw

ISBN: 0-9528184-0-X

- The book contains a list of over 53,000 pieces of organ music by 5,700 composers, with countries and dates of the composers.

- Is the most comprehensive yet published.

- Shows each movement of symphonies, suites; and items in collections, including choral preludes.

- Has 1,134 A5 size pages, hardback, bound in cloth.

- There is also a list showing the number of composers and compositions for each country, and a list of composers by order of number of composition (composers with over 50 pieces).

- Included are a small number of transcriptions which are cross-referenced by transcriber.

- A list of publishers and abbreviations used.

- Useful for finding dates and countries of lesser known composers, many not listed elsewhere.

BARDON ENTERPRISES